How to Paint
Landscapes Quickly
and Beautifully

in Watercolor and Gouache

by Nathan Fowkes

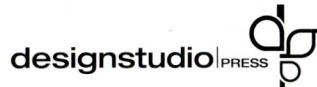

designstudio|PRESS

2 · 23 · 08

Sunny day in Griffeth Park

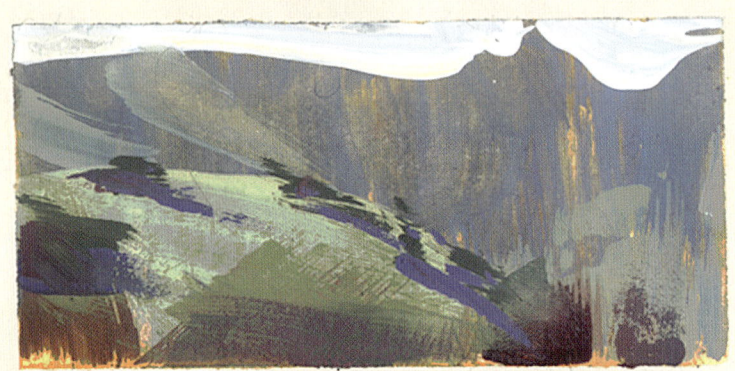

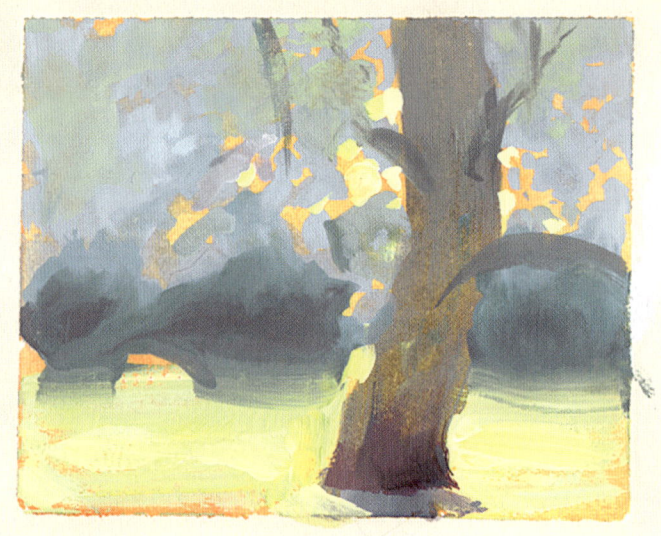

Off the ⑤ in Santa Clarita

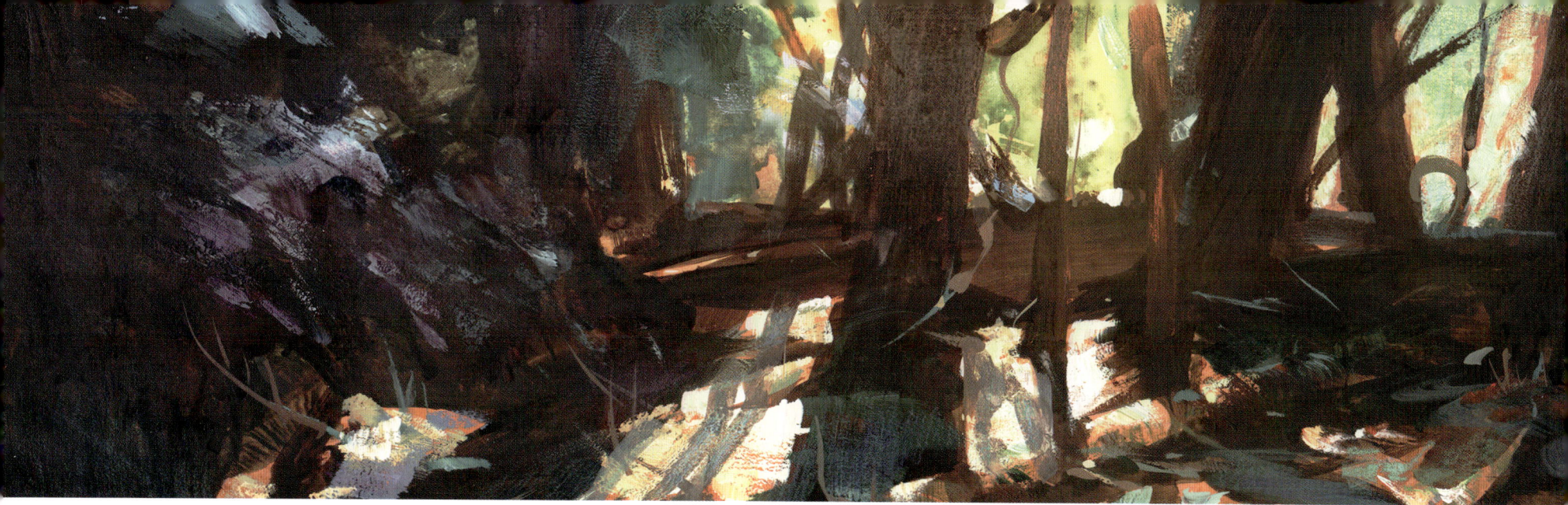

Table *of* Contents

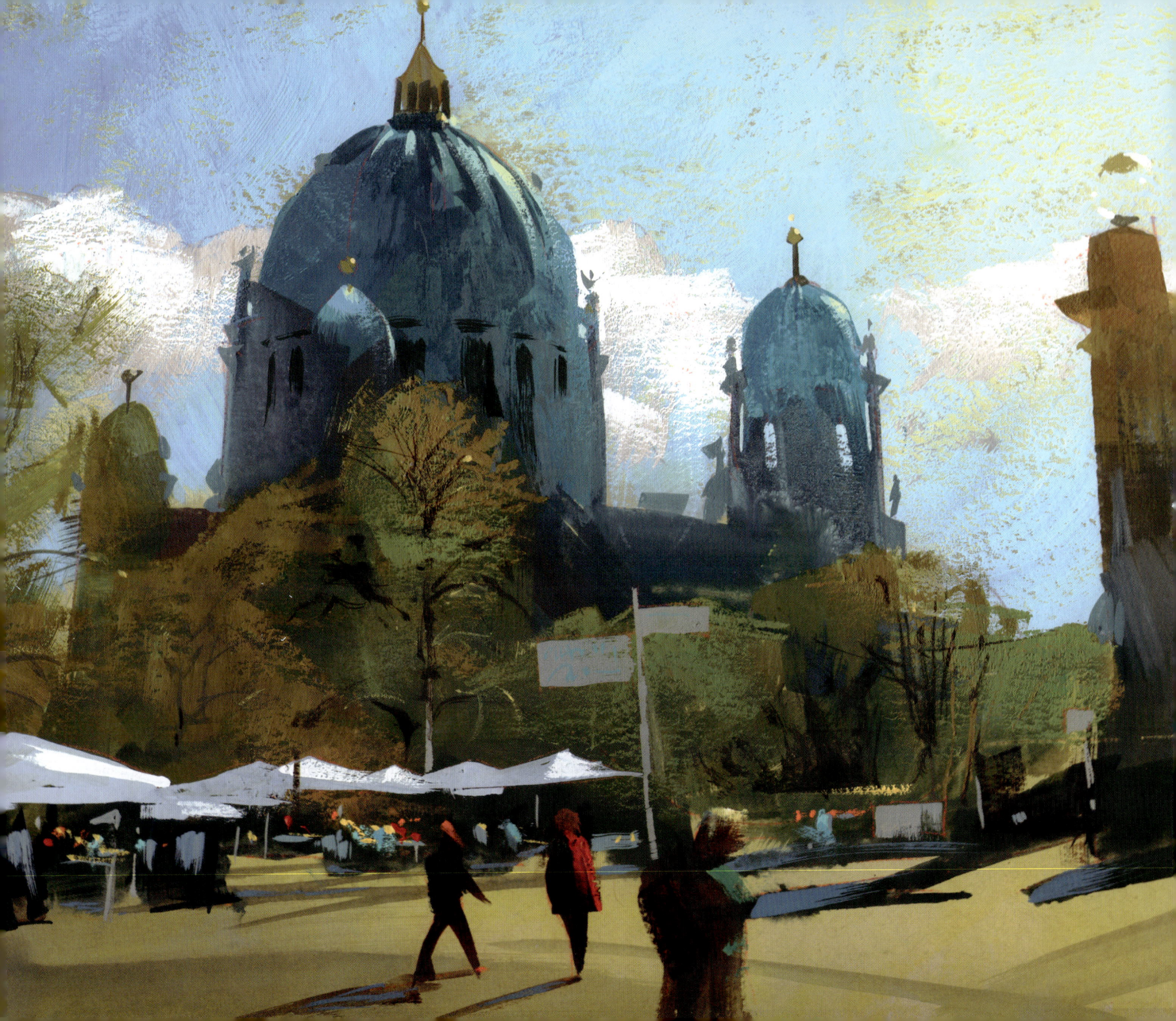

  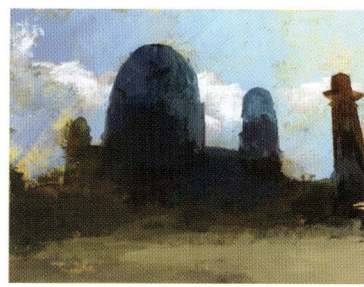 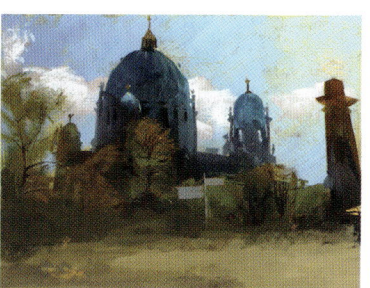 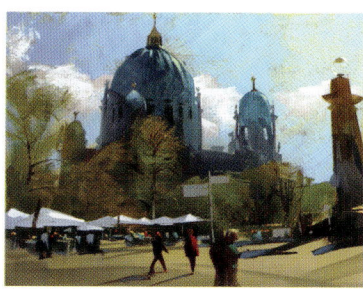

Introduction

My story begins with a French easel and a lot of greasy oil paint. Back in the early '90s I got very serious about venturing outside to learn landscape painting; I was going to get out there, doggone it, and I was going to figure this thing out! I got my bulky easel and oil painting materials prepared and headed out to Angeles National Forest, which is an attractive hiking destination not too far from my home in Los Angeles.

I found a spot to park and had a look around, but nothing jumped out at me that would make a great painting. I kept walking and walking, looking for the perfect spot until, finally, my stomach spoke louder than my desire to paint, and I said to myself, "Look, it's lunchtime already, I guess I need to take a break and have a sandwich." After the break I kept looking, and it will be no surprise to you that the perfect spot never appeared. I knew that I had to do something, and I saw some shadows falling across the ground in an interesting way, it wasn't much, but I thought, Okay, that'll have to be my painting.

I went through the whole process of setting up my French easel, squeezing out all the colors of oil paint, and prepared the whole batch of materials. And finally, I looked up to see that, you guessed it, the shadows had already changed. I was tempted to find another location, but time was passing quickly so I tried to paint the landscape from both observation and memory. Guess how well that went?

Well, here in California, we get the Santa Ana winds blowing in from the desert through L.A., sometimes at gale force. And those winds had kicked up by the afternoon, and they blew my easel and canvas right over into the dirt, which was perfect, because that way I could lie to myself and say: "If it wasn't for the @%#!! wind, the painting would've turned out!" And so I called it a day and headed home.

But I wasn't willing to admit defeat yet. I had shot some photos of the painting location and decided to paint from those in my home studio for practice, and then get out the next weekend, better prepared to paint from life. But I was tired, and the thought of unloading my whole rig of easel and supplies just to set it up again in the studio seemed too exhausting. But I knew that wasn't a good enough excuse not to paint, so I came up with an even better justification.

We had some new kittens at home sleeping in a cozy spot in our garage, and to get at my painting supplies, I would have to open the garage door since my car was a hatchback. And kittens getting outside in the outskirts of L.A., where I live, is certain doom; the area is heavily patrolled by coyotes! I told myself that as an artist, I have a deep and abiding love for all living things, so my artistic decision would be to do no painting, so that those kittens would live!

And so I got no painting done, I had a legitimate excuse not to! My friends, our lives are filled with responsibilities, and there's always a legitimate excuse not to get any painting done. There are always "kittens" so to speak. But we just can't allow that to happen, that's not who we are, it's not how we ultimately want to spend our creative time. We have to prioritize what's most important to us and be willing to make sacrifices. And so I did it, I made the hard choice, I got rid of the kittens . . . of course not literally, I wouldn't dream of such a thing . . . I actually got rid of my French easel.

After a good deal of experimentation, I settled on a small, highly convenient kit of watercolors, and for me, this was perfect. I could open up my kit and be painting within two minutes. And it traveled so easily! I could strap it to my waist for hiking or throw it in the car and paint anywhere and everywhere I went!

My kit was so handy and convenient that I no longer had any excuses not to paint. From then on, painting ceased to feel like a difficult chore and became so much fun that I began painting everywhere I went. Here we are, 25 years later, and I can tell you, the daily practice of painting created artistic opportunities for me beyond anything I had imagined. In many ways, it's been the foundation of my career, and in this book, I hope to inspire you to do the same.

Nathan Fowkes
Los Angeles, California
March 2019

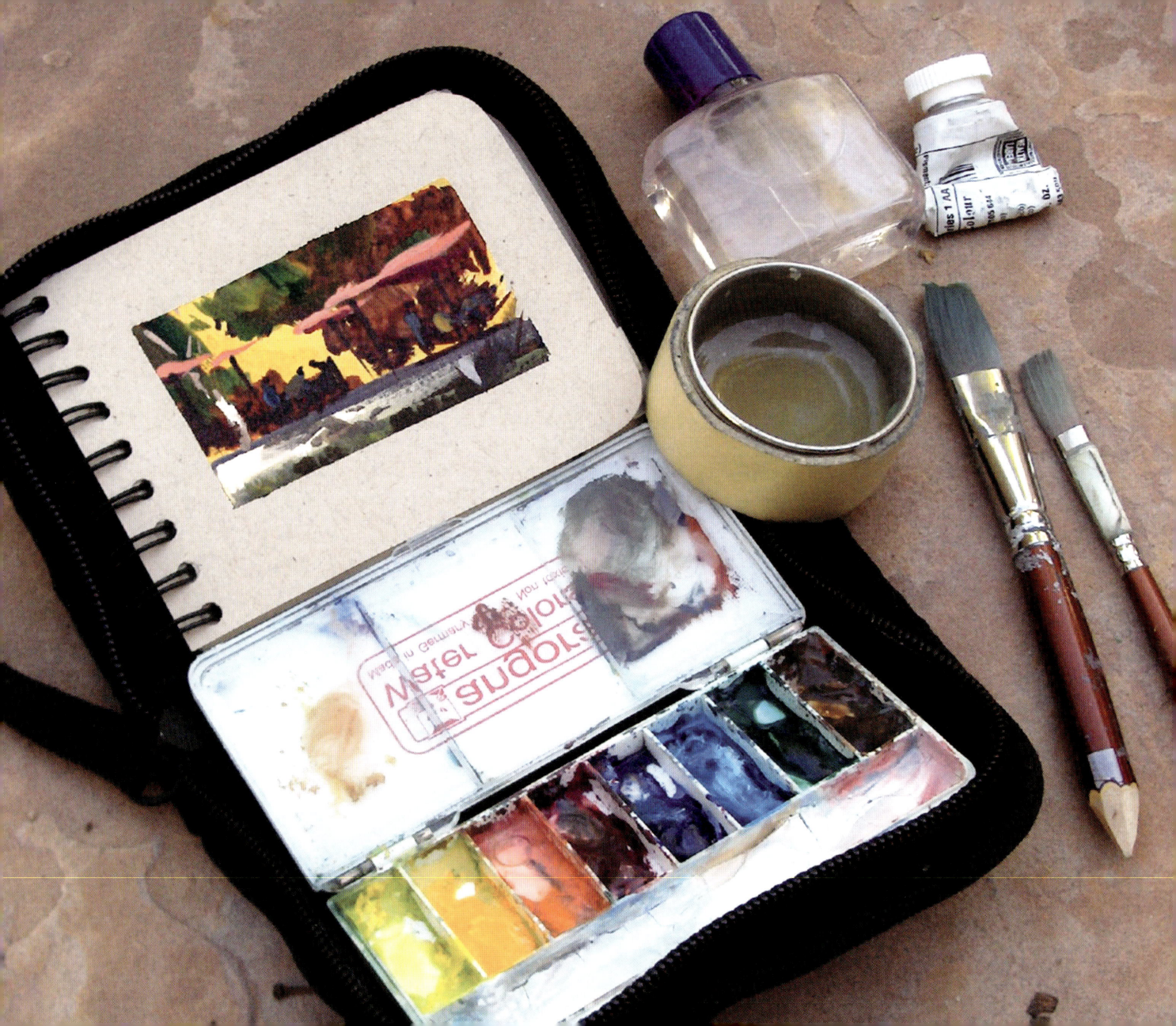

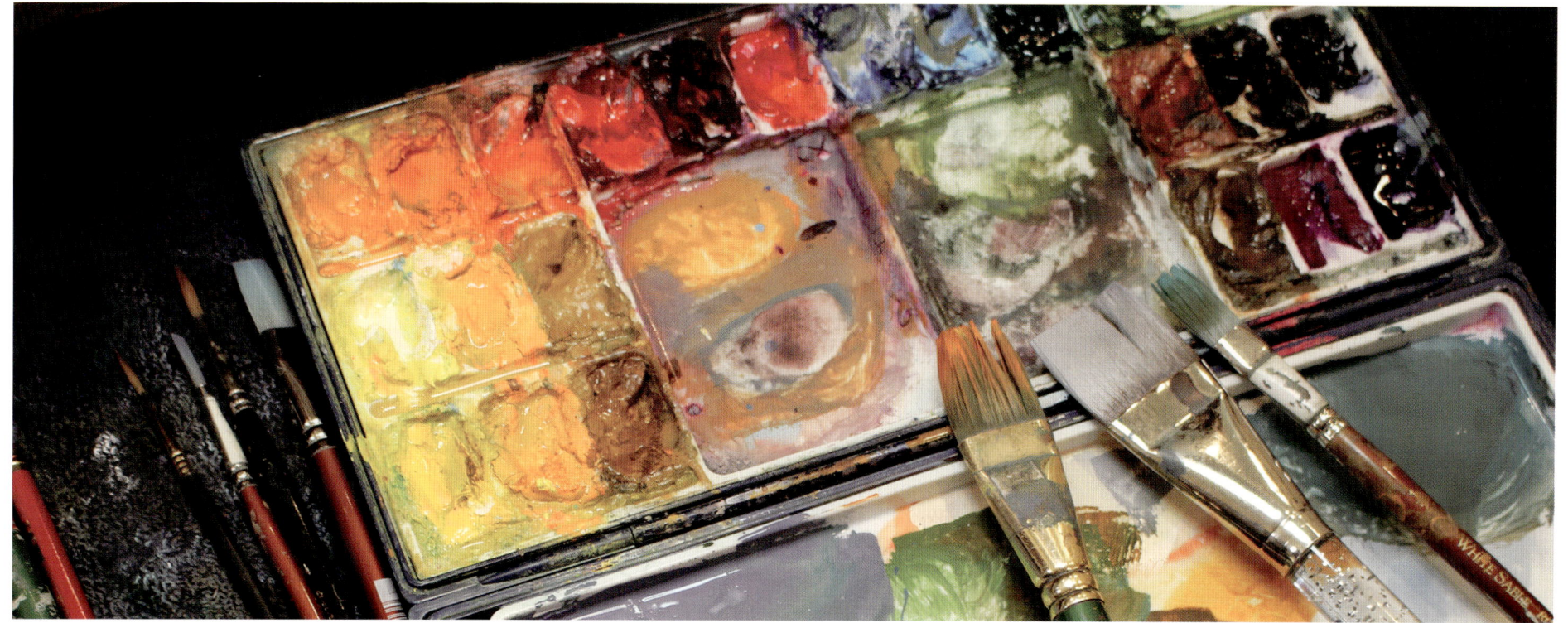

Chapter 1

Materials

Here we go, it's time to get everything together so we can get outside and sketch! There's just nothing better, and possibly nothing more important for the foundation of what we do as artists than sketching, not to mention the pure enjoyment of painting from life!

And at the same time, you're probably well aware of the frustrations of landscape sketching. My suspicion is that many of you have given it a shot, and you're here because your initial experiences have been disastrous. Mine too. You were probably happy to read in the introduction how badly my first efforts went. Nothing worked, and I had to completely rethink my materials so that sketching from life would become so convenient, and so enjoyable that there would be nothing holding me back from doing it at every opportunity. So let's dig in and take a look at the materials that made the difference.

"Choose the materials that will make sketching from life so convenient, and so enjoyable that you'll want to paint all the time!"

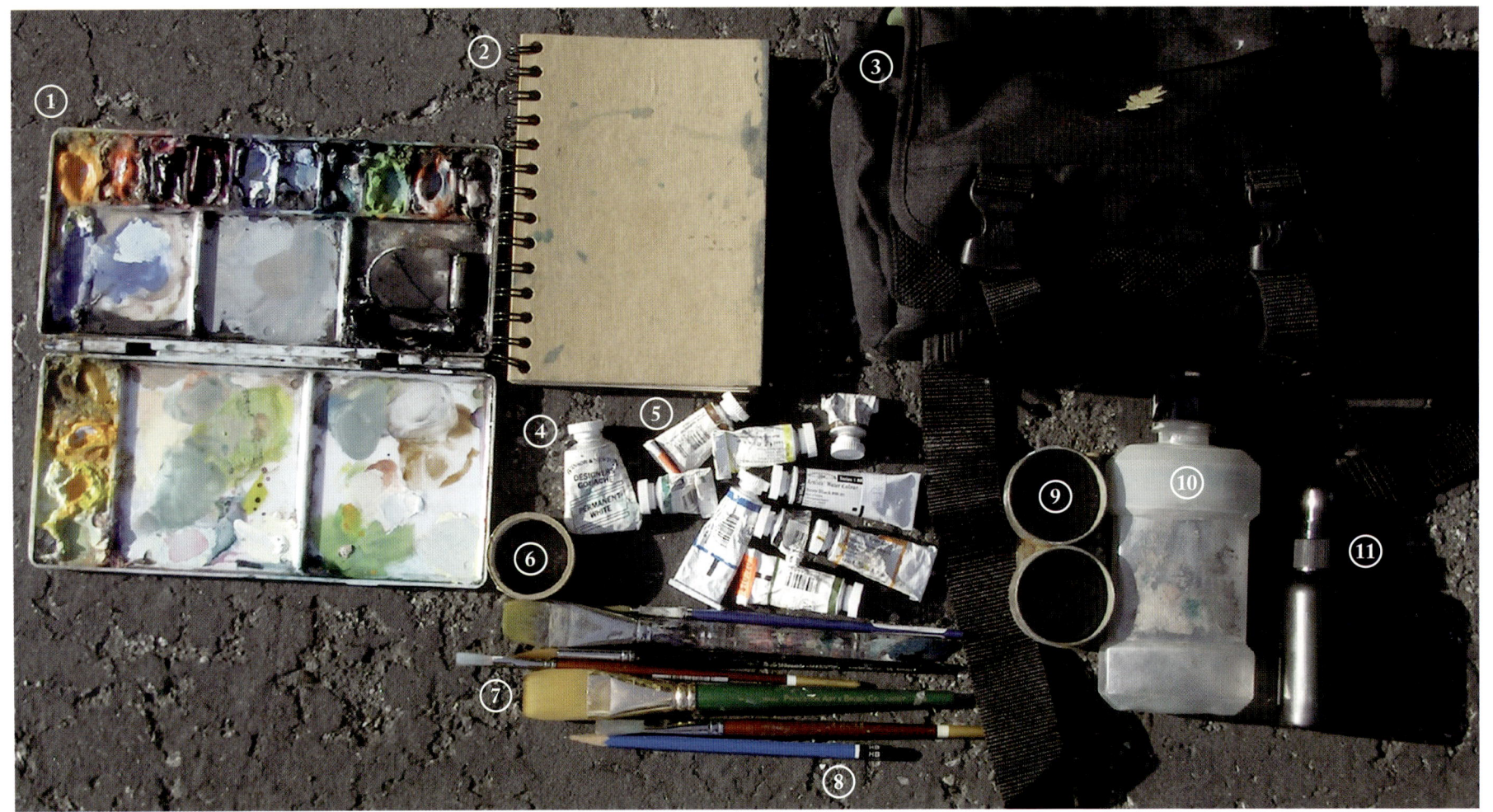

Suggested Materials

Travel size palette (Alvin Heritage Palette) ①

② Sketchbook (see next page for options)

Waist bag ③

④ Winsor & Newton Designers Gouache white

Winsor & Newton tube watercolors ⑤

⑥ Small roll of masking tape

Brushes (see next page for options) ⑦

⑧ Graphite pencil HB hardness
(I also use red and orange Prismacolor pencils)

Metal water container (to clean brushes) ⑨

⑩ Water bottle

Spray bottle for water ⑪

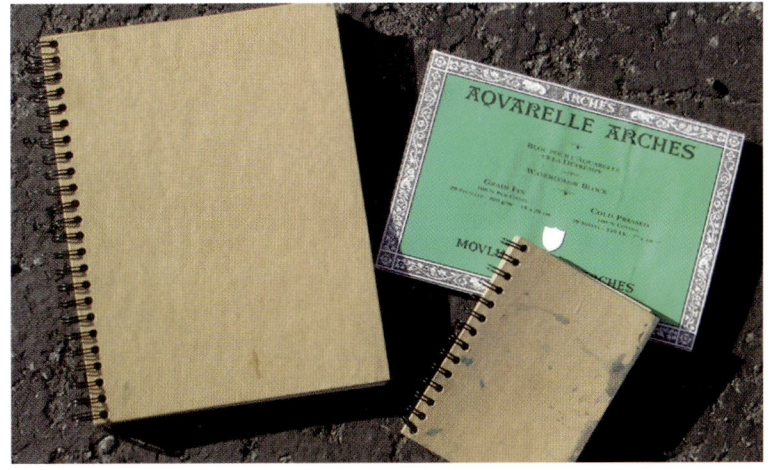

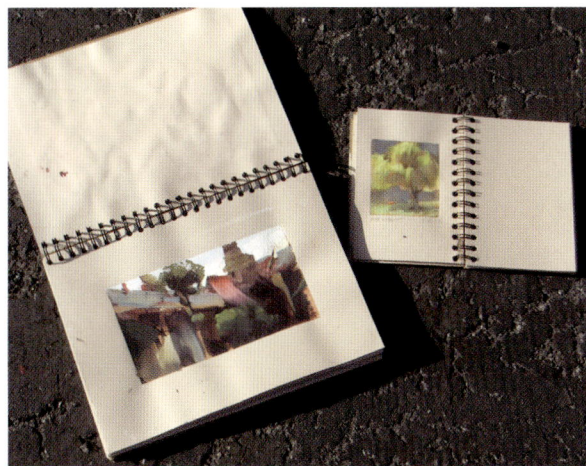

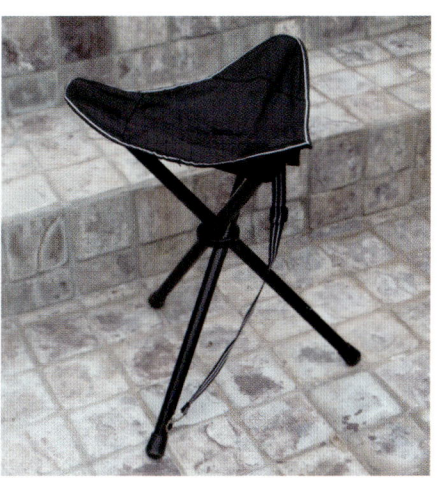

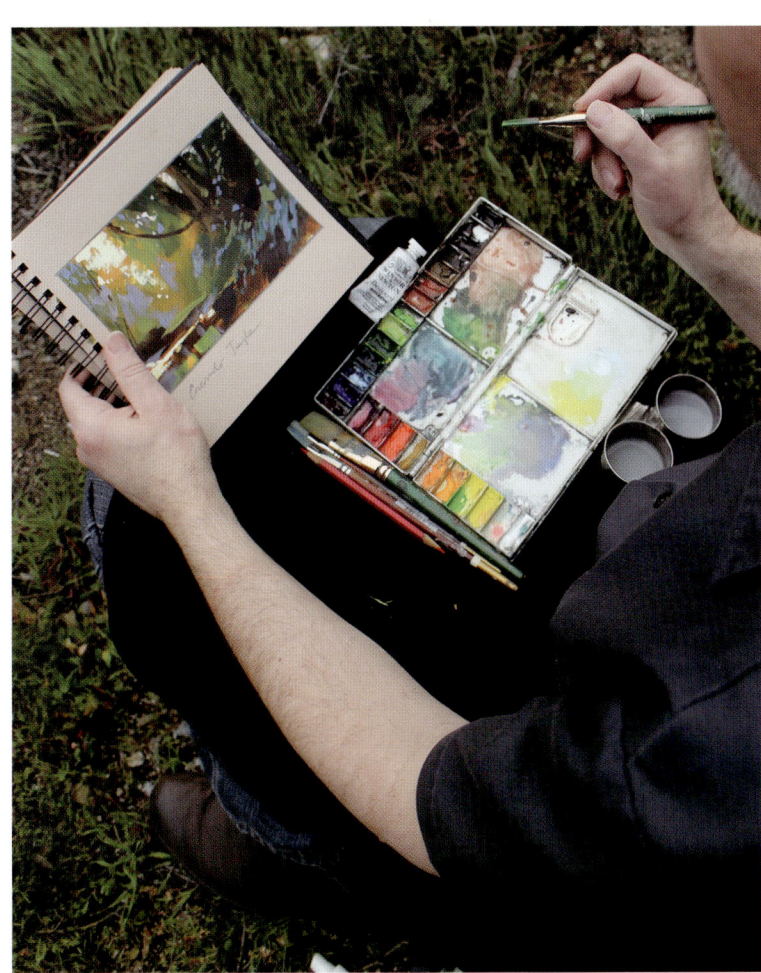

Watercolor-Friendly Sketchbook

Here are a few suggestions:

1. Heavy-weight (heavy cardstock), acid-free, toned mixed-media paper: make your own sketchbook from this, or it can be found in sketchbook form in some areas. I recommend Strathmore Toned Tan or Gray Mixed Media paper, 400 Series; many of my demonstrations are on this paper.

2. Arches cold-pressed watercolor paper block: 7 x 10 inches is an ideal size for sketching.

3. Moleskine watercolor sketchbook

4. Crescent #100 illustration board: cut this to whatever size is ideal for you.

Brushes

1. Princeton flat series 4350, sizes 1" and ¾" (can be substituted with any similar synthetic flat)

2. Robert Simmons white sable series 721 flat, sizes ½" and ¼" (can be substituted with any similar flat)

3. Da Vinci Maestro series 35, long tapered round, size 4 (or any good round sable brush)

Going Easel Free

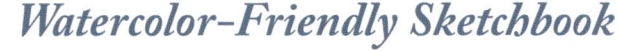

And as you can see here, I do not use an easel! I'm not at all against them, and you should certainly consider using one, but for me, sketching is meant to be as simple, and on the go as possible. As soon as I see a good spot, I plop down in my handy travel chair (above) and lay a small towel in my lap with my palette, brushes, etc. I hold my sketchbook in one hand and my paint brush in the other and I'm up and running in less than two minutes!

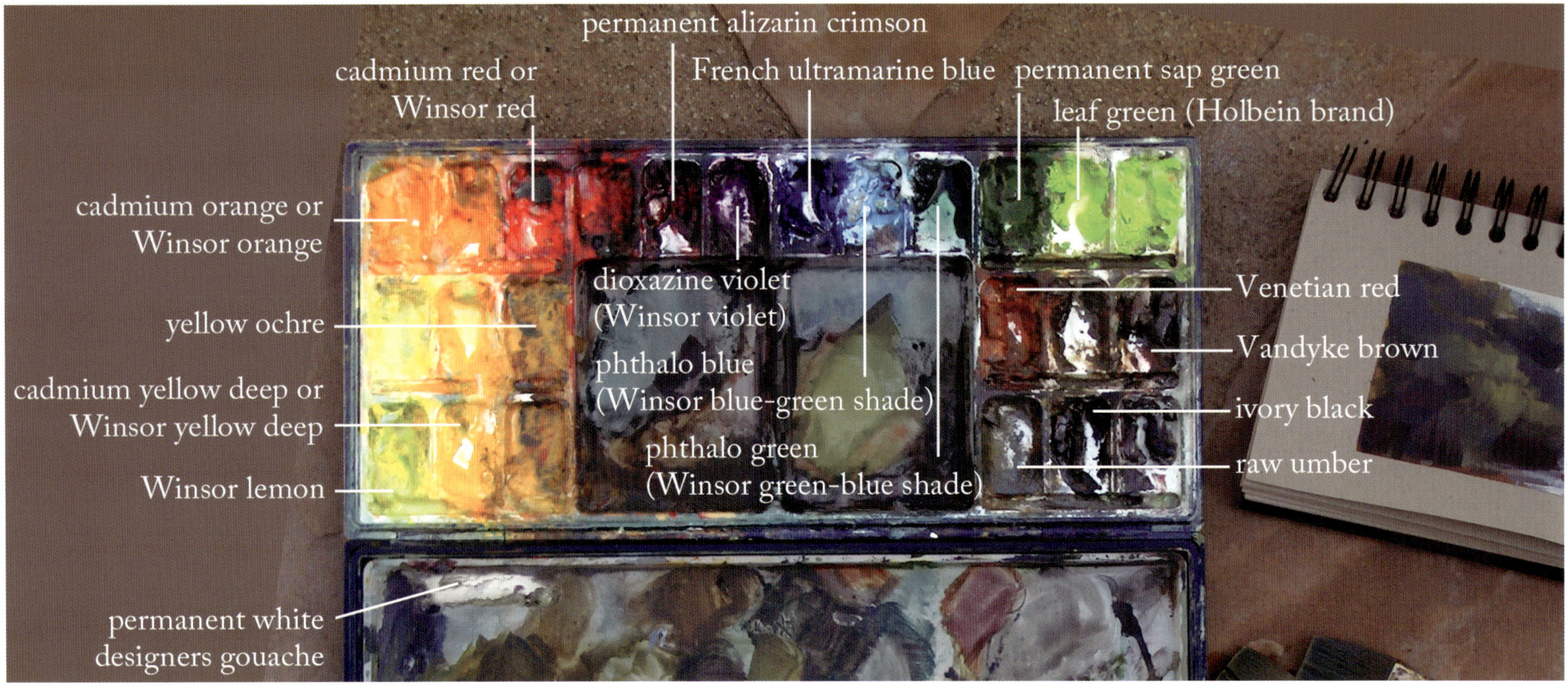

The image shows a watercolor palette with labeled pigment wells and a spiral-bound sketchbook to the right.

Labels (clockwise from top):
- permanent alizarin crimson
- French ultramarine blue
- permanent sap green
- leaf green (Holbein brand)
- cadmium red or Winsor red
- cadmium orange or Winsor orange
- yellow ochre
- cadmium yellow deep or Winsor yellow deep
- Winsor lemon
- dioxazine violet (Winsor violet)
- phthalo blue (Winsor blue-green shade)
- phthalo green (Winsor green-blue shade)
- Venetian red
- Vandyke brown
- ivory black
- raw umber
- permanent white designers gouache

Pigments

Above are the pigments I typically use, all are Winsor & Newton unless otherwise noted. There are many good brands of watercolors, but this one has consistently worked well for me, so I've stuck to it. Keep in mind that these pigments are suggestions, but I also recommend experimentation. Ultimately, the goal is to have a full range of color possibilities available.

For a few of the pigments I've listed cadmium colors, plus Winsor "hue" colors as alternatives. The cadmium-based colors are more brilliant and much more expensive, but the Winsor colors are a good alternative, especially for students.

You might have noticed that some colors are used twice in the palette. These are colors that dirty very easily or that I use frequently. Using them twice is another way I make sure my palette is as useful and convenient as possible. Note that I do not use the dry cakes of pigment that come with some palettes; they're just too hard and require too much work to dig colors out of. The Winsor & Newton colors do dry out in-between uses, but with a spritz of water they come back to life within minutes.

My palette includes white gouache. Gouache is watercolor that has additives to make it opaquer than the normal transparent quality of watercolor. I often use it to create opaque highlights or any time that it will help me mix the color that I need. And because the white dirties so easily on the palette, I tend to lay it in a long strip and use a little at a time, otherwise a single pool of white dirties instantly and is less usable.

Many students ask why I use watercolors instead of all gouache, since I like to paint thickly and opaquely at times. I do love gouache, but when the pools of paint on the palette dry out, they are very difficult to reactivate; I just don't have time to fight my medium. Watercolor rewets beautifully after drying on the palette, and my paintings look about the same as they would with gouache only.

Sketchbooks

I love sketchbooks! I stand by my recommendations on the previous page, but that doesn't stop me from buying every single watercolor sketchbook I ever come across. I end up using different papers and different sizes for different kinds of subjects; the experimentation contributes to the adventure!

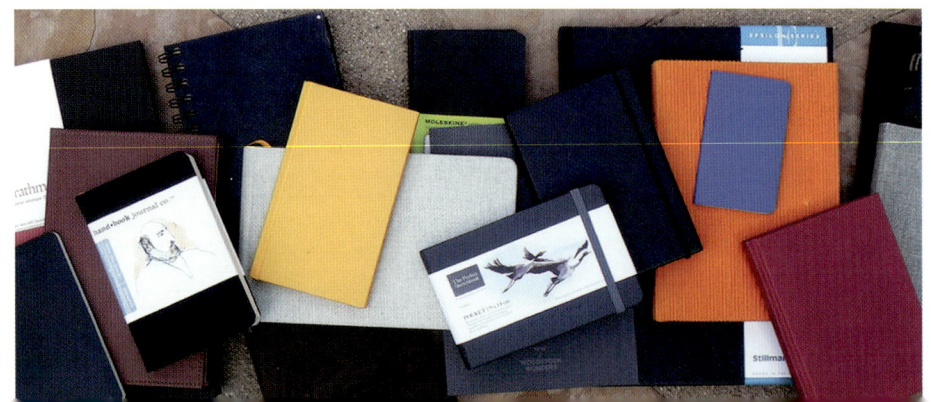

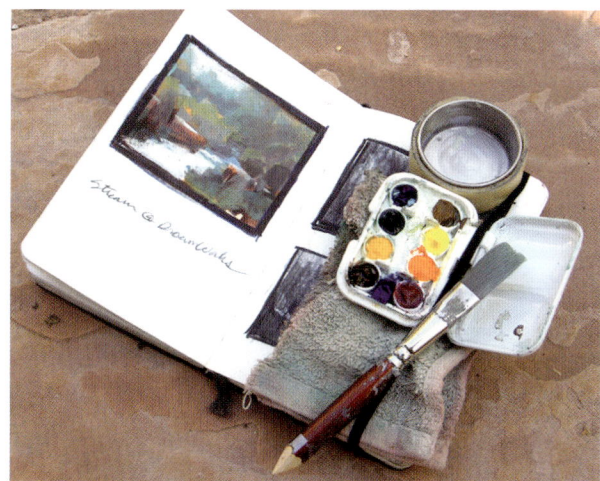

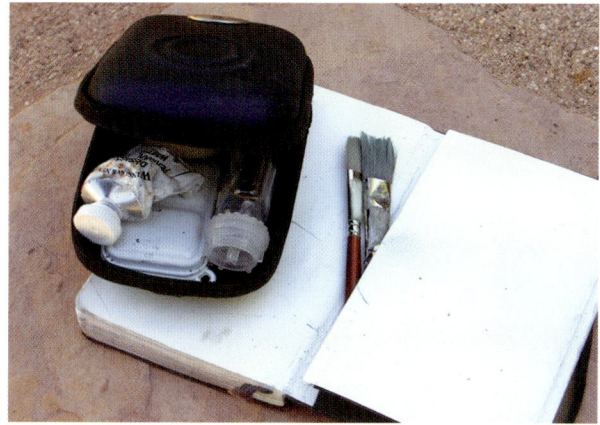

Speaking of convenience, here's a handy little pocket-size sketching kit that I've put together. It's a Moleskine sketchbook and a little novelty palette I picked up at an art store. (I've seen similar ones available for purchase online.) But I definitely do not use the cheap pigments that come with it. Instead, I pry those out and insert my own choice of colors. The case is an inexpensive camera case and the rest are materials previously listed. Now I really can sketch anywhere, anytime!

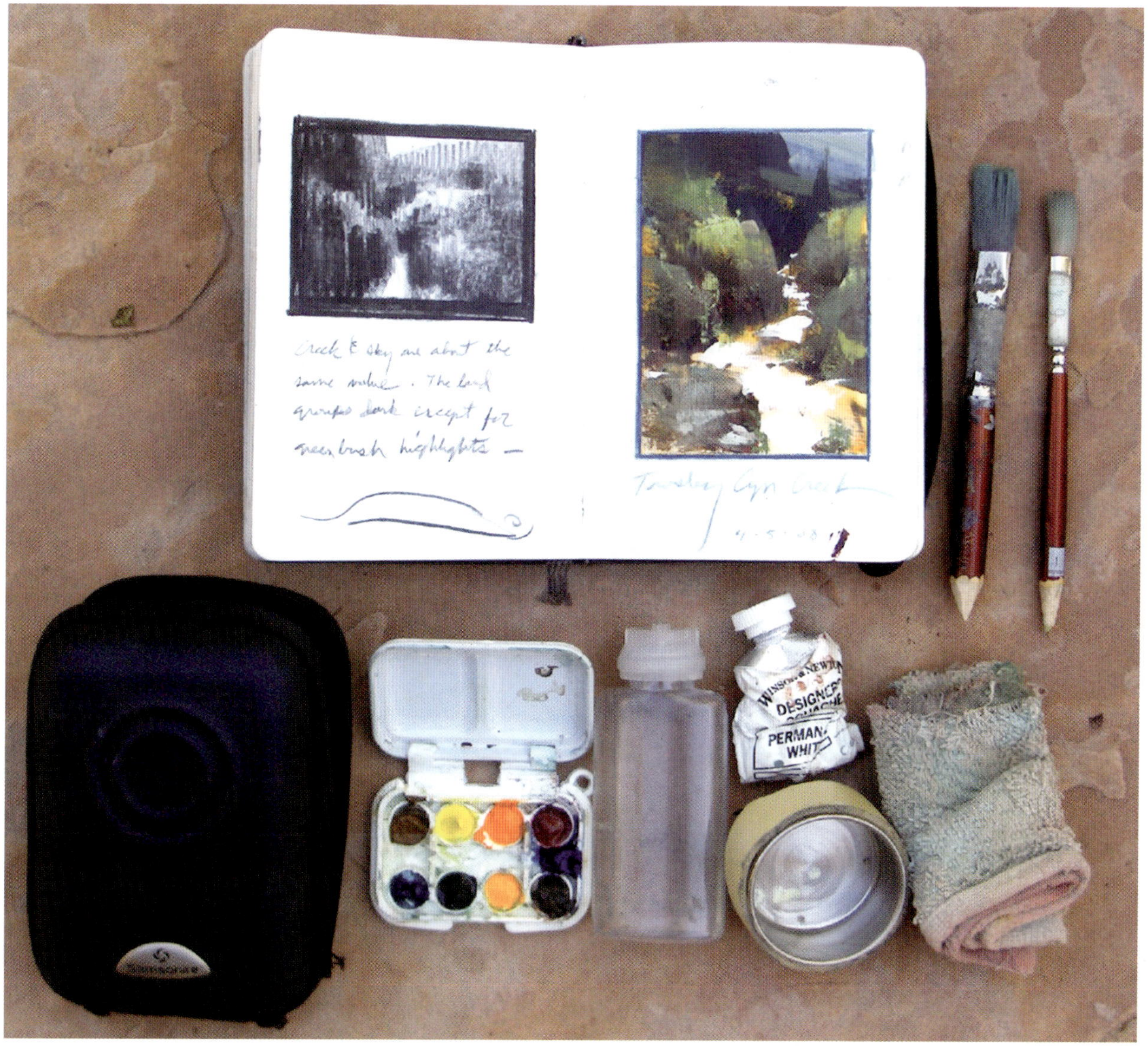

"The goal is to find the materials that let you sketch anywhere, anytime; experimentation contributes to the adventure!"

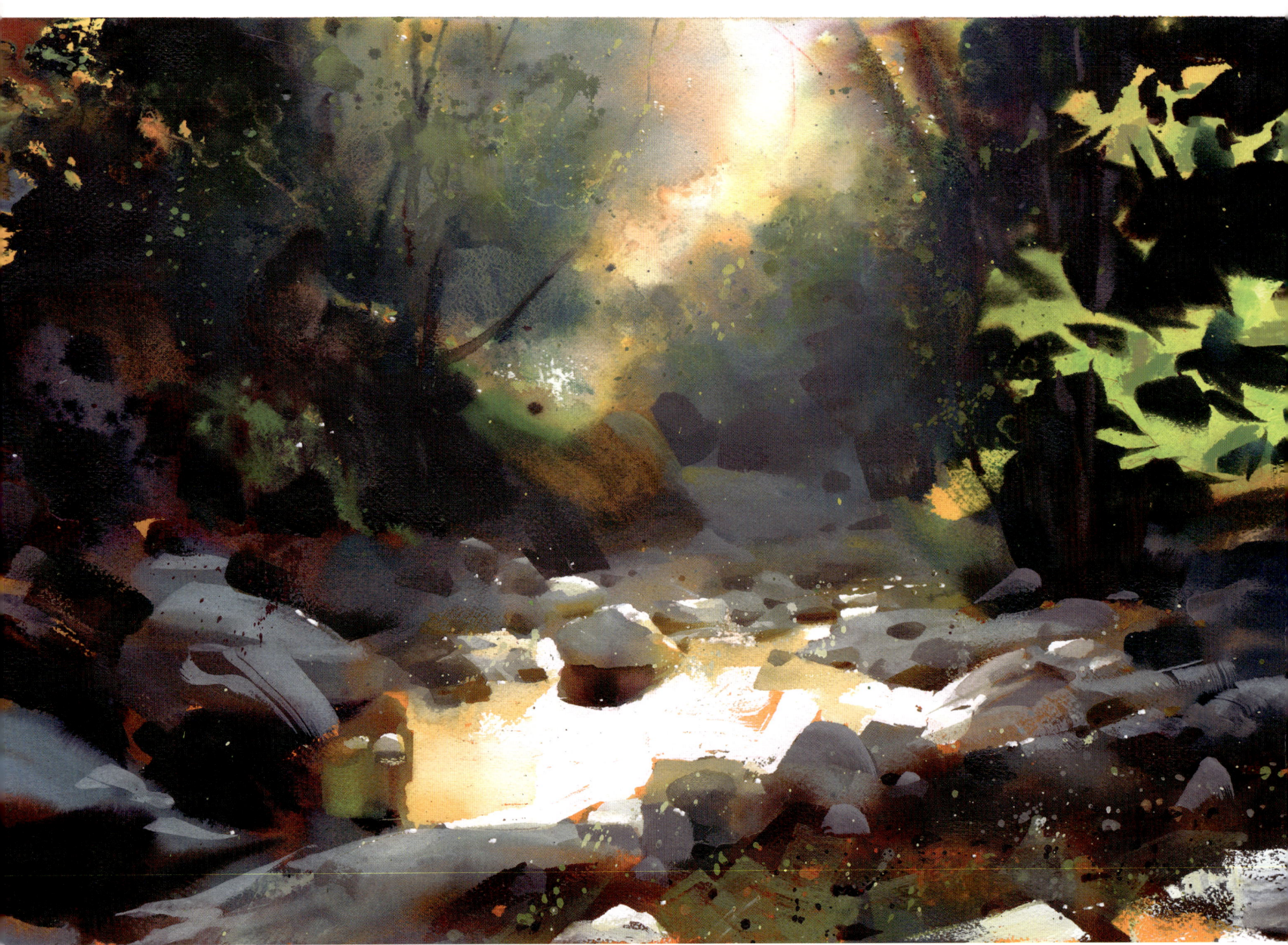

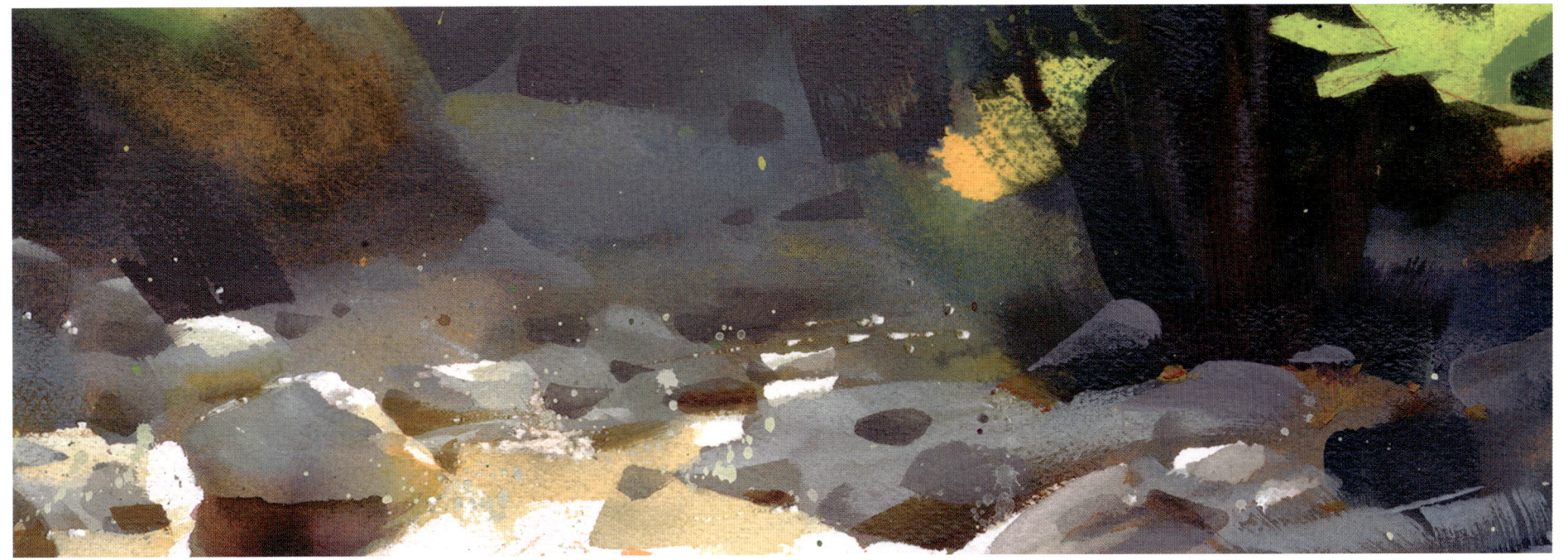

Chapter 2

Using the Materials

Let's have some fun. It's time to get outside and get a feel for the immediacy of the light and atmosphere of your local landscape!

Our primary goal in this book is to create on-location sketches in roughly an hour, before lighting conditions can significantly change. I'll also include an occasional studio painting, created from sketches and photographic reference taken on location.

On the following pages are five demonstrations that show an assortment of materials being used in diverse ways. Head outside and give them a try! Personally, I've found that certain kinds of materials and techniques lend themselves to different subjects; experimenting with them has been incredibly useful because the world is filled with variety! It would be a great shame to use a single, formulaic technique to depict nature.

1. Watercolor on Crescent 100 illustration board

2. Watercolor on Crescent 100 board with opaque highlights

3. Watercolor and opaque gouache on toned mixed-media paper

4. Transparent watercolor on Arches cold-pressed paper

5. Full-size studio painting on Arches cold-pressed paper

"It would be a great shame to use a single, formulaic technique to depict nature."

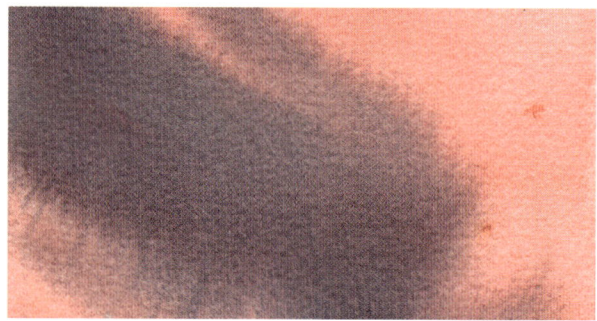

Wet on wet

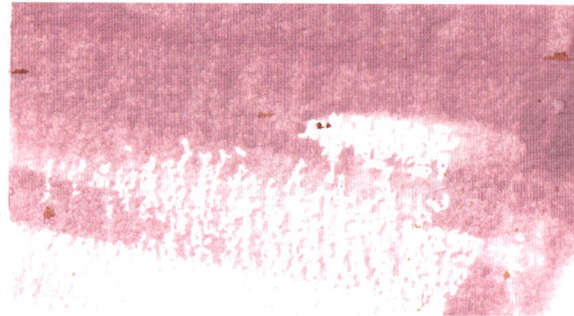

Color wash and dry brush

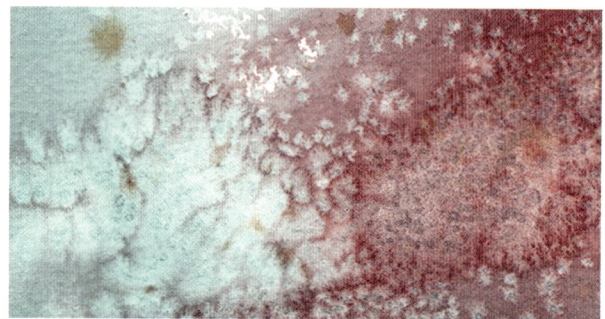

Sprinkling salt grains into a wash.

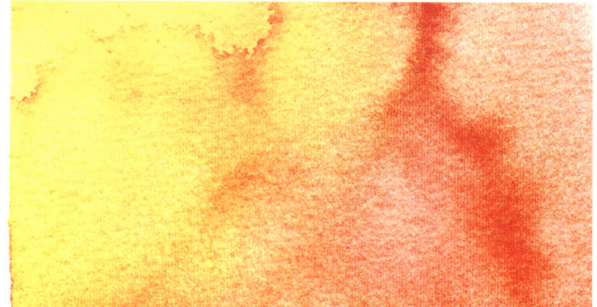

Spritzing water into a wash to create sedimented edges

Layering a wash over previous washes for rich color variations

Spatter

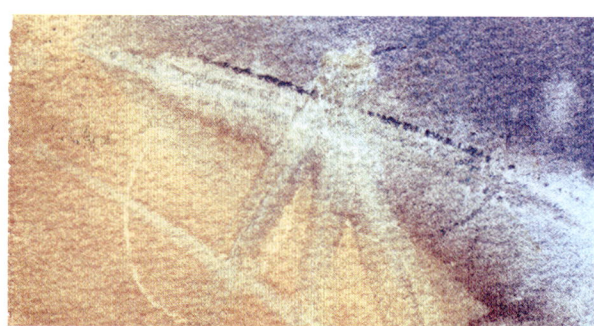

Rubbing pigment out of a wash with a tissue or cloth

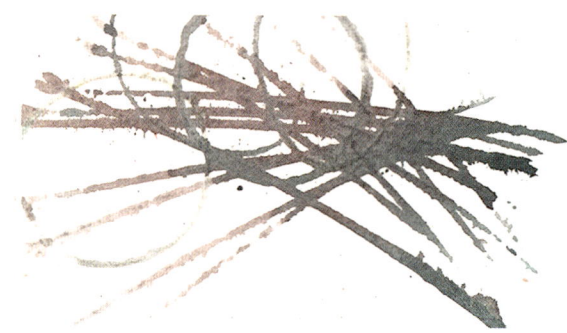

Stamping shapes by dipping objects into paint and applying to surface

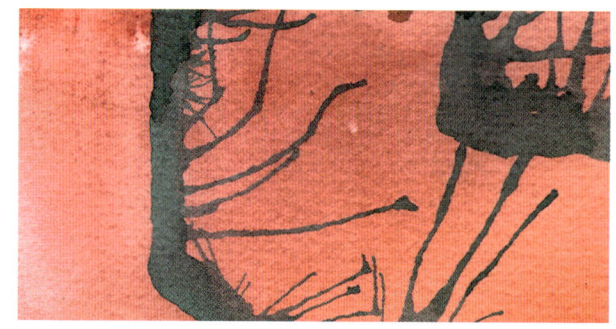

Blowing into wet paint to create interesting shapes

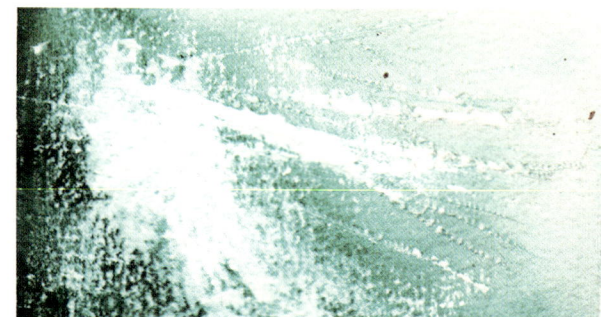

Scratching into dry paint with a razor blade

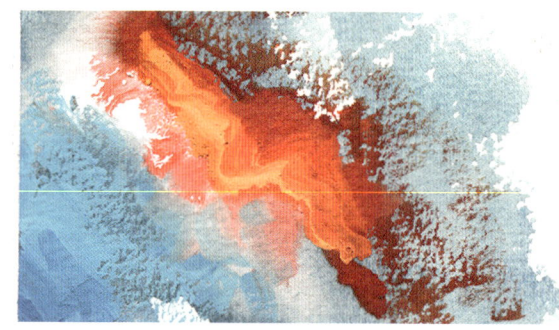

Applying opaque colors

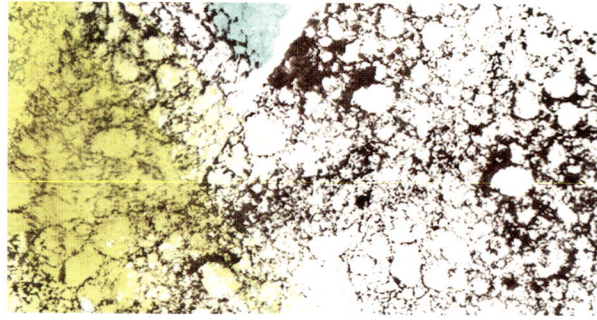

Creating texture with a sponge

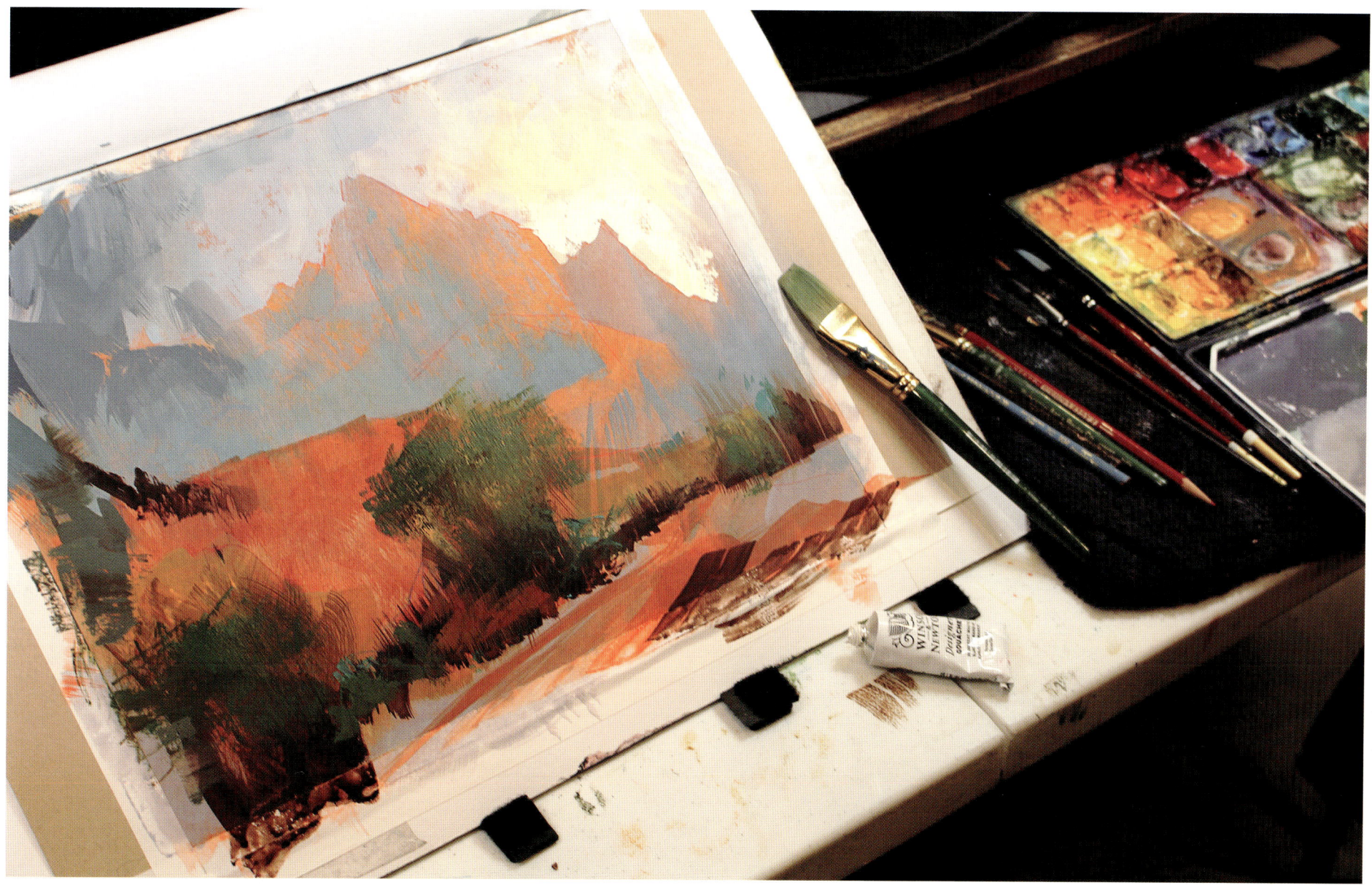

Techniques for Applying Paint

Take a look at the textures to the left and give this exercise a try. Much of painting is about interesting mark making. It's useful to explore the boundaries of what your pigments can achieve.

Above is the initial lay-in for one of the paintings featured later in this book, on page 65. You can see that I enjoy combining washes, textures, and opaque paints to get a variety of effects and describe a variety of objects. The demonstrations on the following pages will show each step of these kinds of techniques.

"Much of painting is about interesting mark making. It's useful to explore the boundaries of what your pigments can achieve."

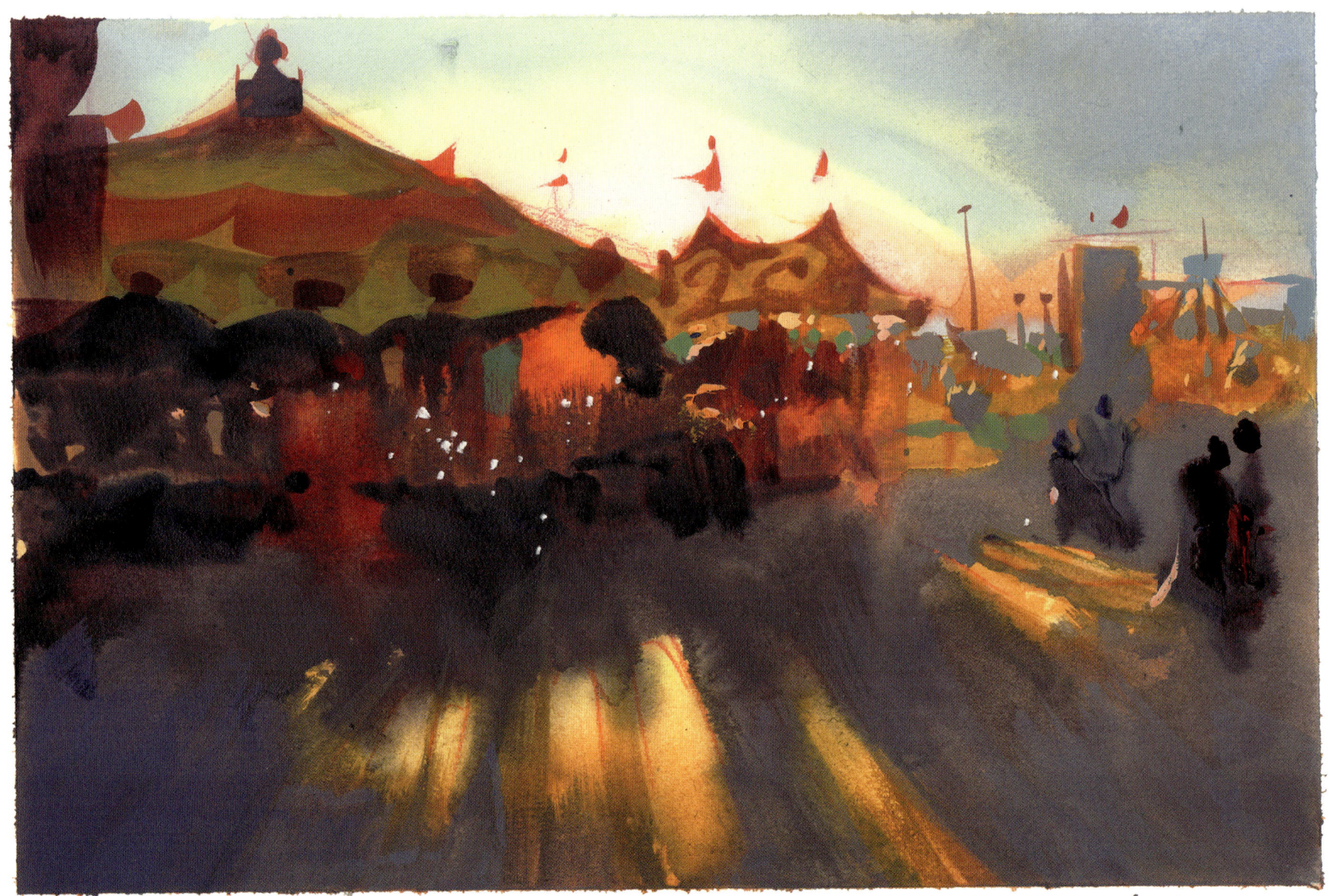

A county fair is a great place and a wonderful challenge for a sketch. And . . . what a huge potential for a painting disaster. Imagine the carnival of people, objects, carousel horses, flashing lights, and endless complexities. How do we deal with all of it in a short enough time to capture the scene before the light changes?

The good news is that the answer is simple: choose the thing that interests you most about the scene and focus on that. (Look for more information on this in Chapter 3: The Simple Statement.) For me, it was the shapes and warmth of the carnival tents with the intriguing cast shadows in the foreground, so that's exactly the simple statement I fought for in this sketch.

Here was my thinking: the sun is placed in the center of the image with a gradating sky to show luminosity and the glowing backlit quality of the tents. That's also where I placed key green accents and little sparkles of light glinting off surfaces, then had the cast shadows radiate out from there. A few fairgoers are loosely indicated plus the pageantry of the flags, and we have our simple statement at the county fair! Let's jump to the next page to go through the actual painting techniques step by step.

1

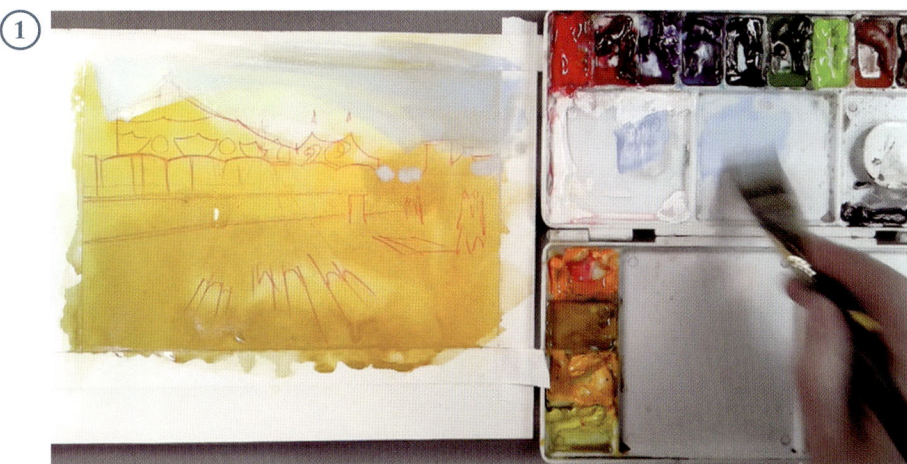

I've chosen to work on illustration board for this painting because it has a sturdy thickness and a beautiful painting surface, the size is 6 x 8 inches. My starting point is to establish the glowing luminosity of the sun, so I begin with a very simple and quick line drawing using a red Prismacolor pencil to indicate simple shapes. I then wash in a vivid yellow with Winsor yellow deep and yellow ochre. I also wash a gradation into the sky using white gouache, ultramarine blue, and the tiniest amount of black.

2

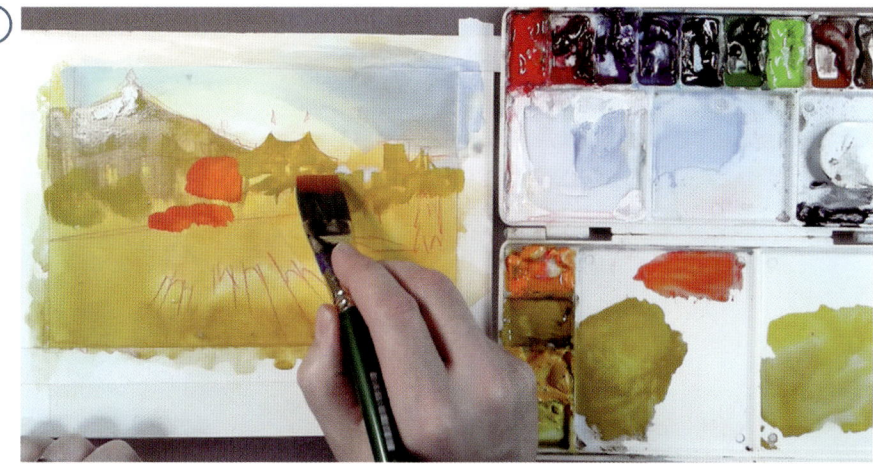

For the tent shapes, I put in a deeper shade of yellow ochre and then start laying in the saturated reds that will give me the backlit feel I'm looking for. I'm using Winsor red with my yellows here. It's helpful to keep the painting surface level for these initial washes so the paint doesn't run into unwanted areas.

3

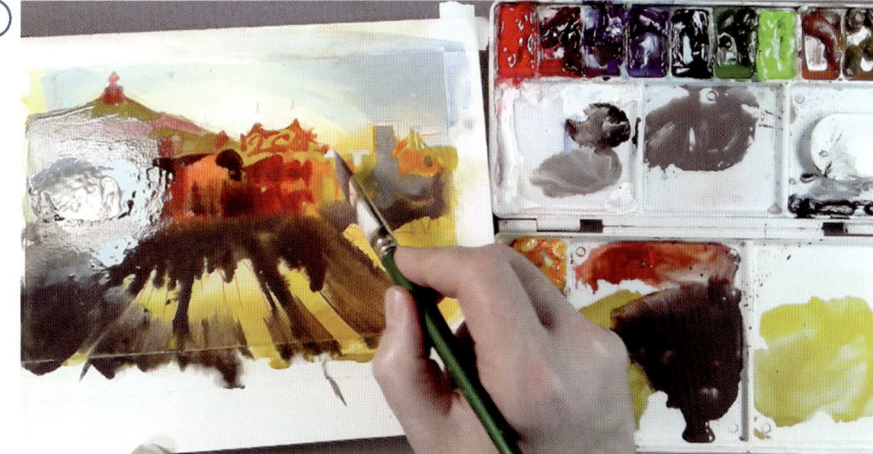

It's time to establish the darks! I'm adding Vandyke brown with a little yellow ochre to create the darker shadow shapes, and then adding red to the mix to get the darker colors in the tent area. Keeping the shafts of light along the ground clear is important, so I use a tissue to dab any dark color that starts to run into that area.

4

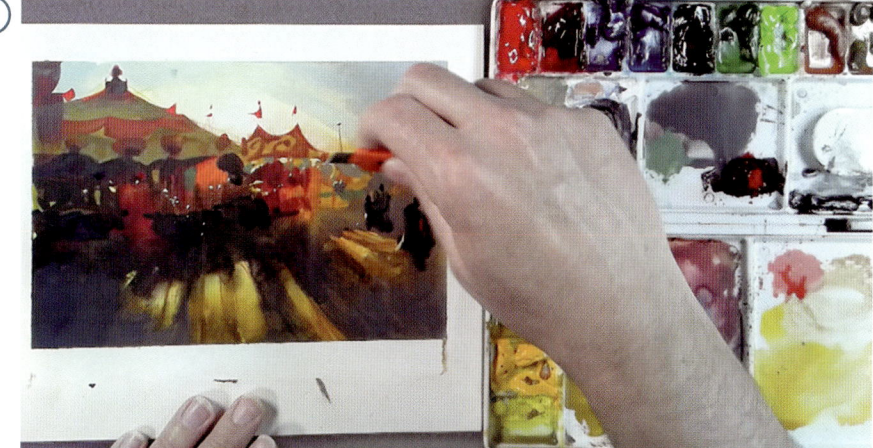

Next, I use some ultramarine blue with a tiny bit of white mixed in to glaze some cool temperatures over the shadows in the foreground. This is important because there's a great deal of blue light from the sky shining down into the shadows. The cool temperatures are a wonderful complement to the warm tones of the scene. I splash in the suggestion of some people as well as some of the decor on the tents and flags. And finally, I use a razor blade to chip out some glints of light by digging right down to the white of the illustration board. These little glints can be a great way to add a sense of finish to a quick sketch. And with that, we're done!

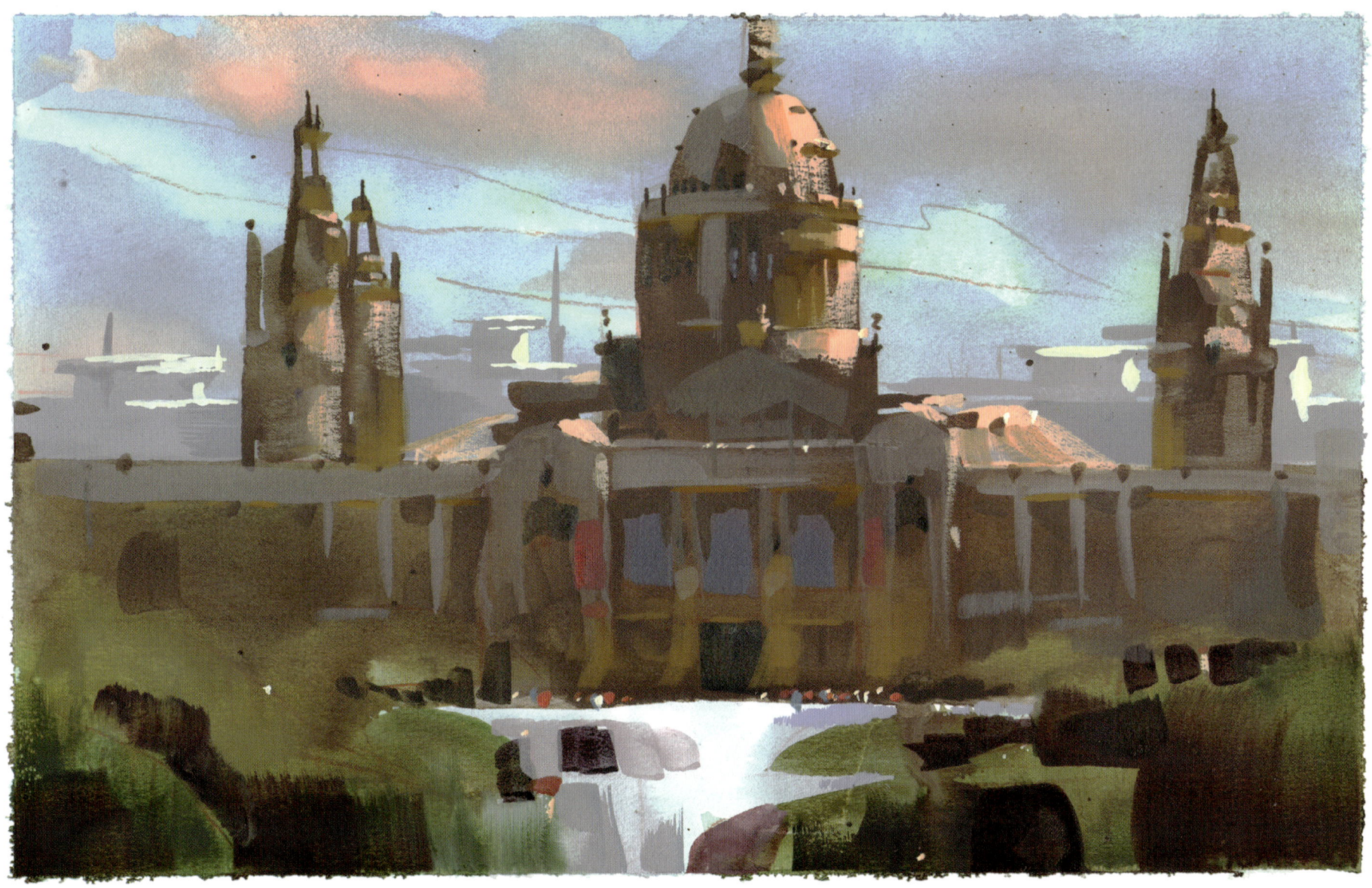

This is Spain's National Gallery in Barcelona. It's a stately building that very much deserves a sketch, especially at sunset!

The primary goal of this sketch (and this book) is to figure out how to capture the moment before the light is gone, so I needed to quickly decide what to emphasize and what to edit in such a complex scene. To me, the captivating quality was the impressive silhouette of the building and the warm sunset light falling across it. To focus in on this quality, I made the big shape of the building and the foreground blend together into one simple shape, then added darks in the foreground for a sense of depth.

By creating this simple statement first, it let me emphasize the more active areas of visual interest, especially the light on the building, the white waterfall and the sweep of clouds. And that's often the answer, to simplify and group what is secondary so that the primary visual interest can stand out meaningfully.

When traveling, I most often work in a mixed-media sketchbook (heavyweight paper that can take wet paint) but for this one I've chosen illustration board. I can easily tip the board as needed to control the wet on wet flow of paint. And even though it's a fairly small painting (6 x 9 inches), I'm hoping it will turn out to be frameable, so I don't want to hide it away in a sketchbook.

You can see a reference photo of this location on page 178/179.

Approach 2: Watercolor on Crescent 100 Board with Opaque Highlights

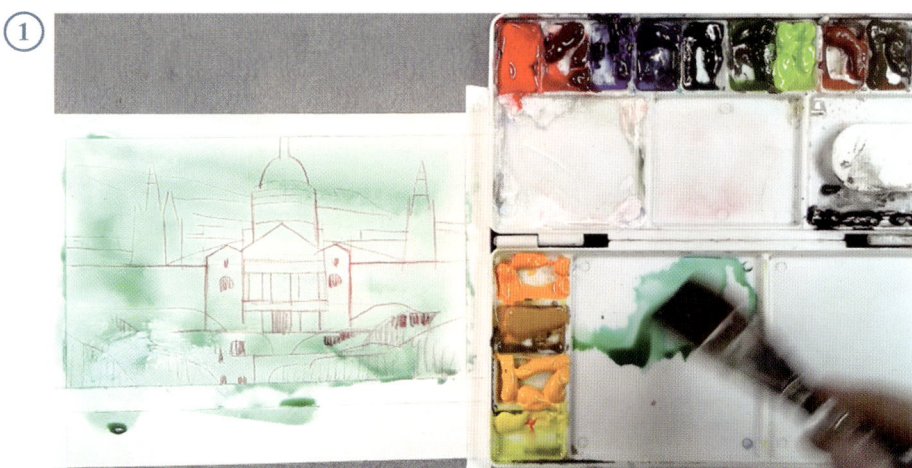

① Once again, I use red Prismacolor to create a very simple drawing, just placing the most important shapes. Next, I lay in a green wash of color over the whole image. This might seem like an odd choice, but the warm light streaming through the sky created a greenish quality in the distance, plus it lends to the green foliage of the foreground. And the emphasis on green is for style reasons as well: it will help the reds of the sunset light really pop!

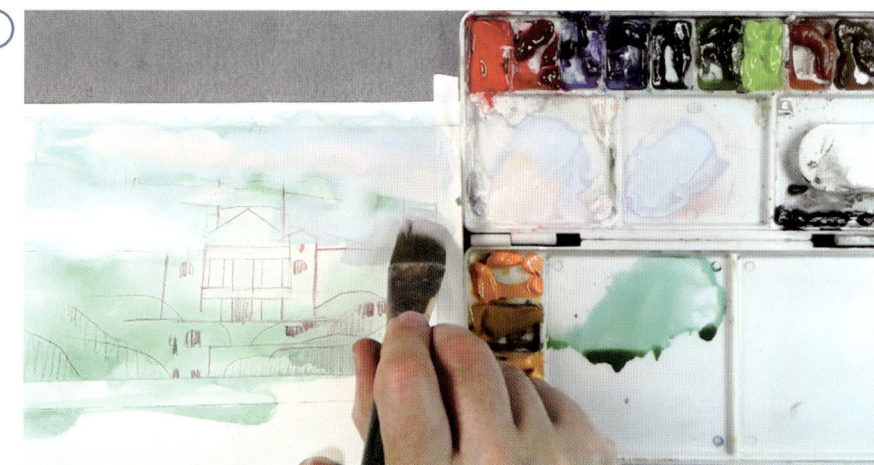

② Now it's time to suggest the sky. I'm using opaque white combined with ultramarine blue to create the cool cloud shapes, then I mix a touch of Winsor red with opaque white to suggest the red sunset light hitting the clouds. All of this is done wet on wet while the underlying green wash is still damp. I hold the painting level during this process so the wet paint doesn't run downward.

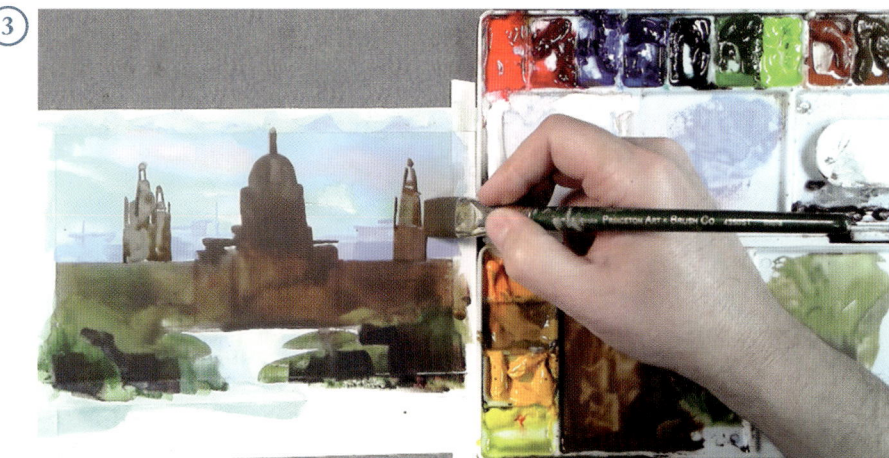

③ To block in the big simple silhouette of the architecture, I use Vandyke brown, then blend in sap green to create the foreground suggestion of foliage. I'm careful to work around the lighter shape of the central waterfall to maintain its light value.

Next, it's time for more opaque color. I mix a tiny bit of red and yellow into white opaque gouache and keep the mixture quite thick. Thin and runny paint at this point will not have the opacity needed to create the impact of the highlights.

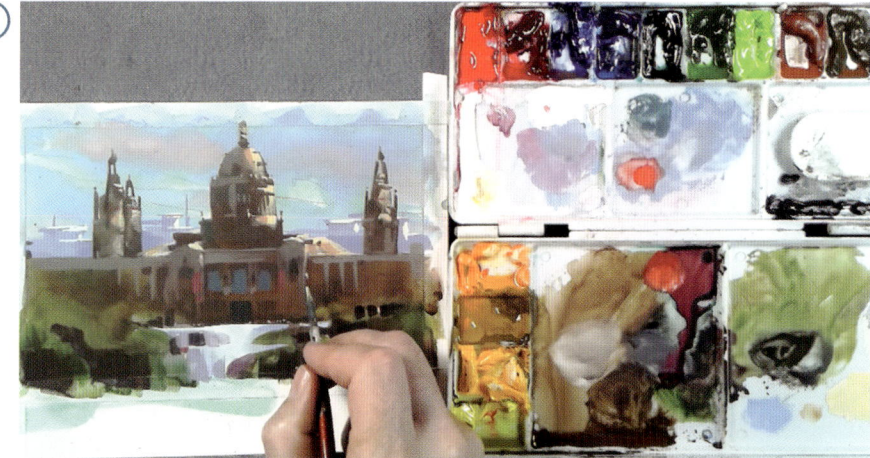

④ I dry brush the paint onto the building, following the curving forms to suggest a sense of volume. I also let the paint drag a little to create texture. Texture in the highlights can suggest visual activity and help a quick sketch feel more finished. There is also cool skylight coming down onto the building, so those are indicated by adding a tiny bit of white into Vandyke brown and applying it to the painting. Finally, I add some accents of color that suggests windows, banners, and a sprinkle of tiny people atop the waterfall.

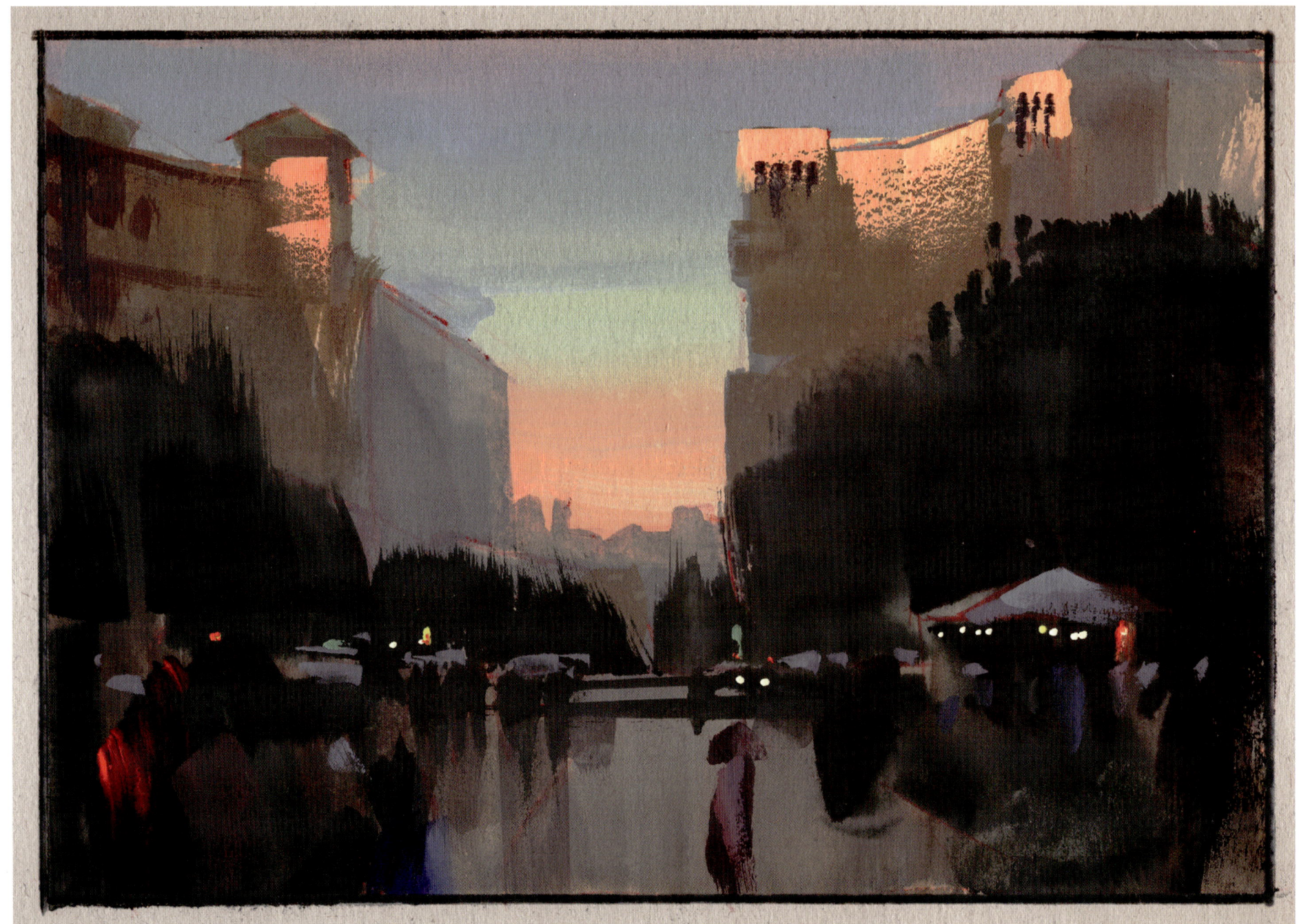

Let's head back to Barcelona for another sketch, this time to Cathedral Square in the city center. Once again, our goal is to quickly sketch the location in less than an hour, which means tough decisions have to be made about what to emphasize and what to edit in the hustle and bustle of the city. The warm lights were quite magnificent, so I gave a strong emphasis to the contrasting greens and blues in the background sky, and painted sunlight on the buildings with thick textural strokes.

The activity at street level created a good deal of visual interest, so I kept the surrounding masses of dark foliage very simple and graphic. This is how we can make our paintings special and unique: think in terms of opposites, or contrast. In this case, I depicted the active versus passive. The toned paper is also helpful, serving as an automatic "ground" of warmth that underlies everything I put down. Let's go through the techniques for this step by step on the next page.

You can see a reference photo of this location on page 178/179.

1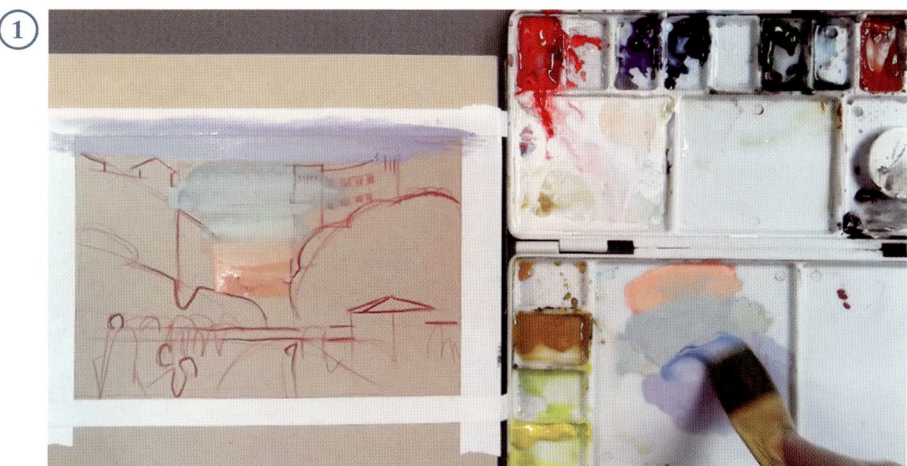

You're familiar with step one by now, start with a simple drawing that places big shapes and then lay in color. The banding of colors in the sky were extraordinary, with contrasts of red gradating into greens and blues, so I begin there, blending the opaque colors together wet on wet. To get the opaque quality, I'm blending white gouache into each of the colors I mix.

2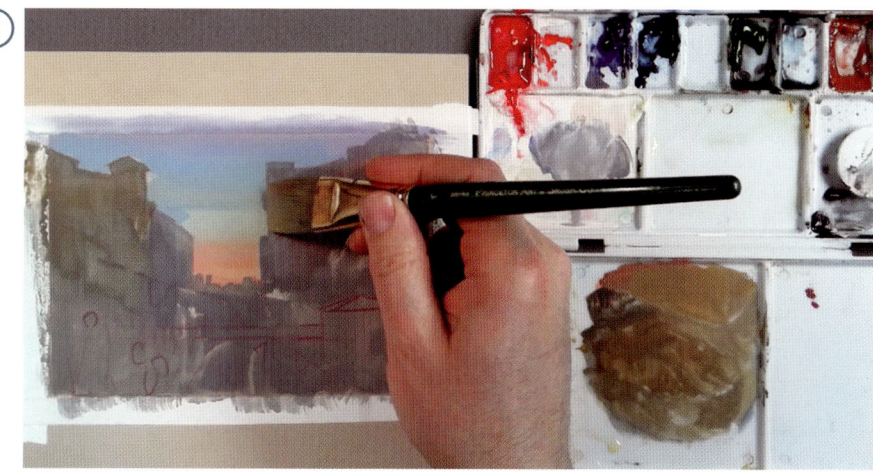

Next up is blocking in the big simple silhouette of the buildings. Remember, I'm thinking in terms of simplicity so that I can add the more active areas over top. A warm mixture of brown, yellow ochre, and a touch of blue does the trick. The paint is just opaque enough for a good coverage, but I'm reserving the really thick, textural paint for the highlights.

3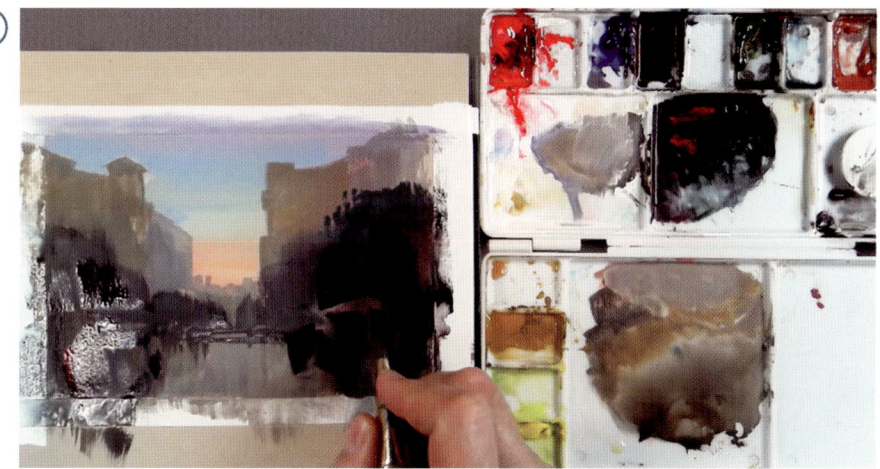

For the dark tones, I'm using a mixture of red and green to get the dark neutral tones of the foliage. The darkness here is very important so that I can contrast the glowing lights and activity at ground level. I'm using a large 1-inch brush for this with quick upward strokes that suggest tree shapes.

4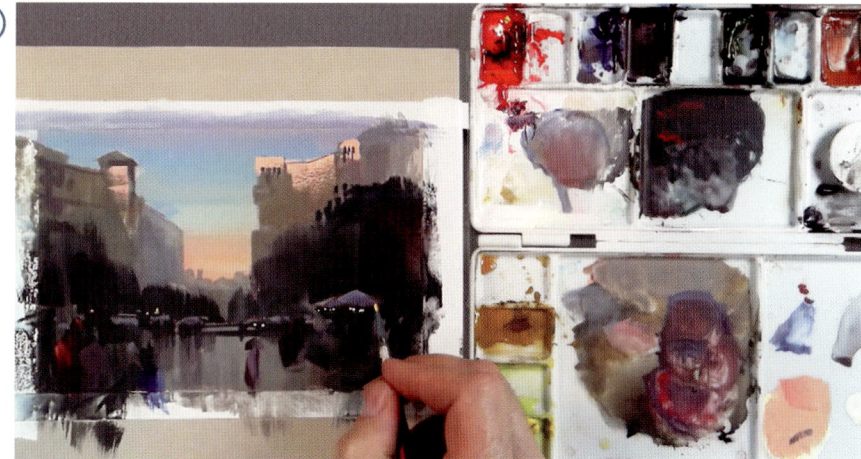

And now, going into the opaque highlights, I'm mixing white with a little red and yellow and dragging my brush for textural sunlight on the buildings. Below I suggest umbrellas and lights as well as passersby in the street. Note that these opaquely painted areas have more vivid colors and more committed edges than the soft and blended masses of trees and buildings, thus staying true to the idea of active versus passive. And with that, we can peel the tape off for the finished piece, as shown at left!

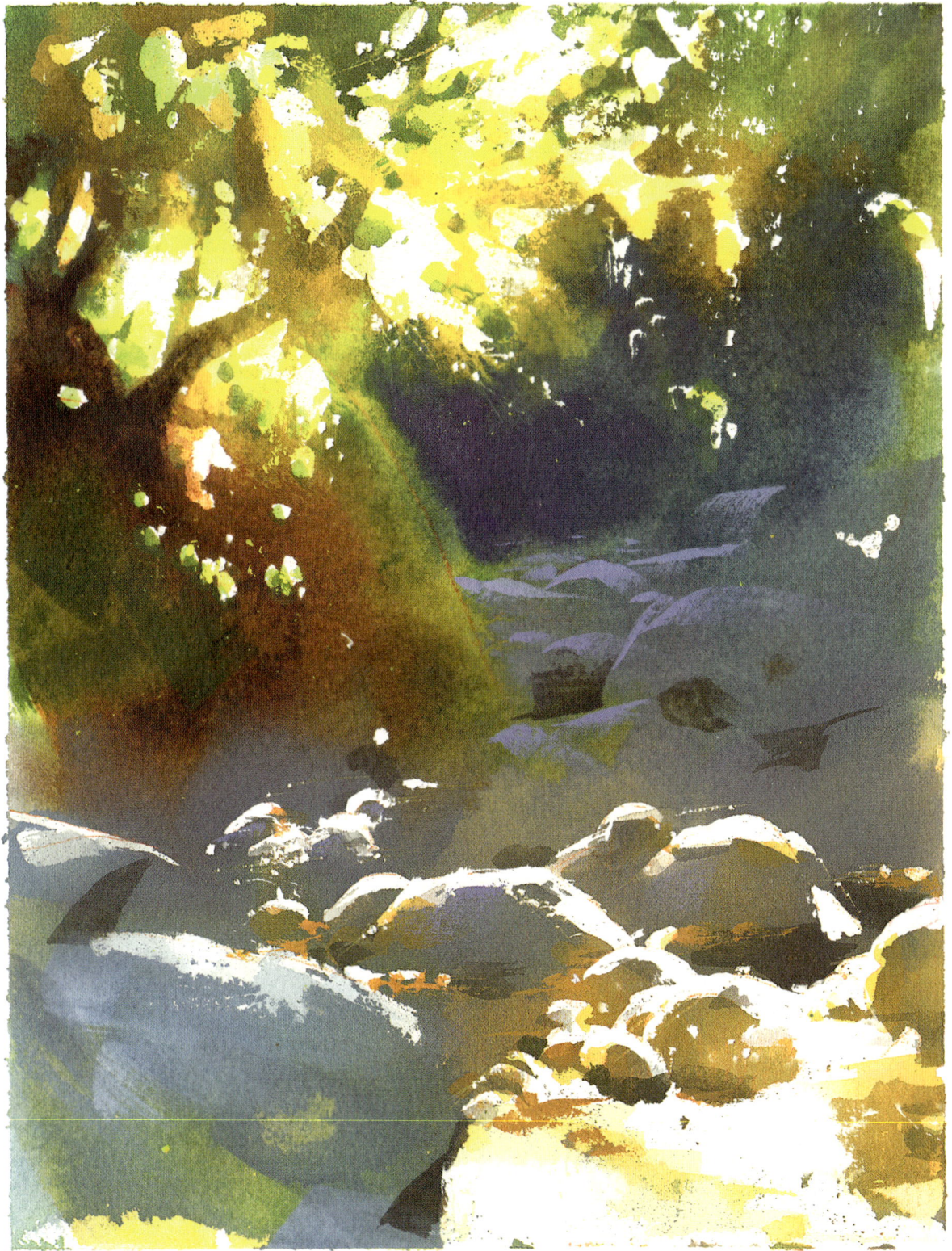

Now, let's move to something that might be considered a more traditional watercolor technique, an approach that relies on washes and taking advantage of the brilliant white of the paper. I occasionally have concerns about this approach because it's been dogmatically followed as the "proper" way to use watercolor, devolving into formulaic techniques of tinted colors that lack the depth of value that a heavier application of pigment can create. That being said, it's a time-honored technique for a reason: it can be absolutely gorgeous in its luminosity.

The technique here is to apply masking fluid to areas that are meant to remain the pure white of the paper. This way, washes can be painted quickly and loosely over top. For me, carefully painting around white shapes is too much of an impediment to quick and expressive painting. I prefer the use of masking fluid for such images.

Masking fluid is easily available from most art suppliers. It is brushed on and needs a few minutes to dry, at which time paint can be laid over top. When the painting is ready, the masking fluid can be easily rubbed off with an eraser or even fingers, revealing the vivid white of the paper. I strongly recommend Arches paper, it's made of 100 percent cotton and takes watercolor beautifully; washes flow better, and color is more brilliant than on lower quality wood pulp papers.

I'll be using a 7 x 10–inch Arches block, which is a stack of papers already secured to a board; the paper is held secure while painting, then is easily peeled away from the block when finished. This keeps the paper from bending and buckling from the wetting and drying process. Let's put this beautiful paper and masking technique to use on the next page. We'll keep to our quick-sketch approach of capturing the immediate effects of light before conditions change too much, finishing in about an hour.

You can see a reference photo of this location on page 178/179.

Approach 4: Transparent Watercolor on Arches Cold-Pressed Paper

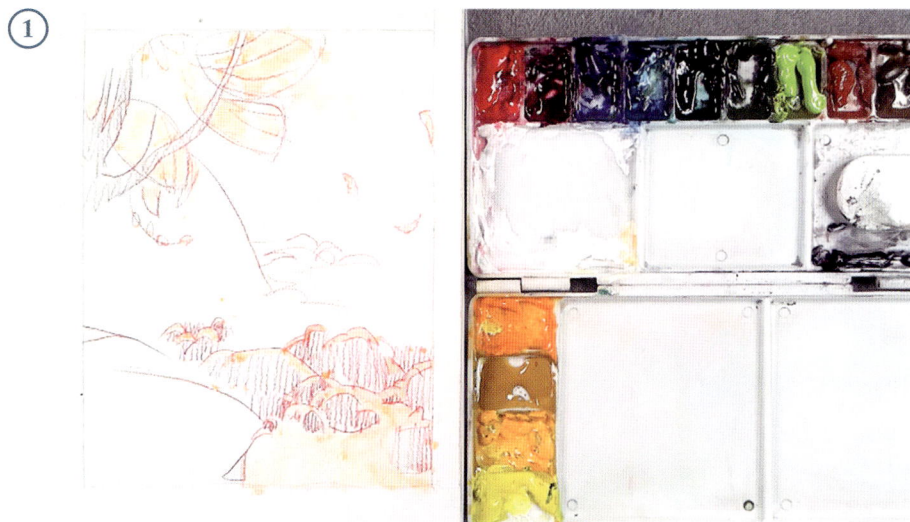

1 A quick drawing in red Prismacolor establishes where the light and shadow will be, then masking fluid is applied to any area where white highlights need to be preserved. The mask will need a of couple minutes to dry until I'm ready to move forward.

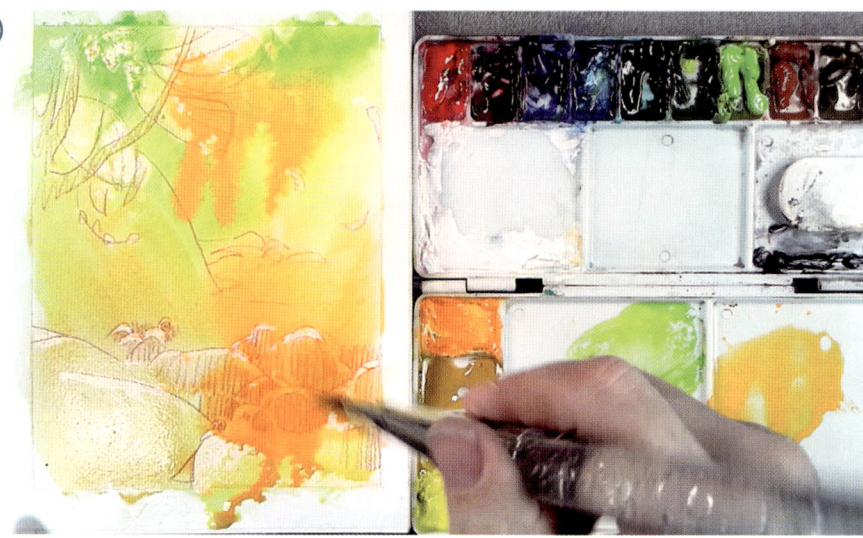

2 Time to lay down the initial transparent washes. This painting is all about the vivid glow of light, so I start with vibrant warms as underpainting for the light filtering through the foliage and splashing onto the ground.

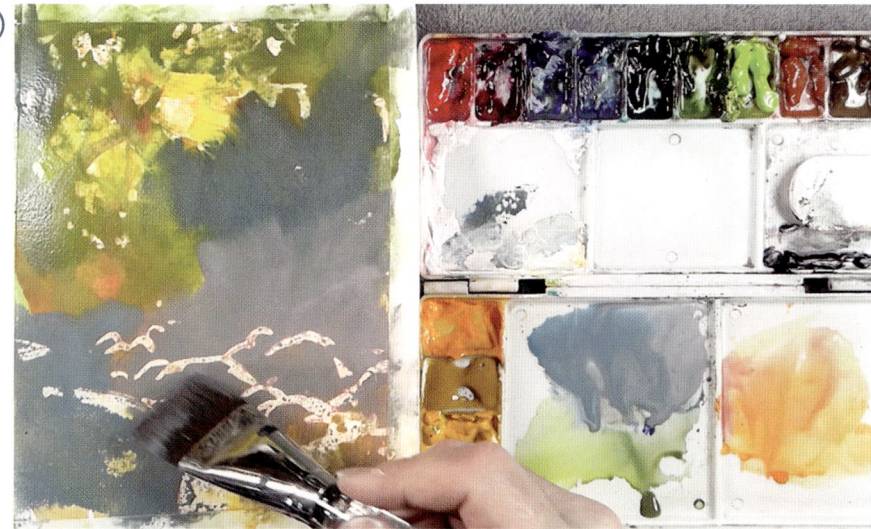

3 Next, I apply darker washes to surround the illuminated areas to create the contrast that I need to emphasize the light. I'm being very careful to preserve the areas of backlit foliage and the warm light in the rocks.

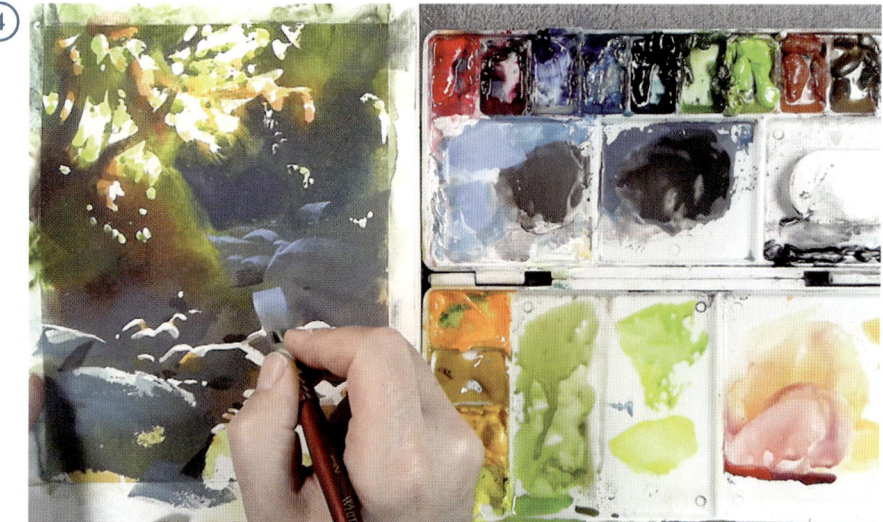

4 Now it's time to rub off the masking fluid and reveal the highlights! This gives me a better feel for the value range of my sketch. Then I add the darkest accents where I feel they're needed. Since I'm not at all a purist, I go ahead and use some opaque color made up of blue and white for some cool light on the distant rocks for a stronger sense of depth. And time's up!

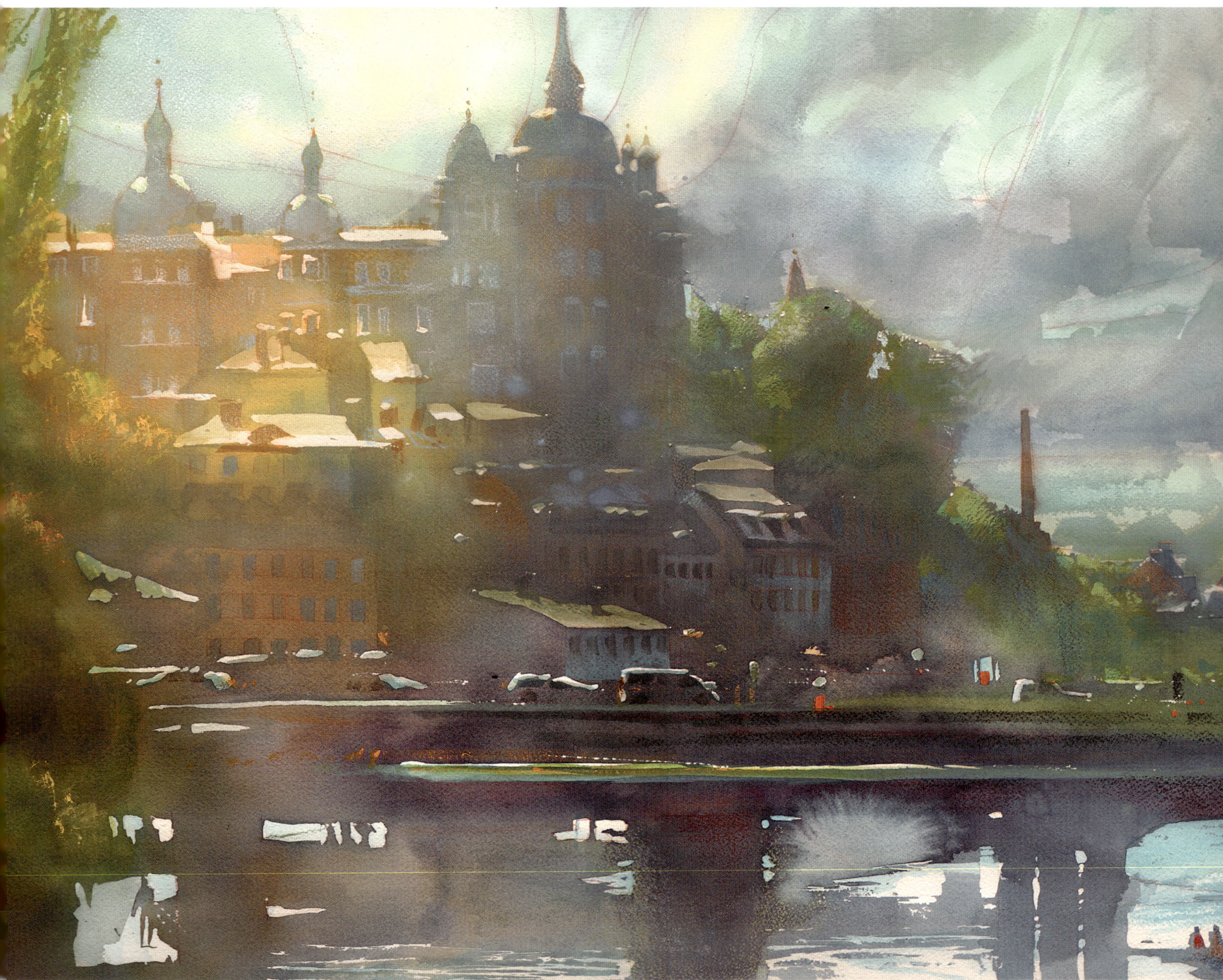

Although the primary concern of this book is to address the challenges of on-site landscape sketching, doing more finished paintings in the controlled environment of a home studio is an important addition to our craft. So for this fifth approach, we will be tackling just that. The paper we'll be using is an 18 x 24–inch Arches block of cold-pressed 140-lb paper.

Welcome to my studio. I use the exact same supplies here as I do outdoors, so the tools and process will no doubt look familiar by now. Probably the only difference is that I use bigger brushes for washes, preferably a Robert Simmons 2-inch Skyflow brush.

And welcome to the beautiful city of Stockholm, Sweden! I was there on business and didn't have the time I would have liked to paint the local cityscape. I was able, however, to paint the smaller study (7 x 10 inches) shown right, and using the study and location photos, I completed the painting shown left in my studio.

To me, the exciting thing about such paintings is that they use the same approaches and techniques as on-site work. And with some planning, they can be completed rather quickly and with the same spontaneity.

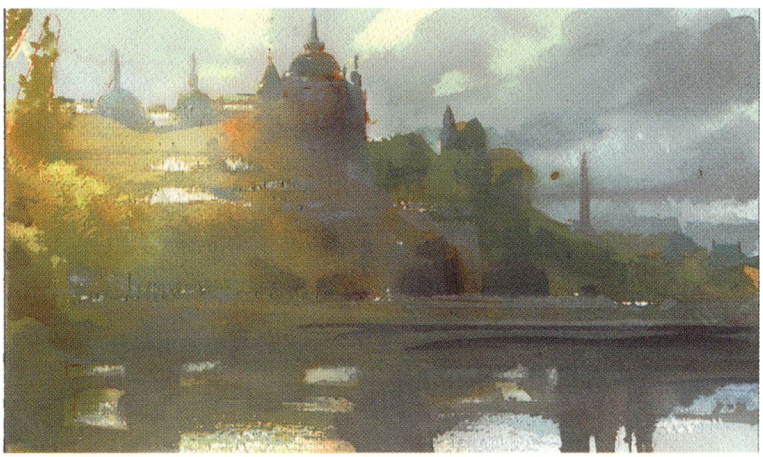

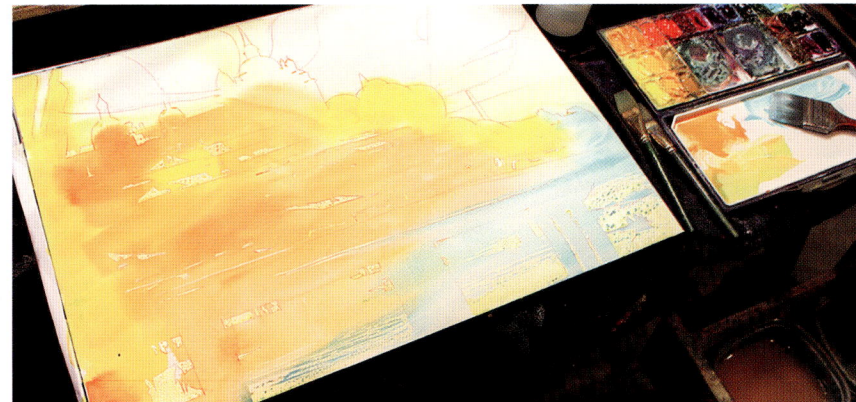

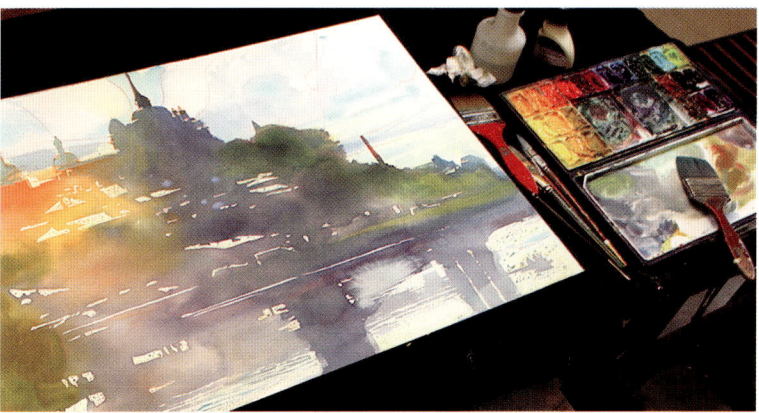

① First comes a line drawing, I'm concentrating on the silhouette of the city as well as where the highlights will be placed. I also plan out the shapes of the clouds since they will help the skyline stand out where needed. Next, masking fluid is applied to preserve the highlights, just like shown in the previous demonstration. Then, I dive right into washes of warm colors to ensure the glowing luminosity of the scene. But the cool temperatures are extremely important as well and I begin washing those into the water and sky.

② This part is tricky but exciting at the same time, I'll attempt to wash in the entire landmass, foliage, and bridge in one wet-on-wet block-in. I premix the colors I'll need on the palette, then begin laying them in to create a big silhouetted shape of the city and its surroundings. I try to keep everything wet on wet at this point and use a spray bottle to mist areas that need to remain damp. But I'm careful not to over mist to avoid paint bleeding outside of the silhouetted shape. I'm sweating profusely and in a near panic by the time I get the washes done, but if I've done it right, I'll have nice transitions from warms to cools and lights to darks. I can now rub out the masking fluid to reveal the highlights then begin painting any necessary details and adding opaque paint in areas that need to be lightened or given texture. And, voilà! We have a studio watercolor painting. It took about two and a half hours to complete, whereas the on-site sketch took about an hour.

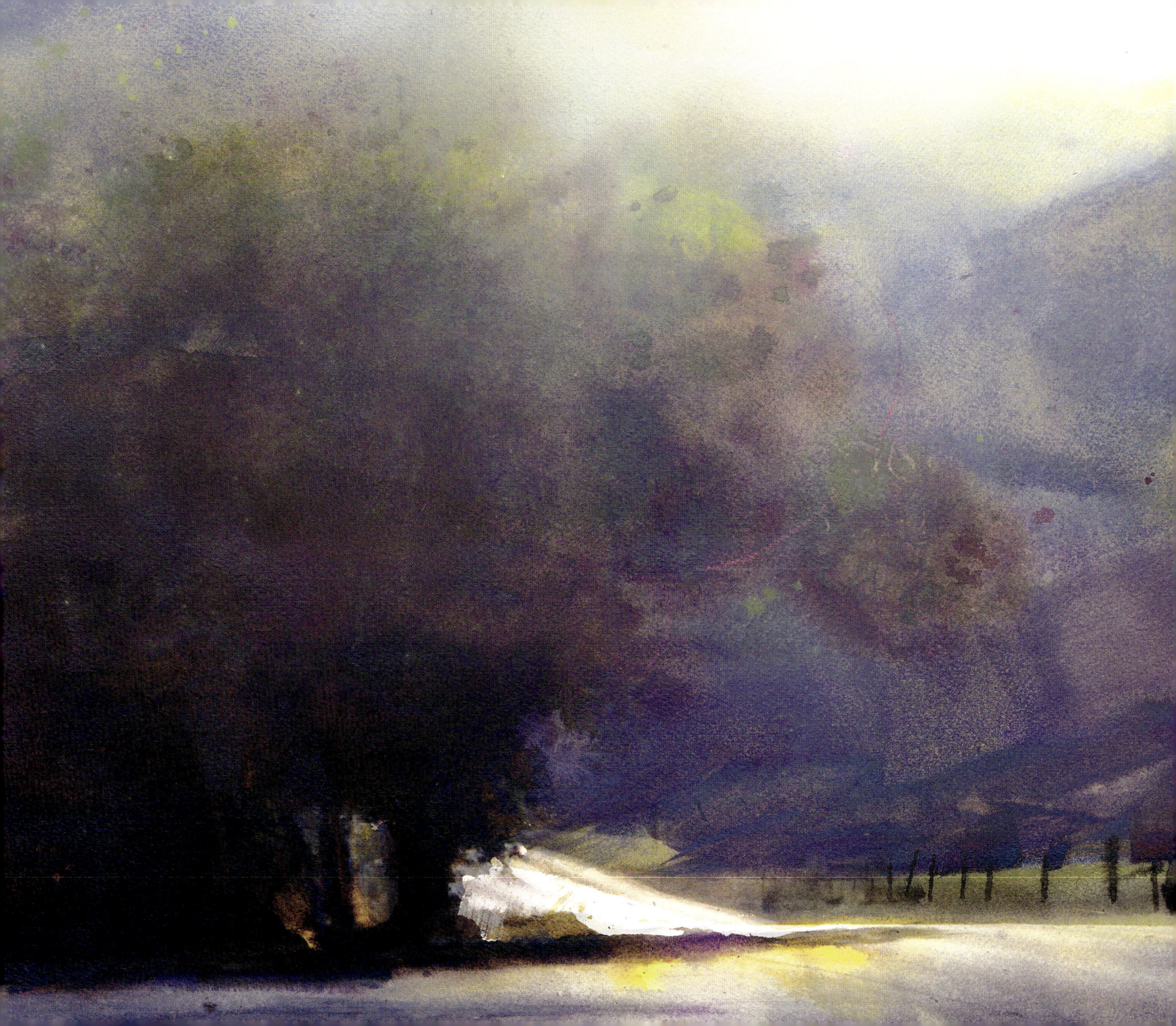

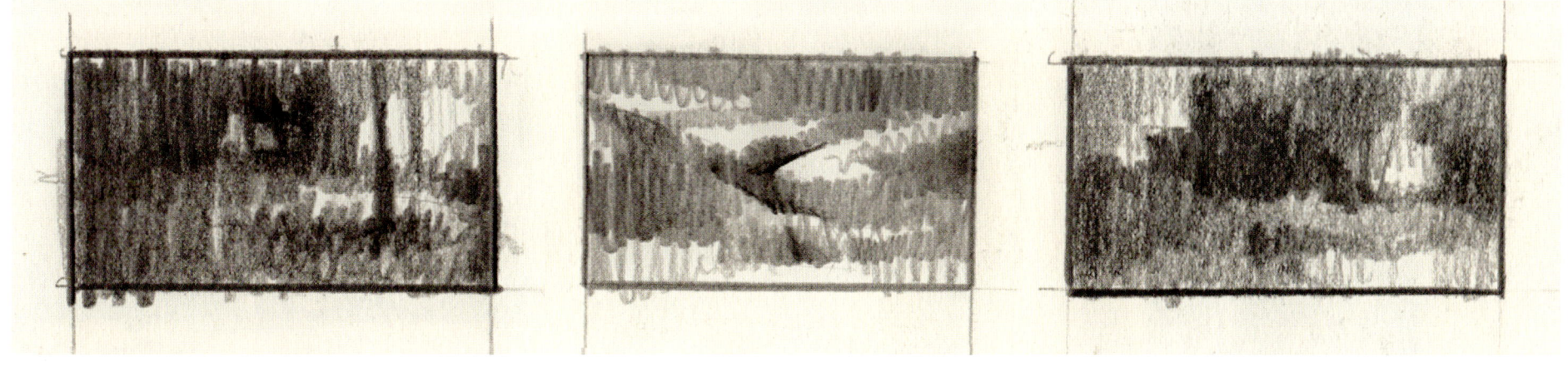

Chapter 3

The Simple Statement

Pretty much everyone has looked at a majestic landscape and been emotionally moved by it. And it's a normal human reaction to want to hold onto it and make it last forever. We can break out a camera and take a pretty good picture, but the camera doesn't feel anything, it isn't selective. You, as the artist, will always have the potential to be better than your camera, because you can develop the ability to bring purpose and emotion to your paintings. And my own belief is that the moment you can visually convey emotion to your audience, you are officially an artist. This is the essence of finding the powerful, simple statement in your work, and it's what this chapter is all about.

"The moment you can visually convey emotion to your audience, you are officially an artist."

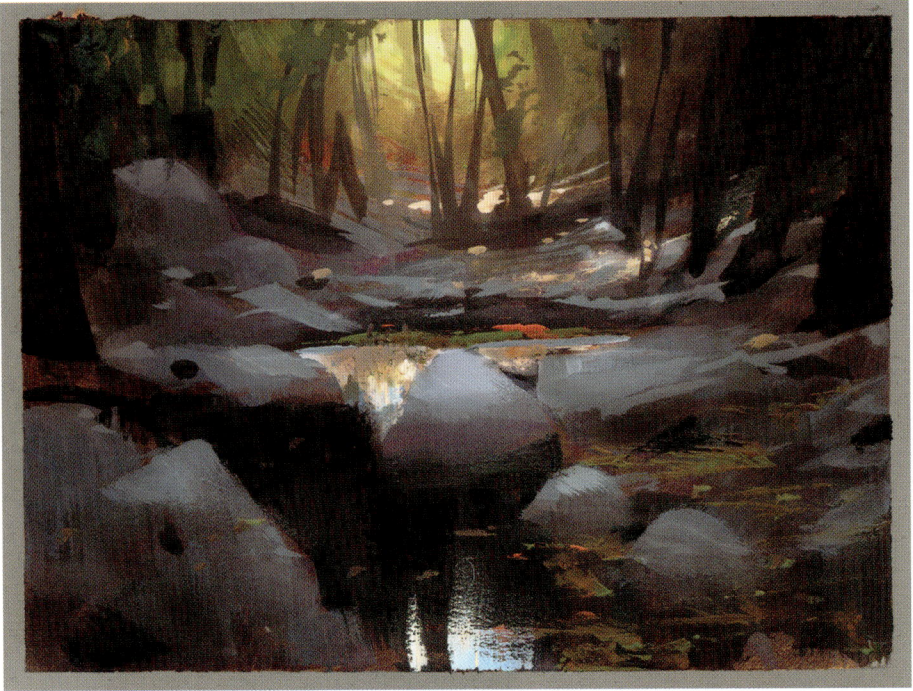

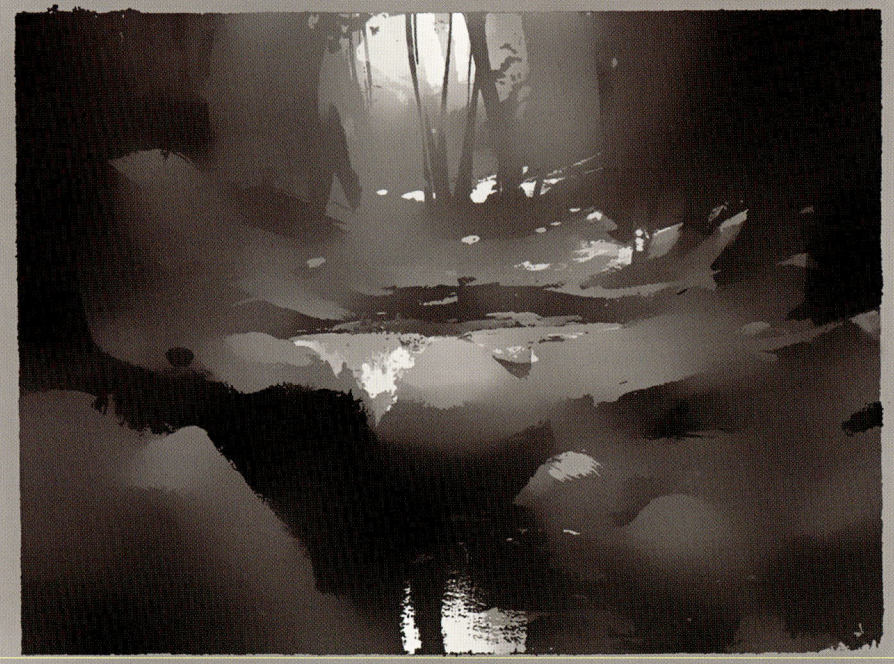

Want to know the big secret of landscape painting? Squinting. Yep, squinting. Let me explain with a story.

From time to time I teach landscape sketching classes on the outskirts of my native Los Angeles, and it was on an autumn day that we went to the location you see at left. It's a beautiful spot in Angeles National Forest with a bubbling creek flowing through granite stones; there's lots of foliage with fallen leaves, and just an extraordinary level of detail everywhere you look. That is why my class had looks of horror on their faces when I told them their first exercise was to sketch it in full color in 20 minutes. Some of them even thought I was joking. But I had to make the same point to them that I make in this chapter. Getting an effective sketch done before the light changes requires speed, and the only way to do it well is to find a simple statement.

So after their initial struggles, I took pity on the class and did the demonstration that you see here, which brings us back to squinting. That's exactly what I did: squinted to see a simpler version of the landscape. When you squint, you're literally looking through your eyelashes. Details start to disappear and color is not as apparent; all you see are the big, simple relationships of value (value is the term artists use for the range of light to dark). In other words, you see a simple statement.

Take a look at the simplified version of this sketch at lower left. I've digitally treated it to look like what we would see when squinting, and I'd like you to notice a couple of things. The central area is open to skylight, and the surrounding foliage creates darker drop shadows along the outskirts with dark trees at the outer edges. Then there are bright rows of dappled light falling across the landscape with light in the far distance. Despite the incredible amount of detail present, there is a very simple value and lighting statement to the scene, and nobody, I mean, nobody sees it like this. Why? People mostly notice the details and contrasts, then they sit down and paint the scene as a bunch of individual pieces of contrast, and the painting predictably turns into a patchwork of disaster. They emphasized the individual parts without the simple relationships of how those parts fit together. This, in a nutshell, is why landscape painting is so very difficult for everyone! We have a natural inclination to approach it in a way that does not work. Let me repeat that: the natural way we tend to look at a landscape is a near guarantee of failure. That's why we're talking up front about finding the big simple statement, and it's why squinting at your subject is incredibly useful.

> *"The reason landscape painting is consistently difficult is that we have a natural tendency to mostly notice and emphasize the contrasts while missing the big, simple relationships."*

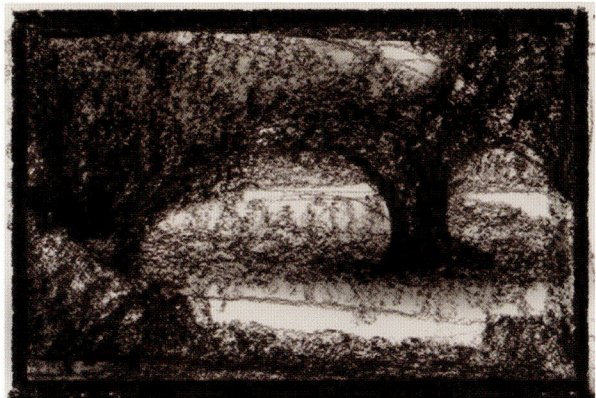

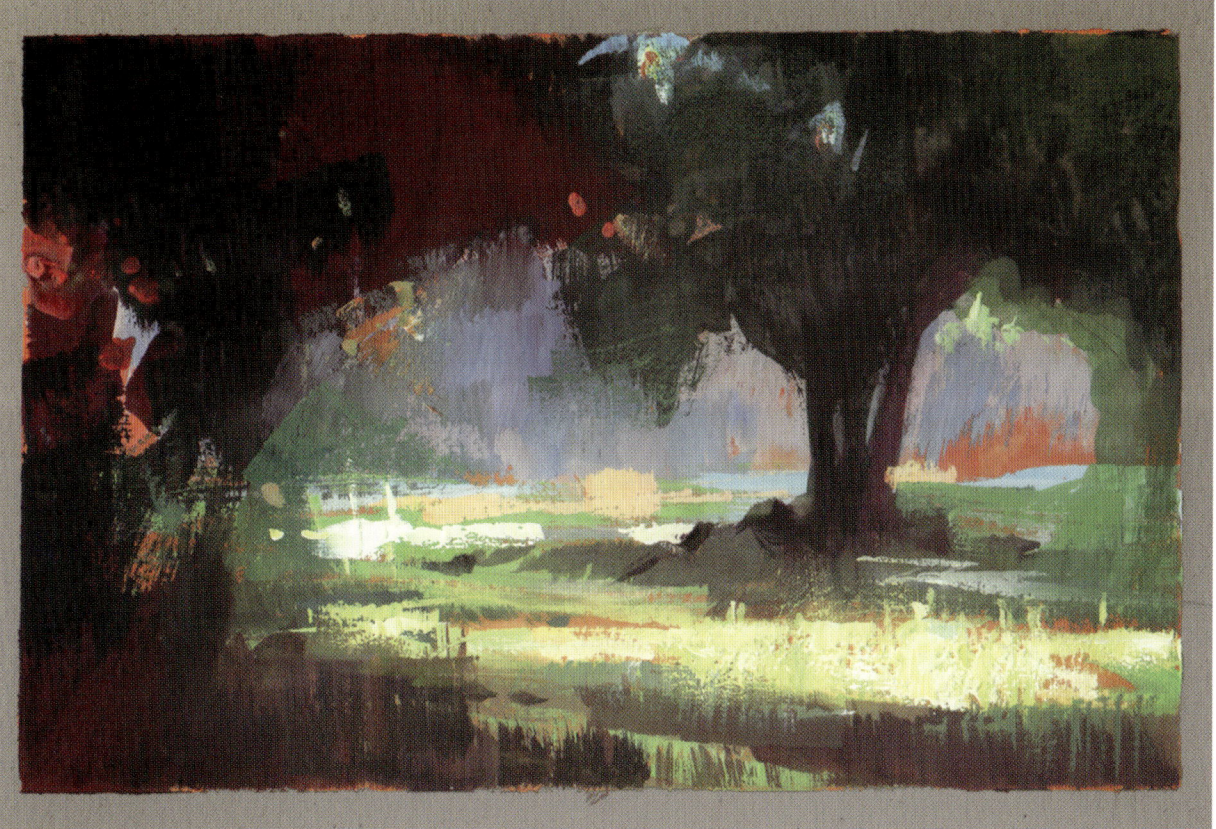

Let's move on to another on-site location sketch that I also did as a class demonstration. And, I'll tell you, doing demonstrations is nerve racking. All kinds of people are looking over your shoulder expecting you to know what you're doing, and if you don't come up with something that looks passably good really fast, it will be embarrassing! I have to force myself to parse the complexity of the scene and capture the simple statement of light and location before those things significantly change. So the first part of my demo was to do a little tiny charcoal sketch to feel out the simple statement of the scene. I always say to myself at the beginning, "It is not possible to paint everything I see, and so I've got to clearly decide what I am going to emphasize and what I'm going to edit out." And, my friends, I'm going to say that one more time, because it cannot be underestimated. Because we cannot paint everything we see, we must make clear decisions on what we will emphasize and what we will edit out to achieve a simple statement. Frankly, I don't believe we can succeed as landscape painters unless we bring this approach to our work.

So may I make a suggestion? Think about what it was that made you stop and want to paint a particular location. Identify that quality and emphasize it in your painting, then your work will more likely become an emotional piece of art instead of a jumble of objects. You're the artist, you're the poet, you can have profound emotional experiences, and you must develop the technical ability to communicate those emotions visually.

Back to the demonstration at hand, what I really loved was the strong contrast of the tree trunk branching up into the soft green foliage, against the reds of the autumn foliage in the foreground and the cool atmosphere of the background. There were engaging shadows falling across the ground plane, and I really liked the simple archway shape that the trees conformed to. And so I did a little tonal study to emphasize these simple shapes and masses, then moved on to the painting, trying my best to hit the target of the simple ideas that had initially interested me.

"It's not possible to paint every detail you see, so ask yourself, What made you want to paint a particular location? Identify that quality and strongly emphasize it in your painting and edit anything that might distract from it."

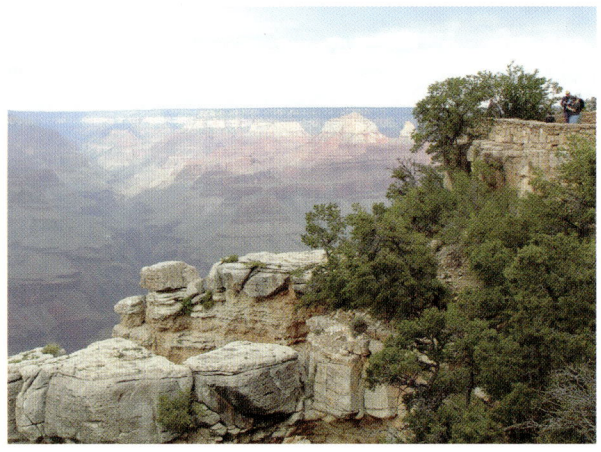

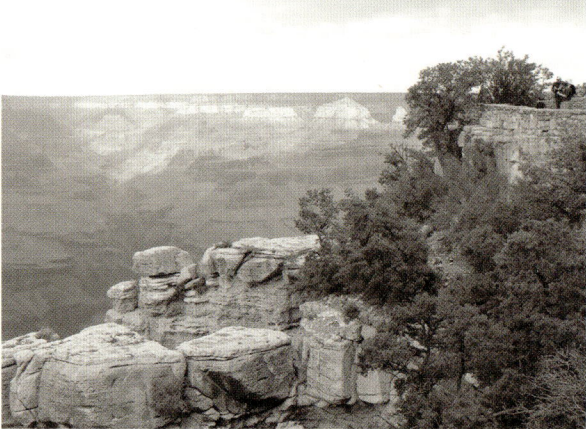

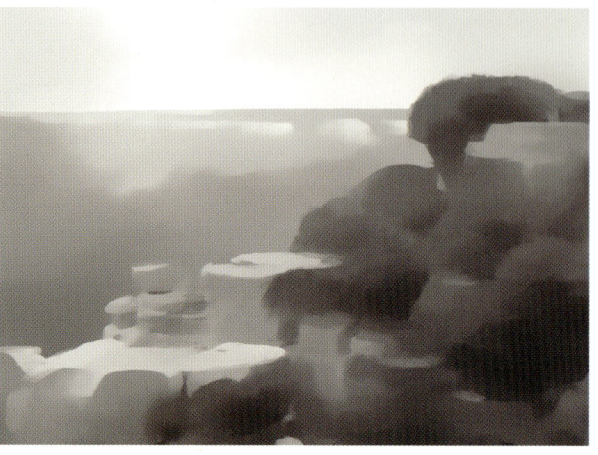

Simple Statement for Complex Subjects

Let's look at a photograph of the Grand Canyon. How would you handle the complexity of this? I mean, it's the Grand Canyon! The level of information here is extraordinary. Are we going to spend hours rendering all of that in paint? There would be nothing wrong with doing that considering all the rich layers of color and visual interest. It's gorgeous!

But once again, this book is primarily about sketching in the moment, so if not all details, which ones? Look at the simplified statement in the third image; it blends away the smaller details and textures and shows us that the values of the scene group quite simply. Additionally, it shows how the complexity of the rocks can be simplified into basic geometry: top plane, front plane, and side plane and the bushes into spheres.

Remember, our job is to recreate the illusion of three-dimensional life on a two-dimensional surface, so emphasizing the simple three-dimensional nature of our subjects is a powerful idea. After all, we're trying to make a little sketch in a sketchbook feel like the vastness of the Grand Canyon. So by combining a simple value statement, an emphasis of three-dimensional form, and a few key details, we can sketch the vastness of the Grand Canyon right on the spot! (And there's a step-by-step demo coming in a few chapters to do just that.)

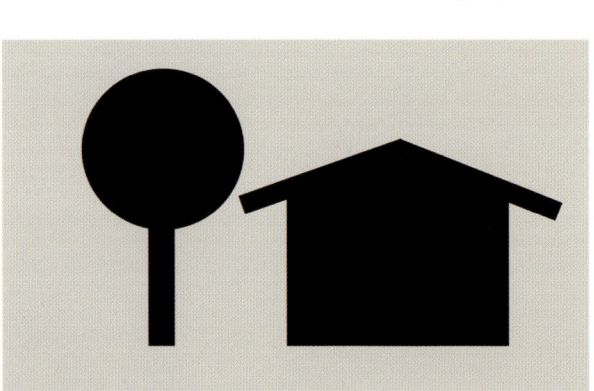

Silhouette

Let's keep looking for useful approaches to find a simple statement in our paintings.

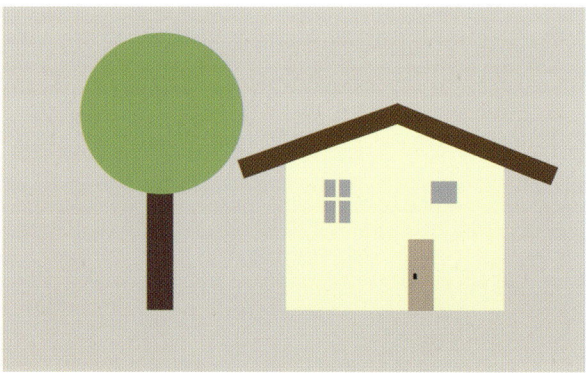

Local value/color

When I'm faced with a difficult scene, I'll start by looking for three simple ingredients: 1) the simple silhouetted shape of primary elements, 2) the local values and colors of objects (local color refers to the actual color of an object independent of the light present), and 3) the simple masses of light and shadow.

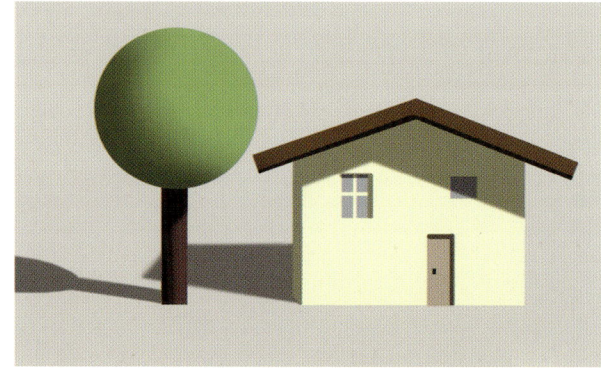

Light and shadow

If I get these three things down clearly in my sketch, it's much more likely to hold together well.

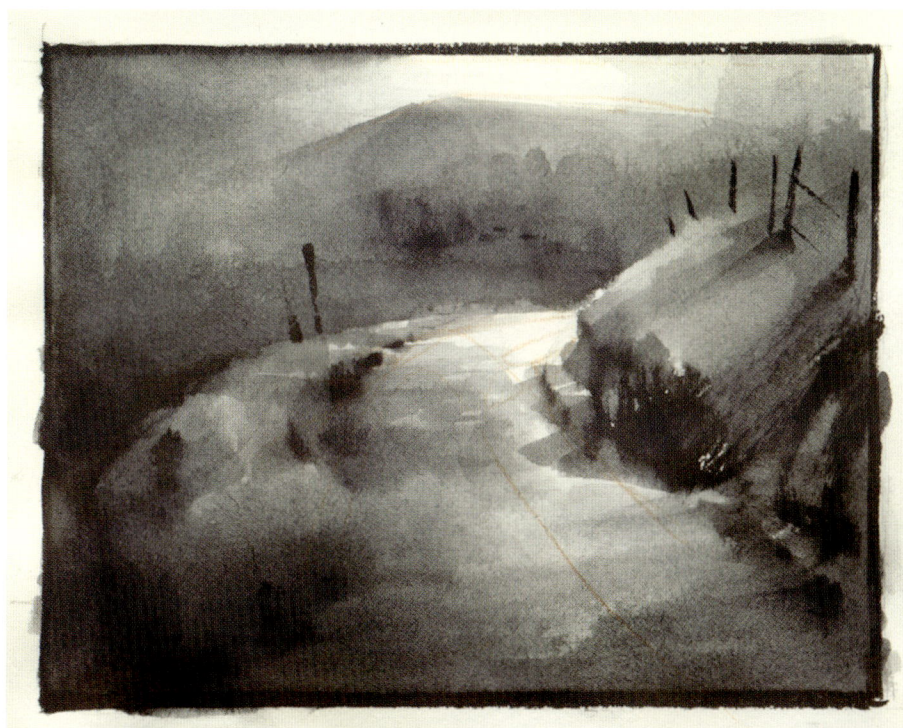

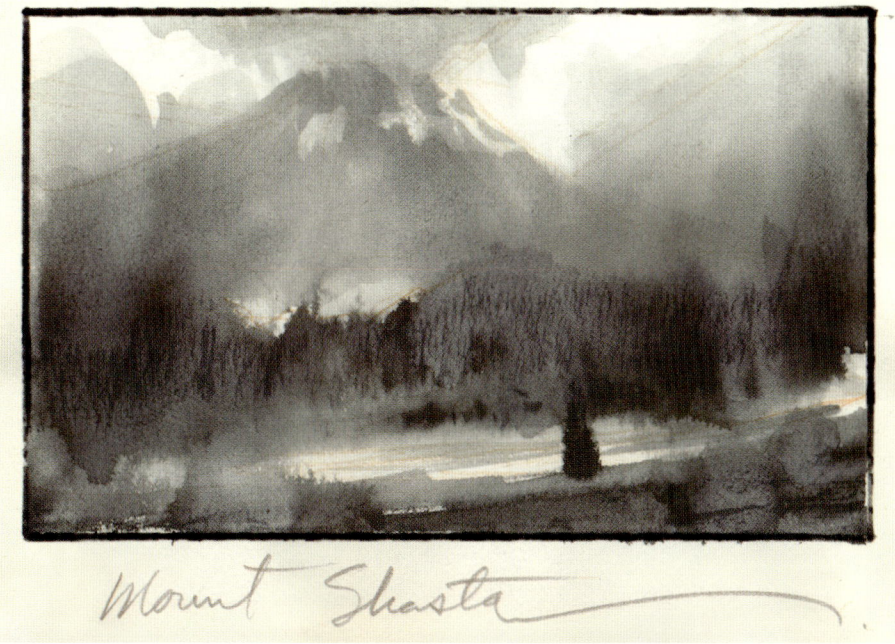

Mount Shasta

Putting the Simple Statement into Practice

Here are a couple of tonal sketchbook studies to illustrate the ideas we've been discussing. You'll find a demonstration on the next page that shows the technique that I am using here. I very much recall the challenge of sketching the top scene: there were grasses, rocks, and details by the millions. But this is a sketch about one thing, a road. Everything else was treated as secondary or edited out entirely. And if you don't mind me saying so, I like the result. It feels like there's a purpose, a journey to see where the road will take us.

The second study is Mount Shasta in Northern California. This is from a car trip through the state and I didn't have much time to spare, but the idea of a simple statement allows for such occasions. Here, passages of light and dark layer from foreground to background, each one creating a simple passive area and an adjacent active area. Boom, boom, boom, and done.

"By combining a simple value statement, emphasis of three-dimensional form, and a few key details, we can sketch any location right on the spot!"

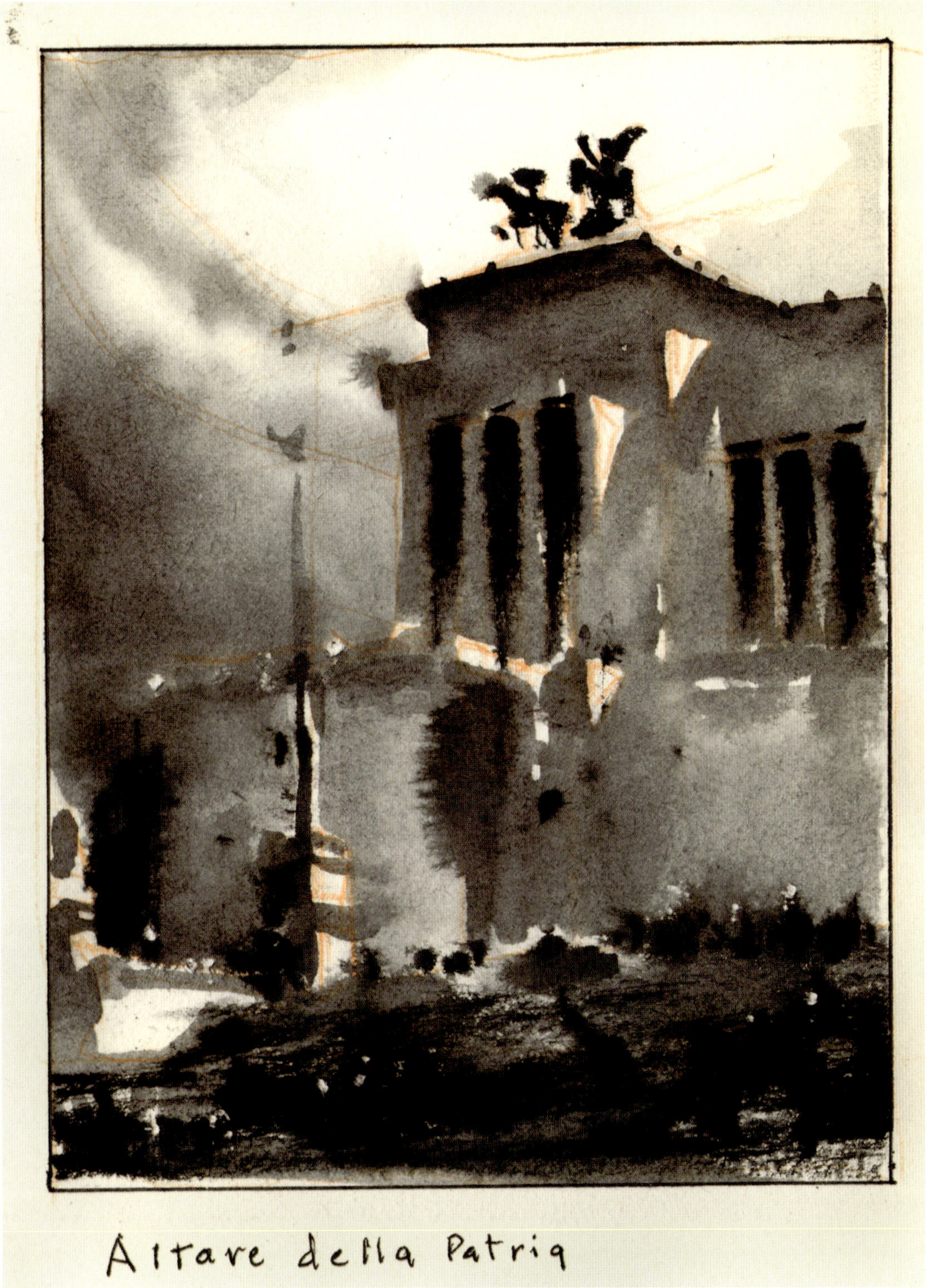

This illustration is of the Altare della Patria in Rome, Italy, and it's done in a technique I like to use for quick, simple statement sketches of complex subjects. The tools are a Pentel #101 brush pen, a water brush pen, and an orange Prismacolor pencil, in a 5 x 8–inch watercolor paper sketchbook. Note that my emphasis is on the shapes of light falling across the building, and the statues on top. The midtone values of building and sky are very grouped and even blend into each other.

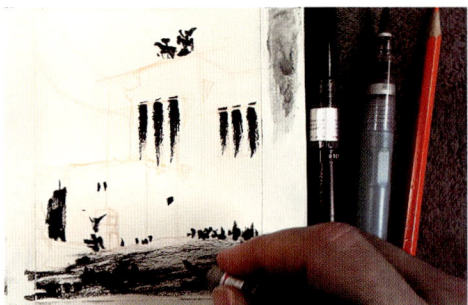

① I start with a simple line drawing for structure and perspective, then use the brush pen to put in the darkest darks.

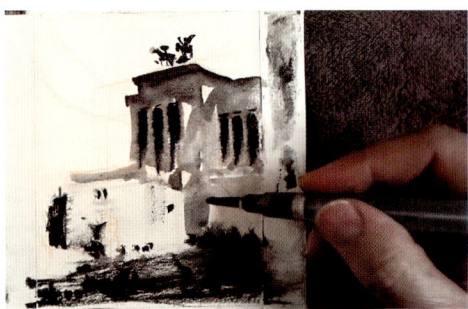

② I use the water brush to pull a little pigment out of the darks and wash it into the shadow areas leaving the white of the paper for highlights.

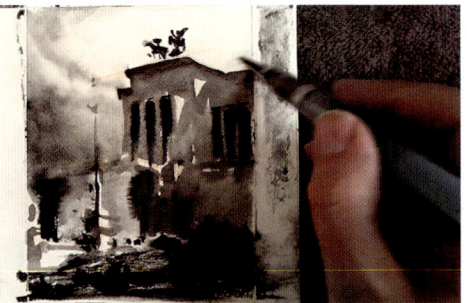

③ Finally, I brush in a value for the sky with the same technique of dragging pigment with the water brush, then add a few dots and dashes to suggest details, and we have our sketch!

Altare della Patria

You can see a reference photo of this location on page 178/179.

Standing on the Shoulders of Giants

Here's my studio from back in the '90s, when I got very serious about landscape sketching. On my desk is a page of landscape studies I did of one of my favorite landscape painters, Edgar Payne, and you can see those studies reproduced below. After some disastrous outings trying to paint on location, I knew I needed help. So I turned to artists that I admired, whose work seemed to capture something clear and beautiful about the places they were painting. Even though I was already working up to 12 hours per day, I made a point to do at least one of these daily, and that cumulative practice helped tremendously. I didn't have to entirely reinvent the wheel; great ideas were out there and I was able to improve quickly by standing on the shoulders of giants. My recommendation to you is to put together a reference file of your favorite landscape paintings, then do small, thumbnail-size copies. Don't worry about lesser details, rather look for the bigger, simpler statement and work at capturing that in less than an hour.

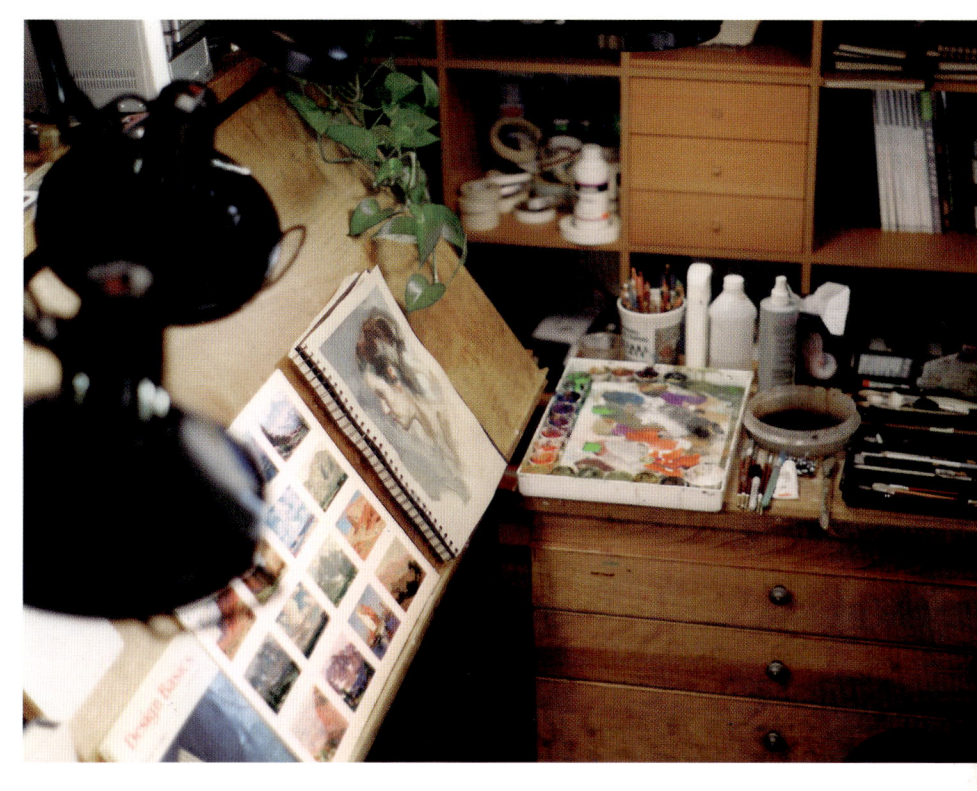

> *"We don't have to entirely reinvent the wheel. By painting frequent and dedicated master copies, we can stand on the shoulders of giants."*

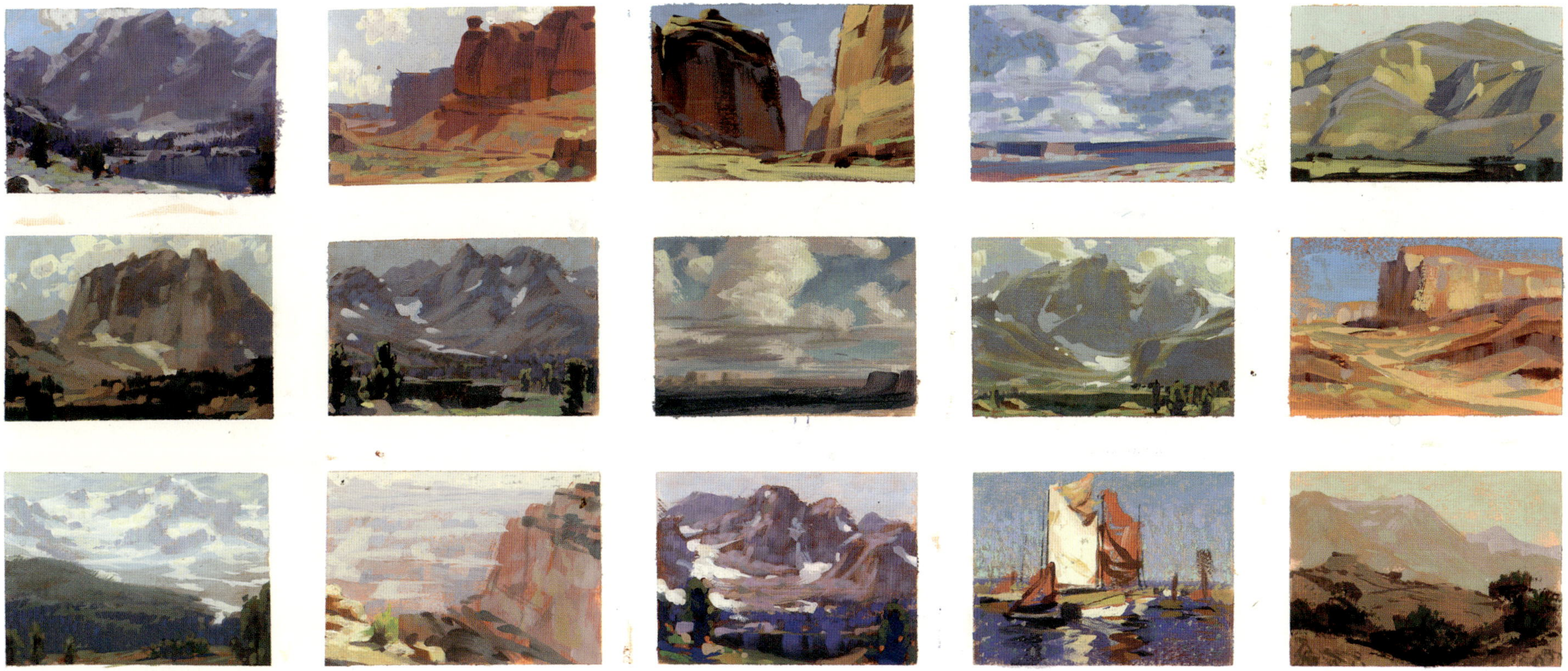

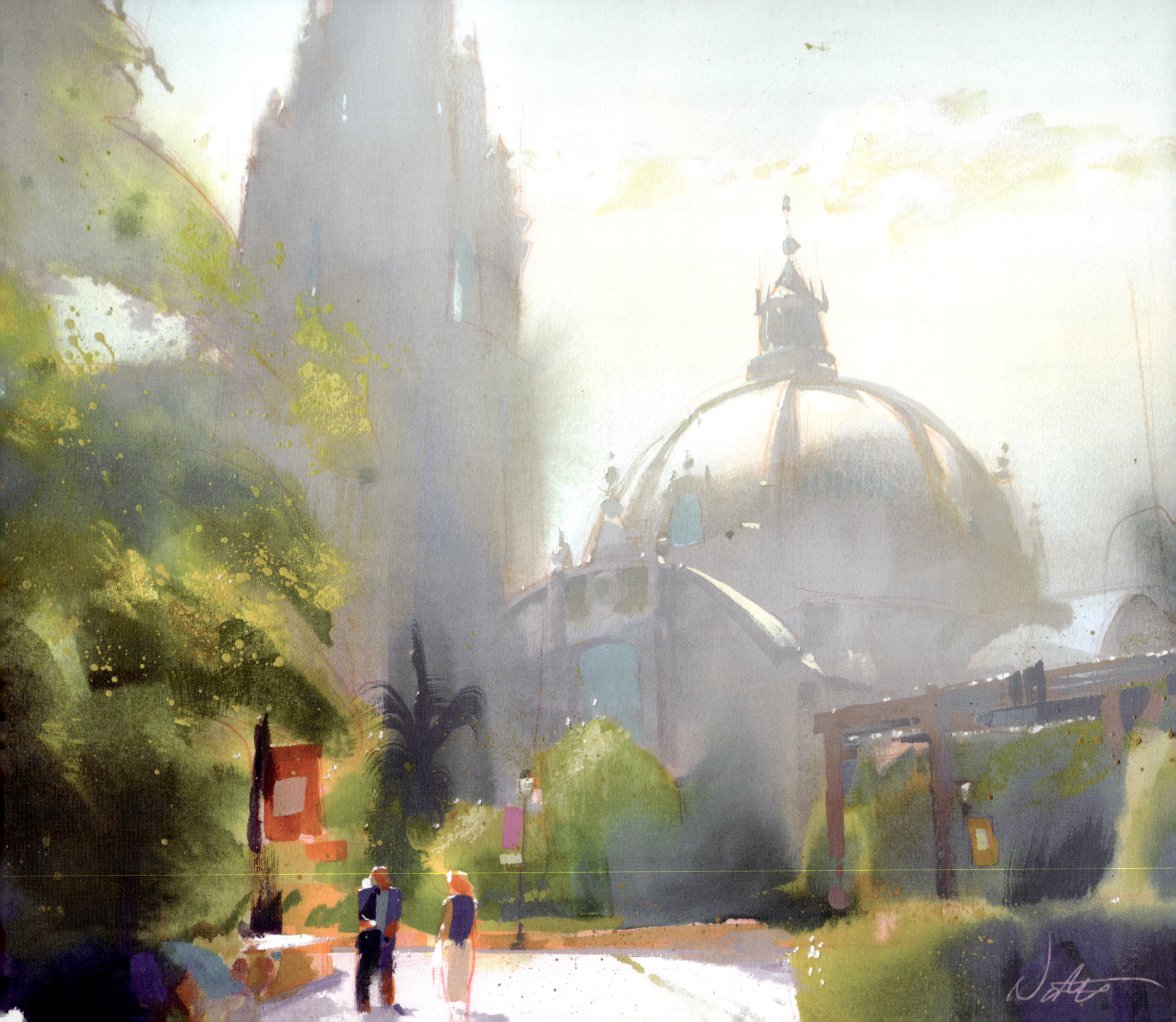

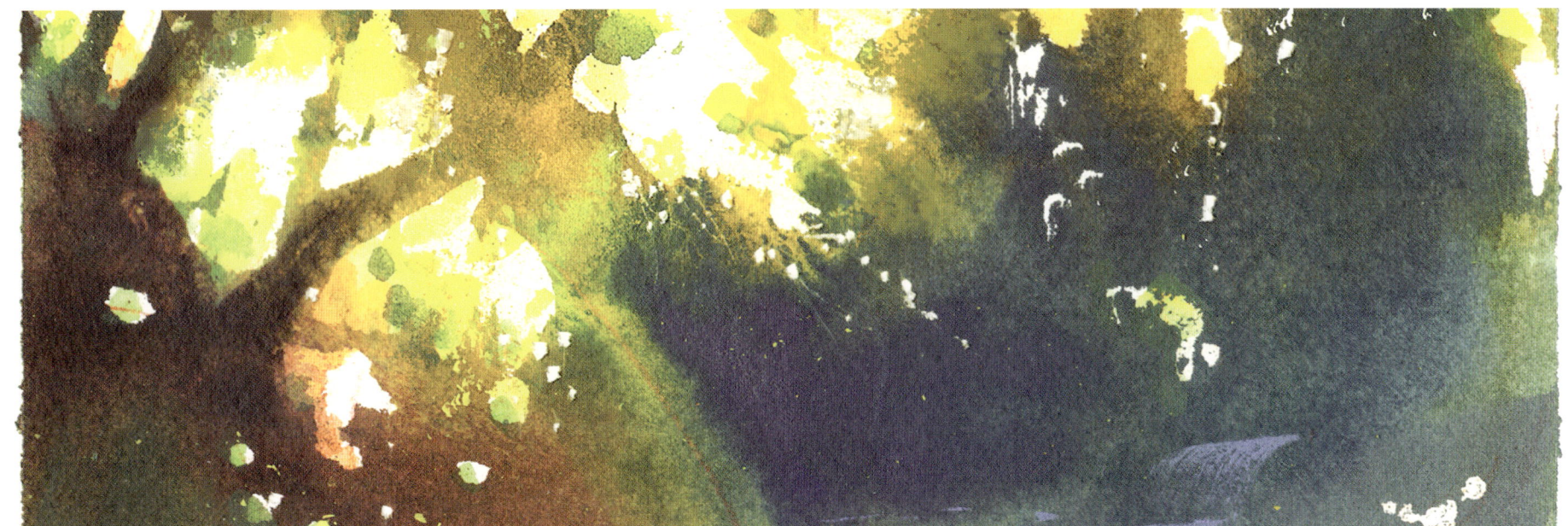

Chapter 4

Light and Value

Up to this point, it's been important to have an overview of the tools, techniques, and ideas that make landscape sketching manageable. In this chapter we're going to identify and deal with yet another cause of failure for hopeful landscape painters.

Back in the early '90s when I was trying to learn this craft, I would take photos of any interesting place I visited, hoping to do some painted studies in my home studio. But the photos were always disappointing because they didn't come close to capturing the feeling of the light that was present on location. Well, of course they didn't!

This was before digital photography, and a printed photograph is just pigment on paper and doesn't have the incredible range that light has; the photo only captures a small amount of the light present. The thing is, that's exactly what our paintings are, pigment on paper. So we need ideas for creating the illusion of real light, even to the point of telling little white lies in our paintings to get to the greater truth of the vivid light we can see in the landscape. This chapter is all about achieving that goal.

> *"Our paintings must create the illusion of real light, even to the point of telling little white lies to get to the greater truth of the vivid light we can see in the landscape."*

You can see a reference photo of this location on page 178/179.

The Big Challenge of Painting Light

There's a misconception that when we paint, we're simply reproducing what we see, but if that's our approach, failure is certain. The chart to the right shows why. What we can see from the brightness of the sun all the way to the darkest shadow (top section of the chart) is an incredible range of value. However, our pigments can't come close to representing what we actually see (value scale at lower section of chart). They simply depict a small portion of the light present. So when we paint, we are trying to represent what we see with a medium that is not capable of doing it.

Do you see the problem here? Being unaware of this issue is yet another reason why so many people fail at landscape painting.

The first two examples below are different camera exposures of the same scene at sunset. In each, something is gained, and something is lost. The first (at left) is exposed to open up the shadows and let us really see and appreciate the buildings. But the amazing sky does not survive the exposure. In the second version, the sunset shows up beautifully but at the loss of information in the dark mass of the shadowed cityscape. Our eyes also work like a camera, their aperture opening or closing depending on how much light is present. But that happens from moment to moment. If we look into a deep shadow, our pupils open to let

in more light, then our eyes flick up to a luminous area, and they adjust to see that. So painting what we "see" is like trying to hit a moving target, which is what the third example is all about. If we randomly mix and match exposures, the value structure of our image falls apart and we lose the powerful sense of light that our painting could have had.

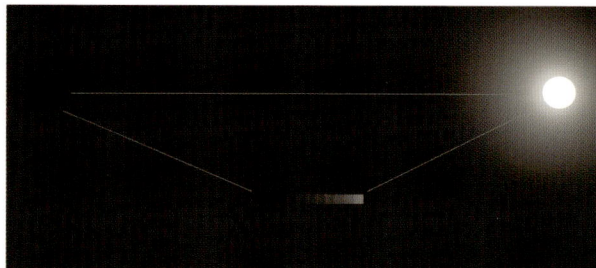

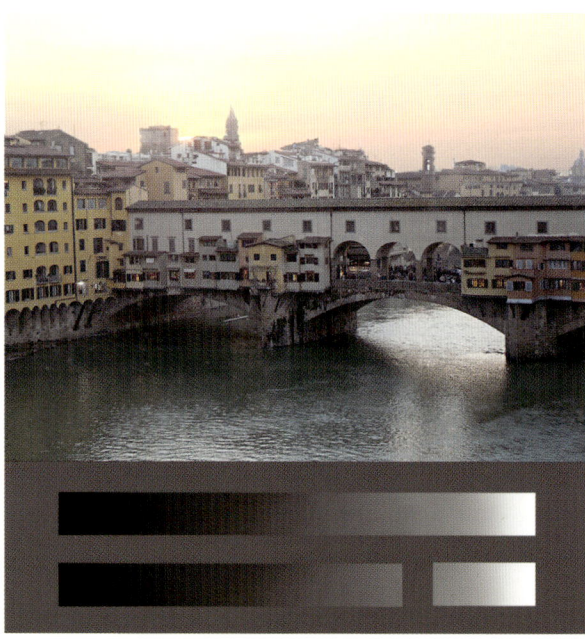 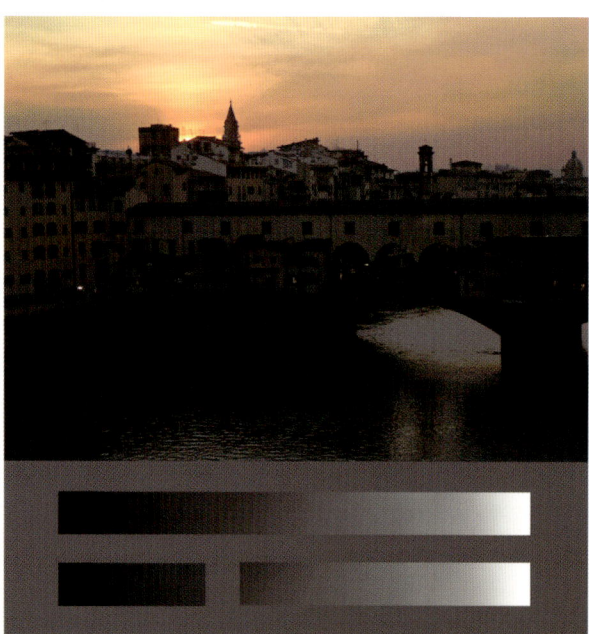 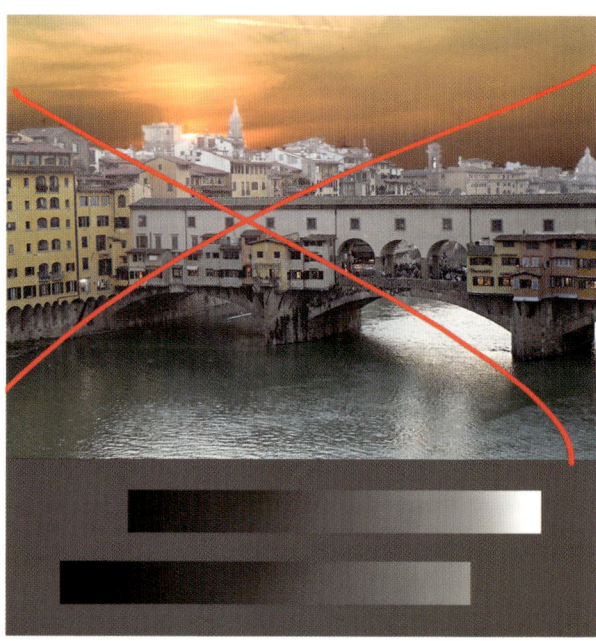

The band of value below each picture shows how the light or the shadow is pushed into a narrower range to open up room for the other. In the third we have two overlapping value structures, which breaks the boundaries of reality and doesn't work. Paintings are about relationships and choices.

And here's the good news, in the previous chapter we covered two very simple ideas to get complex subjects to work for us. Squinting and choosing what the images are about. That's exactly the solution here. We can squint at our subject to see the big, simple relationships. And we must make clear decisions up front what our images are about. Is it more about the rich subtlety of the buildings? Then go with something more like the first exposure. Or is it about the simple silhouette of the city and the amazing sky behind it, as in the second example?

But a choice must be made, or the likely result is a patchwork of parts that do not fit together in a meaningful way—in other words, a painting disaster—and that leaves us wanting to lie in bed the rest of the day trying to recover our sense of self-worth. Nobody wants that.

These are the simple solutions to working within the value limitations of your medium:

(1) Decide what you would like to emphasize about your subject.

(2) Find the simple value relationships of your subject.

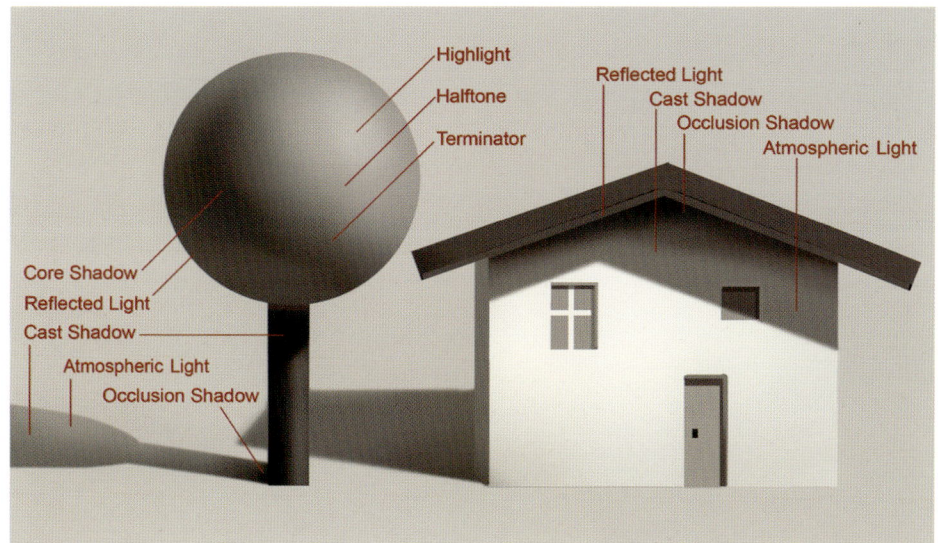

Highlight

Halftone

Terminator

Reflected Light
Cast Shadow
Occlusion Shadow
Atmospheric Light

Core Shadow
Reflected Light
Cast Shadow
Atmospheric Light
Occlusion Shadow

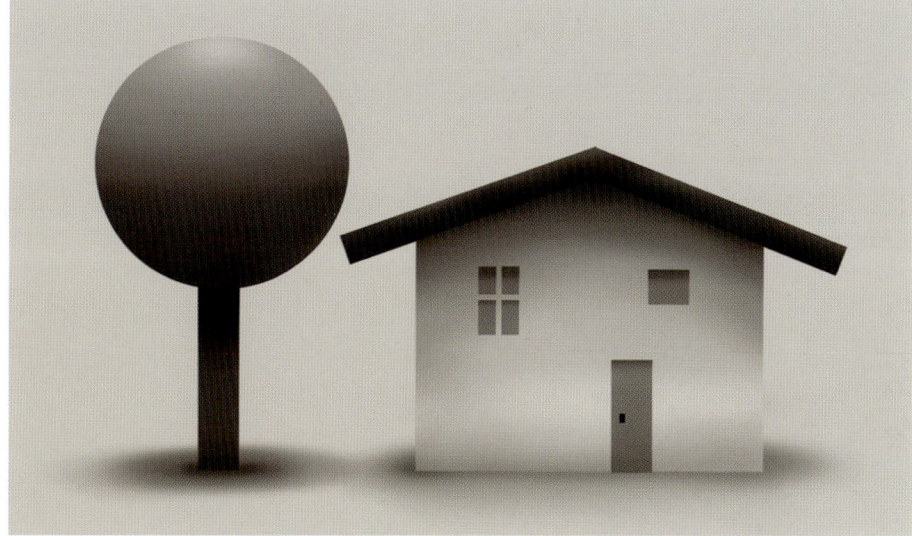

Let's familiarize ourselves with the terminology for light, as seen above, and we'll revisit when we talk color in a later chapter. Being clear about the values of light and shadow is important because this is what gives form to our subject. As landscape painters, we mostly deal with two kinds of light: direct sunlight and overcast light, as seen on a cloudy day.

Direct sunlight creates a great deal of exciting contrast and overcast light can have the benefit of softening our subject. In fact, some artists prefer an overcast day because it allows for a longer painting session before the light significantly changes.

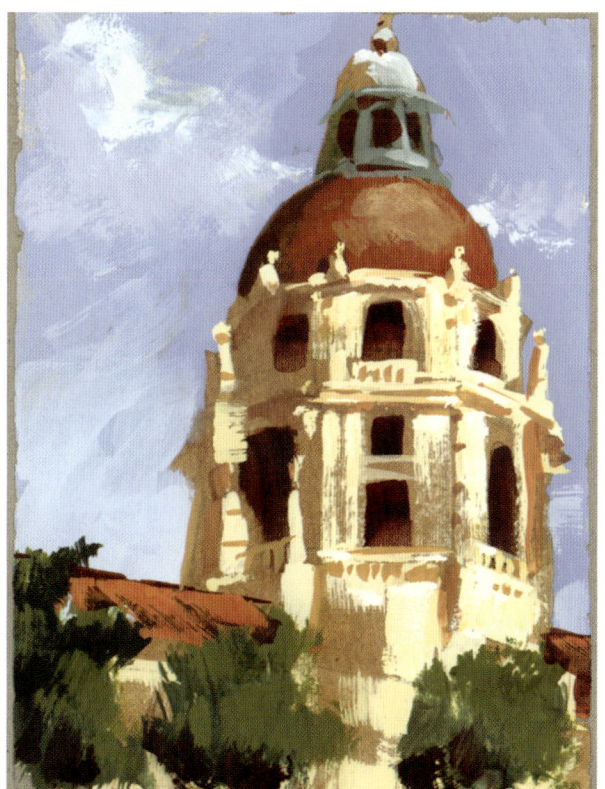

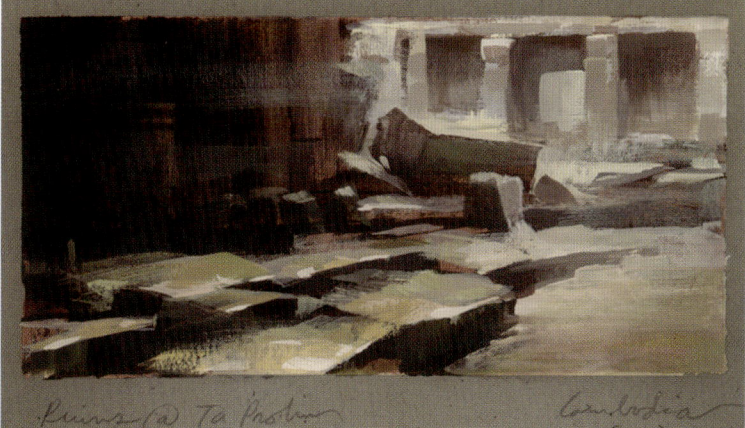

Here are a couple of examples of direct sunlight and overcast light. To the left is Pasadena City Hall in Southern California. You can see the strong contrast of light and shadow and the spherical form of the dome. The other image is from a trip to the temple ruins of Cambodia. The misty softness is an example of overcast light. It doesn't have the sharp cast shadows of full sun, but there's still a good amount of contrast because our eyes adjust to the lower light levels of the scene.

"It's not possible for our pigments to reproduce the range of value we see with light, so painting landscapes is always an interpretation of what we see."

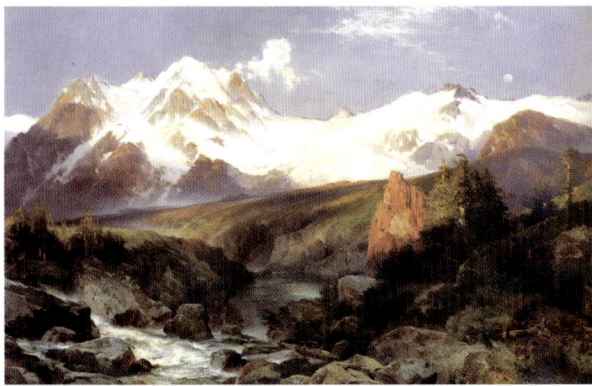 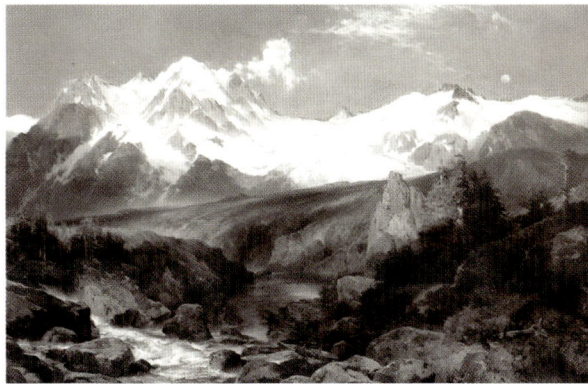 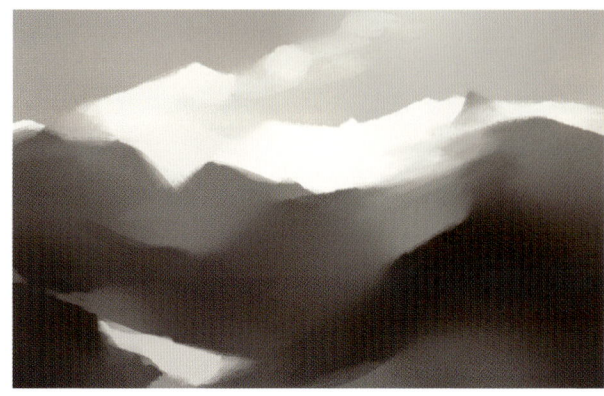

Many of the great (and highly complex) landscape paintings have an elegantly simple tonal structure. This is a studio painting by Thomas Moran (1837–1926). It must have taken a great many hours to complete, and yet it uses the same solution that we've been discussing for our one-hour sketches: a very clear and simple underlying value statement. At the same time, I don't want anyone to believe that I'm against detail and complexity in a painting. You can layer in as much detail as you want (and have time for), as long as it does not disturb the underlying simple value statement.

"Your paintings can have as much or as little detail as you want, as long as those details do not disturb the underlying simple value statement."

Now let's head to Rome, Italy, for a quick value demonstration to illustrate the ideas discussed thus far.

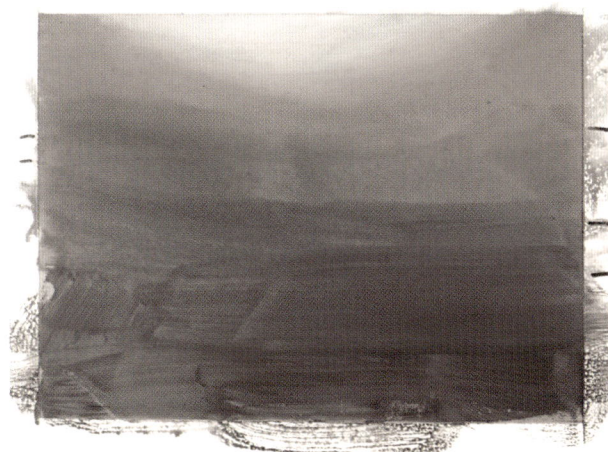 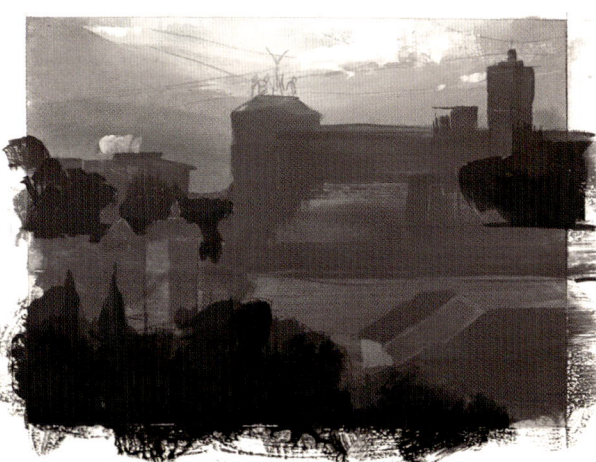 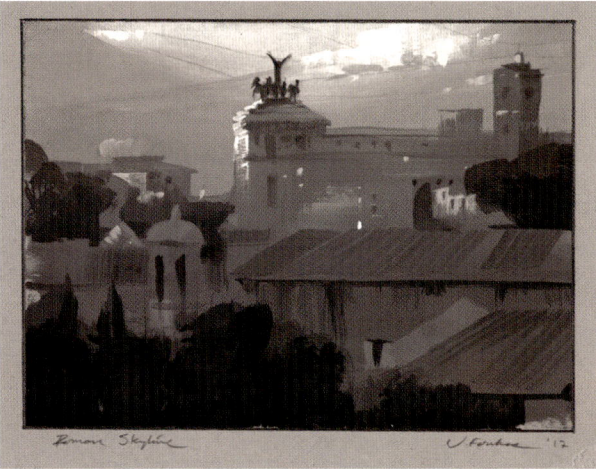

Toned mixed-media paper, 6 x 8 inches

(1) For this scene, I was struck by the majestic silhouettes of the buildings against a luminous sky, and the glints of sidelight. That's my simple statement idea, so I start with a gradation that will create my sky and suggest a darker foreground.

(2) Despite the dozens of buildings and thousands of details, I stick to a simple silhouette, then add the dark accents of surrounding trees. I also indicate the illuminated clouds above. What I've done so far is simple and manageable for just about anyone and look at how far it's taken me, historic Rome is starting to appear!

(3) I'm ready to drop in a few significant details like windows and roof lines. I also use my opaque white to lay in a few vivid highlights along the upper buildings. Notice that I've planned ahead and been very careful to keep the buildings dark enough so that the lights pop. Remember, it's all about planning out the value relationships. And that's how you paint the Roman skyline in 20 minutes!

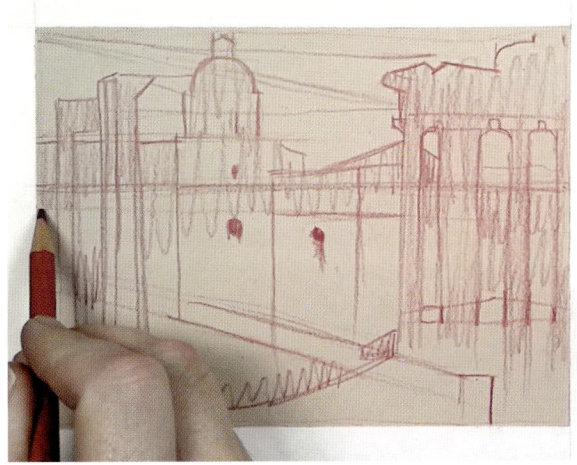

Let's stick around Rome for the next study, this time the ruins of the Forum.

(1) To begin, I put down a simple line drawing that emphasizes perspective and a simple silhouette. It's always helpful to start with your horizon line when placing your perspective.

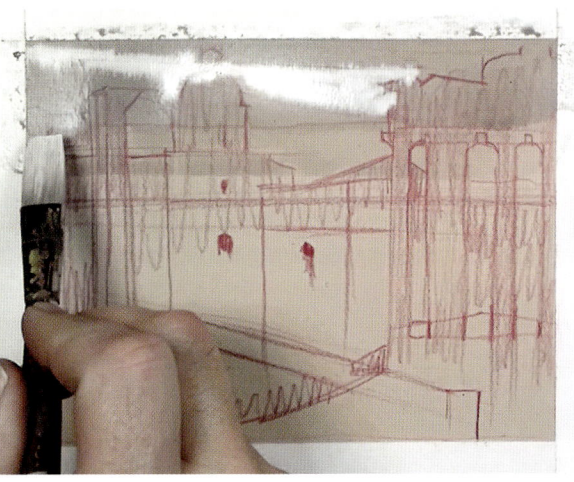

(2) I plan to emphasize the simplest value statement, in this case the light sky against the mass of the land and buildings. I begin by dampening the paper in the sky area, then blending in some opaque white for soft-edge clouds.

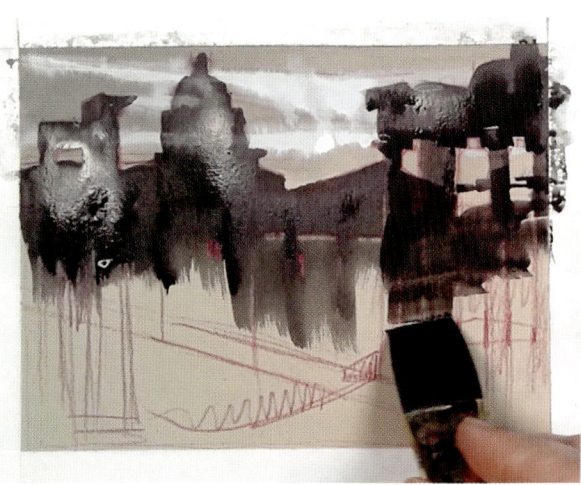

(3) For the landmass, I'm using a big one-inch brush, no kidding around here, I've got to quickly block in those simple shapes. Remember that the goal is to paint at a speed that let's us sketch anyplace, anytime, anywhere. So I'm just filling the entire landmass with one value. As promised, we're going for the simple statement first.

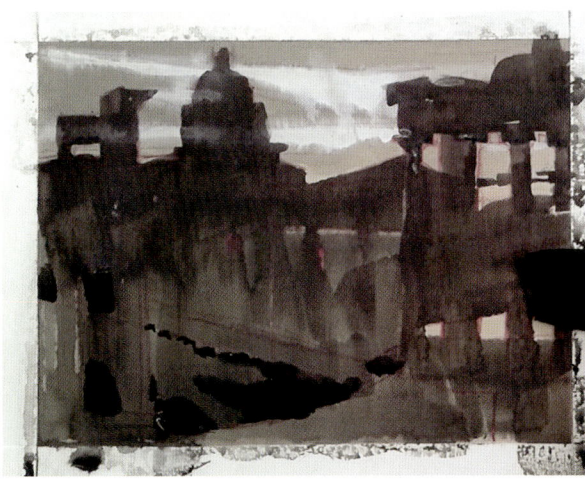

(4) Now let's put in the darks to get in a strong range of value. Remember, we're not putting them in randomly but rather with great purpose. They are calculated to reinforce the perspective, chisel out important shapes, and sprinkle in visual interest in areas where needed.

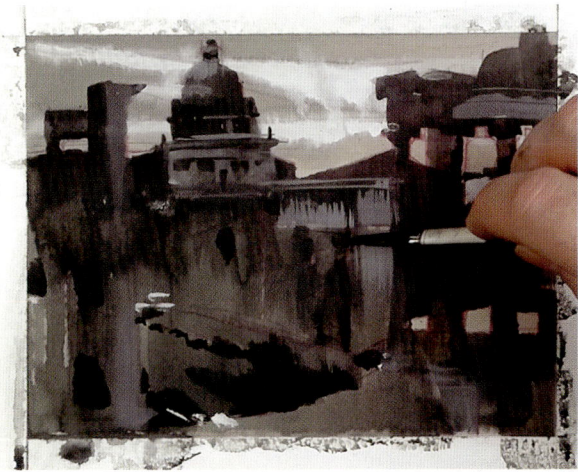

(5) The dome will be a bit of a focal area, so I'll concentrate some accents there. There are also a few areas in the landscape that have a lighter local value, so I'm sprinkling a few of those in, carefully following the perspective and keeping to areas where I want more visual interest.

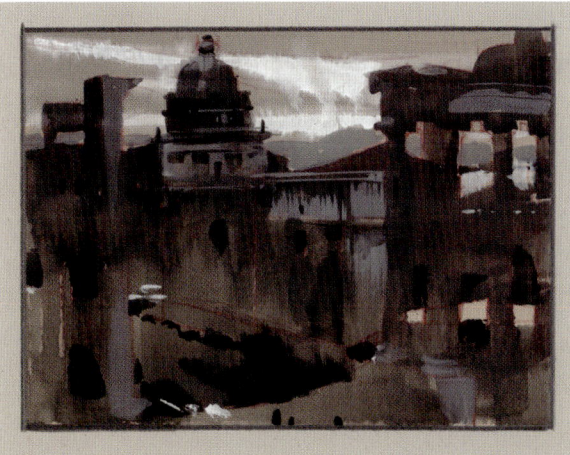

(6) There are a few distant mountains, so I'll indicate those, and some final dark accents and indication of windows, especially in the dome area. And with that were done!

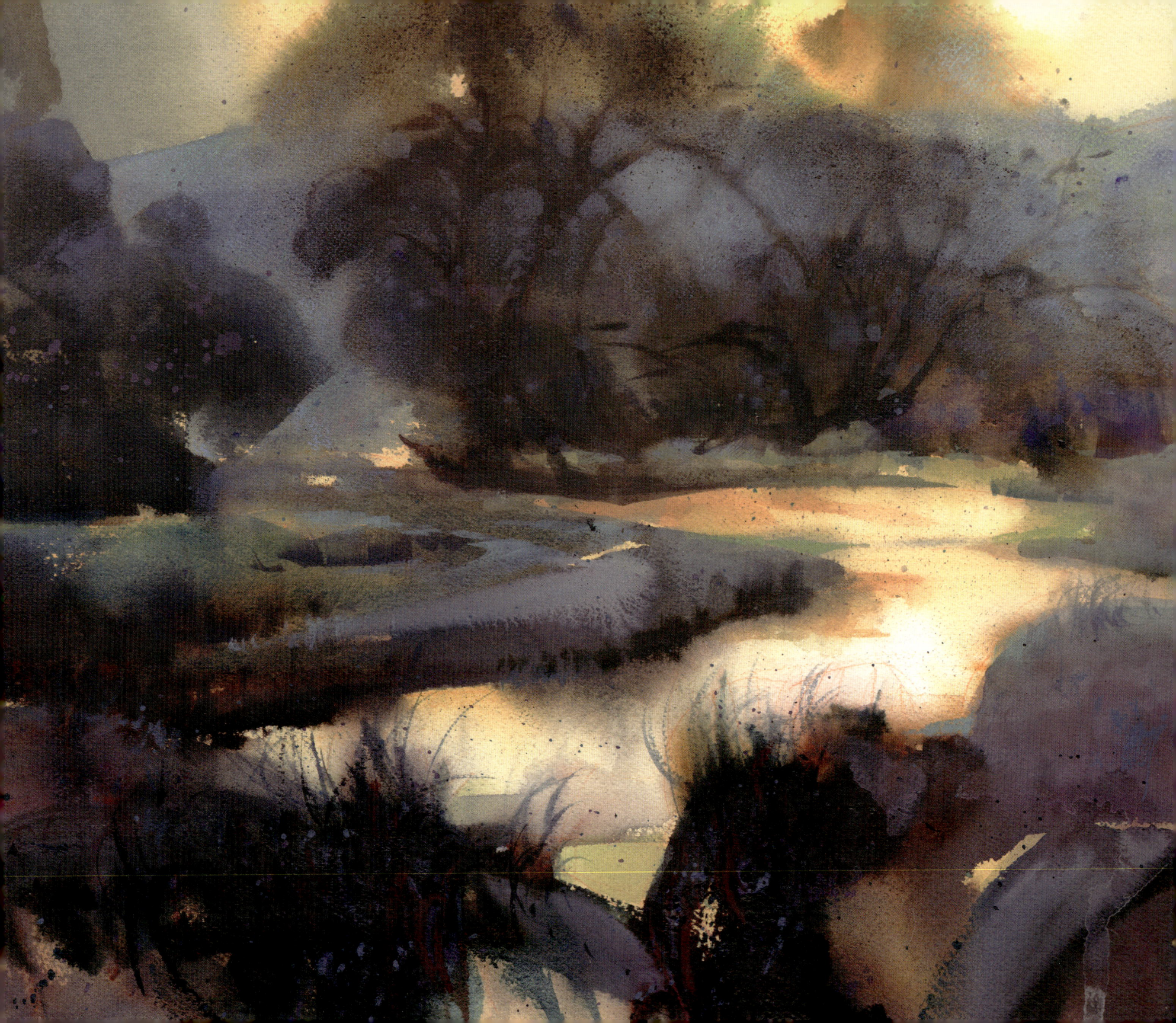

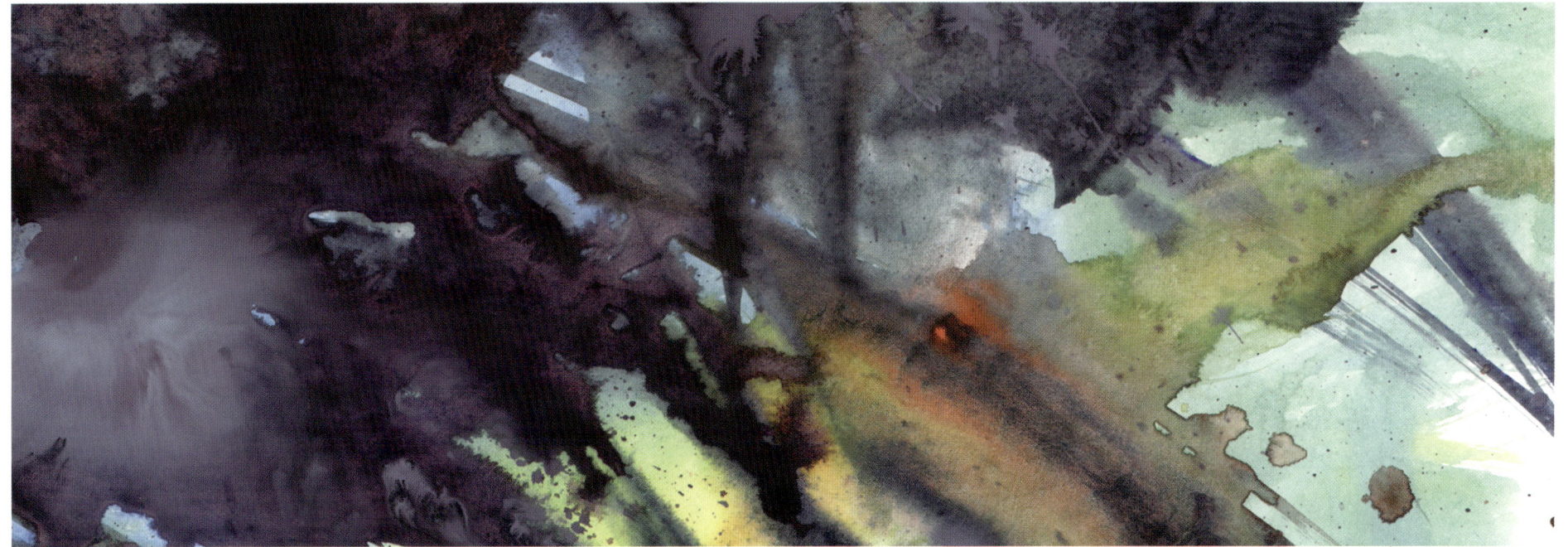

Chapter 5

Edges and Textures

Take a look at the scene to the left, this is a creek in Angeles National Forest, not too far from where I live in Los Angeles. You've seen sketches of this location already in this book. and you'll see more before we're done. I come back to this area over and over because it's so luminous in the late afternoon sun and so difficult to paint, I'm never quite satisfied with what I do here. But I do have two ideas to add to our bag of tricks that I feel give me a shot at succeeding in a place like this: the design of edges and textures.

So let's review my tips so far:

① Identify the primary reason you want to sketch a particular spot.

② Squint to see the simple value relationships.

③ Design shapes and silhouettes.

④ Use light and value to convey form.

⑤ Design edges and textures to create emphasis and depth.

⑥ Strongly emphasize the concept from step one in every subsequent step.

"The design of edges and textures is a simple concept that helps me tackle difficult subjects."

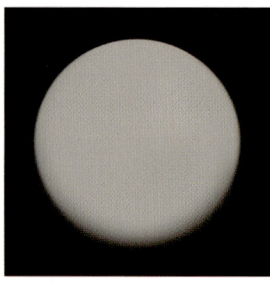

① An example of hard and soft edge: note that the harder edge tends to demand more of our attention.

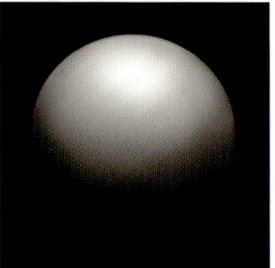

② Lost edge and found edge: the shadow disappears completely into the background to give a strong emphasis to the light.

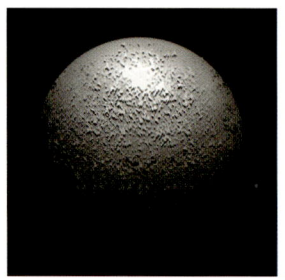

③ With texture added: there's an even greater emphasis on the light and stronger sense of form.

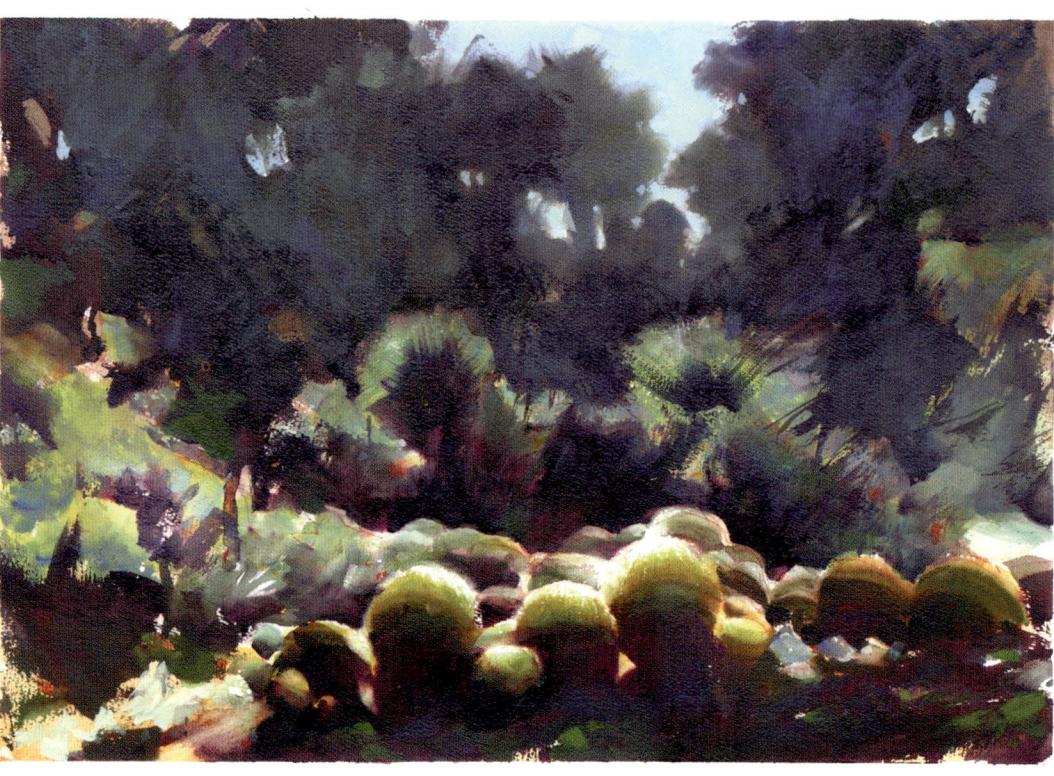

Adventures with Golden Barrel Cacti

Our landscapes will get better with good edge design because they'll have a greater sense of purpose. The bonus is, they'll also get easier because there's so much you can let go of and let disappear into mystery rather than fighting details. That was very much the case with this study featuring golden barrel cacti in the foreground (done on Arches cold-pressed 140-lb paper, 16 x 20 inches). I was a bit daunted by the level of information at this spot, so I thought through the process that was laid out on the previous page. I wanted to feature the foreground cactus and dramatic backlighting, then let rocks and foliage in the scene become less important as they receded.

I also chose to simplify the shadows to an extreme for a powerful statement about the light. This is an example of lost and found edges.

Note how the foreground has stronger contrast through texture, edge, light, and shadow; then the background foliage becomes soft and nondescript to not distract from the main event. These simple ideas have allowed me to emphasize my chosen subject as well as create a sense of depth in the landscape. On the following page we'll take a close look at the techniques used plus a few bonus ideas.

"Edges do two valuable things, they create emphasis and depth in our landscape."

Techniques for Edges and Texture

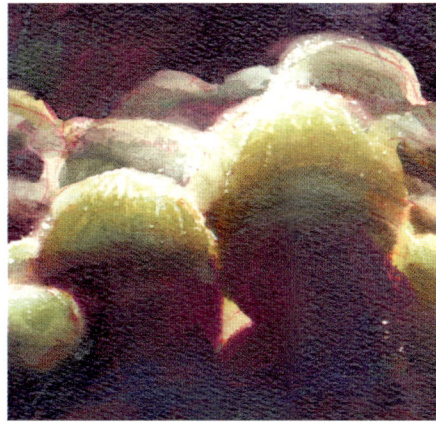

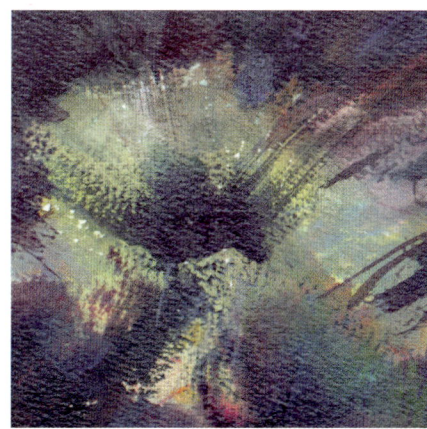

1 Here's a close-up of the simple handling of the cactus. The textures are literally scratched into the page with a razor blade to create this effect. I'm using heavyweight watercolor paper to be sure I don't scratch through!

2 In this close-up, I'm dragging the brush (drybrush) to give a texture to the foliage. I like this technique because it suggests detail without the need for rendering.

3 In the far background, I'm painting wet into wet; I need soft edges for a sense of faraway depth and a glowing sky.

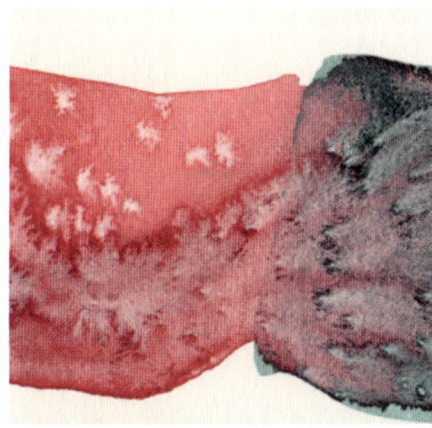

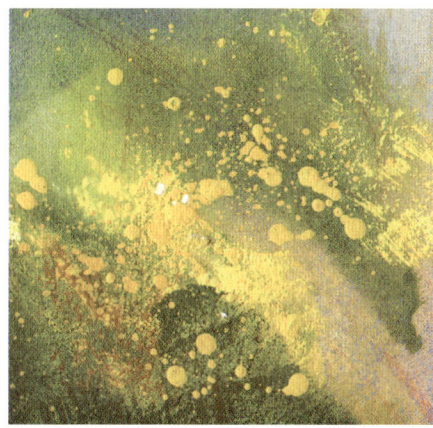

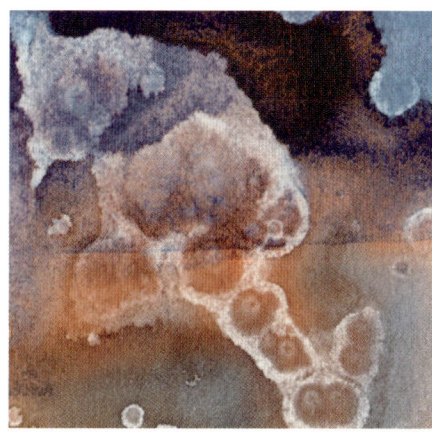

4 An additional textural technique is sprinkling salt onto a wash. The grains absorb water and create a unique quality of texture. I really like this one because I can suggest passages of detail without doing any rendering.

5 I often use spatter in a textural foreground. I'll load up a brush with thick paint and flick it onto the painting, or I'll use a toothbrush and flick the bristles with my thumb to spray on finer textures. Be sure to block off the rest of your painting, the spatter has a tendency to go everywhere!

6 A surprising texture can be created by spraying or dripping isopropyl (rubbing) alcohol into a wet wash. The alcohol repels water and dries at a different speed to create the effect shown.

Examples from the Field

Toned, heavyweight, mixed-media paper sketchbook, 3 x 5 inches

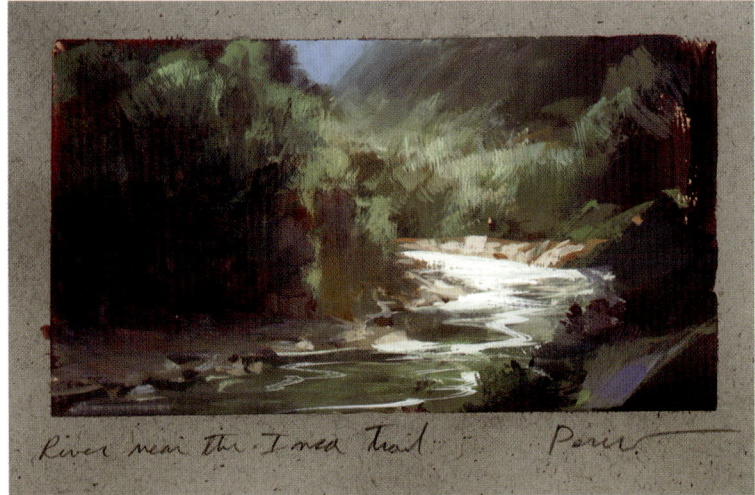

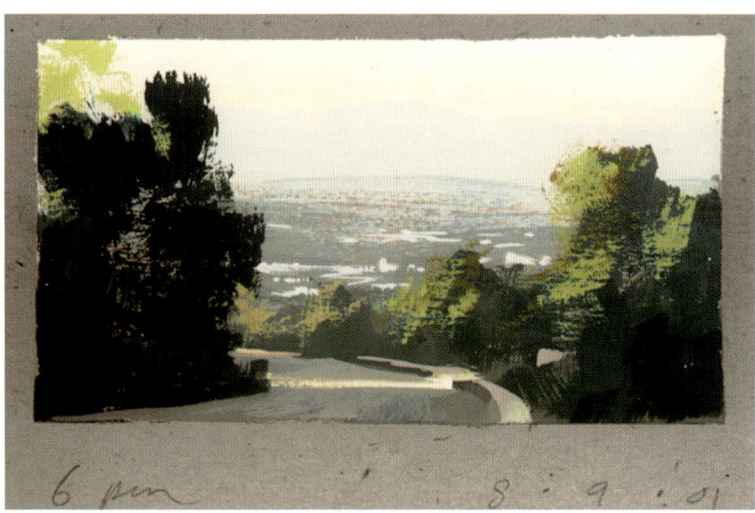

① This sketch is from an extraordinary trip across the Inca Trail in Peru. This is the point where we met some lost travelers who had been abandoned by their guide and were very relieved to find us. There was an oppressive overcast and dampness from the overnight rains and the river was beginning to rage. I focused in on the soft textural sheen of the foliage and the white water of the river and let go of just about everything else.

② I pulled over in my car after work to sketch this scene from Mulholland Drive in Los Angeles. I knew the light would be changing in minutes so there was no time to waste. Blocking in the background with soft tones then stamping in the dark foreground with a larger brush allowed me to work quickly and get a strong, atmospheric depth. Then I drybrushed thick paint in the sunlit areas for a textural suggestion of leaves until time was up, and the light was gone!

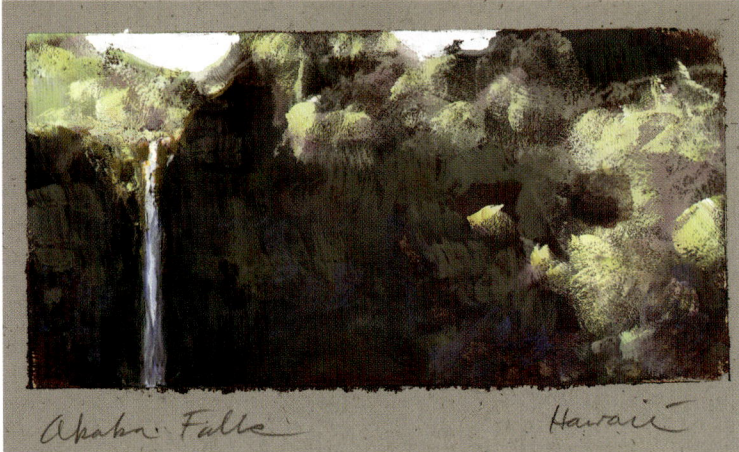

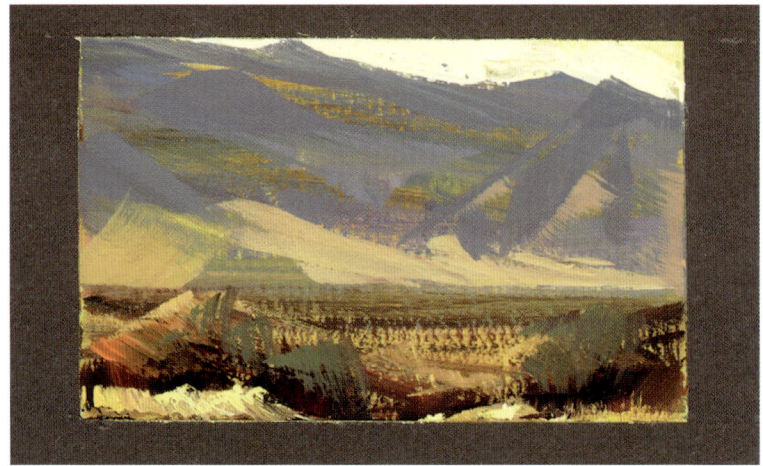

③ This is from a hike on the Big Island of Hawaii. Though far away, the sheer drop of the waterfall was breathtaking, and I conscientiously decided to eliminate detail in the shadow so the waterfall and illuminated foliage could pop. That was my concept and I stuck to it.

④ I had the need for speed with this quick sketch, specifically because it was over 120° F/48° C outside. It's from a trip to Death Valley, California. You might be disappointed to hear that I did it sitting inside my car with the air conditioner blazing. I was nervous about the car overheating while sitting there idling, so I worked quickly. My solution was to use heavy textures and contrasts in the foreground created by drybrushing for a strong sense of depth.

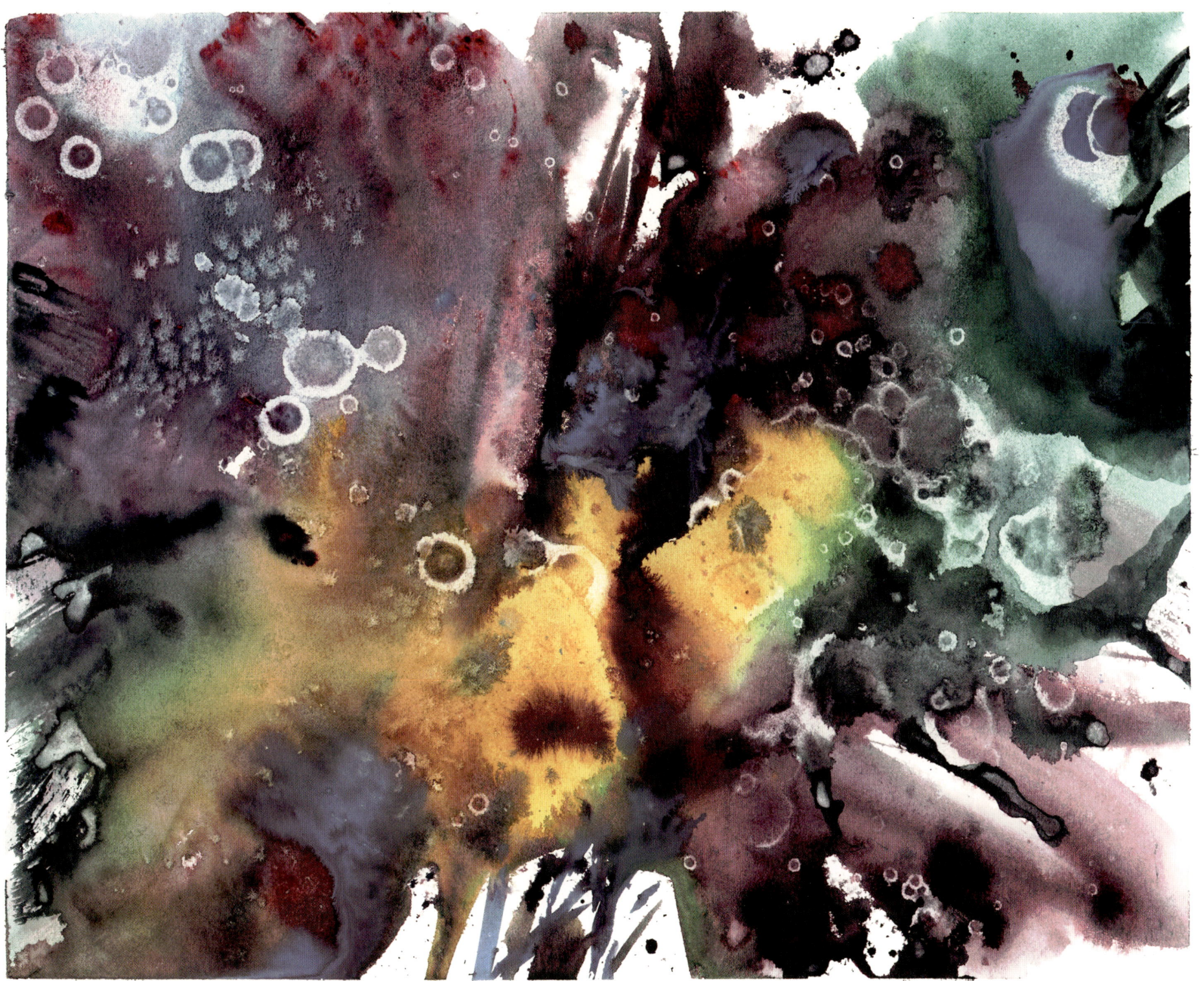

Experiment!

Demonstration Sketch: Land and Sky

We haven't focused on sketching a sky yet, and it's a perfect subject for dealing with edges and textures, so let's do it!

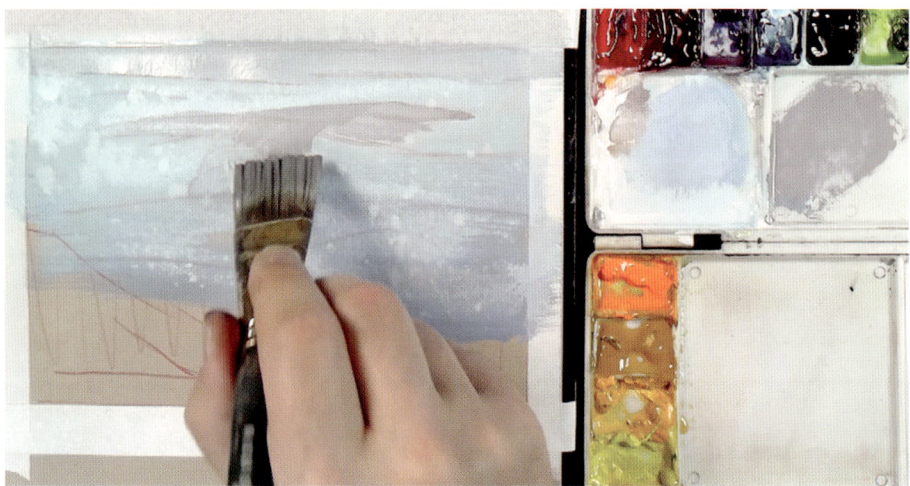

(1) As always, I decide what to emphasize, which will be the brilliant warm light set against the darker clouds. To set that up, I start with a wash that has a temperature and value that will allow darker clouds and lighter highlights to be layered over top. If I start too light, the highlights won't stand out enough, if I go too dark, the sky will not feel luminous.

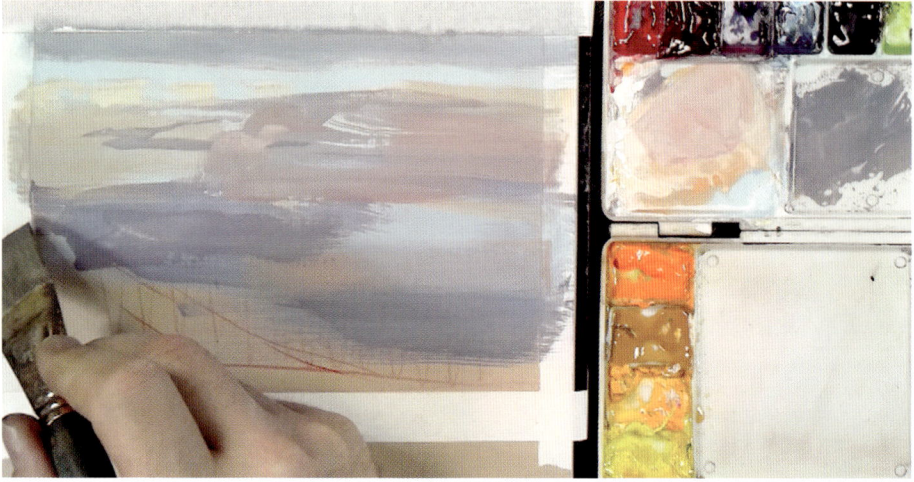

(2) While the wash is still damp, I brush in the shapes of darker clouds using a one-inch brush. The wet-on-wet technique allows for some aggressive brushstrokes while maintaining an appropriate softness.

Strathmore 400 Series Toned Gray Mixed Media pad, 6 x 8 inches

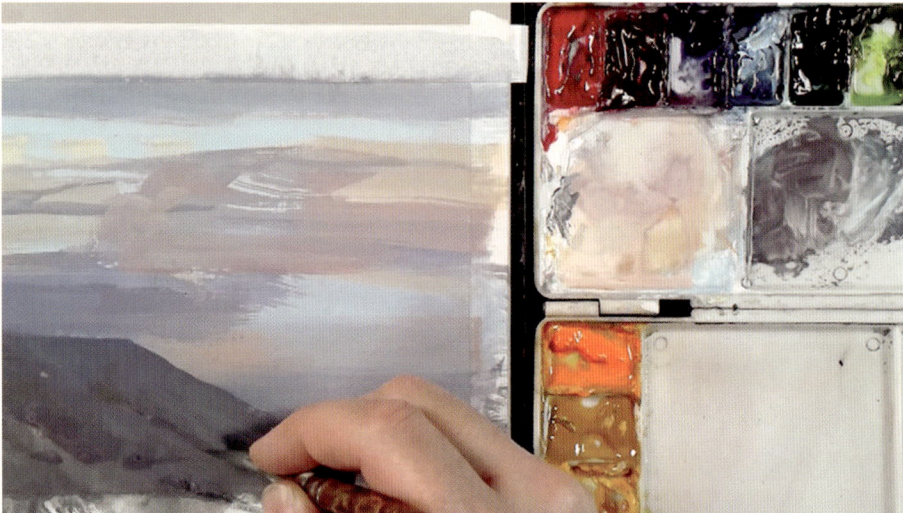

(3) Next, it's time to brush in the land. I make sure that the furthest area is soft-edged and blends into the distant haze to create depth. Finally, I mix some orange with opaque white gouache and drybrush it into the clouds for the key highlights. And it's a wrap!

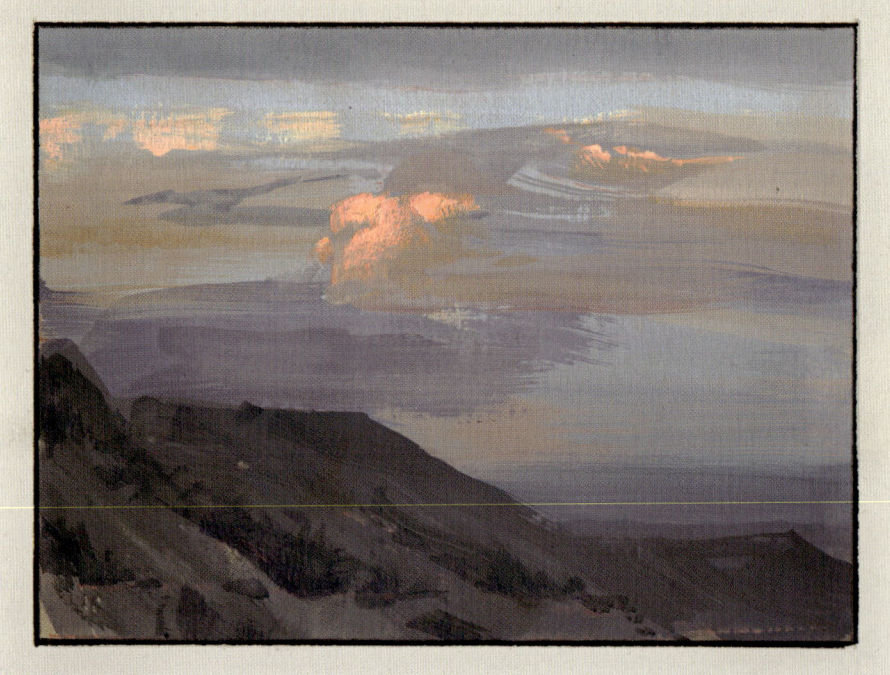

You can see a reference photo of this location on page 178/179.

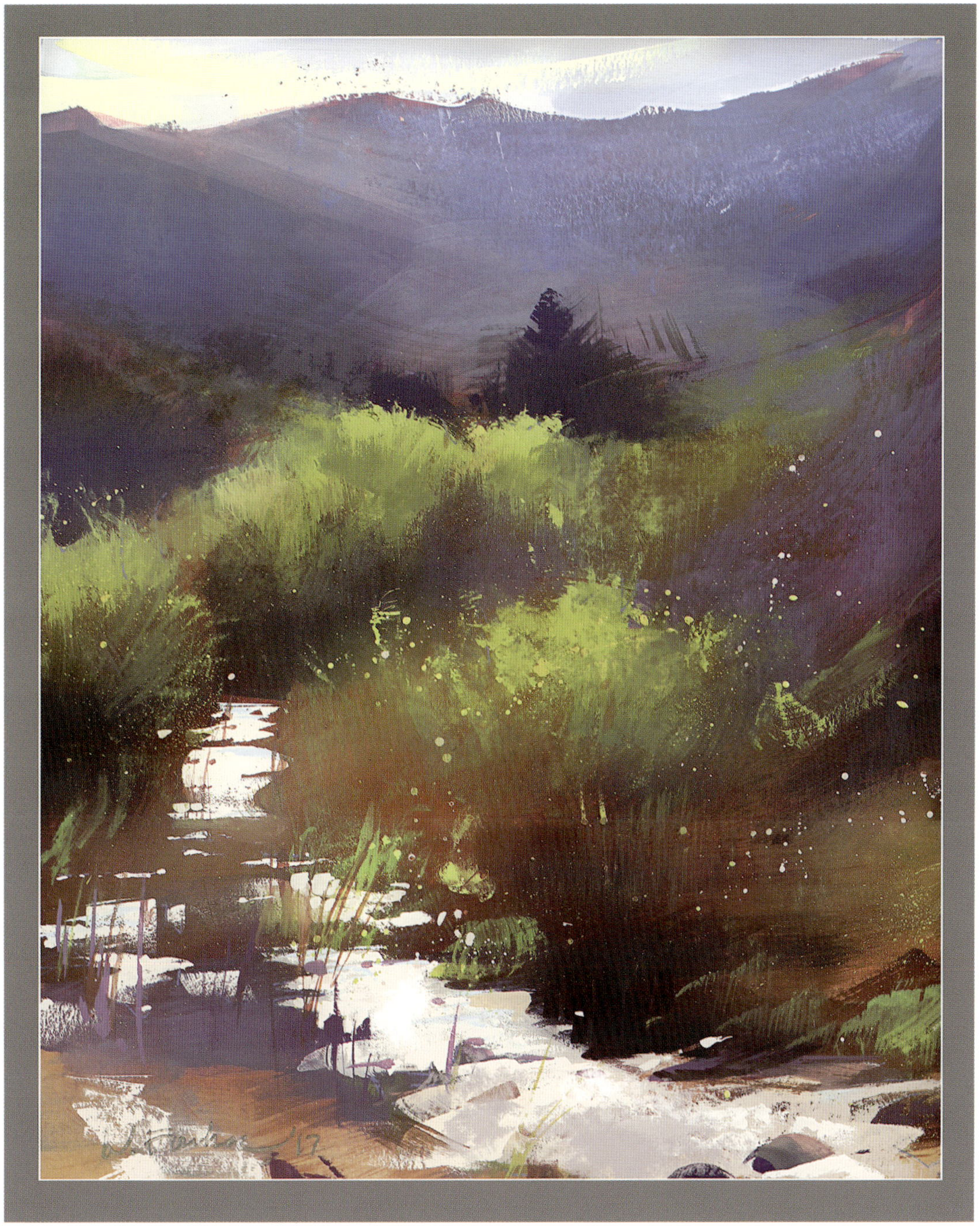

Strathmore 400 Series Toned Gray Mixed Media paper, 14 x 11 inches

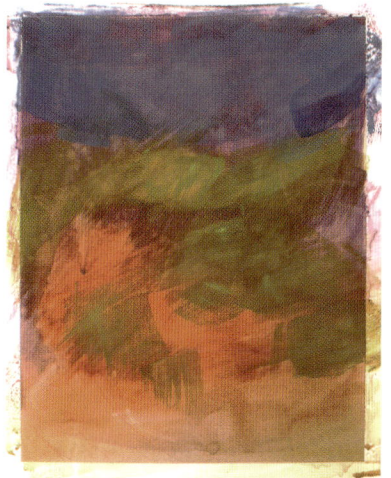

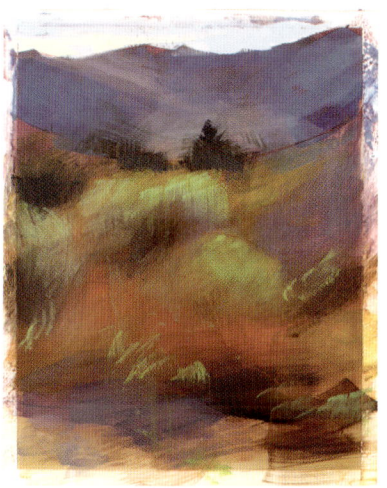

Demonstration: Mountain Creek

For this image, I'm taking textures and lost and found edges to an extreme. I want the creek, green foliage highlights, and the dark upper pine tree to pop, and so I keep everything else extremely blended and simple to set up the concept.

In step one I scumble in color from warm to cool to suggest the depth of the scene. To scumble is to use the brush to rub the paint into the paper rather than a drippy wash. In step two I add the contrasting elements, then use opaque paints (white gouache and thick tube watercolors) and drybrush in the creek and green foliage highlights. My final step is adding the suggestion of vertical grasses then using spatter for a final indication of detail in the lights.

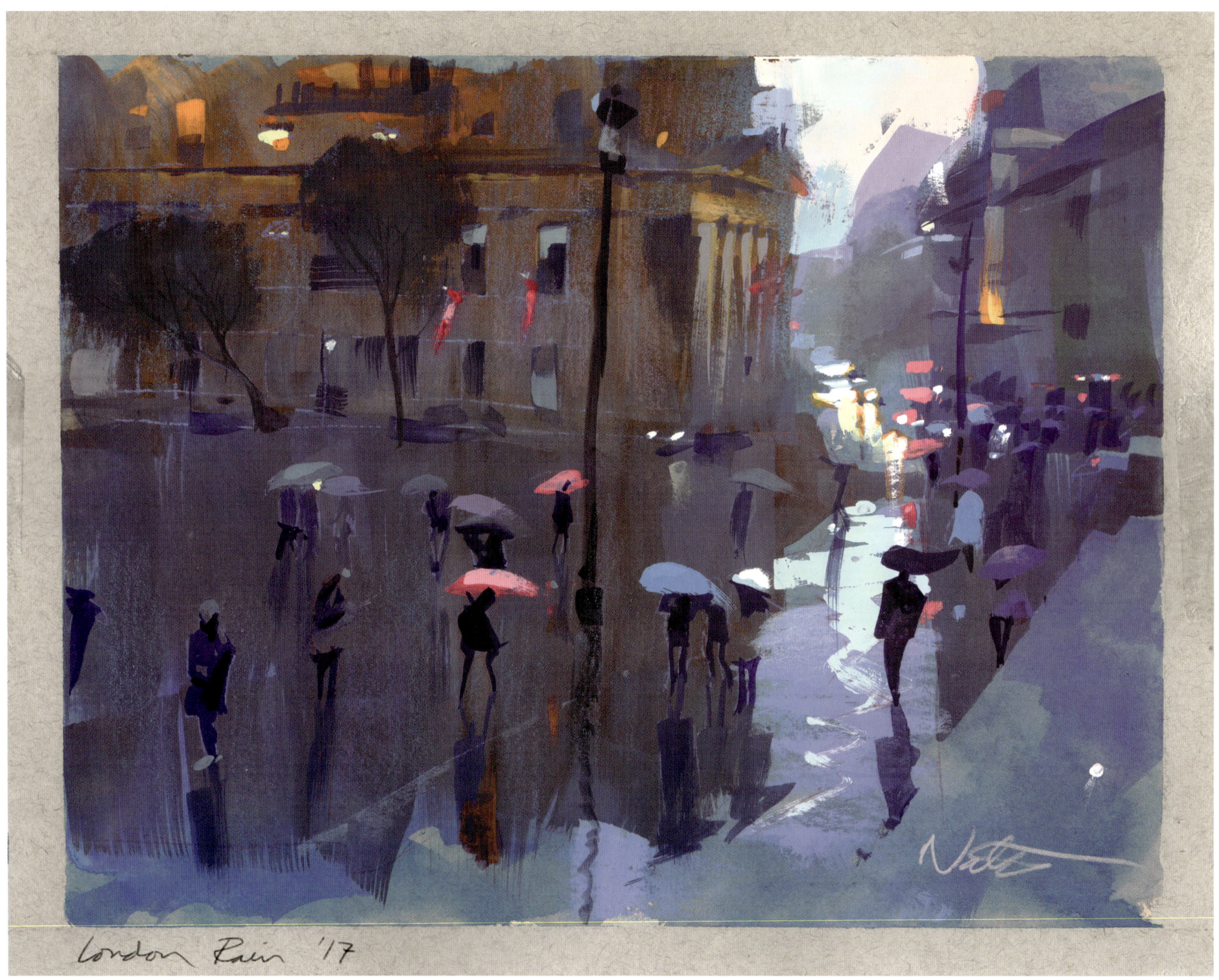

London Rain '17

You can see a reference photo of this location on page 178/179.

Demonstration: London Rain

Strathmore 400 Series Toned Tan Mixed Media paper, 9 x 11 inches

Let's do one more demonstration here to take on a cityscape using our principles of simple concept, value, texture, and edge. This is from a trip to London, on a typical rainy, overcast day, which set up great reflections and an interesting pattern of umbrellas. I'm using the usual combination of watercolors and white gouache.

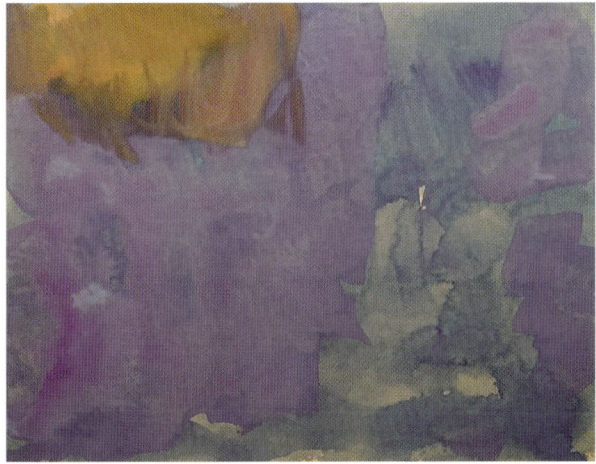

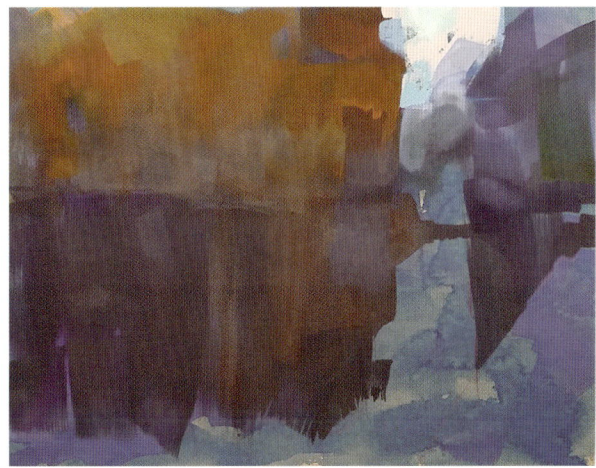

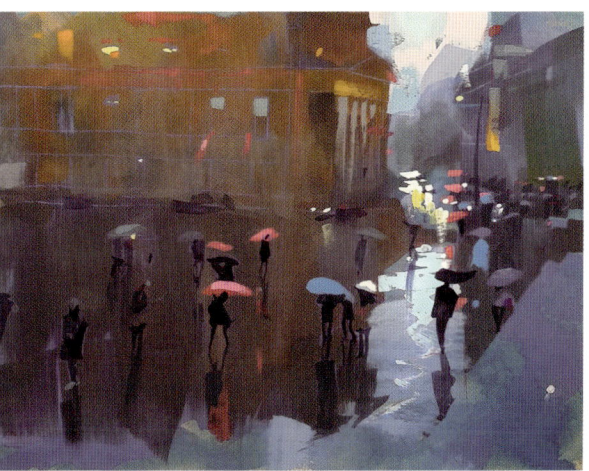

① Step one is all about underpainting to prepare for the higher contrast elements. You might say that this is the unifying aspect of the painting to which I'll add the variety. I get started by washing in the cool tones of the reflected sky onto the ground plane, then put down a brown to prepare for the upper-left building.

② Now it's time to suggest buildings and reflections. The upper-left building has a warm local color, which is a nice contrast to the cools of the environment. I get that roughed in, then use more opaque tones for the sky. There are some surprising warms and cools present up there, so I carefully paint in those relationships.

③ Now it's time to really dig in! I use fairly thick paint to lay in the sky reflections, car lights, and pedestrians with umbrellas. All that's left to do is to suggest architectural elements and trees. I'm careful to follow the perspective of the scene as I indicate windows, columns, and rooflines, and I finish off with a few lamp poles and trees. I scribble on my signature and it's done!

"Step one is all about underpainting to prepare for the higher contrast elements. You might say that it's the unifying aspect of the painting to which I'll add the variety."

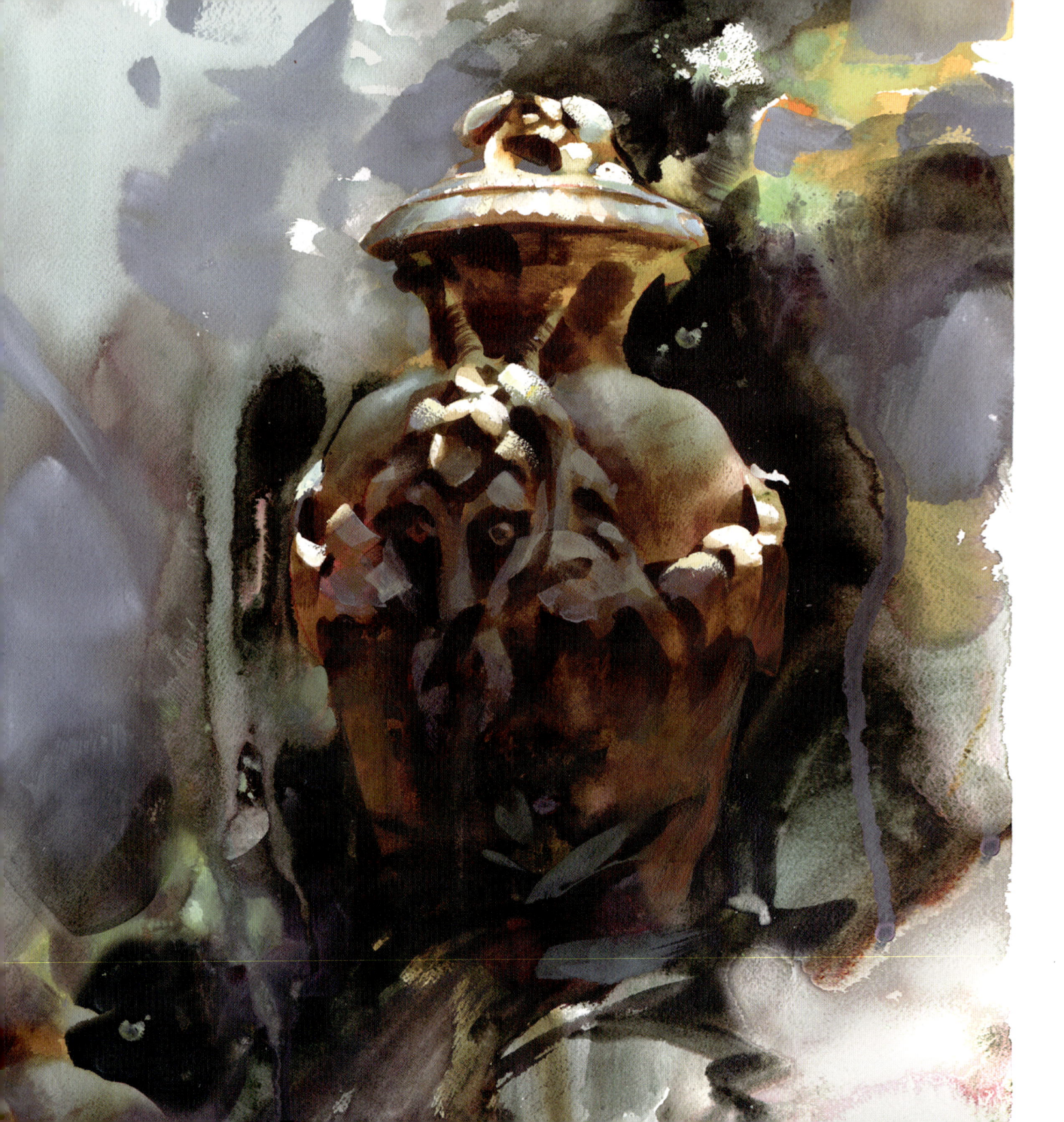

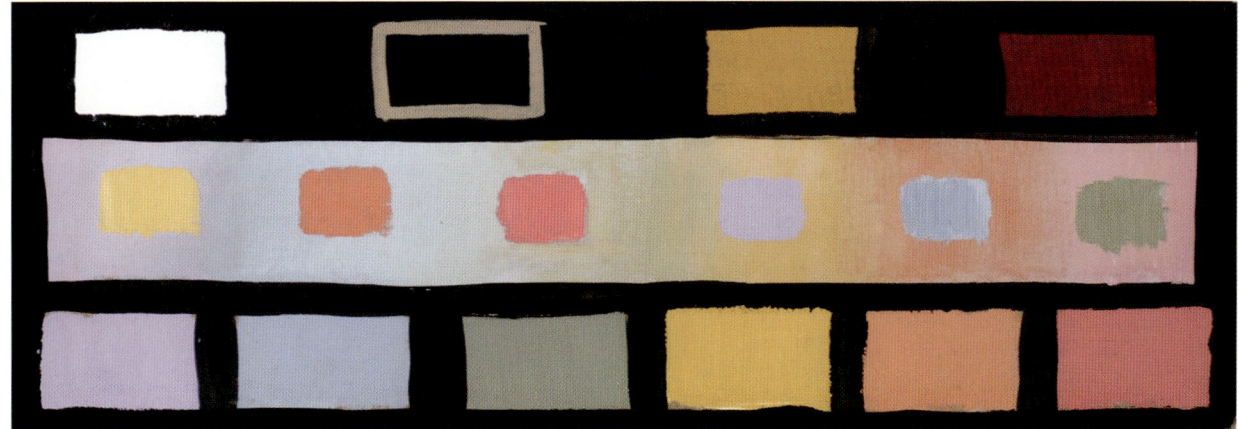

Chapter 6

Color: Limited Palette

Many years ago, an artist I was working with let me in on a big family secret. I won't give any names or places to protect his privacy, but he confided in me that his dad, who had been a painter at a major animation studio, was color blind, and had never revealed it to the studio.

The artist in question had studied art in the late 1930s, primarily focusing on draftsmanship and working in value. In the 1940s he was drafted into World War II as an aircraft electrician, and when he could not distinguish some of the colored wires, he discovered he was color blind! Despite this, he wanted to continue as an artist, and his black-and-white work was of a quality that brought him to the attention of the animation studio. But he was required to do color work, so at the end of every day, he put his current artwork in a satchel and brought it home where his wife would help correct any misplaced colors. His color abilities were limited but his draftsmanship and value design were exceptional, and on that strength, he managed a successful lifelong career.

Color is wonderful, it's amazing, it can enhance everything we do as artists. But the moral of this story is that it's not more important than the concepts we've been discussing thus far. We have to think of color as the frosting, not the cake; good color relies on an underlying structure of draftsmanship, value, and design.

We all know that color is complicated and challenging, which is why we're starting with a limited palette. It's not because good landscape painting requires it, it's simply to make the learning process manageable, as we take on the color challenge. When you have just a handful of tubes of paint, you can work more quickly; you're less likely to get lost in all the possible choices, and color mixing doesn't require as much time. Rather than drowning in too many choices, we need to get comfortable with our medium first, then move forward from there.

And you'd be surprised how much variety of color we can get with just a few pigments. Take a look at the color swatches above. Everything you see there is mixed from the top four pigments: yellow ochre, alizarin crimson, black, and white. Yep, just those two colors plus black and white created what appears to be a full rainbow of color! Please note that I don't actually recommend those four colors for landscape painting, but the chart helps make this valuable point.

Okay, let's get started with color. On the next pages, I'll lay out my suggested pigments for you.

"We have to think of color as the frosting, not the cake; good color relies on an underlying structure of draftsmanship, value, and design."

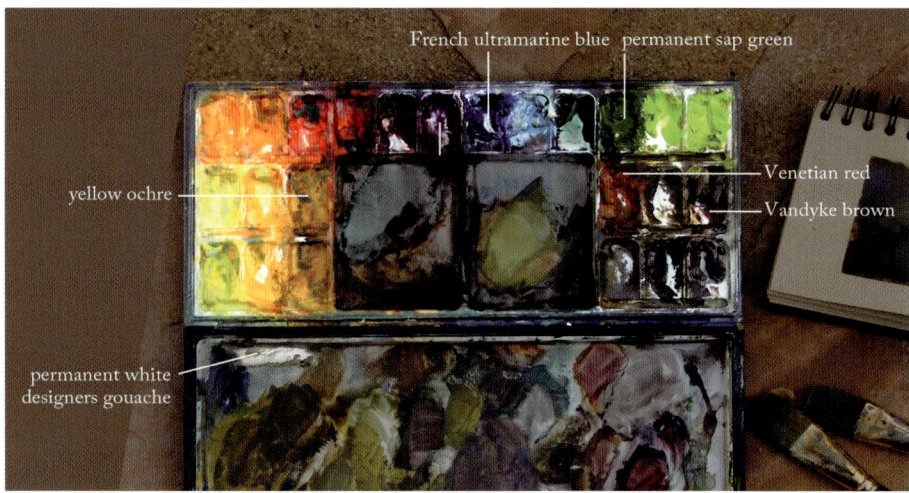

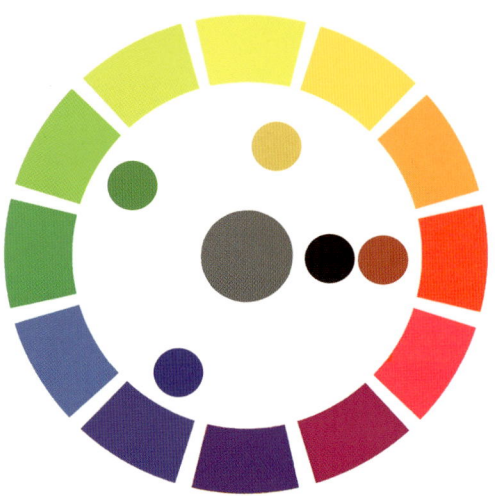

The Pigments

Above are the colors that I recommend for your "training" palette. It's a good basic bunch of pigments, capable of getting much of the rich, earthiness of nature, but they are not highly saturated colors and therefore, easier to control as you go through the learning curve. And most paintings you do will be a limited palette of some kind, meaning that you won't use every single possible color in them. So eventually, we'll need a full range of pigment so you can take on the challenge of any subject you see; we'll add those colors in the next chapter.

Pigments in Context

Here's our limited palette in the context of the color wheel. You can see that our pigments are fairly evenly spaced. This gives us a good range for mixing a full variety of colors while managing complexity by only using five colors plus white. For instance, the blue and Venetian red can be mixed to create a useful gray-purple, and so forth.

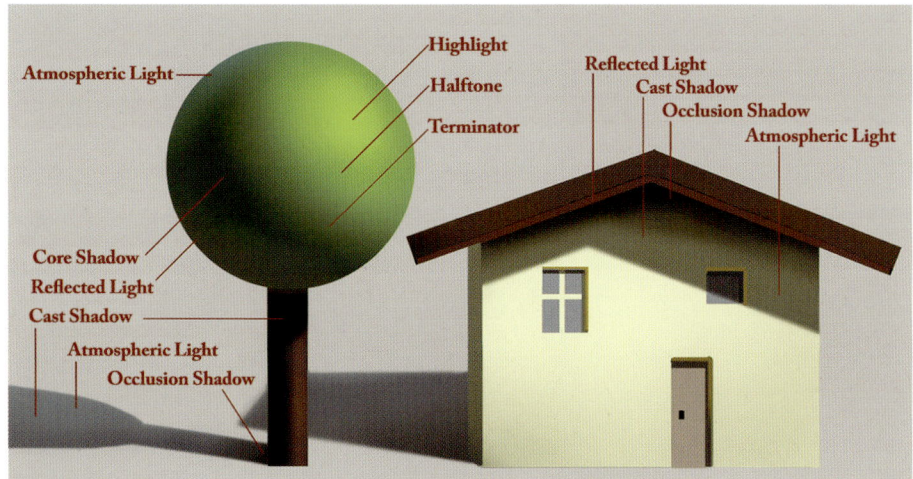

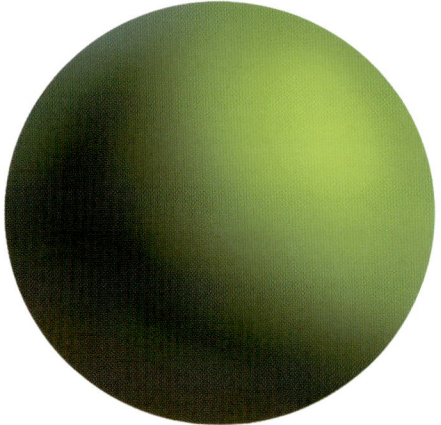

The Terminology of Light Revisited

We've looked at lighting terminology before, and now it's time to look at it in the context of color. A useful way to think about color is that it's a combination of local color and light color. Local color refers to the actual color of an object and light can have a variety of colors depending on the source. We can illustrate this idea clearly by taking a look at the green sphere to the right.

Light and Local Color

This, of course, is a green sphere but it also has a hint of yellow, blue, and orange; those are from the influence of light. On any object, the highlights tend to be more the color of the light source, and in this case, we have yellow light from the sun, blue light from the sky, and warm reflected light coming from below. So the highlights show the color influence of the light, but as the form curves away, we see more of the local color, in this case, green.

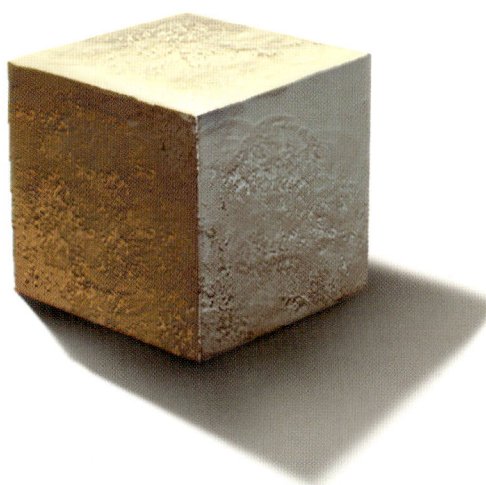

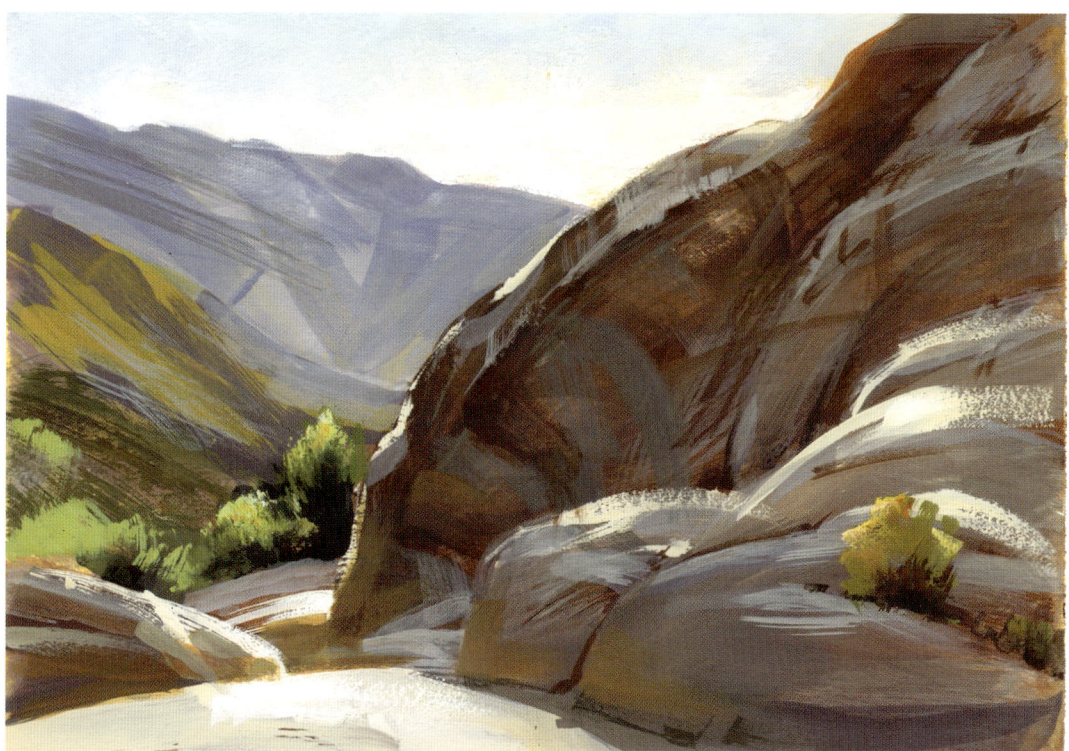

Color and Light to Convey Form

We've discussed the importance of conveying three-dimensional form in our landscapes, and color can be a big assist with this. In this rocky cube, form is conveyed not only by light and shadow but also the warm bounce light and the cool atmospheric light. These secondary light sources come from different directions and show plane changes in the shadows; this can be very useful when sketching forms that are primarily in shadow, as in the rocky sketch to the upper right.

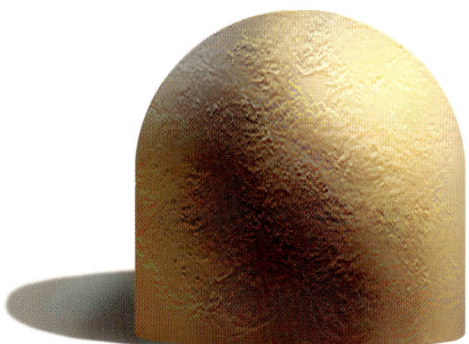

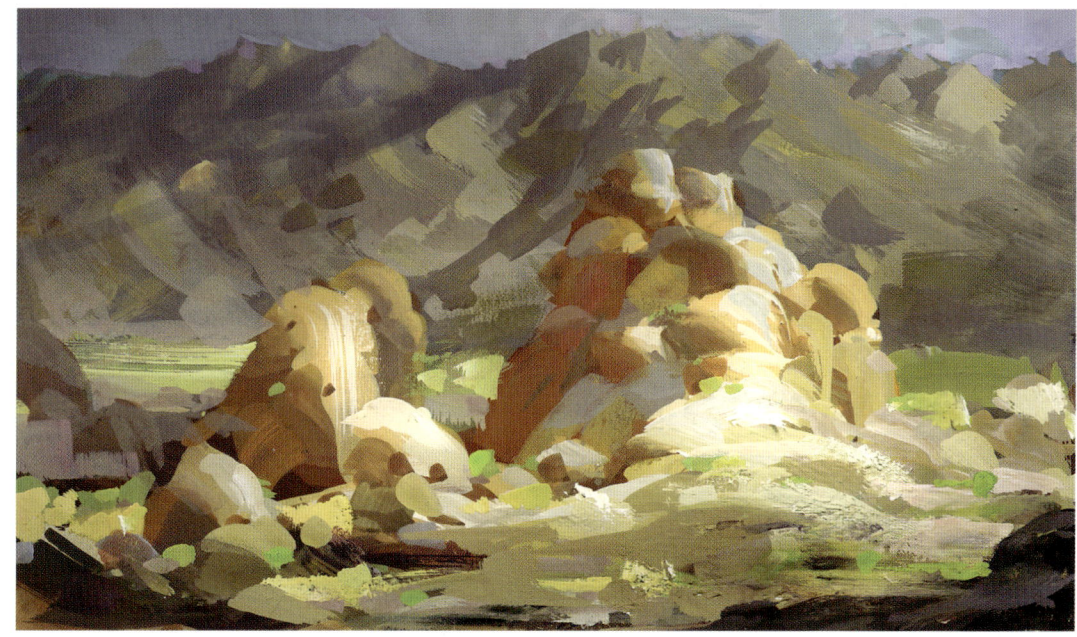

And here's another example of light on form as suggested in the sketch at lower right. These are unusual rock formations found in Joshua Tree National Park, California. They were tricky to paint in less than an hour, but treating them as simple 3-D forms made the process manageable.

Grand Canyon: 30-Minutes Limited-Palette Study

Heavyweight, mixed-media paper sketchbook, 7 x 10 inches

Now, how about an easy subject to take on? Let's see if we can sketch the Grand Canyon with our limited palette… in 30 minutes! To deal with the incredible complexity of this subject, I squint my eyes way down as I've discussed, to see how the scene groups in value. And it's late afternoon so we have maybe 30 minutes before the light goes away and painting will become challenging if not impossible. Can we do it? Of course we can, if we fight hard for the simple statement.

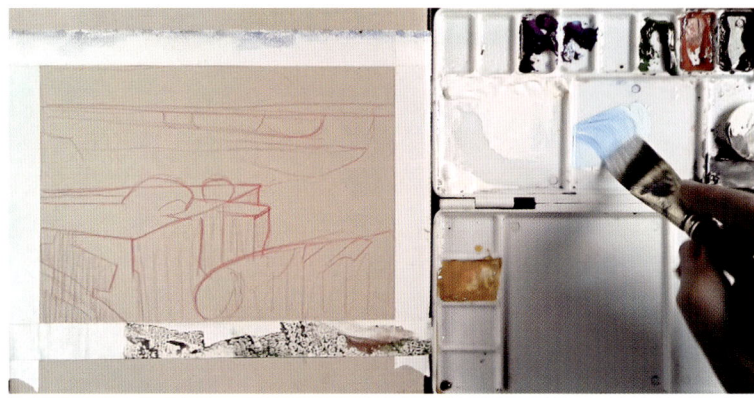

1. Let's start with a drawing using our red Prismacolor pencil. Notice how much I'm focusing on the very simple geometry of the scene; it's also important to establish the far horizon line.

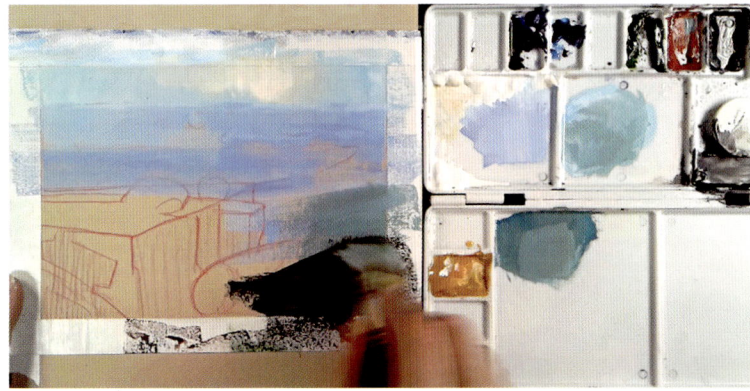

2. I paint in the blue sky, and while the paint is still damp, I add in the central clouds using white with a hint of yellow ochre, and then use a scumbling technique for the far landscape. Scumbling leaves some of the brown paper revealed which contributes to the rich warm/cool effect of the background. And let me admit that I've already cheated on our limited palette (not to worry, a limited palette is a flexible tool, not a dogma), the range of blues is critical to create the effect of distance, so I use a little phthalo blue with white in the sky then transition to the land by adding ultramarine blue.

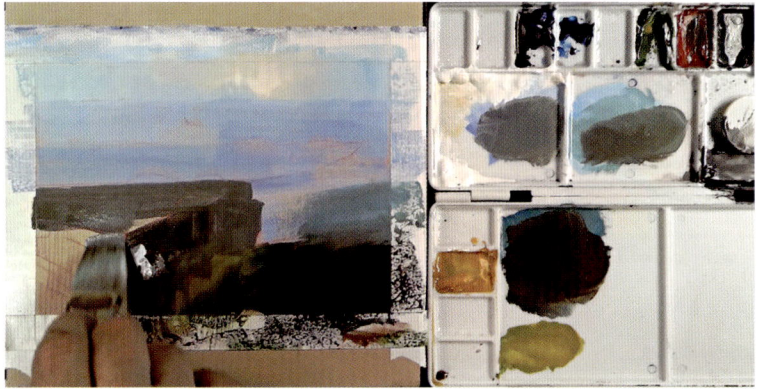

3. Next, I quickly block in the simple shape of the foreground. I'm using Vandyke brown for the dark side then adding a little white to create slightly cooler and lighter tones in the top and front planes. This value and temperature change is a product of cool skylight and helps convey plane changes in the simple geometry of the rock.

You can see a reference photo of this location on page 178/179.

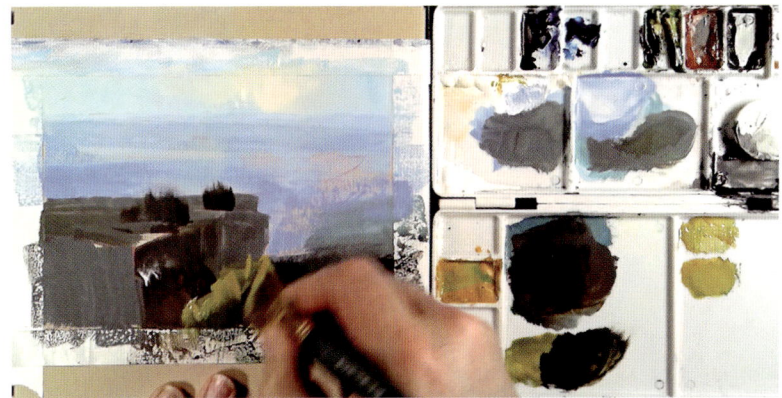

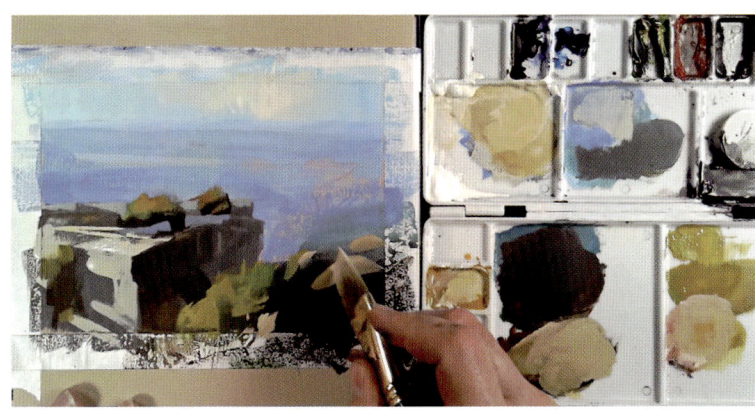

4 The bushes growing atop and in front of the rocks add a nice accent, so I focus on them next. I add a little green to my dark mixture and indicate each bush with a single upward pull of the brush. Now I'm ready for highlights! I make a thick mixture of sap green, yellow ochre, and white, and lay it into the foreground brush. In my experience, the most common mistake with this technique is too much water in the paint; this will lift up the underlying paint and quickly turn into a mess. The paint needs to be opaque for this technique to work!

5 And now we're ready to put some lights on the foreground rock! I'm being very careful to keep the geometric planes organized: the front plane will be lightest, the top plane a bit darker, and the side plane will remain in shadow. I mix yellow ochre and white, and let my brush drag in the direction of the perspective; brushstroke direction can be a great aid in suggesting form. And now I blend some directional light onto the foliage at the lower right and the scene is already starting to emerge!

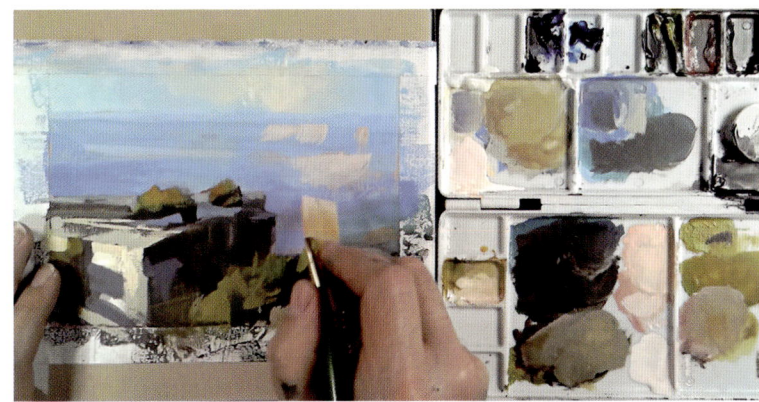

6 Finally, there's the warm sunset light hitting the far canyon wall. Even though there are some complicated forms back there, there's no time to render them, they must be suggested. So I mix a little Venetian red with opaque white, and let the direction of the brush bristles do the work. Then a few little accents and we're ready to pull the tape off and see what we have—the Grand Canyon in 30 minutes!

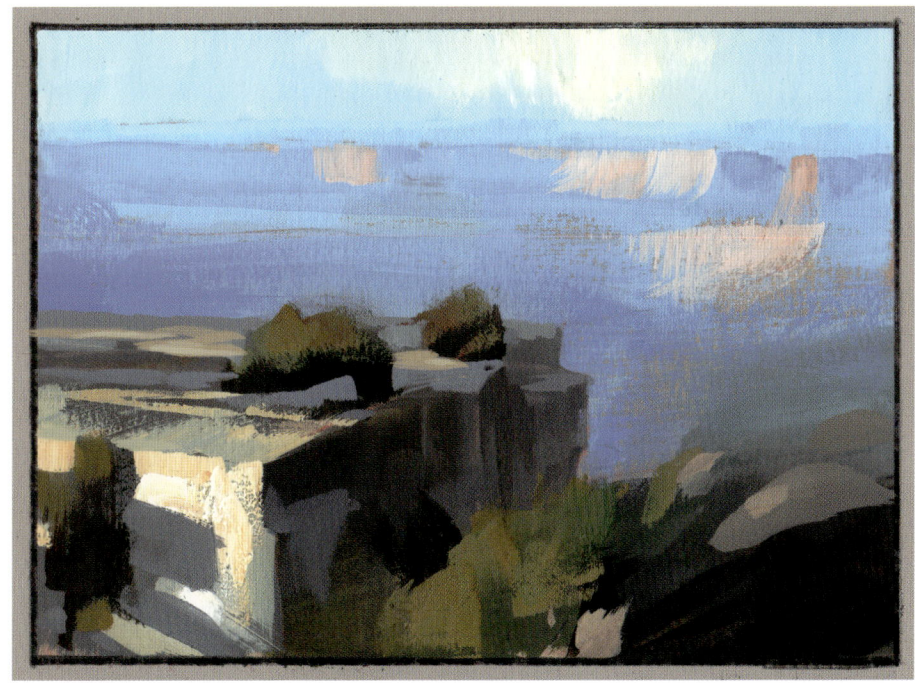

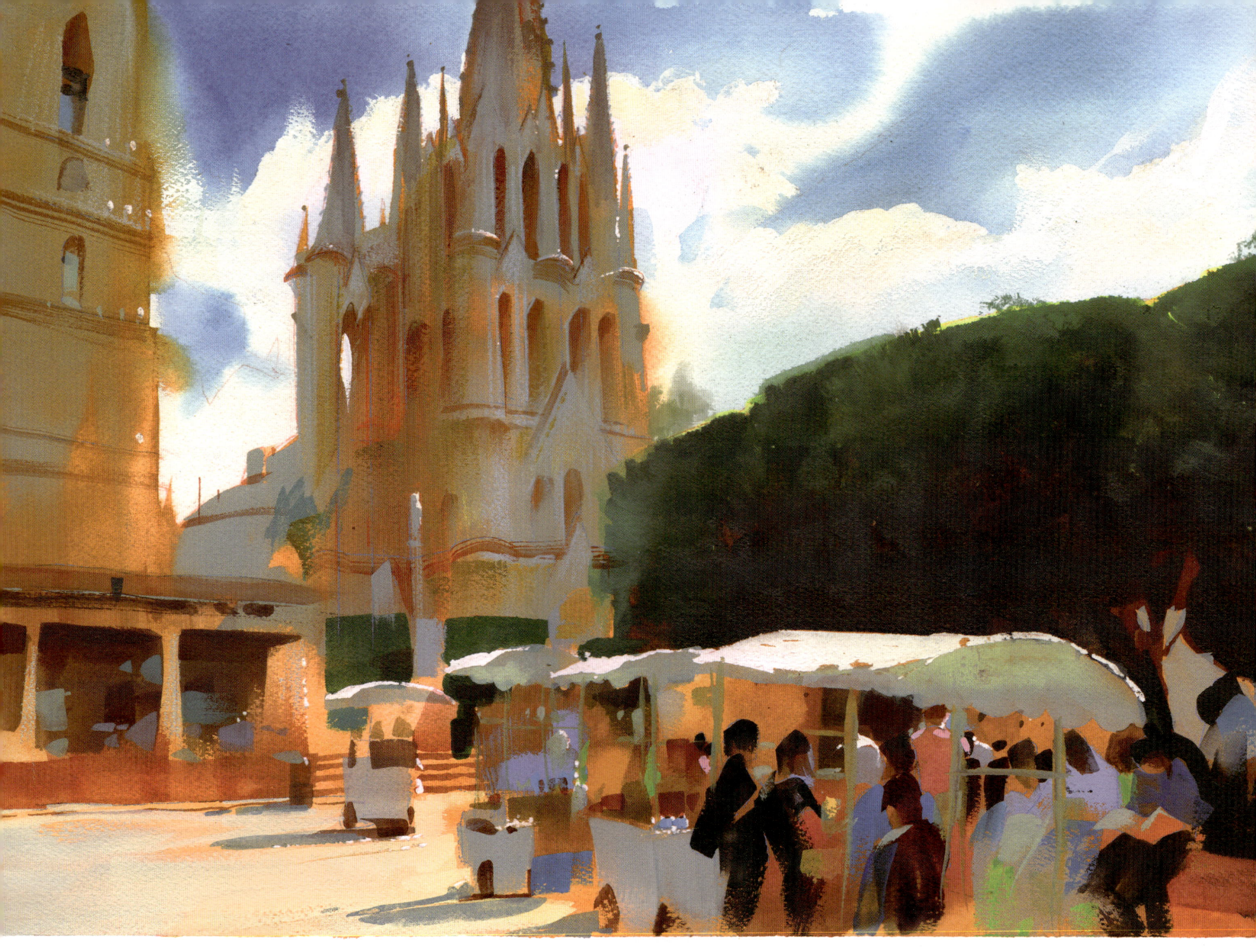

San Miguel de Allende, Mexico: Limited-Palette Demonstration

Arches 140–lb cold-pressed watercolor paper, 12 x 16 inches

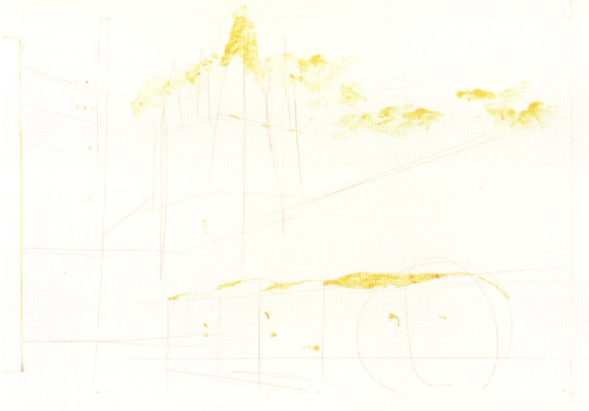

Let's use our limited palette to take on a beautiful but challenging spot, the town center of San Miguel de Allende, Mexico. For this painting I'm using the masking technique from Chapter 2: Using the Materials. The limited palette will give me everything I need to create the warm/cool and value contrasts of this scene.

(1) As usual, we begin with a quick drawing that emphasizes the simple shapes and perspective of the scene. I've decided that this painting should emphasize the white clouds and canopy of the market set against the dark trees and cathedral spires. To prepare for this I use masking fluid to preserve those areas of white.

(2) It will make most sense to start with the background sky, so I prepare the paper by spritzing it with clean water and allow it to dampen for a moment. I wash in ultramarine blue and take advantage of the wet into wet softness of the paper; the lighter more luminous sky to the right is a thinner mixture of pigment with the tiniest addition of yellow ochre for warmth. The buildings and foreground have a warm local color and luminous quality, so I lay in a wash of Venetian red and yellow ochre. Then I begin painting the shadow colors into the buildings. The cools are a mixture of Vandyke brown and white (no blue added). I know this is a counter intuitive way to create a cool temperature, but trust me, on top of the vivid warm, it feels relatively cool. In fact, I suggest that you think of opaque white as very light, cool gray, because that's the effect it has on most everything it's mixed with. The darkest darks are vividly warm and I begin to brush those in as well.

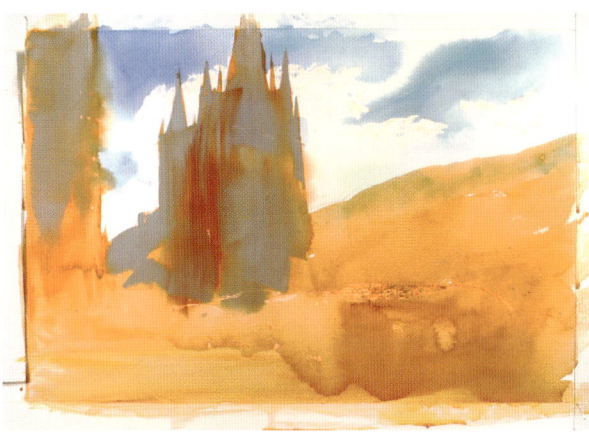

(3) The dark trees at middle right are very important for contrast, so I block those in with sap green that's neutralized with a little Venetian red, then rub off the masking fluid to reveal the white of the scene. The windows and architectural elements of the cathedral are what give it character, so I focus on those with a warm, dark mixture of Venetian red and Vandyke brown. Next, I lay in some warm and cool underpainting to suggest the visual activity of the foreground market. Light falling across the ground plane and cast shadows are indicated, then it's time to suggest people and activity in the foreground. My final step is breaking out a razor blade and chipping little bits of highlight into key areas. This gives the suggestion of light glinting, for a finished quality to an otherwise gestural painting.

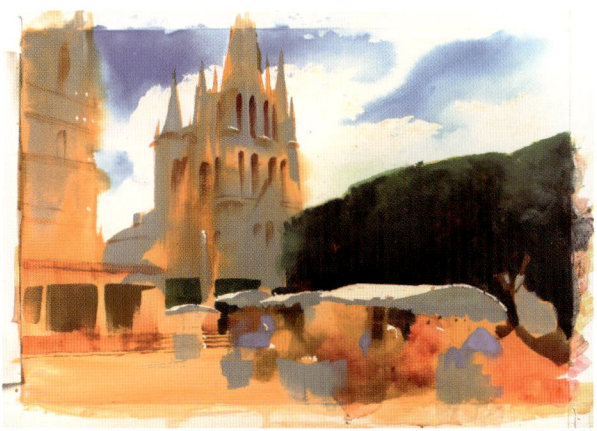

"The limited palette gives me everything I need to create the warm/cool and value contrasts of this scene."

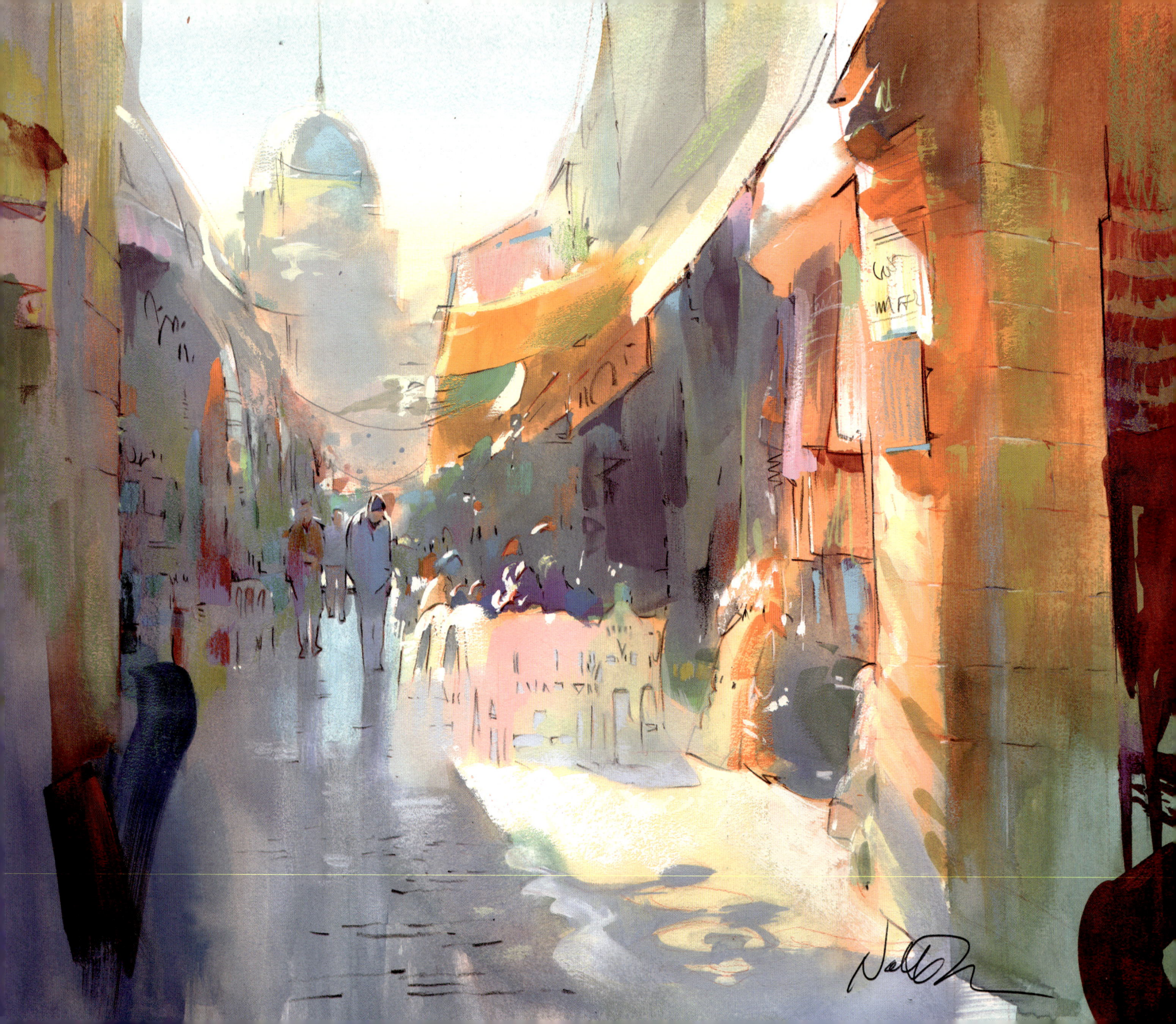

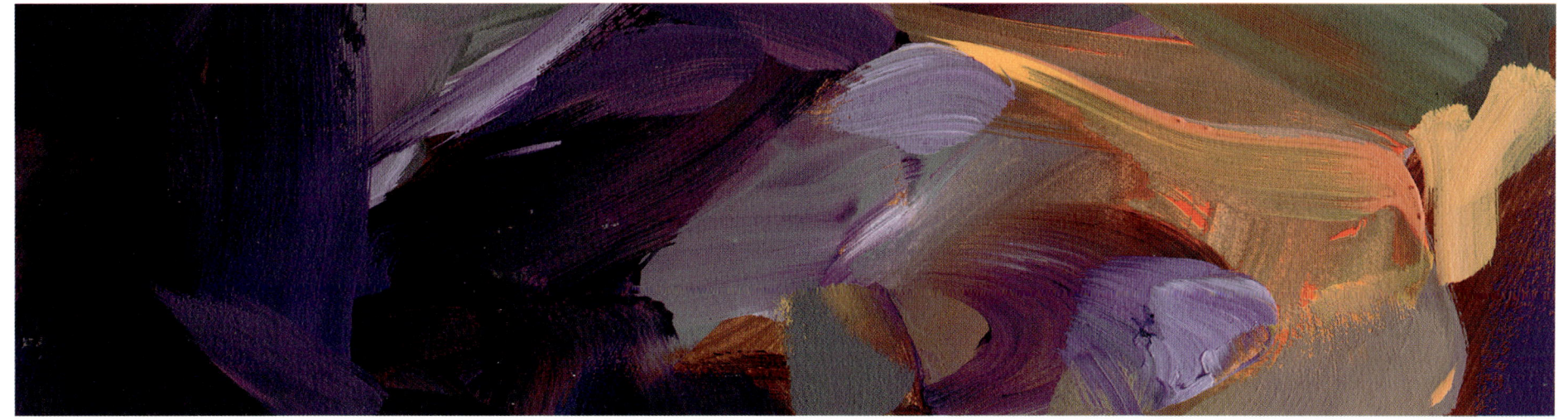

Chapter 7

The Design of Color

Probably most of us have had the experience of visiting a local art fair and seeing some nice paintings of the local landscape, but inevitably, there are booths where less experienced painters don't yet have the abilities with color to match their enthusiasm. They use paint as if bright, saturated colors are good, and more are even better. The results are paintings that are so weighted with layer after layer of sugary color that we feel the need to turn away in hopes of something more palatable elsewhere.

All of us have seen paintings like this, but we've also seen, for instance, an Impressionist masterpiece. Both have bright saturated colors; one draws us in with its beauty while the other turns us away with its garishness. What's the difference, do you know? Let's figure it out on the following pages.

"What's the difference between a painting that's garishly saturated with clashing colors and an Impressionist masterpiece? Both are filled with bright, saturated colors. The key to color design is knowing why the one works and the other fails."

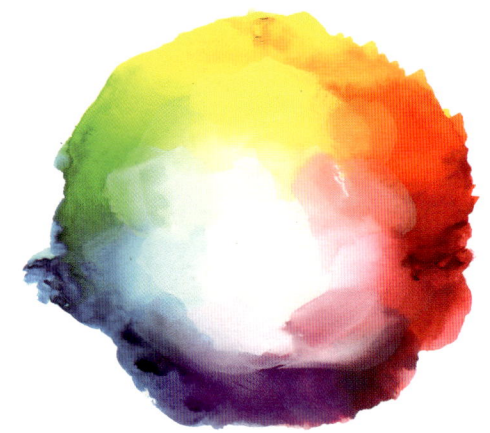

Why a Color Wheel?

There are lots of ways to chart and arrange the varieties of color, so why a wheel shape? The reason is that it places colors in opposition to each other; red is opposite green, yellow opposite violet and so forth. These colors are in direct contrast with each other, they are as different as any two colors can be. This is a product of our brains interpreting wavelengths of light in a way that lets us better distinguish one object from another and successfully make our way through the world. And as artists, much of what we do is about the design of contrast; we've discussed over and over ideas about where to put visual interest in our paintings and where to leave it out. Visual interest is synonymous with contrast, hence the useful nature of the color wheel.

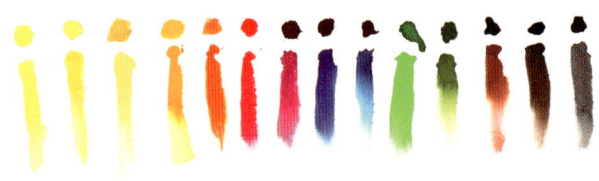

Know Your Pigments

If you're new to this, take a little time to get to know your pigments. Put down a dab of thick paint on a good watercolor paper. (I recommend Arches cold-pressed paper.) Then brush some clean water up against it and let the pigment bleed into it. This gives you a chart of the qualities of the pigments in thick and thin application.

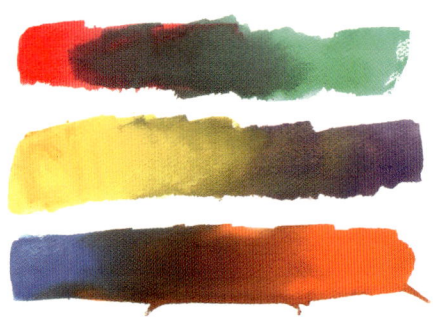

Mixing Opposites

Pigments opposite each other on the color wheel have an interesting property, they neutralize each other when mixed as shown. I find this quality useful because much of the beauty of nature is in the rich variations of neutrals. Ochres, gray greens, browns, cool grays—these colors enhance each other when side by side as found in nature. I like to mix these colors by blending opposites together but leaving the pigments marbled for a rich subtlety that mimics the variety found in nature.

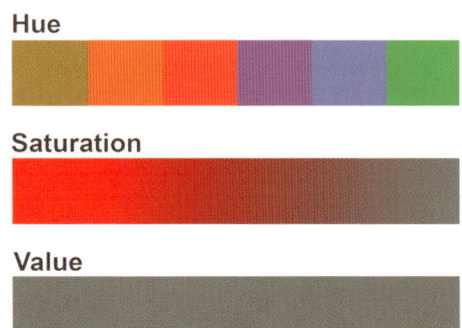

Hue

Saturation

Value

The Three Properties of Color

The three properties of color are hue, saturation, and value. Everything that you ever see is a combination of these three properties; in terms of vision, there is nothing else. Hue is our brain's interpretation of the various wavelengths of light. Saturation is a product of the combination of those wavelengths, and value is simply a perception of how much light is present.

And this is great news, because the human eye can distinguish millions of color variations and all those possibilities can be crippling for an artist. The fact that we can break color down into just three simple properties can be a real lifesaver. I recommend you do exactly that. As you're judging color, first be sure the value is correct, then the hue and saturation. Forget about the millions of possibilities, just these three considerations can give your paintings great color.

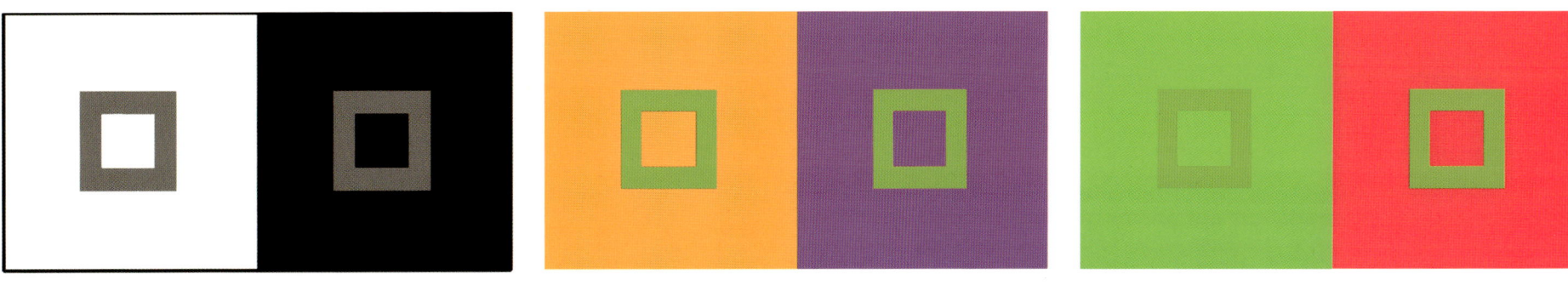

Color Relationships

Value: In a painting, colors are always seen in context with each other, and can strongly influence how we perceive them. For instance, both center squares above are the same value, but we tend to think of the one on the left as a little darker and the one on the right as a little lighter because of their different surroundings.

Hue: Again, the center squares above are exactly the same color, but the one on the left feels relatively cool green compared to the one on the right which feels more yellow-green in hue. This is another example of how our perception of color varies by context.

Saturation: The same principle applies to this property of color. The square surrounded by green appears to be desaturated, but the exact same color appears to be a more saturated green when surrounded by a highly saturated red.

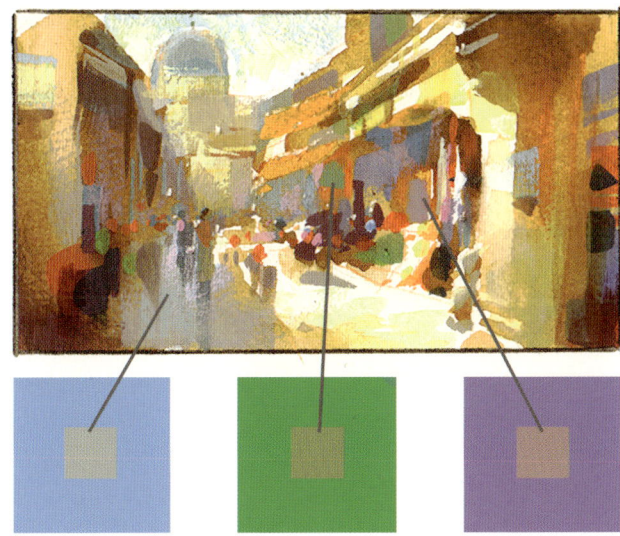

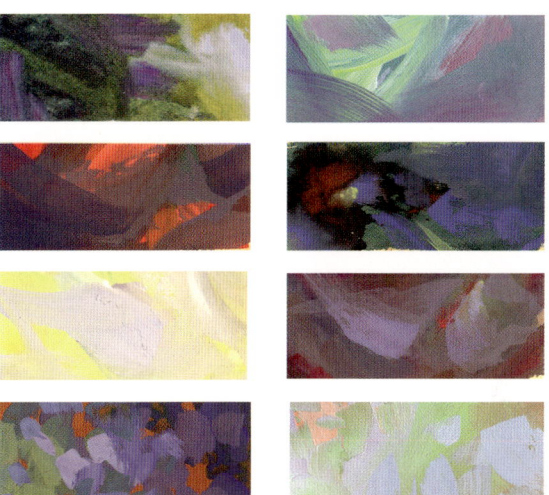

Why Color Relationships Matter

The swatches of color at the top of this page are interesting enough, but why do they matter to a painter? Let's take a look at the street scene above. It is, in fact, the rough sketch that I did in preparation for the painting that leads this chapter. It's also a good illustration of colors influencing each other in a painting. Look at the three colors that are pointed out: a blue in the lower left, a cool green in the middle, and a grey purple to the right. Each appears to have a distinctive cool hue in the painting, but put them in a different context and suddenly they all feel warm! This is the answer to the question posed in the introduction to this chapter. An experienced artist will design how colors feel relative to each other, but an amateur will simply say "it needs to be blue" and paint an actual blue, ending up with the clashy color combinations that I warned about on the previous page.

A Useful Exercise

Back in the '90s, when I was trying to figure all of this out, I was very serious about my commitment to daily practice, but I would come home from long days of over-time exhausted and incapable of painting more pictures. Determined to keep the dream alive, I simply spent five minutes taking three contrasting colors plus white and attempted to blend them together in a visually interesting way. These five-minute exercises turned out to be one of the most useful things I did, because they helped me understand how to paint color relationships.

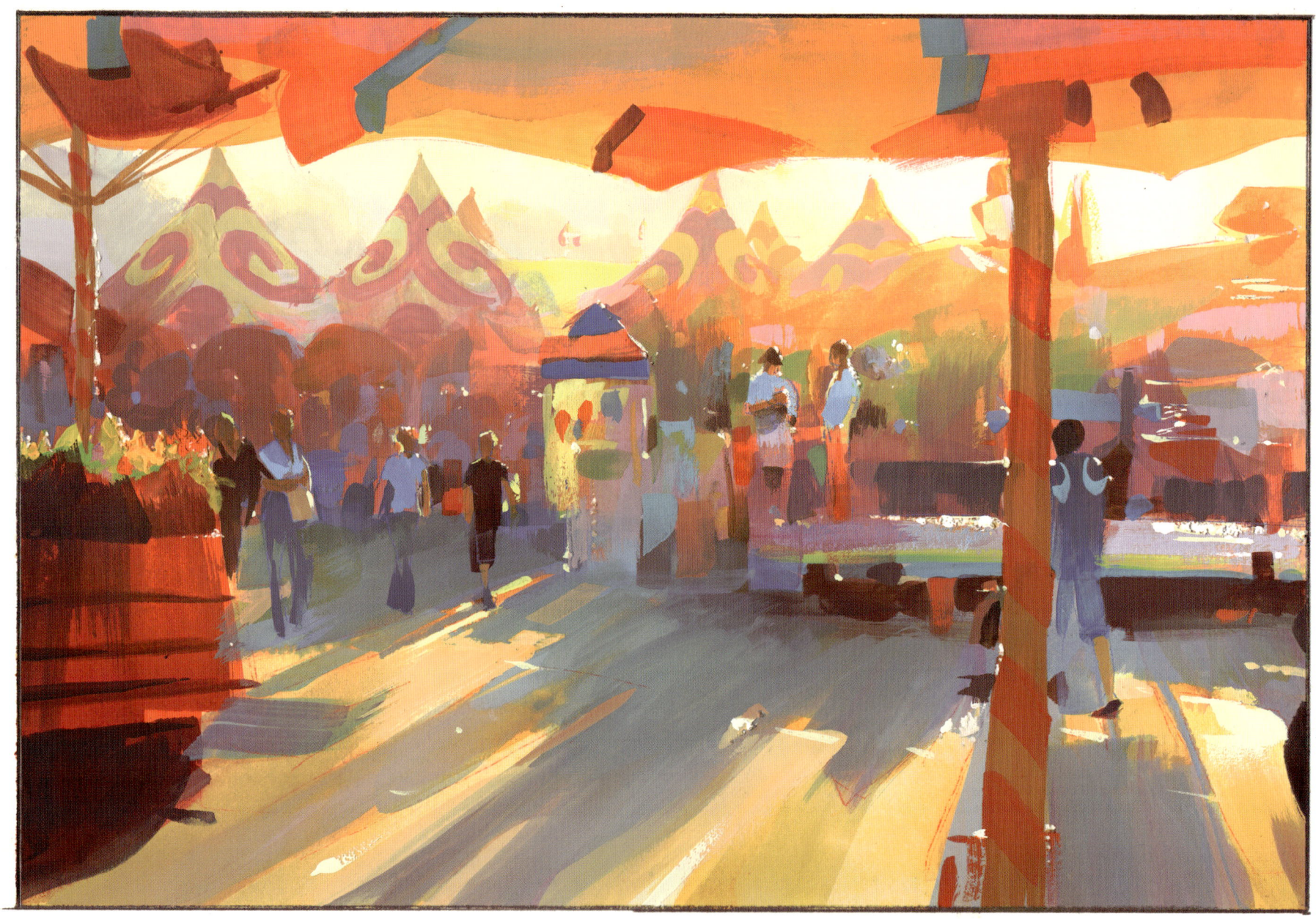

County Fair L.A.

N Fowlee '17

The County Fair: A Color Case Study

Illustration board, 9 x 12 inches

Here's a sketch I did of the L.A. County Fair, and I have to admit, it was a real challenge. The place was loaded with stuff, I mean, everywhere! People, games, shiny prizes, swirling shapes, a beautiful chaos! My only shot at coming up with a meaningful painting was, you guessed it, finding the simple statement. On the following page I'll show you what the thinking was to achieve that goal.

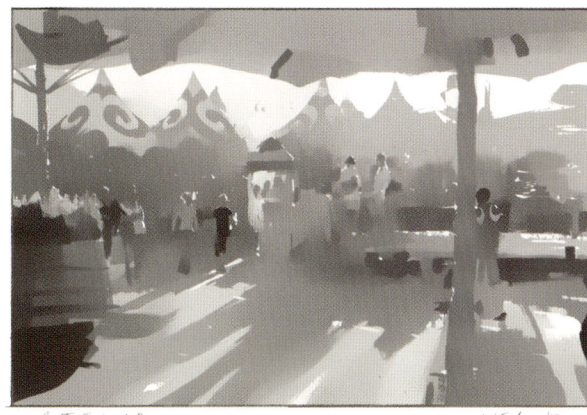

The Simple Value Statement

To illustrate the simple statement of value in this painting, I've turned it to grayscale and added a noise reduction filter to blend away the smaller textures and details, so we can clearly see the underlying value structure. Notice how the light areas group together, and the areas in shadow group together very simply as well. Simplifying these areas allowed me to focus on a sprinkle of contrast across the center of the painting. As usual, this simple value organization was the key ingredient of the painting.

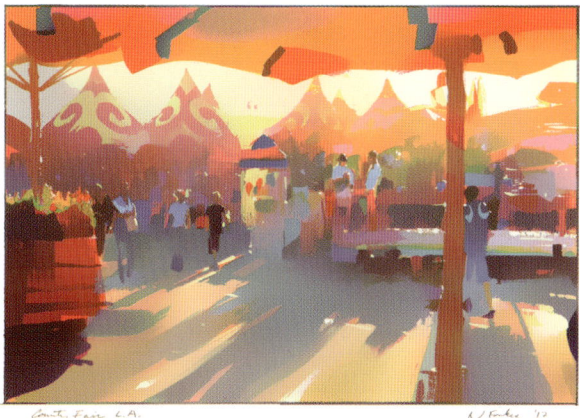

The Simple Color Statement

The scene was characterized by warm colors: red and yellow tents and sunset light streaming in. Even the blue of the shadows is really just a cool gray that feels blue in this context. And that left me wide open to cheat a little for visual effect. The people up on the stage really were wearing blue company uniform T-shirts that contrasted beautifully with the warms of the environment. I ran with that idea and gave other people blue shirts as well and added a few dark value shirts for variety. I told a little white lie about the color of a few of the shirts to get to the greater truth of exciting contrasts in the scene.

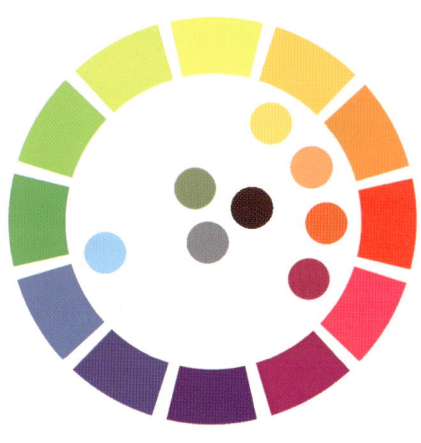

Unity with Variety

We can chart these color choices on the color wheel to confirm how the colors unify and vary from each other. Notice the primary influence of warm colors plus some neutrals, then small accents of cyan blue to create an exciting color contrast. Take this idea of unity with variety to heart next time you're struggling with color. If your color feels clashy, simply find a way to create unity by reducing the contrast of hue and saturation, and if your color feels dead and boring, find some accents of contrasting colors to create variety.

① Here's the step-by-step process. Right up front I observe that the scene unified beautifully around warm temperatures of color, so I start with a glowing yellow wash to suggest that influence throughout the painting.

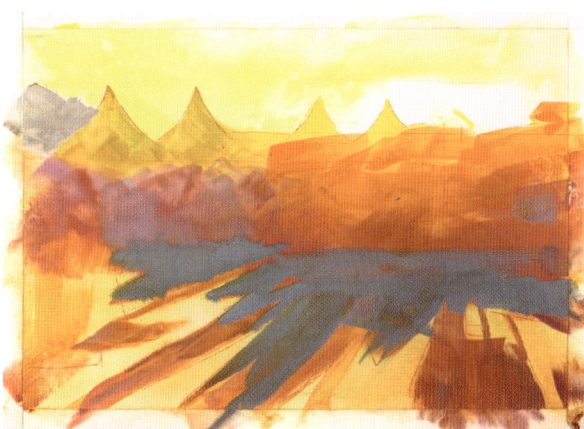

② Next, I block in the simple mass of the tents and add the cast shadows. The influence of cool skylight brings some exciting contrast to the scene, so I begin laying that in as well. This setup helps emphasize the backlit glow of the sun in the distance.

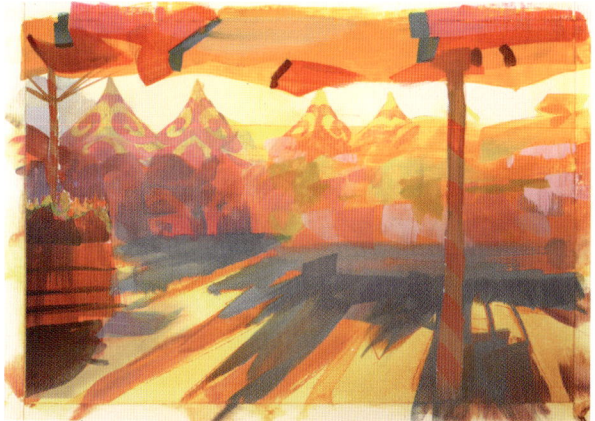

③ The next step is to add the foreground elements, which create a good framework to lay in the primary contrasts in the scene as shown in the final image. To do this I use opaque paints, then break out the razor blade to chip out useful glints of highlight throughout.

Impressionism on the Fly

I sometimes think of the artist Georges Seurat (1859–1891); you know, that pointillist Impressionist artist? The one who spent hour after hour, dot after dot, creating colors that visually blend when you stand back from them. And though I am a fan of his work, I often think, That poor man, the tedium of it! But the truth is, it was brilliant, it was a breakthrough idea. But even if you are an exquisitely patient artist, there's just not time for it under the rapidly changing conditions of sketching outdoors.

And yet, I have often looked at a luminous blue sky that somehow feels warm, or a field with thousands of bits of contrasting colors and wished I could do it the Seurat way. This is what led me to attempt Impressionism "on the fly," or what I sometimes call "poor man's Impressionism." I found that I could simply drybrush contrasting colors over top of each other to create a combination of colors that optically mix on paper, rather than being first blended on the palette. The result is a far more lustrous and visually interesting painting that approximates the richness and luminosity of nature.

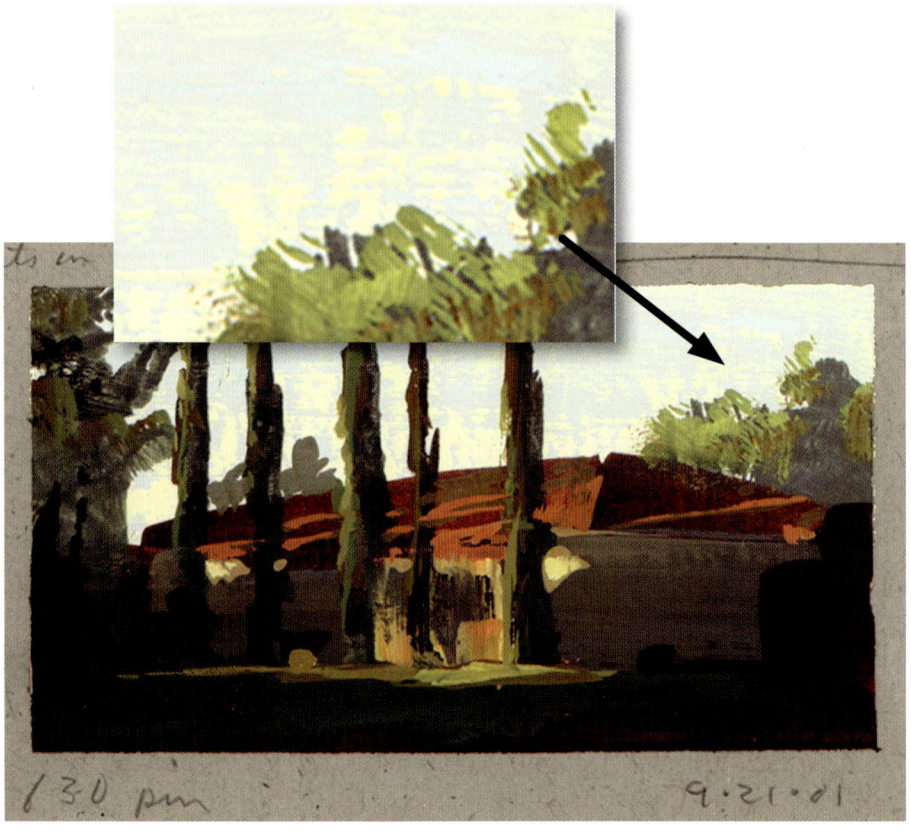

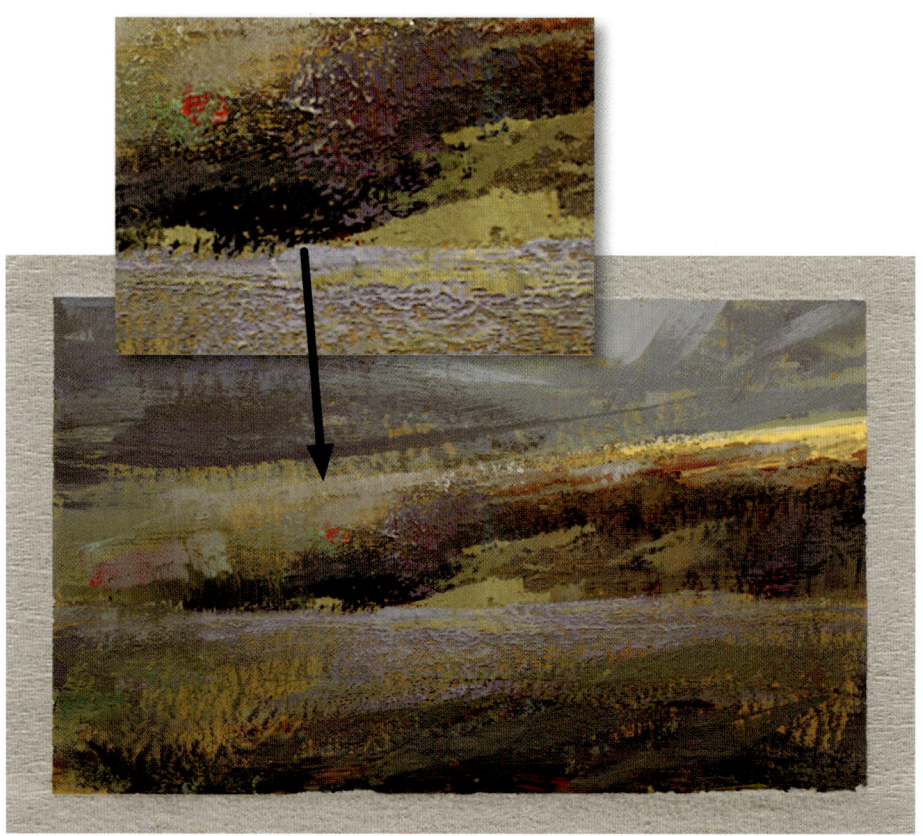

Here's my sketch of a neighborhood house. At the time, as mentioned above, I remember feeling that, even though the sky was bluish, it had a warm luminosity that would be tricky to represent with paint. So I began with a very light warm color of white and lemon yellow covering the mass of the sky, then, while that was drying, I mixed a tiny bit of phthalo and ultramarine blue with white and drybrushed that color over top. Note that it was critical that the blue was nearly the same value as the yellow. Colors of contrasting hue but similar value often feel like they're vibrating with brightness. This effect is referred to as simultaneous contrast, the key ingredient for the luminous quality of impressionism.

Here's another example, this time in a field rather than a sky. I was struck by the contrast of colors of this place: the yellow-grass-covered ground, the cool light of the sky, plus a velvet cover of light purple flowers in the mid ground. But the light was fading fast. The solution? Poor man's Impressionism! Take a look at the detail view to see how there are several layers of paint drybrushed over each other to approximate the variety of color and light present on location.

Let's demonstrate this idea step by step in Zion National Park, Utah! This is a vivid and atmospheric moment, perfect for an impressionistic layering of color.

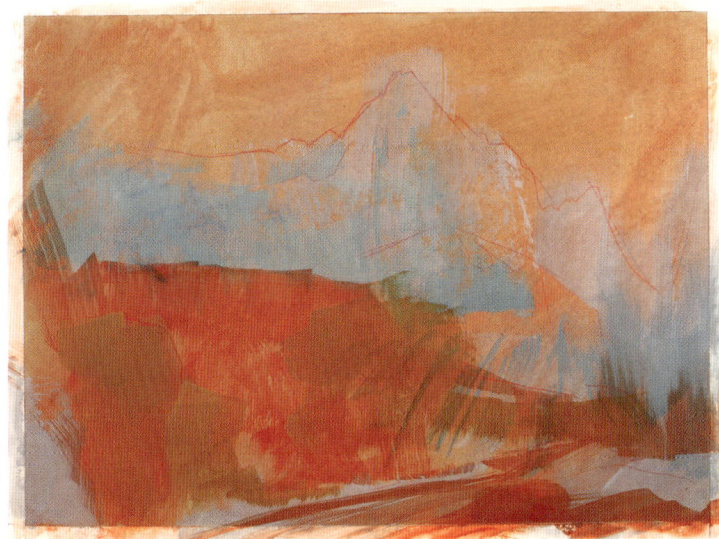

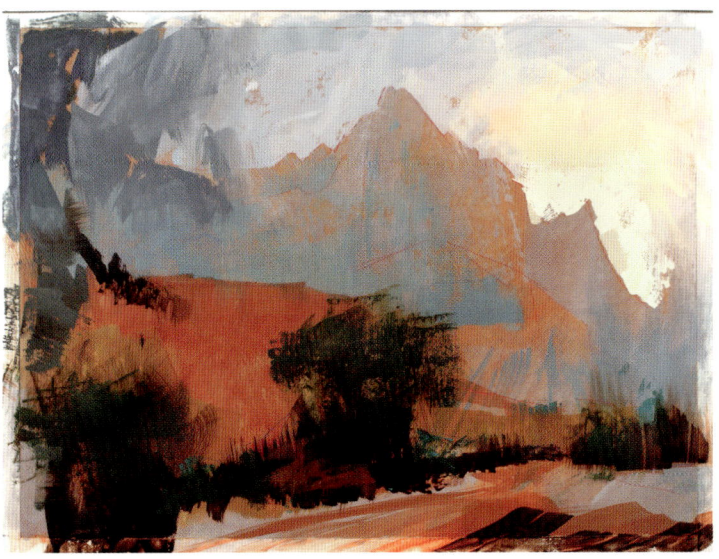

(1) There's a warm glow of sun from the back right, with lots of cool sky and skylight in the distance, so I begin with a warm wash to layer the cooler colors over. I'm using fairly thick paint and drybrushing it on to create the overlapping speckled effect of both warm and cool for simultaneous contrast.

(2) Now I lay in the sky with opaque paint and am drybrushing to allow the underpainting to show through. I place my dark accents below using warm browns then scumble cooler greens over the top to create the underpainting of foliage.

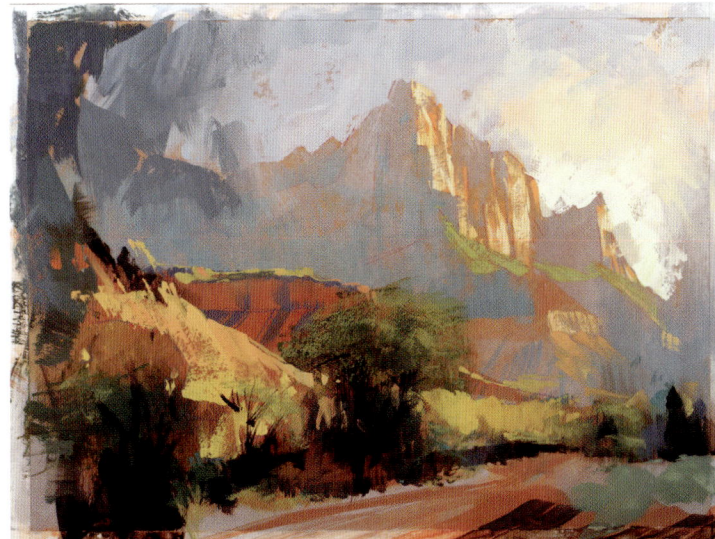

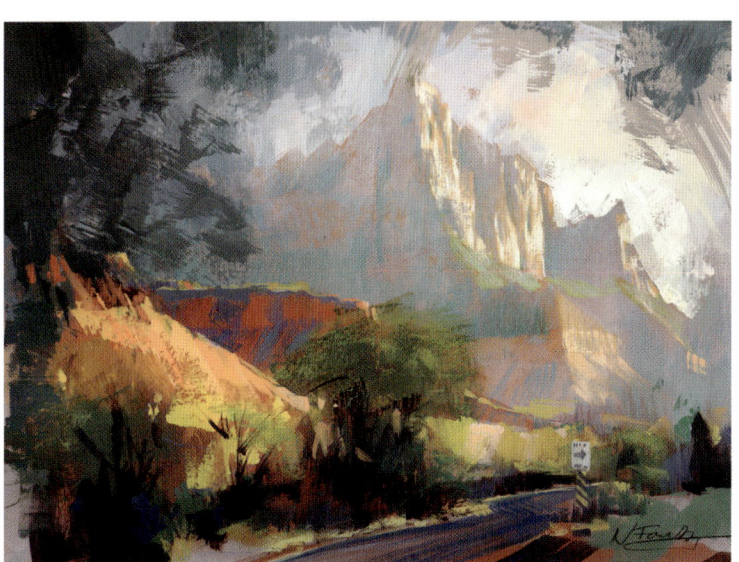

(3) Now it's time for highlights. I'm using very thick opaque paint, being careful to maintain the warm temperatures of the sunset light. I'm heavily drybrushing, especially with warm greens into the foliage for extra texture.

(4) Finally, I frame the scene with the suggestion of foliage and paint the road into the ground plane. My final step is lightly drybrushing more cool colors into the background to finalize the sense of atmospheric distance; I'm being careful that the added paint is about the same value as the area it's applied to. I add a few dots and dashes where needed to suggest detail and the painting is complete!

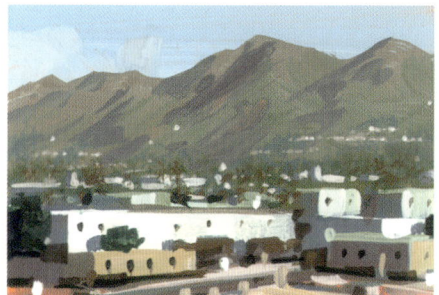 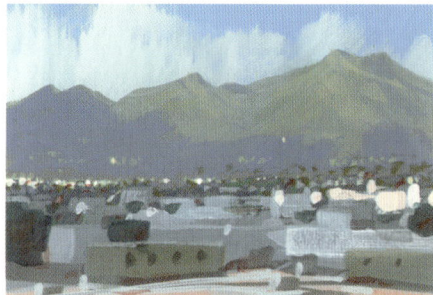 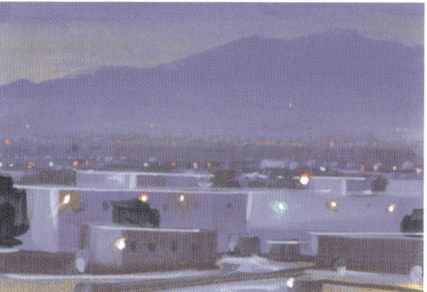 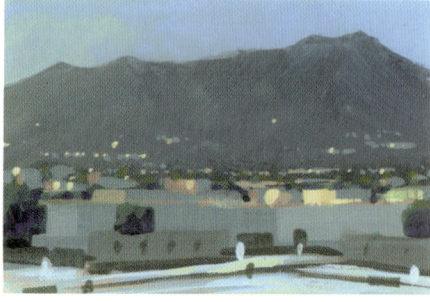

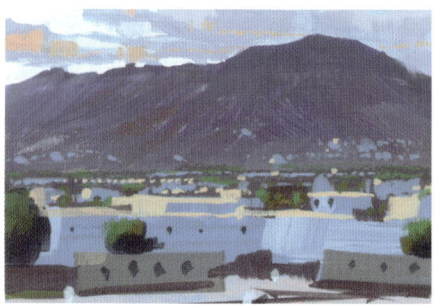 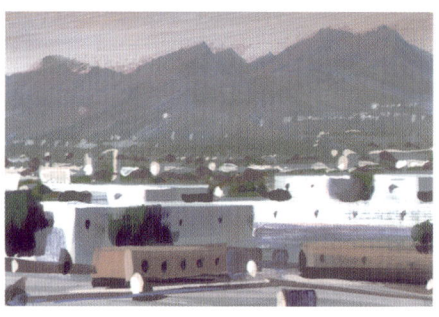 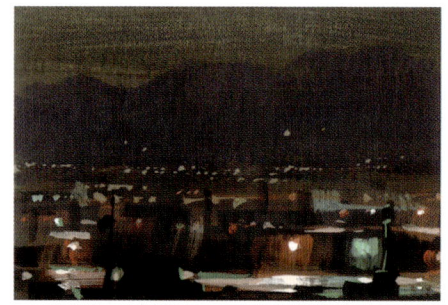 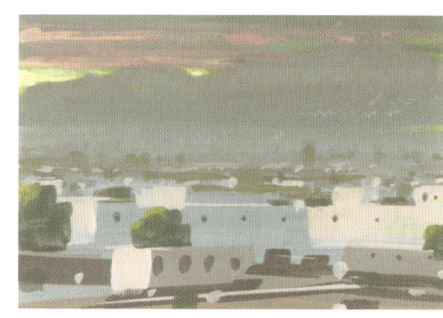

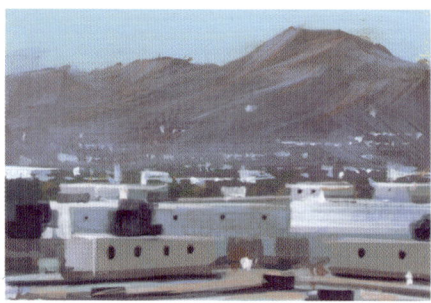 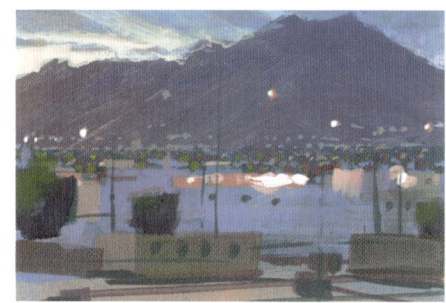 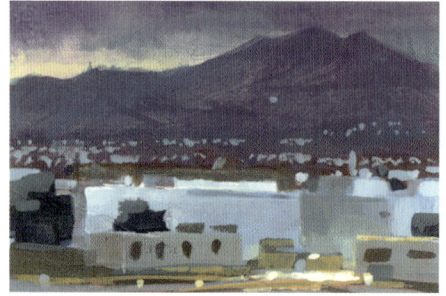 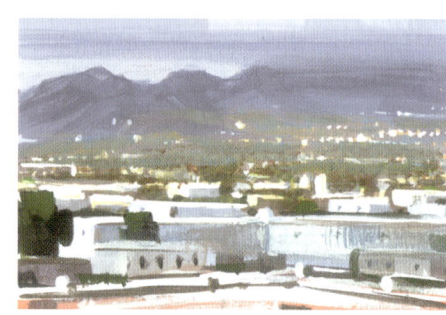

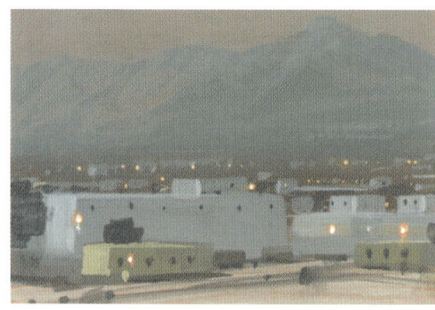 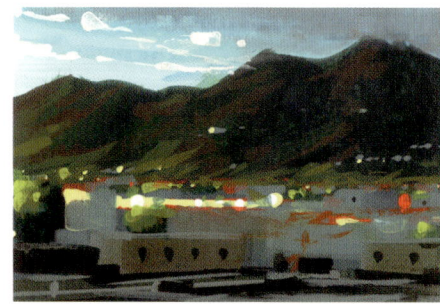 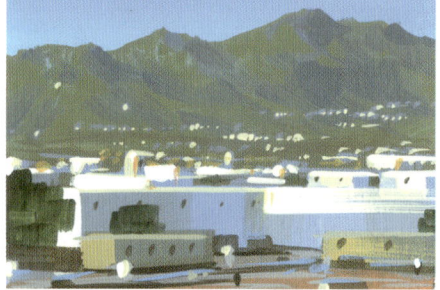 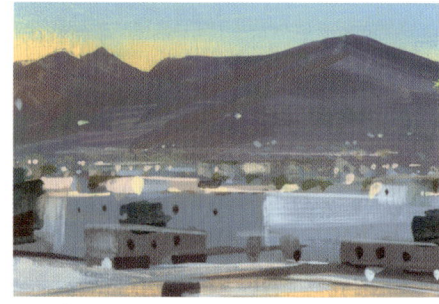

The Influence of Weather and Atmosphere

Toned mixed media paper, 4 x 5 inches

This was the view out my office window while I was working at DreamWorks Animation Studios in Los Angeles. These are painted at a variety of times of day with a range of outdoor conditions.

Here's how this all got started: I'm the same as anyone else; sometimes at work I just want to stare blankly out the window, but I had my whole palette of paints right in front of me so why not turn it into a sketch? So all of these images are a careful chronicle of me doing something other than what I was being paid for, but, hey, we've all gotta take a break, right? So I did all these studies over the course of several months, and the variety was quite surprising; changes in weather and atmosphere made the exact same scene have quite a different mood from day to day.

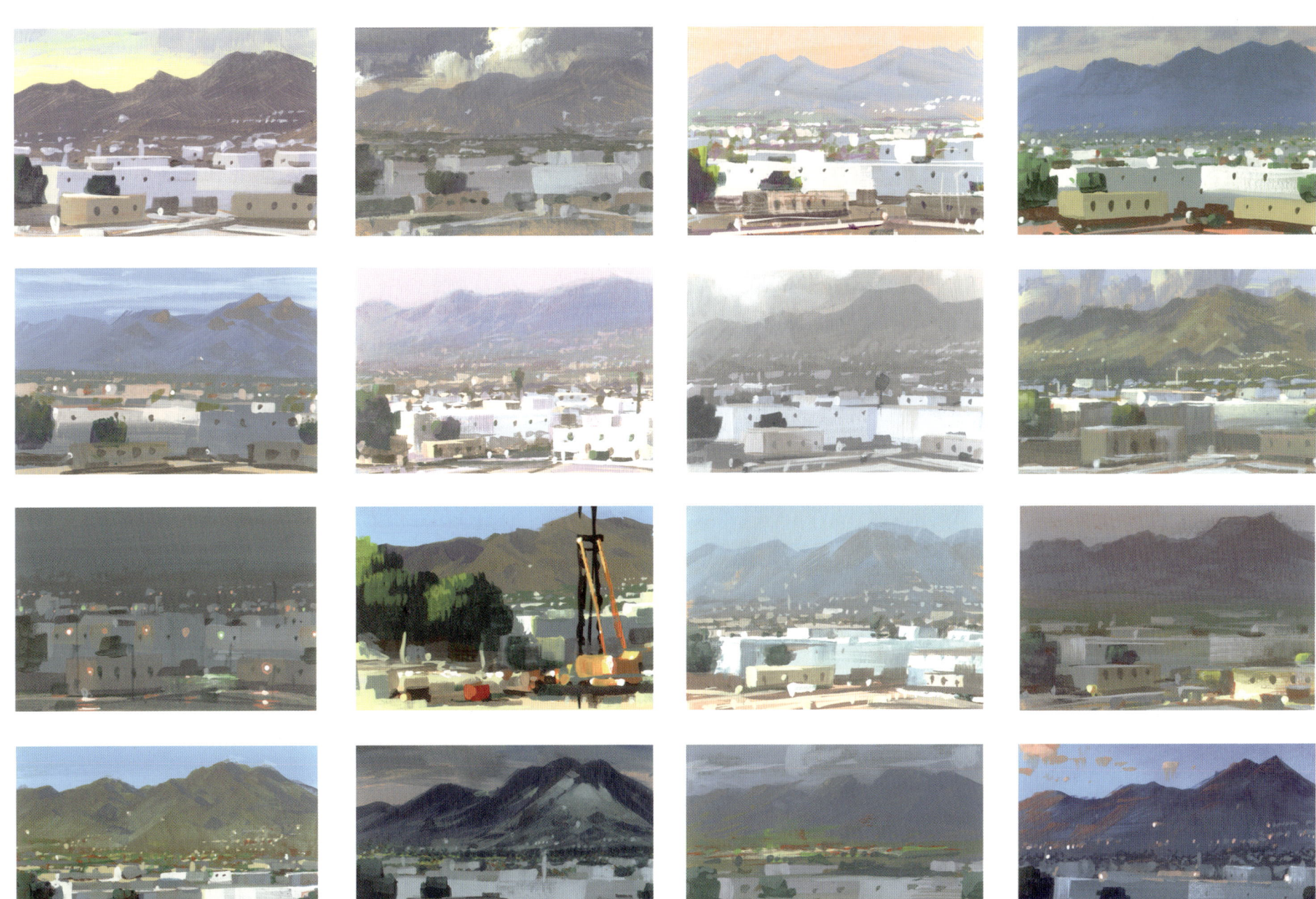

Turn It into an Exercise

I recommend you try this! It could be out your window at home or at work, or any place where you can observe the same scene at different times and under different conditions. Catch the sunrise and the sunset, and paint at night! I think the experience of doing this will be highly instructive and make you a much more sophisticated artist.

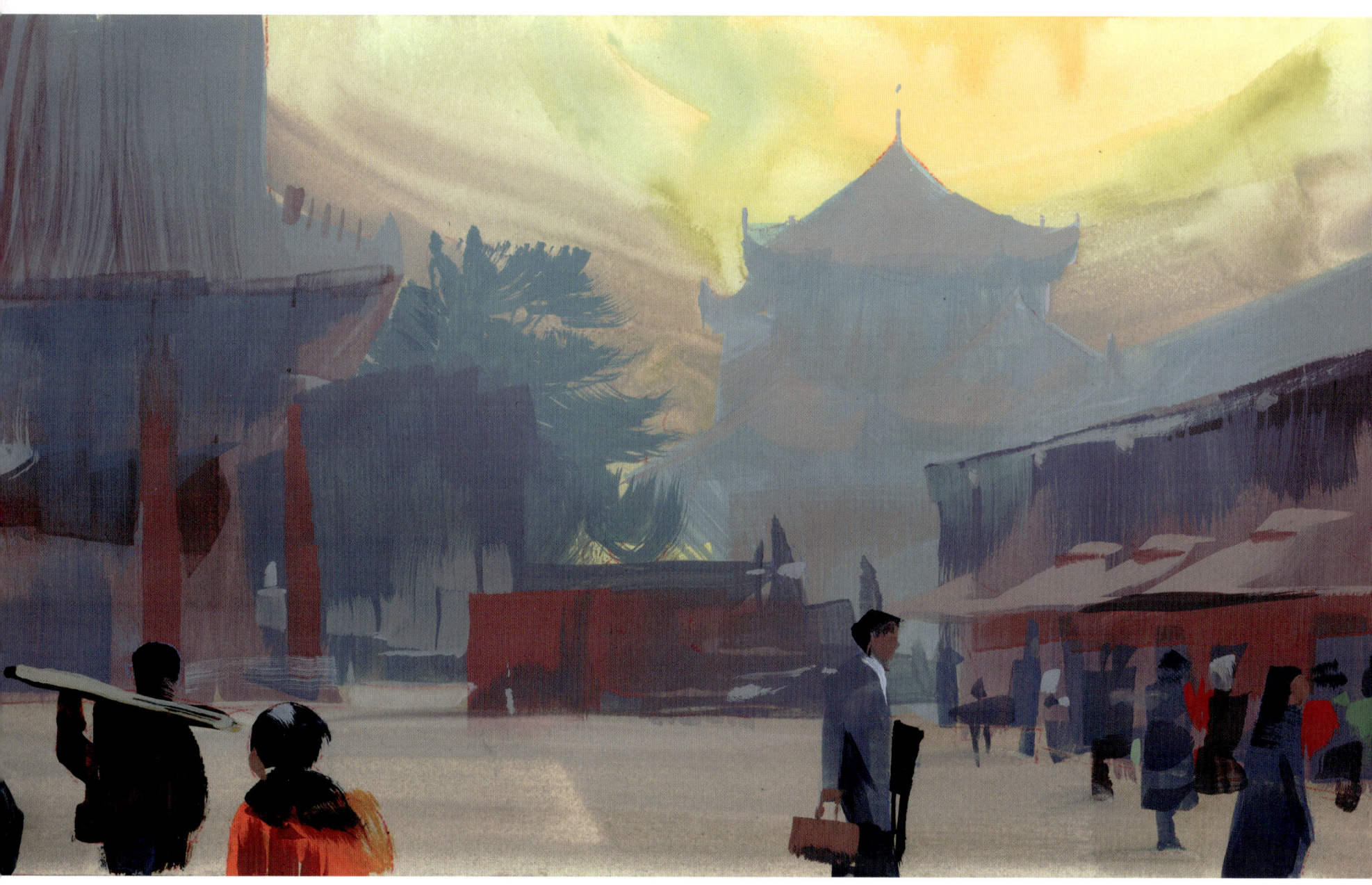

Forbidden City Beijing   N Forbes

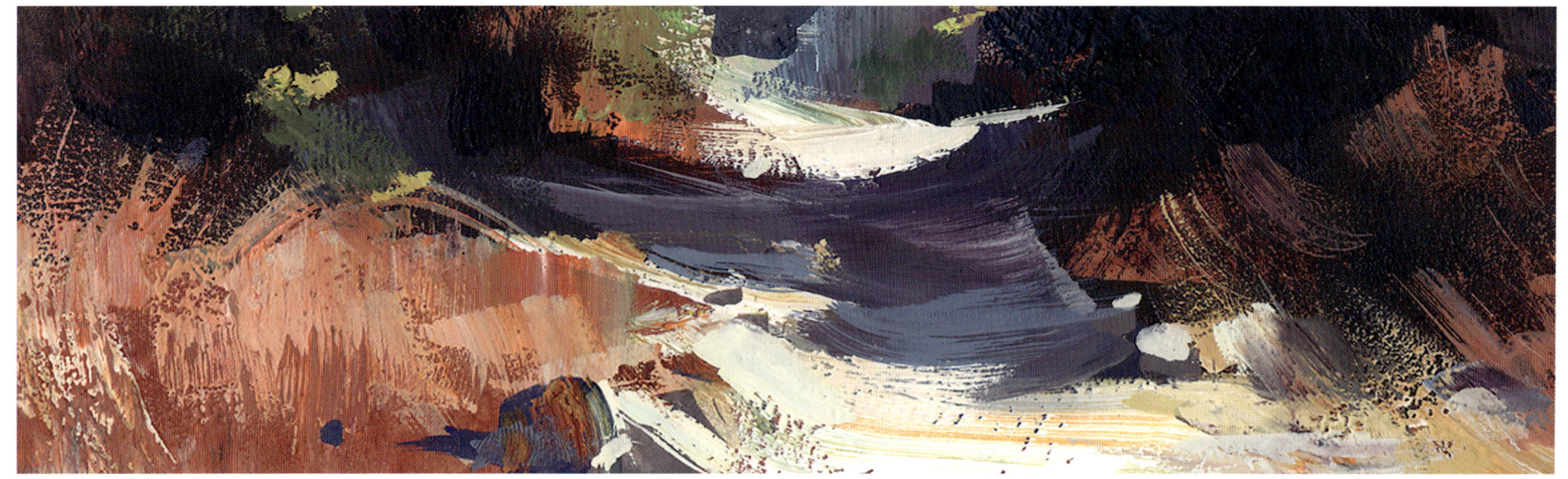

Chapter 8

Depth

I teach classes and workshops when my schedule allows, and I've often had students tell me that they did many more sketches for their homework but threw away the bad ones out of embarrassment. Ugh! It's the worst possible thing they could do! So now I insist that they bring in their worst efforts and take a photo of the location they were painting. Then we sit down and figure out exactly what went wrong, and sometimes, to their shock, nine or ten well-placed strokes pull the sketch together. And in my experience, many of those lifesaving strokes are ones that convey perspective and depth. My friends, if you learn to use simple depth cues to emphasize space in your work, you might just come out the other side with a sketchbook full of meaningful moments, places, and spaces that you've captured and made permanent.

I've freely admitted that my early efforts at landscape sketching on location were poor if not disastrous. Despite my love of doing small sketches, I found it difficult to convey the vast depth of the landscapes I was trying to capture. So I committed to taking reference photos while on location, then, I later painted over my bad location paintings until I figured out how to make them work. This "in-studio" process turned out to be nearly as valuable as the time spent painting outdoors. Developing the technical ability to create the illusion of space on our little sketchbook page, gives our work a compelling believability and emotional authority.

Over the next pages I will share simple ways to dramatize depth, even in a small, one-hour outdoor sketch.

"Learn to use simple depth cues to emphasize space in your work, you might just come out the other side with a sketchbook full of meaningful moments, places, and spaces that you've captured and made permanent."

How to Create a Sense of Depth

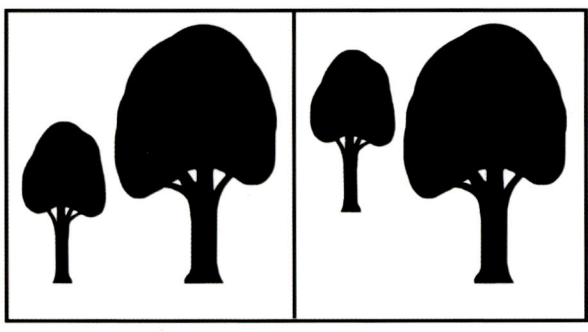

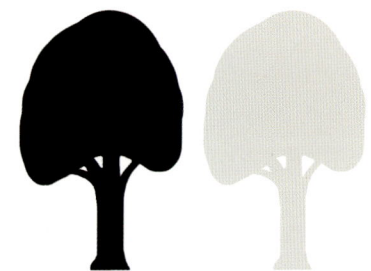

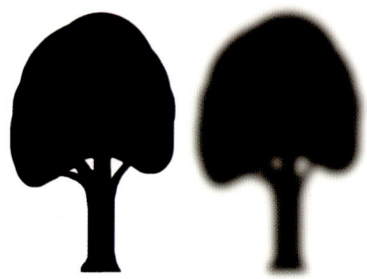

Relative Position

The careful placement of objects in the picture plane is a simple and clear indication of depth. In the image on the left, we perceive a smaller and larger tree, but move the smaller tree higher on the picture plane and we immediately perceive it to be a larger tree in the distance. This is because the horizon is usually well above the ground plane, and the closer an object is to the horizon line, the further away it feels.

High Contrast vs. Low Contrast

In this graphic, the right tree with lower contrast seems to recede compared to the left one. High and low contrast can be easily achieved, just think of the three properties of color, far away objects tend to have less contrast of hue, saturation, and value.

Hard Edge vs. Soft Edge

Hard edges tend to advance, and soft edges tend to recede. Take a look at how the hard-edged tree at left feels noticeably closer than the soft edge tree on the right even though they're both the same size and position.

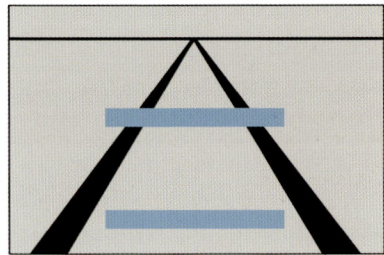

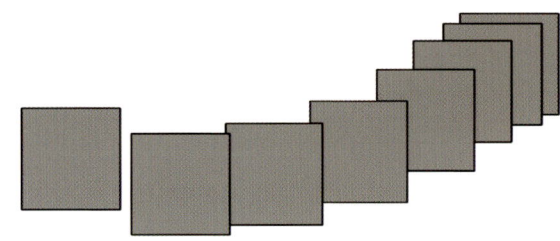

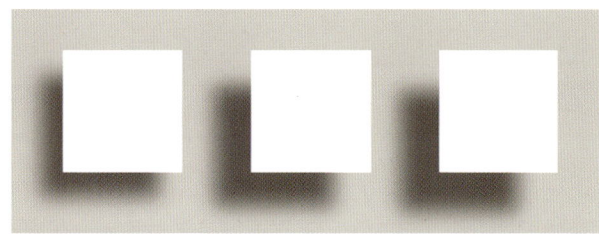

Perspective

Perspective is one of the simplest and most powerful ways to create depth. Look at the optical illusion in the graphic above, both blue bars are the same length but the higher one feels longer because we perceive it to be further away. And it's just those two converging perspective lines that creates the illusion. Many artists will add a path, a fence, or fallen log into the foreground of their painting to suggest perspective lines and create a greater sense of depth. Remember, we're telling the truth about how the landscape feels, so go ahead and do whatever it takes to create the feeling of depth.

Overlap

In the squares above, all are exactly the same and yet they appear to be moving away from us, this is achieved by simple overlap. Personally, this is one technique that I'm always emphasizing, I look for opportunities to layer rocks, trees, buildings, or any object, one in front of the other.

Shadows

We've discussed a good deal about how light and shadow convey form, and form is an illusion of depth. In the graphic above, the placement of shadows creates the illusion of varying heights for each of the white squares. The way that shadows fall across a landscape can give clarity to its space and form.

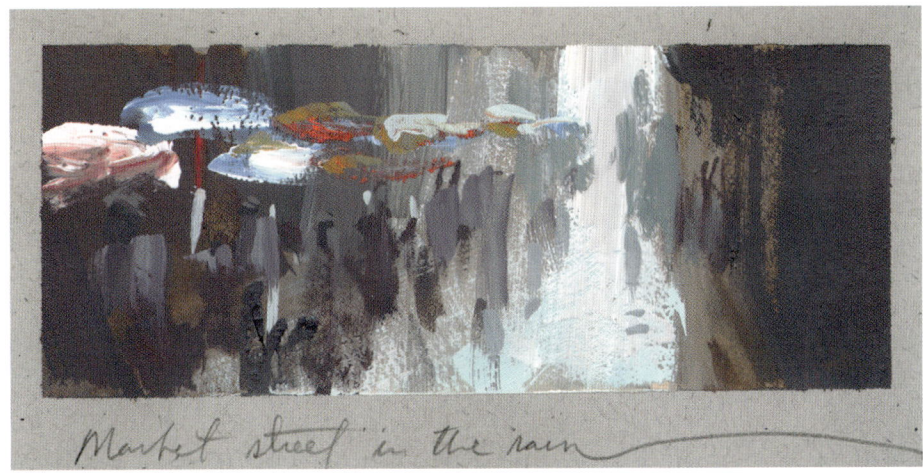

Market street in the rain

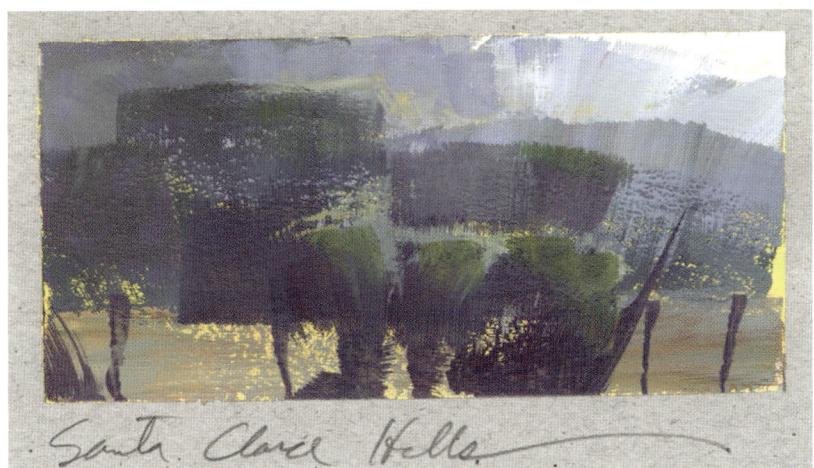

South Clarel Hills

Using Contrast and Perspective

Here's a very quick sketch of a street in the rain, the receding perspective is well defined with the converging perspective lines of the street. There are also extremes of contrast, the foreground umbrellas have an extreme contrast of hue, saturation, and value, and the further the object, the lower the contrast.

Using Overlap, Relative Position, and Texture

This is another very quick sketch, but I'm trying to give it substantial depth, with an overlapping of fence line, trees, and hills. I'm also keeping an eye out for relative position, the further the object, the more it rises in the picture plane toward the horizon. Also note that contrast of texture is a highly useful approach to get foreground to advance and background to recede.

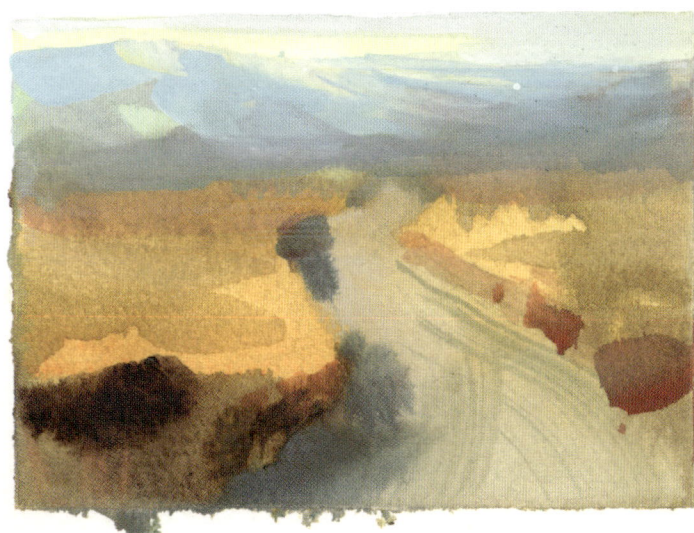

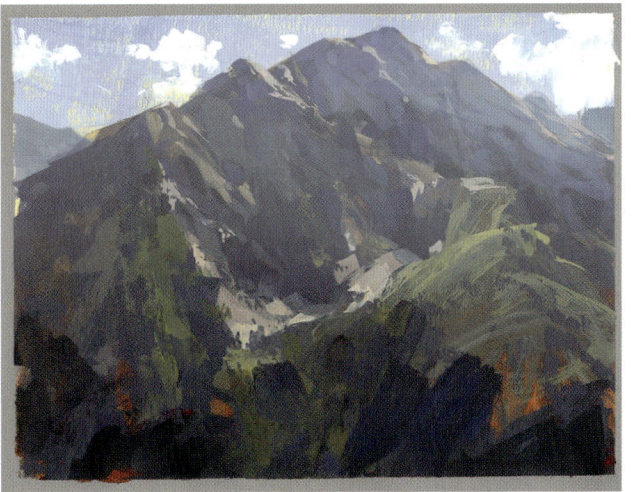

Using Warm vs. Cool and Edges

Here's another quick and simple sketch, and yet I'm throwing everything I can at it for an immediate quality of depth. We haven't mentioned warm vs. cool yet and this is a good example. I've especially emphasized the warms in the nearest foreground, which helps it to advance, while the distant cool temperatures strongly recede. I'm also emphasizing edges, with firmer edges and textures in the foreground, gradually moving to softer and softer edges in the distant background. And of course the perspective of the pathway is immensely helpful for depth.

Using Brushstroke Size

This mountain scene covers a distance of many miles, so I'm using most of the ideas we've been talking about. See if you can identify what they are. Let me also introduce the idea of brushstroke size. I've often noticed that my students will use the exact same size brushstrokes for distant objects that they use in the foreground. This automatically works against the depth of the scene. Bigger, more textural foreground strokes graduating to smaller and smaller ones in the distance is a useful painting technique.

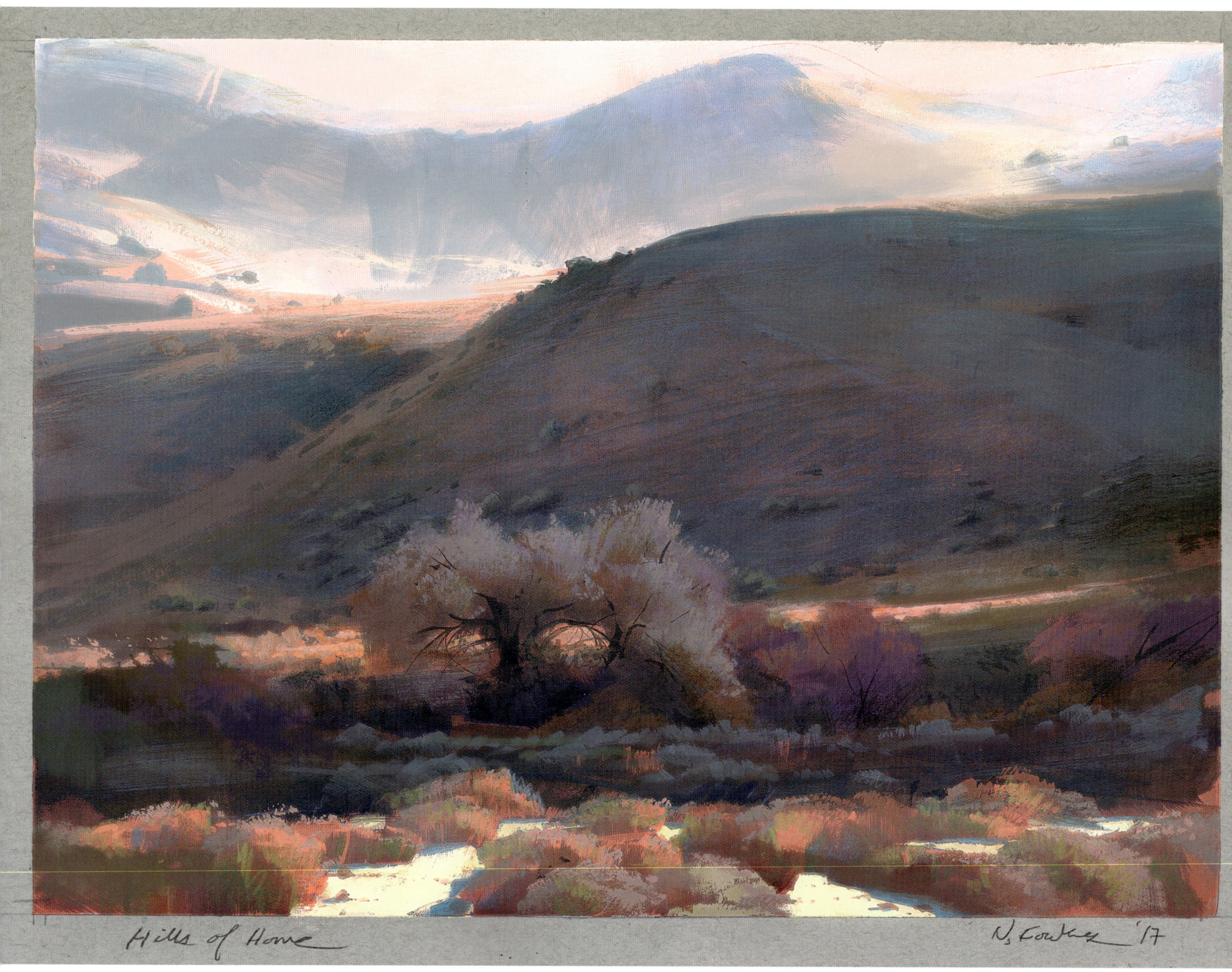

Hills of Home

N Cowdrey '17

Demonstration: Creating Depth

Strathmore 400 Series Toned Gray Mixed Media paper, 14 x 18 inches

These are the rolling hills of Central California where I grew up. As a kid, I hiked over many of them, but no matter how far I went, there were always more receding into the distance, and it felt like they went on forever.

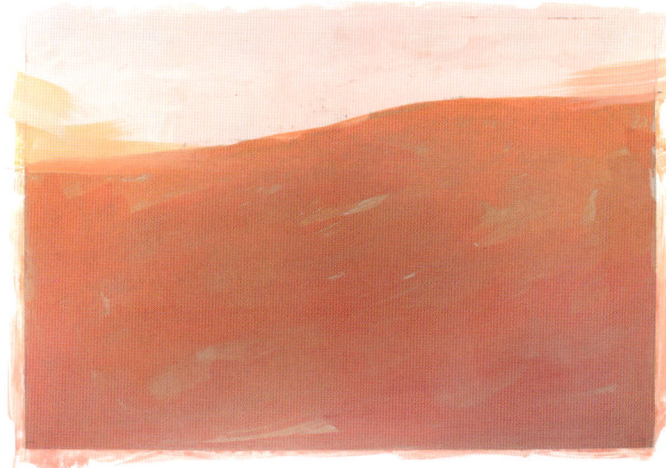

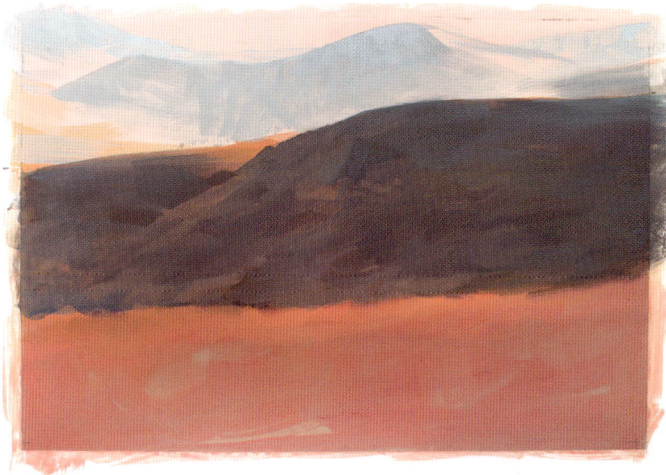

(1) I absolutely love the patterns of light and shadow created at sunset in this place, so that's exactly what we'll emphasize. Let's start with the warms that will reinforce that quality of light. For our first depth cue, there's higher saturation in the foreground and lower saturation in the distance.

(2) I brush in the cooler shadows of the far distance, creating many overlapping shapes, then start to mass in the warm darks of the mid ground. I'm already thinking about the form of the middle hill; it has cooler skylight on top and warm bounce light on its left side.

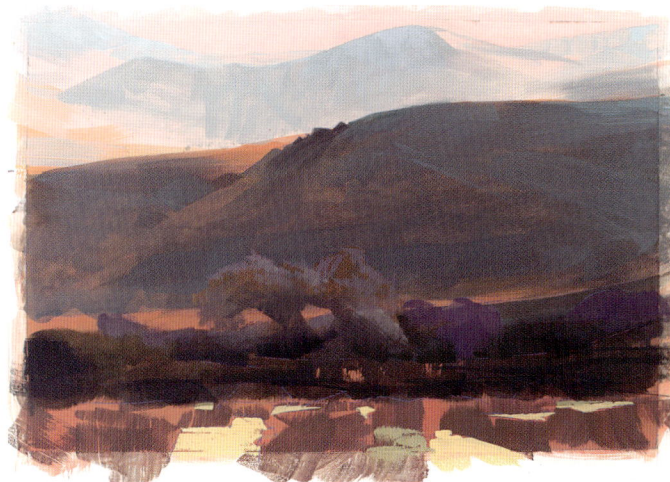

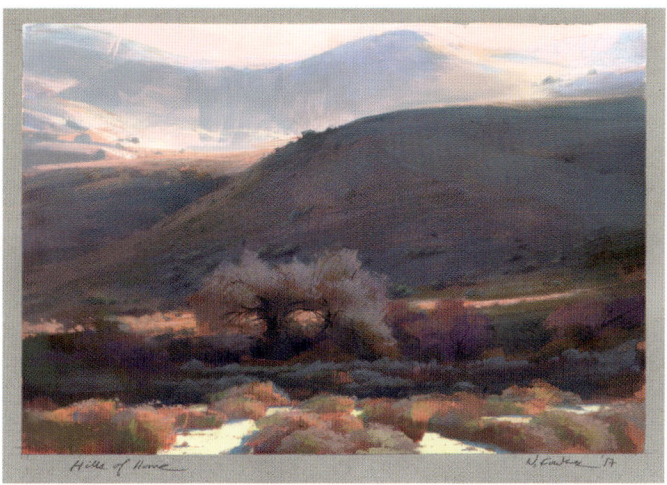

(3) I'm able to get good depth in the foreground as I lay dark over light, so I want to introduce one more concept here that I call "banding," repeating bands of light and shadow over and over as the picture plane recedes. Notice how this image goes from light to shadow, then light and shadow again into the distance. You can create extraordinary depth by using this approach, I've even used it for clouds in other paintings to create receding space in the sky as well.

(4) I finish off the painting by emphasizing many additional depth cues: cool skylight coming down onto top planes, lots of overlapping bushes in the foreground loaded with texture and warmth, and strong perspective lines that lead us into the scene. And I hope I've done justice to the hills of home.

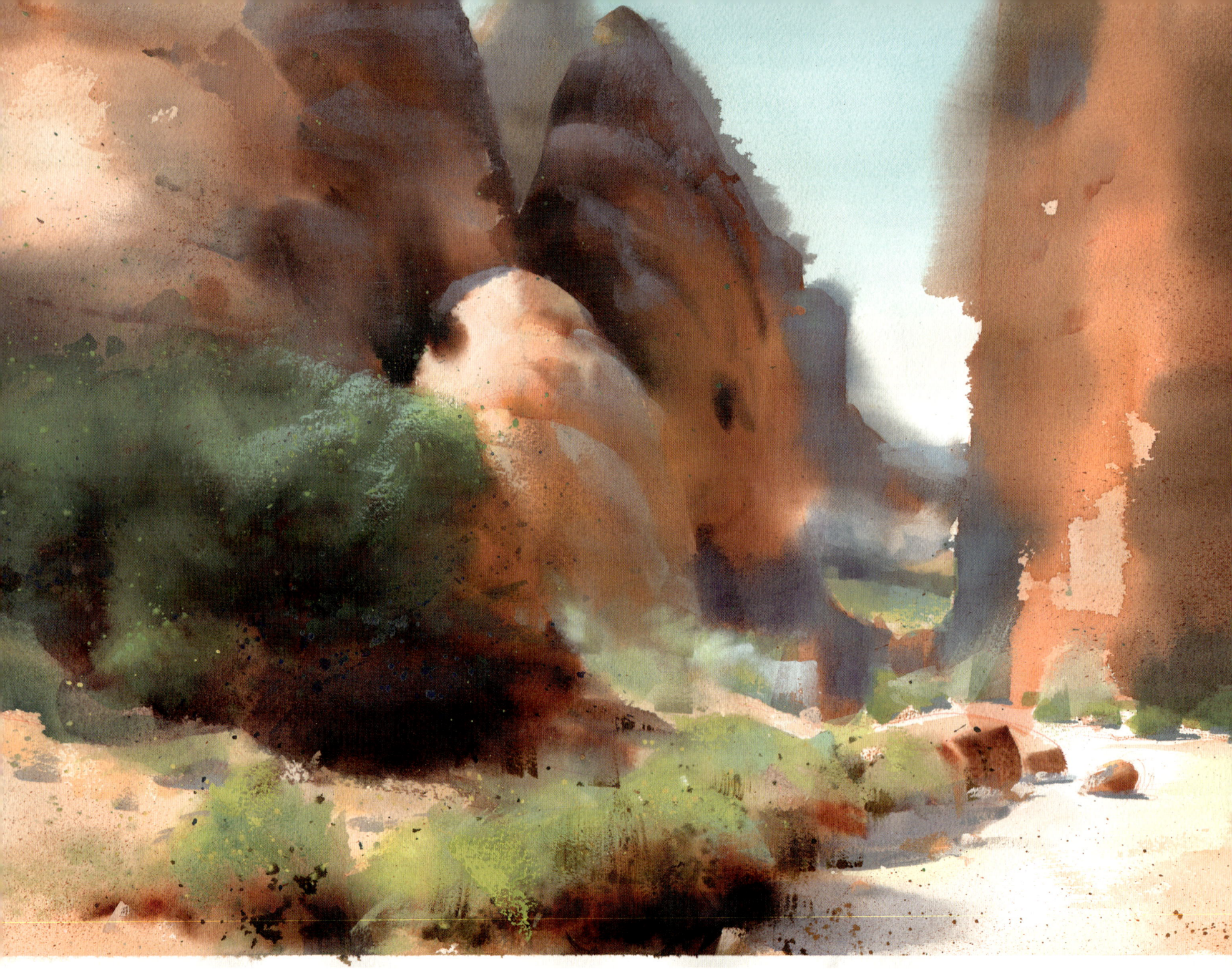

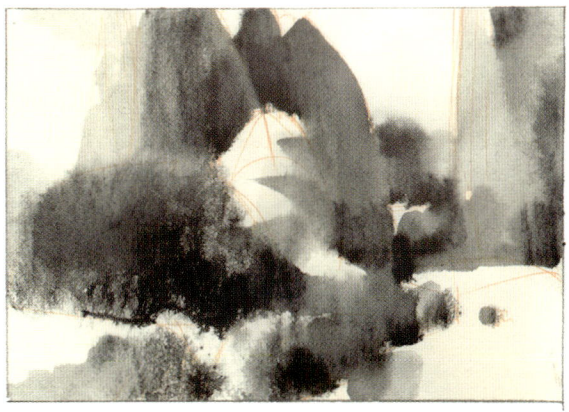

Value rough

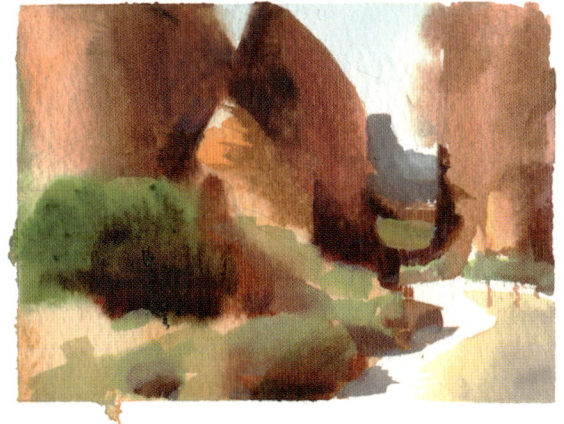

Color comp

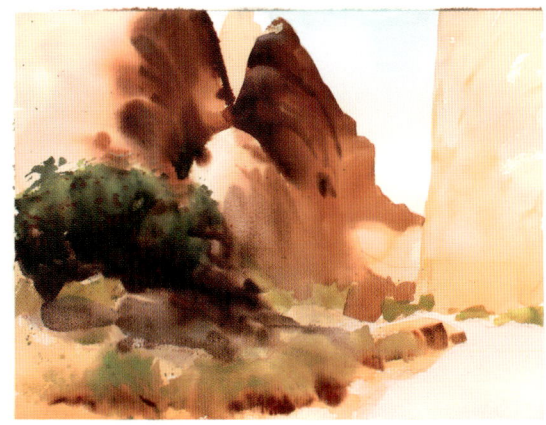

Final lay-in

Composition

In this book, we've extensively discussed the complexities of landscape painting, trying to find ways to make the process manageable. My experience is that it's never easy, and we need a wide range of tools and ideas to successfully take on the challenge, so my hope is that this chapter just might be a breakthrough for you!

Take a look at the painting to the left, these are the majestic red rocks of Utah's Monument Valley. As you can imagine, there was an extraordinary amount of information present with pebbles, textures, foliage, individual leaves, etc. But what struck me was the white path leading to the illuminated rounded spire in the middle left, and how that formation is framed by shadows and complemented by the green brush surrounding it. To me, these were meaningful relationships that deserved to be painted!

Above you can see my process for figuring out what I wanted to emphasize; the tonal sketch attempts to state my idea as clearly as possible, and the middle sketch is meant to find the simple color statement. The third image is the block-in for the final painting, which I completed in my studio from my references.

As I went through the decision-making process, there were eight useful compositional considerations to help me parse the complexities of the landscape:

① Grouping ⑤ Rhythm

② Focal area ⑥ Framing

③ Balance ⑦ Eye level

④ Structure ⑧ Emotion of line

"Composing a scene is never easy. In my experience we need a wide range of tools and ideas to successfully take on the challenge, so my hope is that this chapter will be a breakthrough for you!"

Foundational Principles of Composition

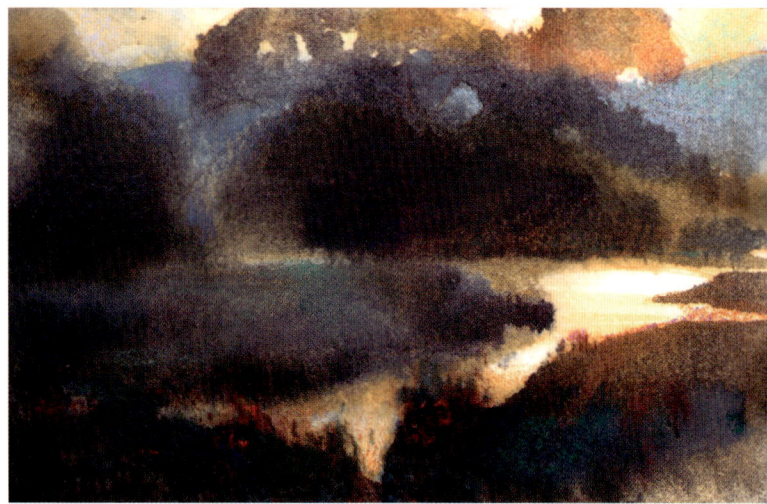

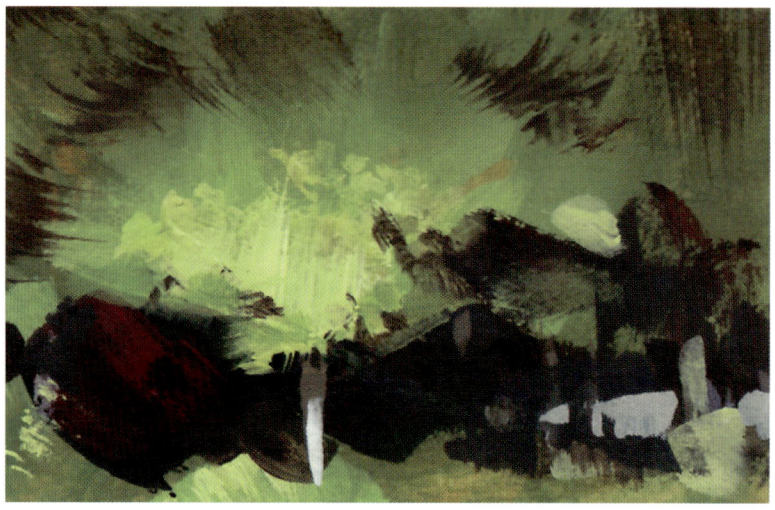

Value grouping

Here's a concept that we've covered quite thoroughly in previous chapters, and it's being put into practice for this sunset sketch. The landscape groups into simple masses of value to allow emphasis of the brilliant reflections of the sunset in the river.

Focal area

This sketch is simply about a tree. If we try to make our paintings about everything, then by default, they end up being about nothing. Picking areas of primary focus is a way to give our images purpose. We look out at a landscape and decide what's most special about it, and how do we give emphasis to that special idea? Emphasis comes through contrast; our eyes are naturally drawn to areas of high contrast. And how do we get contrast? It's back to those three properties of color: contrast of hue, contrast of saturation, contrast of value.

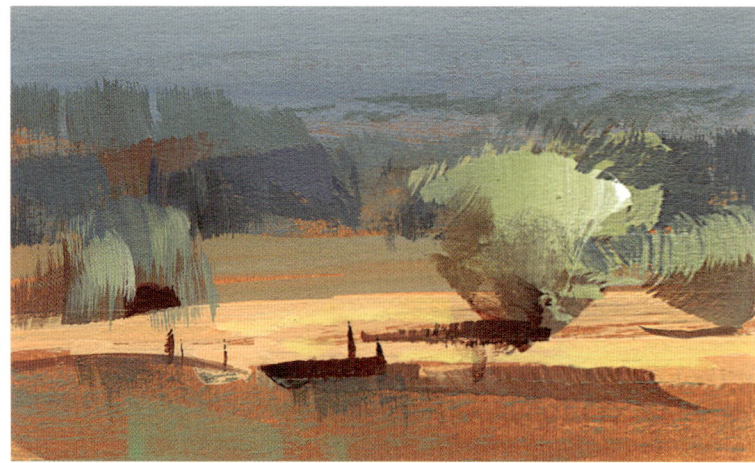

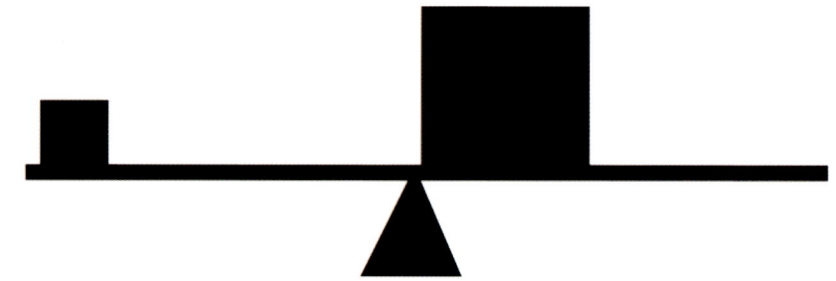

Visual balance

Every movement that we ever make is balanced against the force of gravity. It's an ever-present consideration that we tend to handle at an unconscious level. So it makes sense that an image with visual balance would feel right to our viewers. The sketch here is simply a field with distant trees, but there's a satisfying quality to the asymmetrical balance of a large tree near center balanced by two smaller outlying trees.

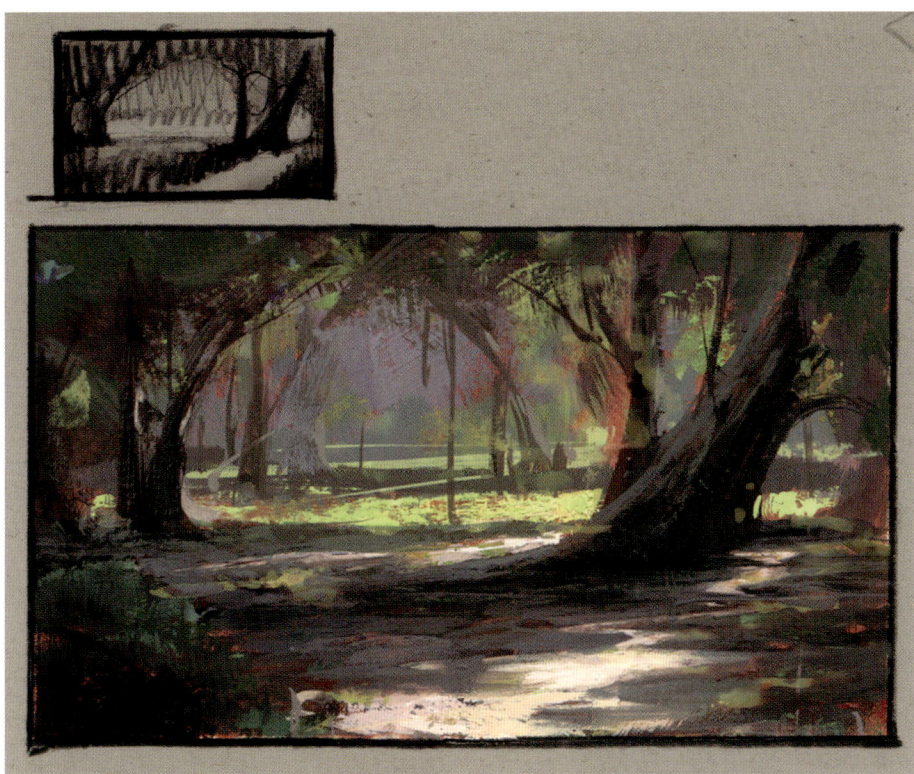

Structure

We can often find meaningful alignments and groupings in the scenes we observe. Emphasizing a simple organization can act as a unifying framework for the abundance of details that might otherwise turn into chaos in a sketchbook study such as this one. As you can see, I worked out my simple idea in pencil, which allowed me to dive into the painting with confidence!

Emphasis comes through contrast; our eyes are naturally drawn to areas of high contrast. And how do we get contrast? It's back to those three properties of color: contrast of hue, contrast of saturation, contrast of value.

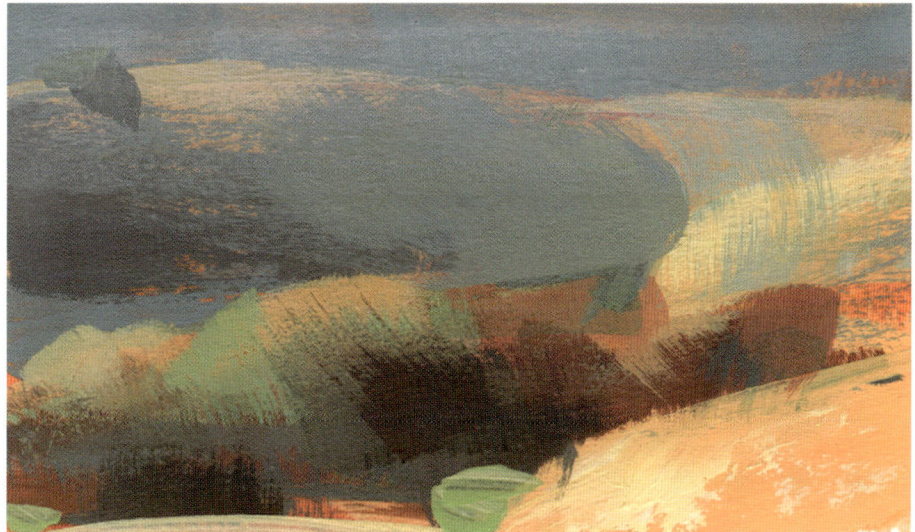

Rhythm

Rhythm can be defined as a meaningful repetition, it's a useful way to create a sense of unity in an image. At this location, I was struck by the repetition of rounded shapes; the bushes, hills, and even the cast shadows had this quality. Emphasizing these rhythms gave the sketch a sense of purpose.

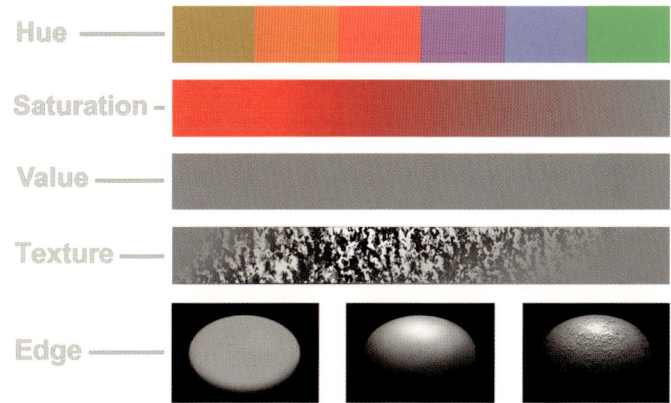

The design of contrast

Every principle we've discussed here is about the design of contrast, so the chart above is a review of five primary ways to create contrast where it's needed. And there's one more important form of contrast to add to the list: psychological contrast. For instance, we're more likely to pay attention to a house than we are to a tree, and we're more likely to look at a person than we are a house. Some objects are simply more important to us psychologically, so they carry more visual weight.

Composition on the Fly

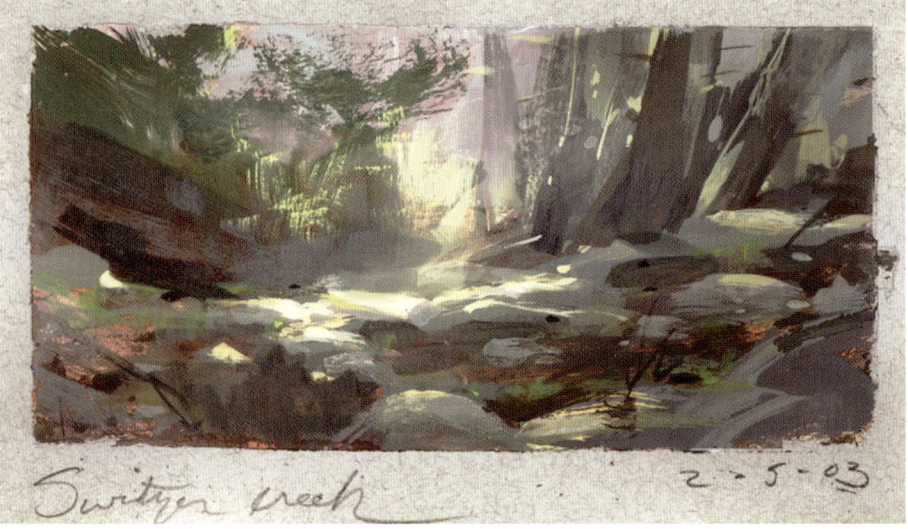

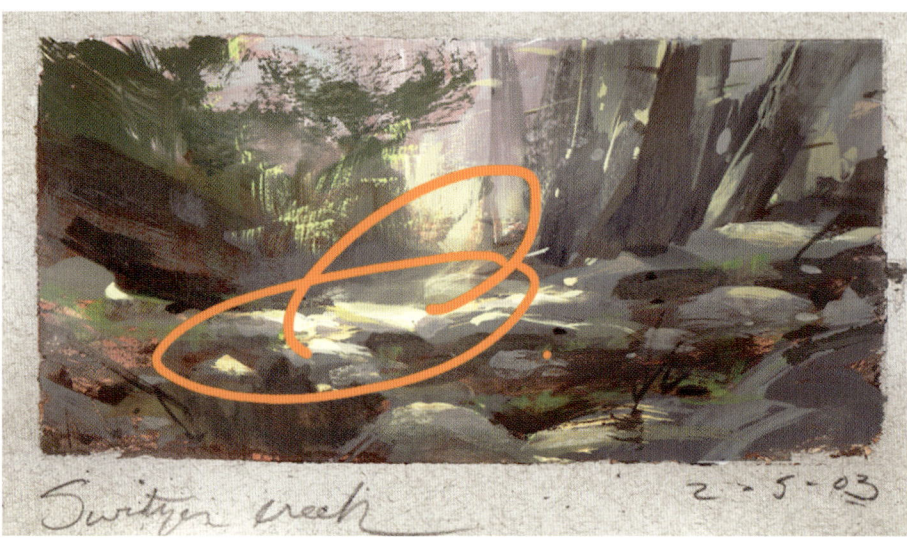

At the end of a long day of painting in Angeles National Forest, I came across this spot as I was leaving. I had somewhere else I needed to be, and yet, the light was irresistible. I had about 15 minutes I could squeeze in, was a sketch possible? I'll let you judge the level of success, but my solution to meet the challenge was to apply each of these principles of composition plus depth cues and color choices.

There was a pool of light in the mid-ground that led into the distant opening in the trees that I felt would make a strong focal area to center the image around. The areas of shadow were kept relatively grouped in value to allow the primary contrast to be the lights.

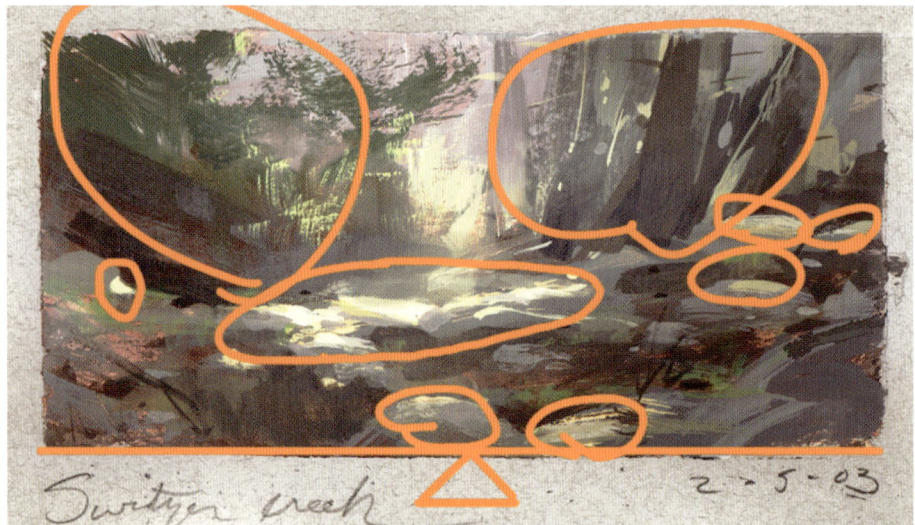

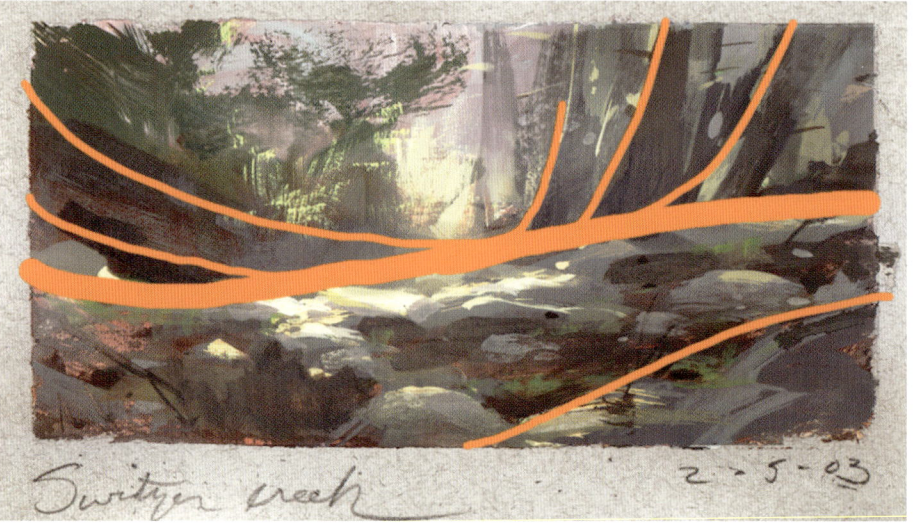

As I worked, I was careful that the areas of greatest contrast kept a visual balance across the image.

The creek bed had a nice flowing structure that moved across the scene and curved into the bushes and trees. I emphasized that quality to maintain the sense of rhythm and structure that was present in the environment.

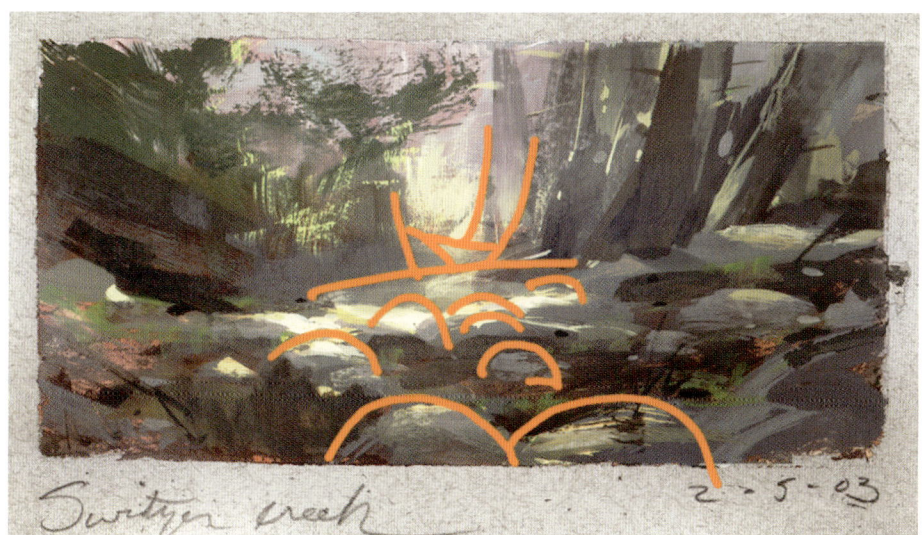

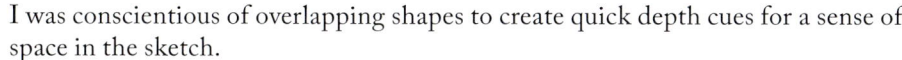

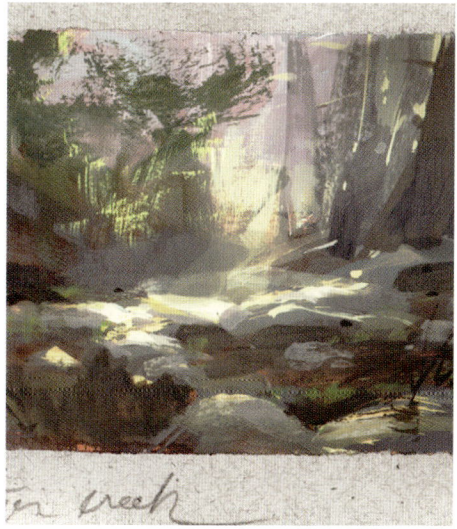

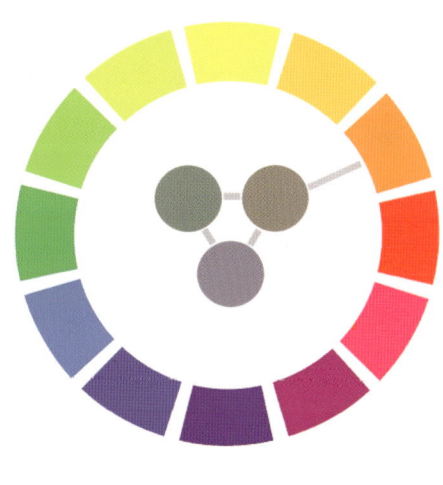

I was conscientious of overlapping shapes to create quick depth cues for a sense of space in the sketch.

Emphasizing a simple organization can act as a unifying framework for the abundance of details that might otherwise turn into chaos in a sketchbook study.

And I made a decision about color as I began the image. The richness of the warm browns contrasted by the leafy grey greens and the atmospheric, distant purples were brilliant together. In the foreground, there was a complement of fallen leaves that created accents of a brilliant orange. I've charted these simple color relationships on the color wheel. It's an example of unity with variety of color.

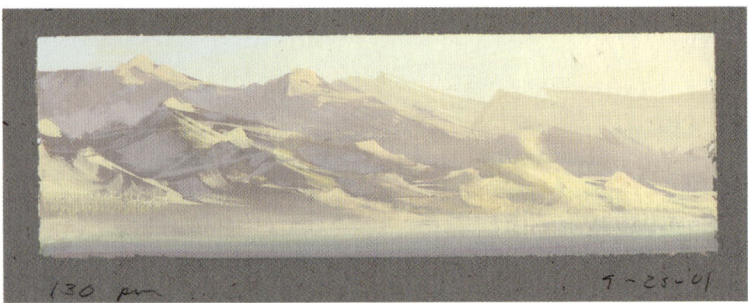

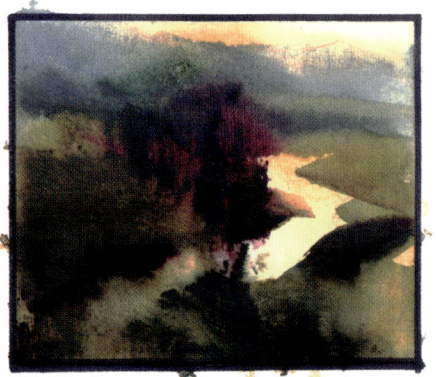

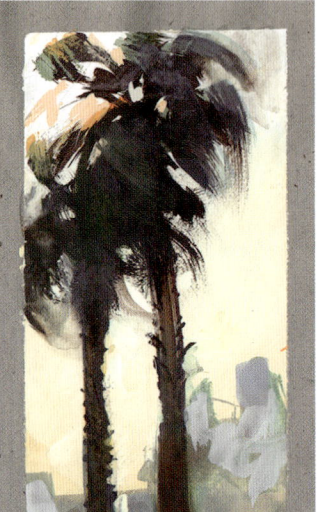

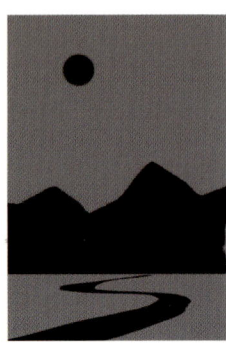

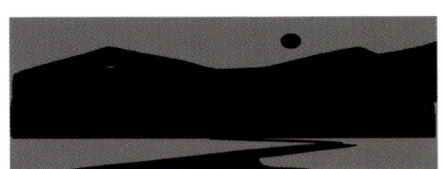

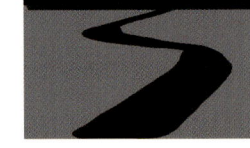

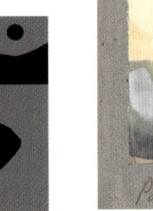

Framing and Eye Level

The way we frame our images is a major compositional consideration. If we're going to make our sketches and paintings about what's most meaningful to us, then it makes sense to carefully design the framing of the scene. By "framing," I simply mean the way the scene is cropped: vertical, square, or horizontal. We can crop our scenes in a way that makes sense for their primary quality, by asking the question, would the image be well served by a panorama? Or maybe a square would fit the scene just about right, or even a tall vertical framing.

Horizontal images are most common simply because we are much more prone to look side to side than up and down. In the images above, the long stretch of hills at sunset was best suited as a long, sweeping panorama. The middle image is primarily about the river flowing toward us, so the long panorama would be a distraction. The square is a much better framing solution, and, of course, the tall palm trees deserved their own unique vertical framing.

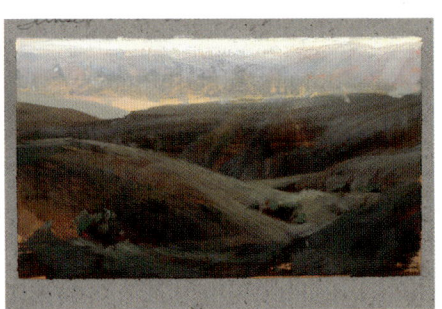

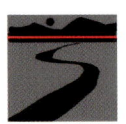

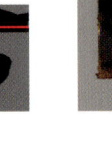

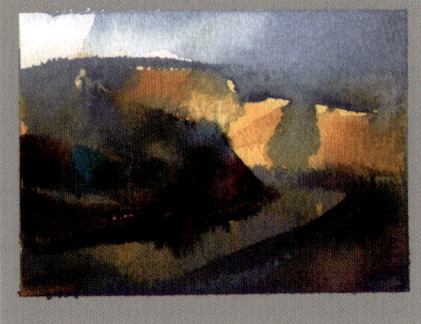

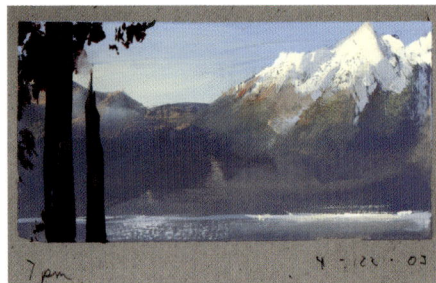

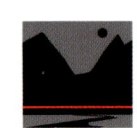

The eye level or horizon line position (they're the same thing) is often missed or forgotten by beginners, but it's of critical importance to the feel of a landscape. In the above rolling hills, we're looking down into the canyon, so the horizon line needs to be very close to the top of the image.

In this sketch there are two considerations, the road leads from below up to the eye level, then the sunlit hill rises above it. It makes sense to keep the horizon centrally located in the picture plane.

In this sketchbook study of Glacier National Park, Montana, the vertical grandeur of the mountain scape was the major consideration. It made sense to place the eye level very low, to give the feeling of looking up into the height of the mountains.

Line and Emotion

There's something very interesting and useful about the way that we unconsciously respond to lines. Take a look at the graphic at right, no big deal, they're just three different lines; horizontal, vertical, and diagonal. But because gravity is an ever-present consideration in how we respond to our surroundings, we tend to feel that a horizontal is at rest, a vertical stands firm, and a diagonal is in motion. This "anthropomorphizing" of line is shown in the second graphic and illustrates how we feel about lines.

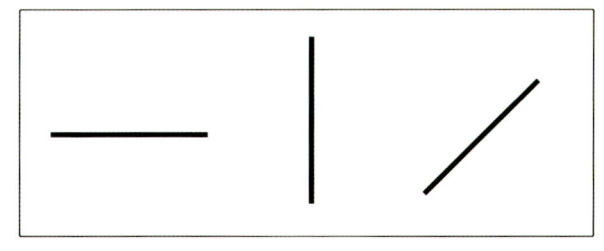

This is a very simple but useful way we can suggest an emotional quality in our landscapes; below are three examples of the emotional quality of line.

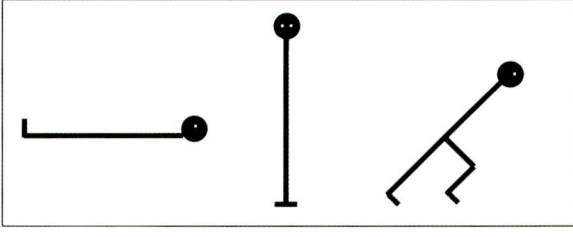

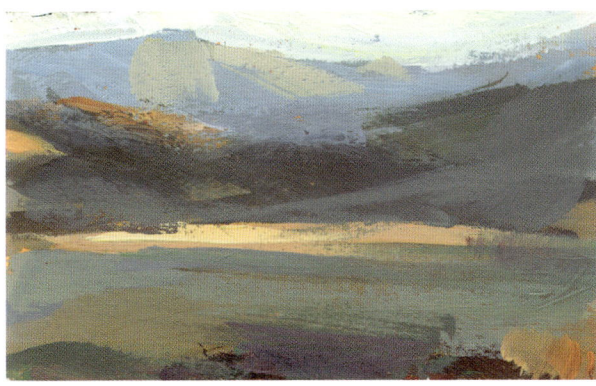

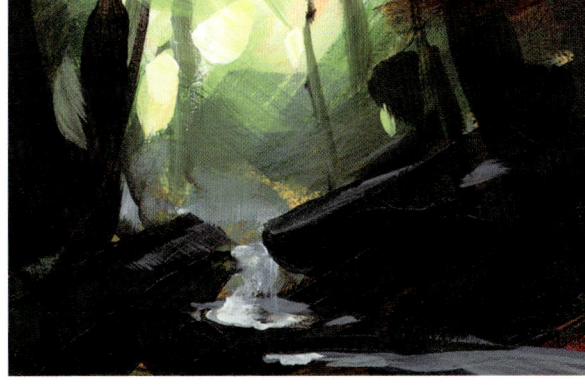

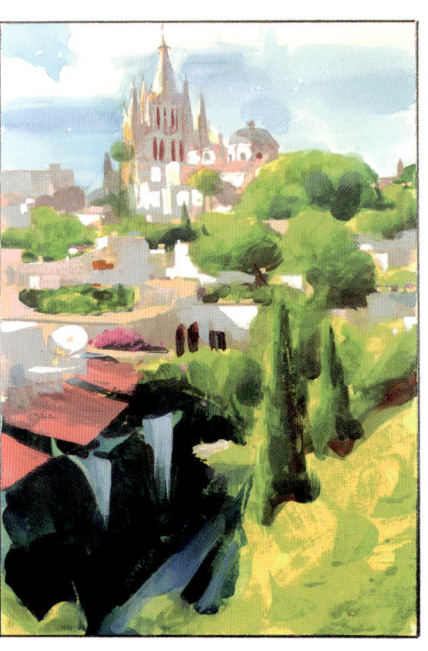

This example is a relatively calm and peaceful moment in a landscape. The mountains and hills were actually more steep and jagged than I've represented here. The sketch is not about the literal truth of the landscape, that would be pointless since my camera is better at "the literal truth" than I am. This sketch is about a calm and peaceful moment, richly illuminated at sunset. As is often true, art is about the emotion.

Here's a more dynamic scene where the wind blew strongly and the water of the stream rushed by. The shadowy rocks of the landscape had a strong diagonal that emphasized a greater sense of energy and motion.

And here's a vista from a hotel roof in San Miguel de Allende, Mexico. The thing I hoped to emphasize here was the majestic verticals of the distant church. I was careful to reinforce that idea with the vertical cypress trees as well as a few windows and architectural shapes that echoed the vertical quality throughout.

> *"Angle of line is a very simple but useful way we can suggest a powerful emotional quality in our landscapes."*

Painting with Purpose

As we fight to sketch from life despite the limitations of time, medium, and changing conditions, the idea of painting with purpose cannot be overemphasized. We've come at it from many different angles thus far, and my experience with teaching (and my own struggles) suggests that we need constant reminders. It is so easy, and even natural for our paintings to deteriorate into mindless rendering of individual contrasts and details. So let's look at a photo of temple ruins in Cambodia that have a great deal of texture, detail and information. Those textures and details are beautiful, but there are literally billions of them on location; none of us would attempt to render them all, so which ones should be left in, and which edited out? The answer is simply, the ones you admire most in the scene.

Here's my take on what I would emphasize in this digital reworking of the scene. I find that the foreground pathway that leads to the person enhances the purposeful quality of that image, so I strengthen the perspective of that area. The carved faces in the middle left, and the columns from center to right, create a remarkable rhythm through the scene, so I choose to emphasize that aspect. I'm also emphasizing the value of the buildings against the background so they can maintain their bold, monolithic quality. That's what stands out to me personally, everything in my rework really exists, I'm just making an artistic choice to give my own sense of purpose to the image. How about you, how would you approach this extraordinary place?

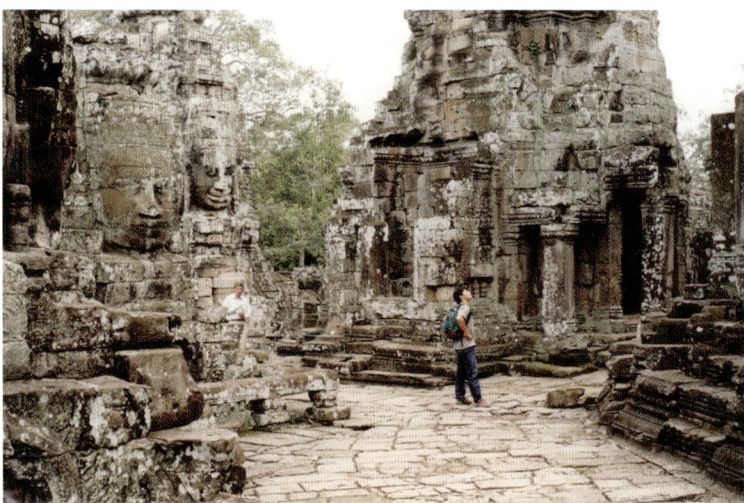
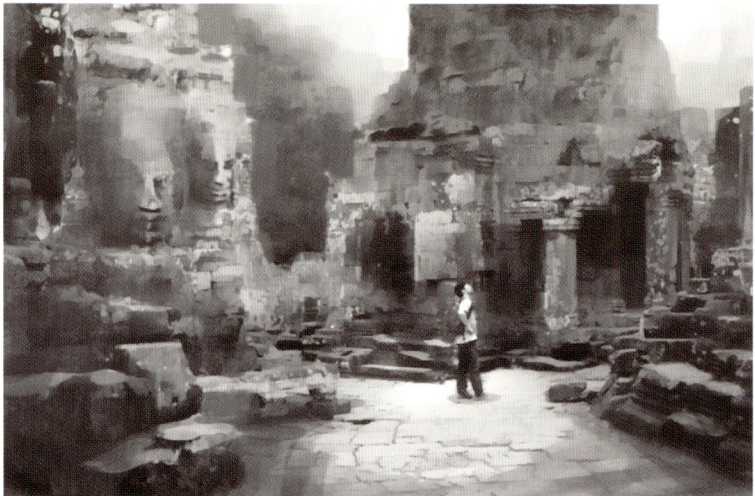

> *The idea of painting with purpose cannot be over-emphasized. We've come at it from many different angles thus far, and my experience with teaching suggests that we need constant reminders.*

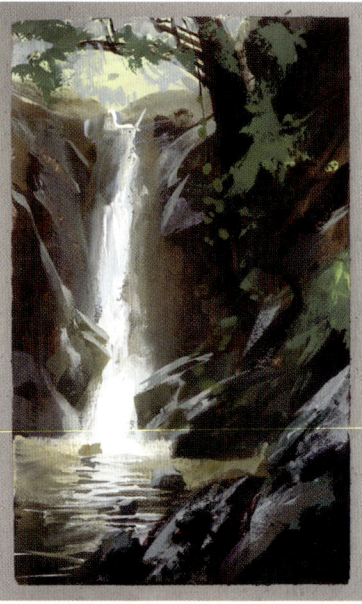
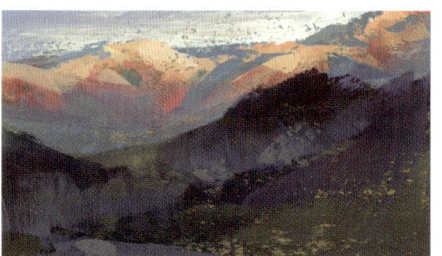
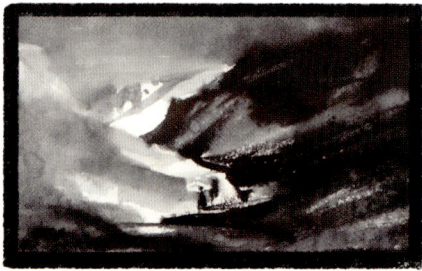

The three sketches here are quite simple, and in my opinion, better for it. The scene to the left is simply about the vertical quality of a waterfall, and the rocks and trees that frame it are generally grouped in value. The truth about the middle scene is that it had contrasting rocks in the foreground, but I wanted the sketch to emphasize the color and pattern of light across the distant hills, so the foreground rocks had to go! And the third sketch is even quicker and simpler. The emphasis here was the zigzag of light through the canyon that framed a couple of hikers in the lower middle; everything else was limited to value and brushstroke direction.

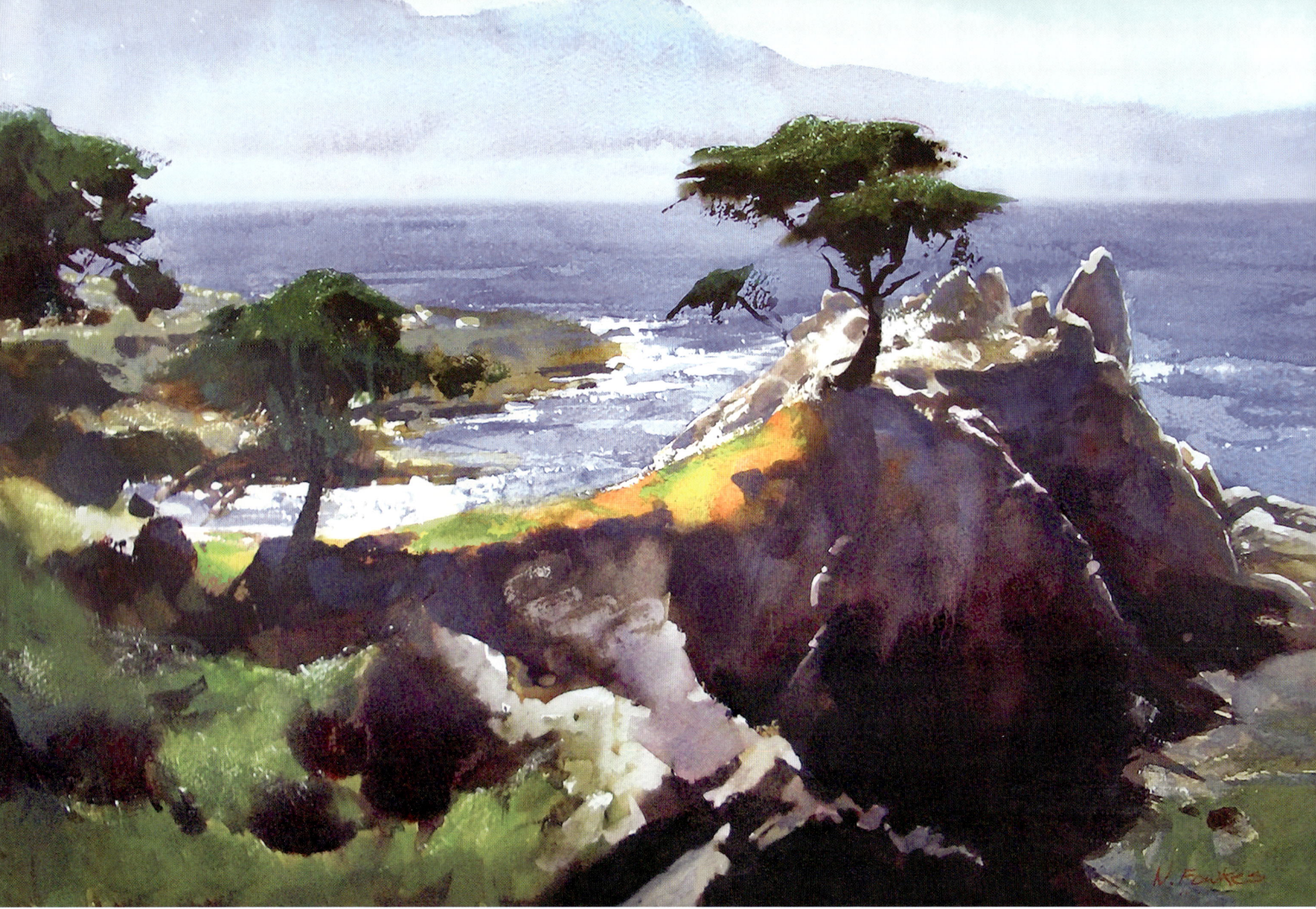

Portrait of a Place

When we paint a portrait, we are not merely rendering surfaces, we are selectively representing the character of a person. That can be, and maybe even should be, our approach to landscape painting: when we paint a landscape, we are not merely painting a view, we are selectively representing the character of the landscape.

I consider the scene here to be a portrait of a cliffside tree overlooking the ocean. To create this quality, I follow each of the compositional elements from the previous pages. The center right tree and rocky outcropping are the focal area, which is reinforced by the intersection of the horizon line and the tree. The shapes of light from the bottom and left lead to the tree, and help give a stable structure to the image. Also, the trees at left are a visual counterbalance. All these compositional elements are present, but I hope not heavy-handed or overly obvious. Good design is invisible design; it's meant to serve the purpose of helping the image simply feel right. Most important of all is the feeling of a salty sea breeze blowing, and light sparkling across the water and landscape. Once again, it's the emotional connection that counts most.

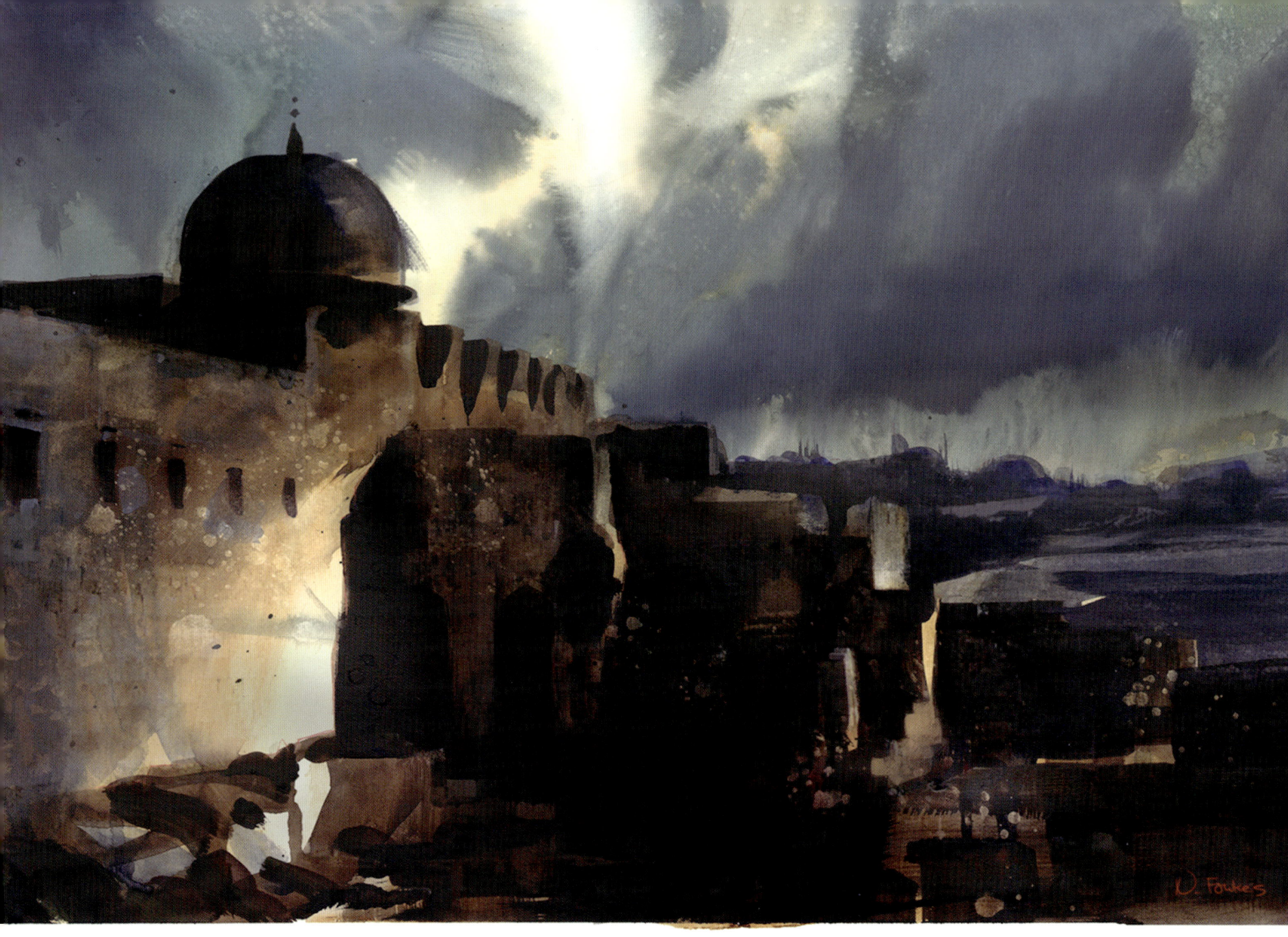

Transparent watercolor (no gouache was used) on hot press (smooth surface) illustration board, 16 x 20 inches

This painting was inspired by a trip to Jerusalem and its ancient architecture. The stormy weather was an impediment to the trip, but created a great mood for the painting, which I did in my home studio from photo references taken on location.

As much as I talk about the need for speed on location, it was a great luxury to take my time and think through how to emphasize the important elements of the scene. I invite you to look for them in the form of simple value grouping, focal area, visual balance, and a rhythmic repetition of elements.

Demonstration: Composing an Image

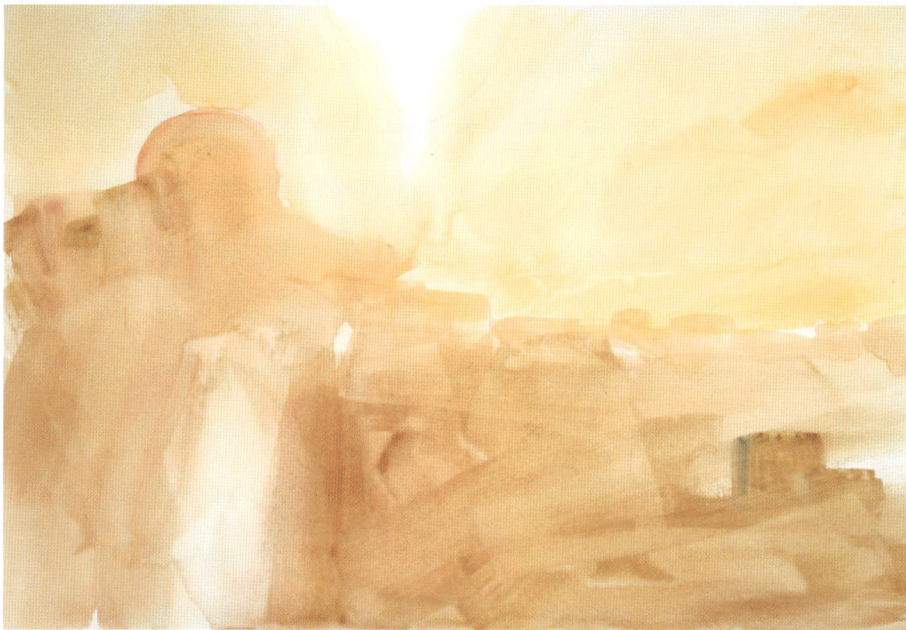

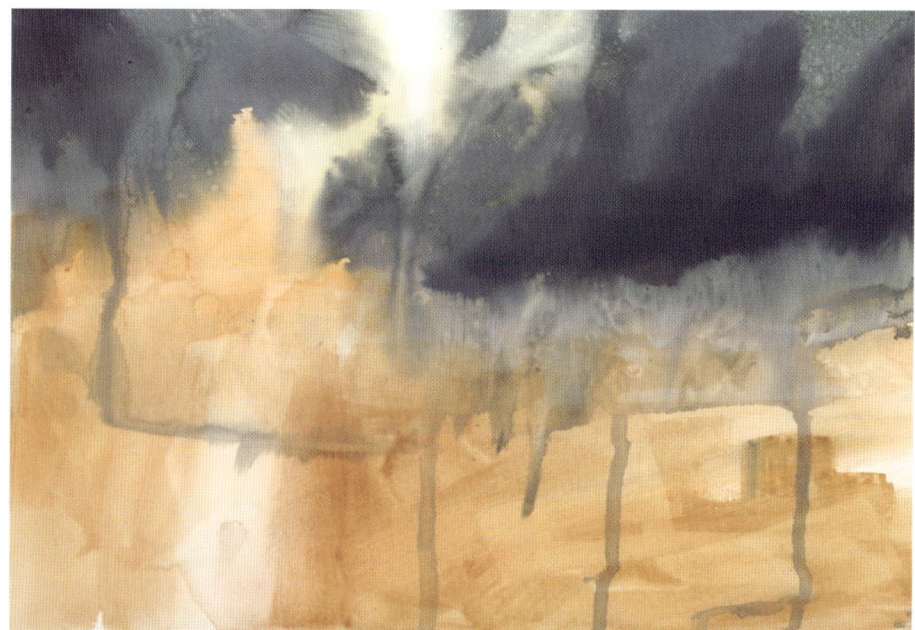

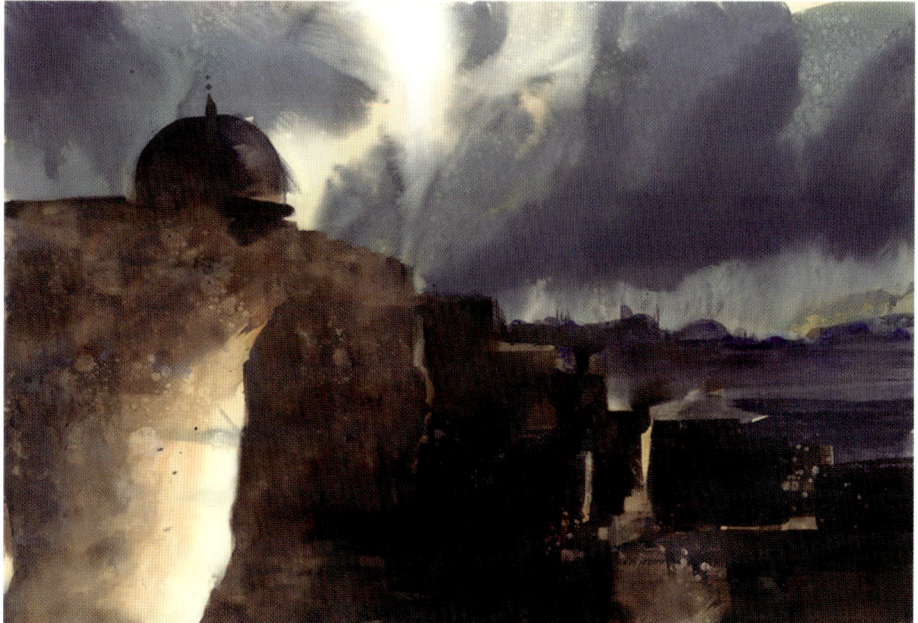

1 Despite the cold, drizzling weather, warm sunset light infused the scene, so I begin with a warm wash to establish the big shapes. I've planned out where the lights will be, so I maintain the white of the board in the top center sky and the lower left of the building; those illuminated areas will become major compositional elements.

2 Time for the sky, this is a wet-on-wet process that is both fun and nerve-wracking. After the underpainting dries, I mist the sky area with a water bottle to prepare for a wet-on-wet technique. I carefully brush in the cool grays with only one stroke each to avoid lifting up the underlying warm paint. I add some darks to the underside of the clouds for the feeling of a brooding storm, then let the wet-on-wet technique take its natural course. Even though I'm allowing for the spontaneity of the technique, I'm very careful to maintain the top center light area in the sky, which will lead the eye to my focal area in the next step.

3 It's time to lay in the landscape; the elements here are the dome, the distant vista, and the areas of light falling across the buildings. I have these areas mapped out ahead of time so that I can carefully paint around them, preserving the lights of the underpainting. The aged texture is very important also, so I spritz on isopropyl alcohol while the darks of the buildings are still wet. This creates the bubbly textural quality that you see in the final. I also use spattering of dark paint into the lighter areas of the buildings for additional texture.

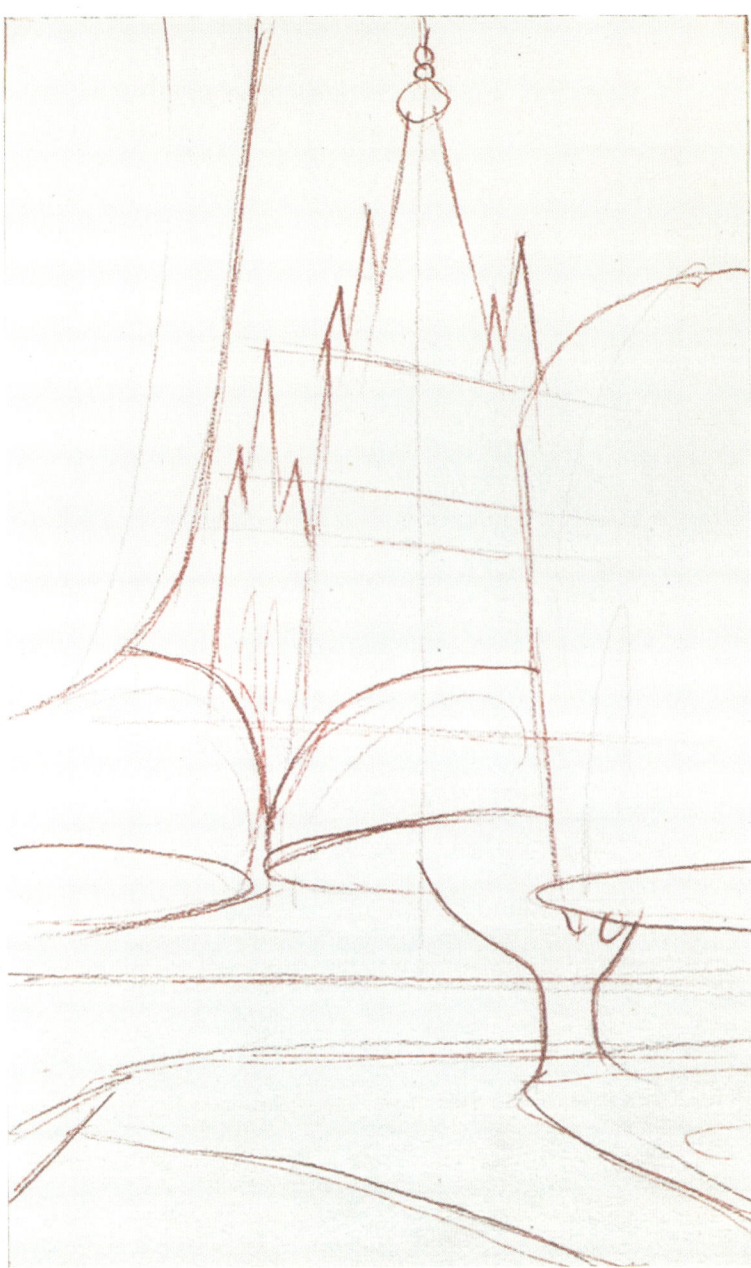

Cold-pressed illustration board, 12 x 8 inches

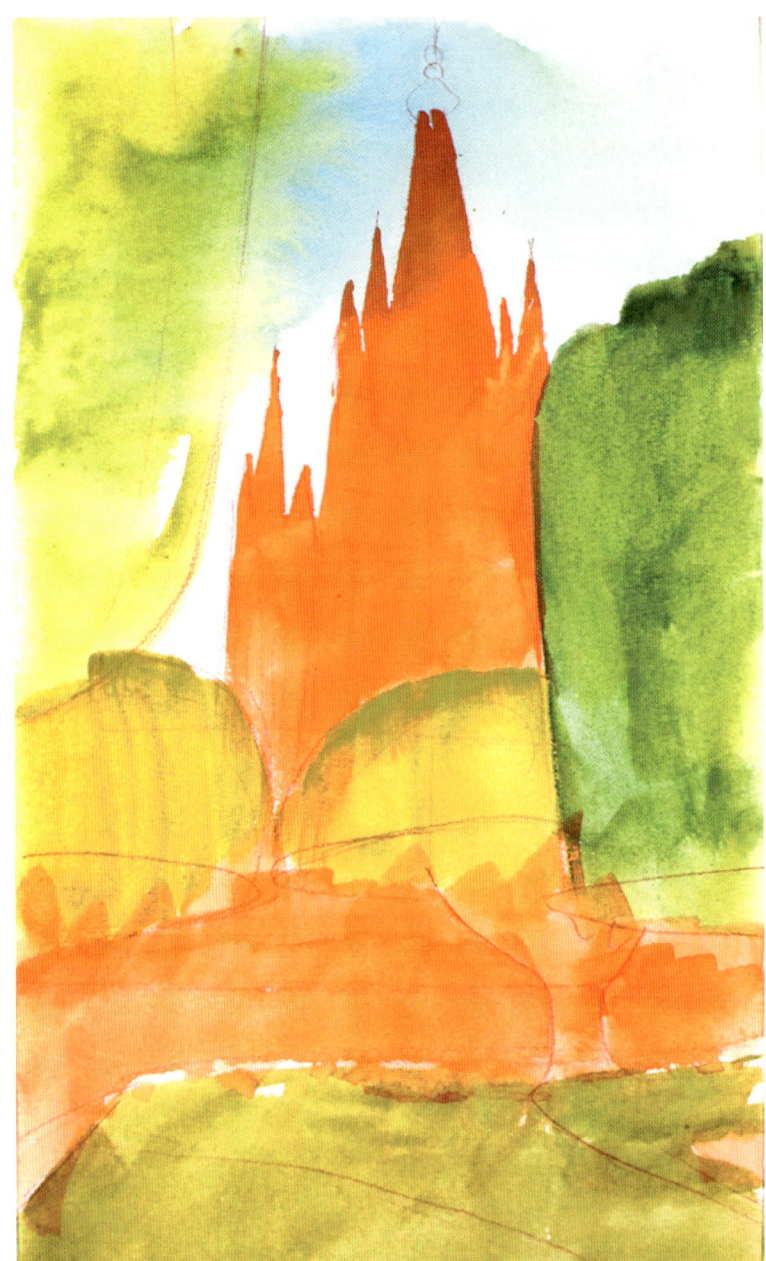

(1) Here's a painting of the town center of San Miguel de Allende, Mexico. It's a lively and colorful place, and I hoped to catch that quality in this image. To begin, I decide that a strong vertical composition will best illustrate the feel of the place. This allows me to emphasize the tall spires of the church, framed by the carefully groomed trees of the city center. My initial drawing using red Prismacolor pencil emphasizes these elements, and places the horizon line low in the image to give the quality of looking up at the church.

(2) The vibrant underpainting here ensures that that image will maintain its colorful quality, even though there will be several layers painted over top. The lighting transition in the sky is also an important consideration, it suggests a strong quality of sunlight radiating into the scene.

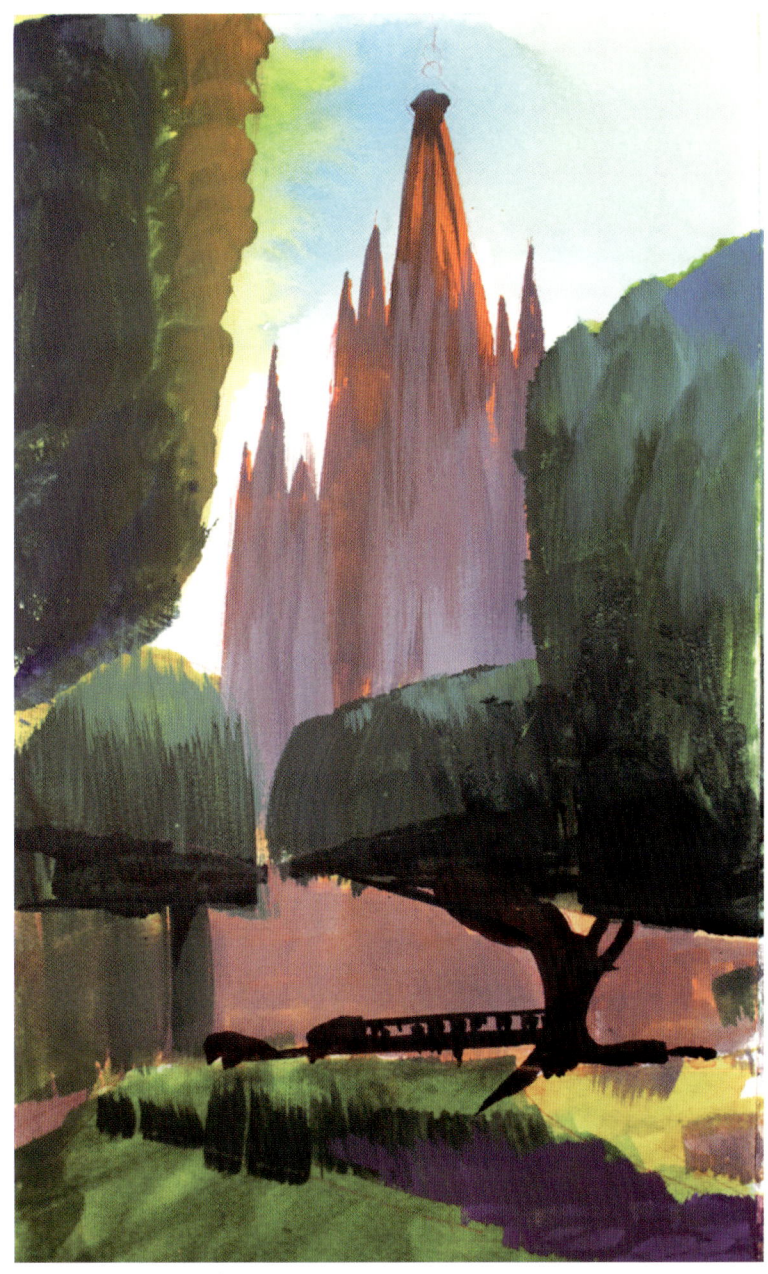

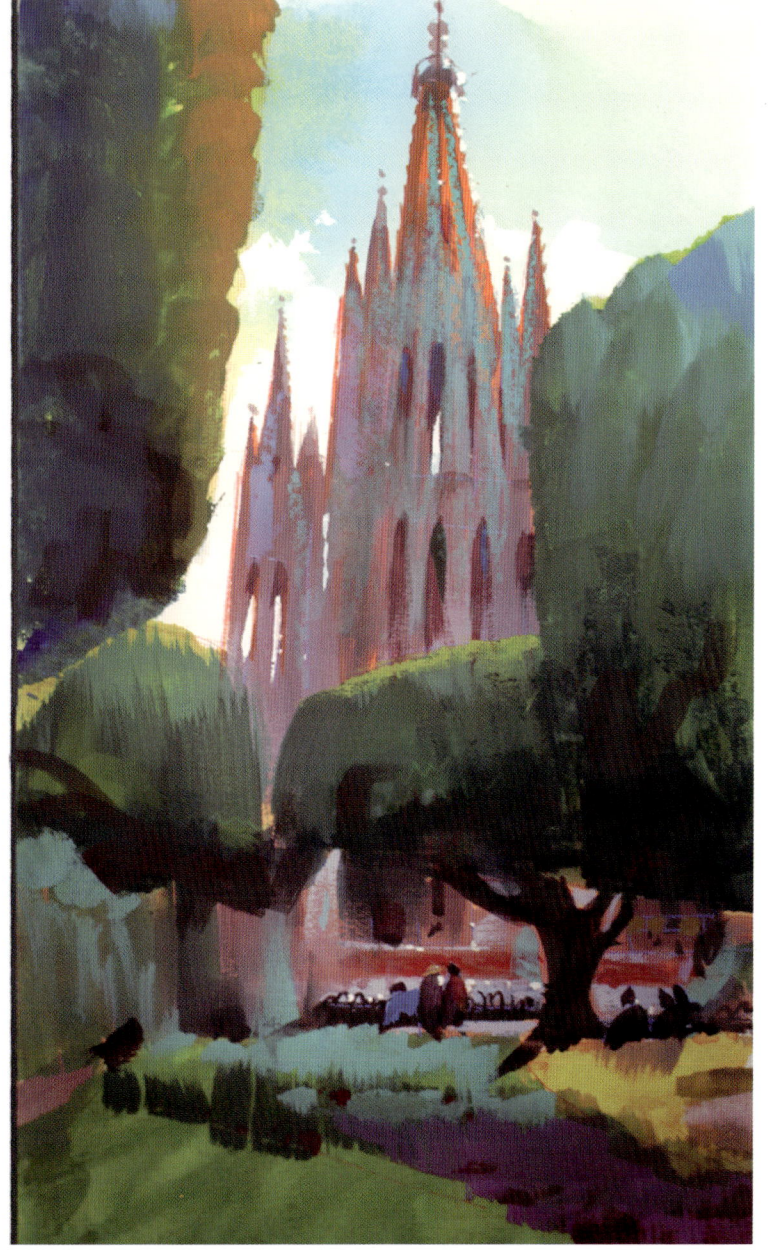

③ Now it's time to get to the guts of the image. Most everything here is in shadow, so I block in the dark local colors of each element. The grouping and rhythm of the trees is important, so I emphasize their simple shape and geometry, adding cool light on top and darker shadow underneath. The focal area created by the church has a backlit glow, so I emphasize the warms and cools there for a strong contrast.

④ For the final stage, I add more cool light to the top planes; this is truthful to the quality of light, and it creates a brilliant visual interest against the warmer elements of the scene, especially in the cathedral spires. I finish off with details that are limited to textures in the landscape and architectural elements in the church. And finally, a sprinkle of paint is added to suggest people in the distance enjoying the Sunday afternoon.

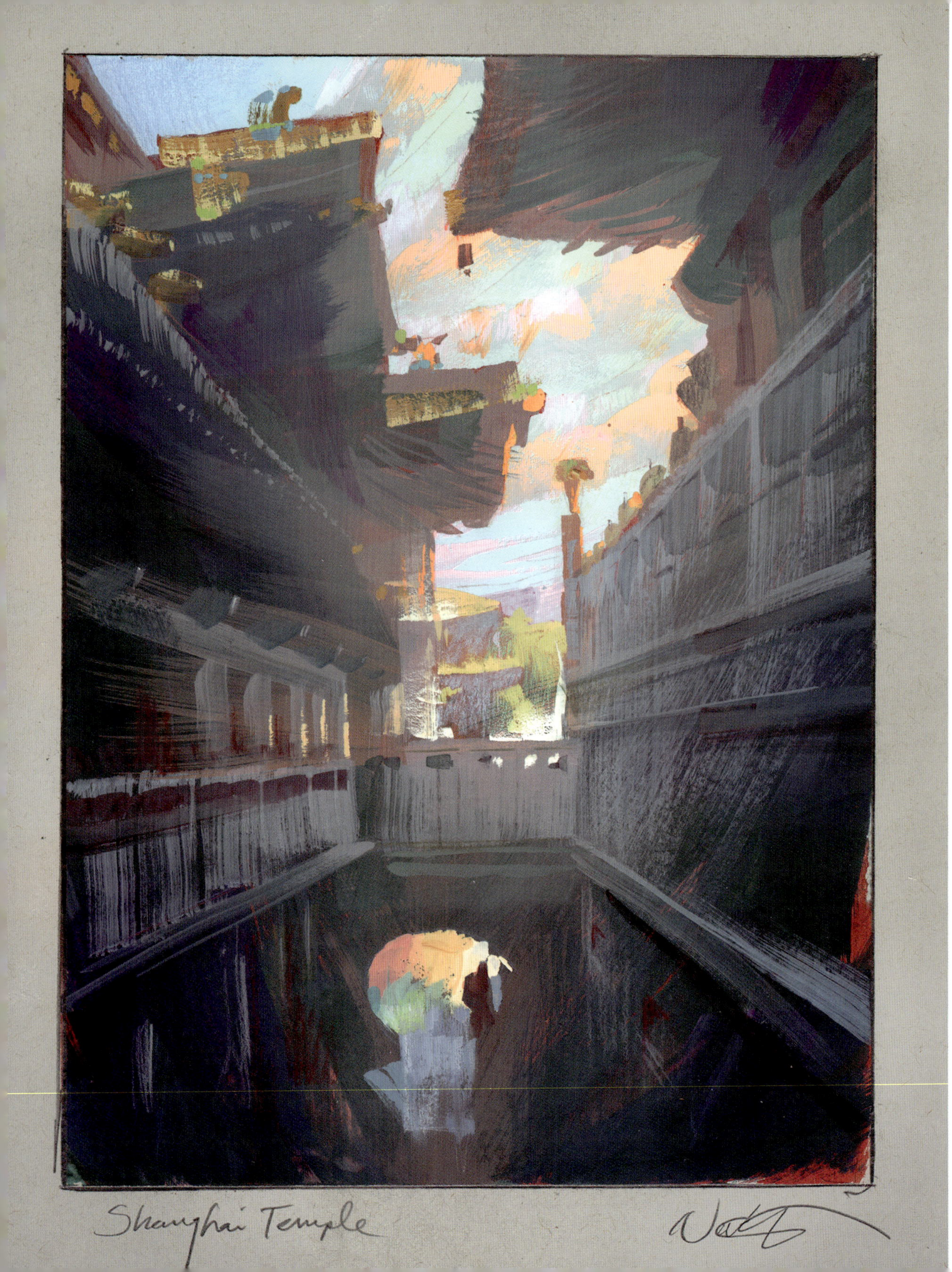

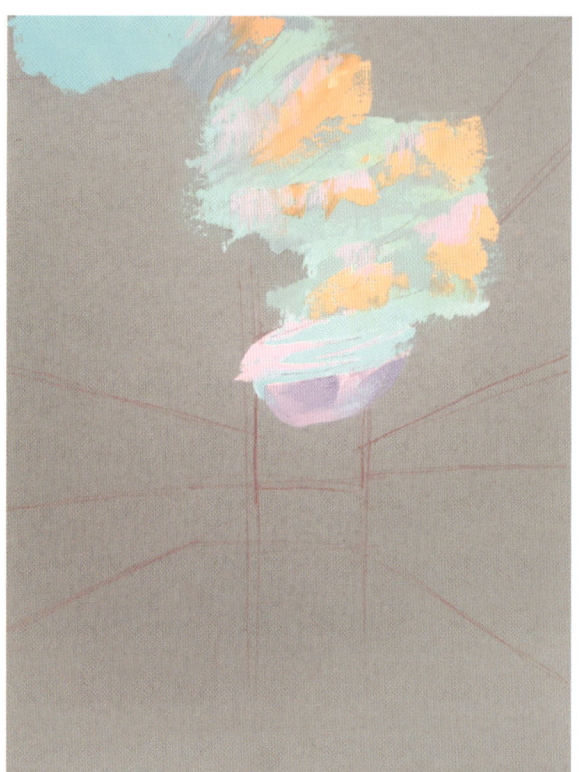

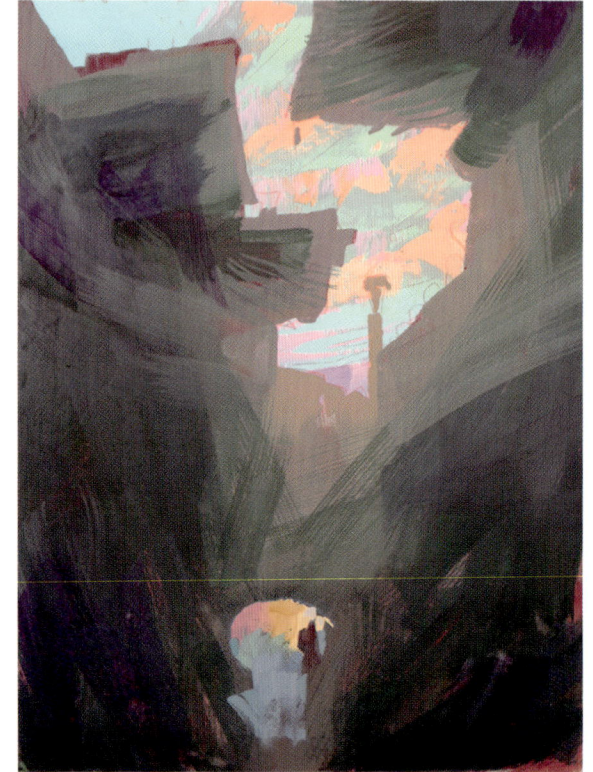

Shanghai Temple

It's About the Big Shapes...

Watercolor and white gouache, Strathmore 400 Series Toned Gray Mixed Media paper, 16 x 12 inches

Here's a scene from a Buddhist temple in Shanghai, China. There is an extraordinary, ornate quality throughout the architecture, and yet the most captivating aspect to me is how the buildings frame the multicolored sky, ending in the tunnel below. To emphasize this quality, I rough in the sky, giving a perspective to the clouds, then block in the big shape of the architecture. I add the one-point perspective lines and the ornamentation along the edges of the silhouette. That's all that I need for my "big, simple statement" idea.

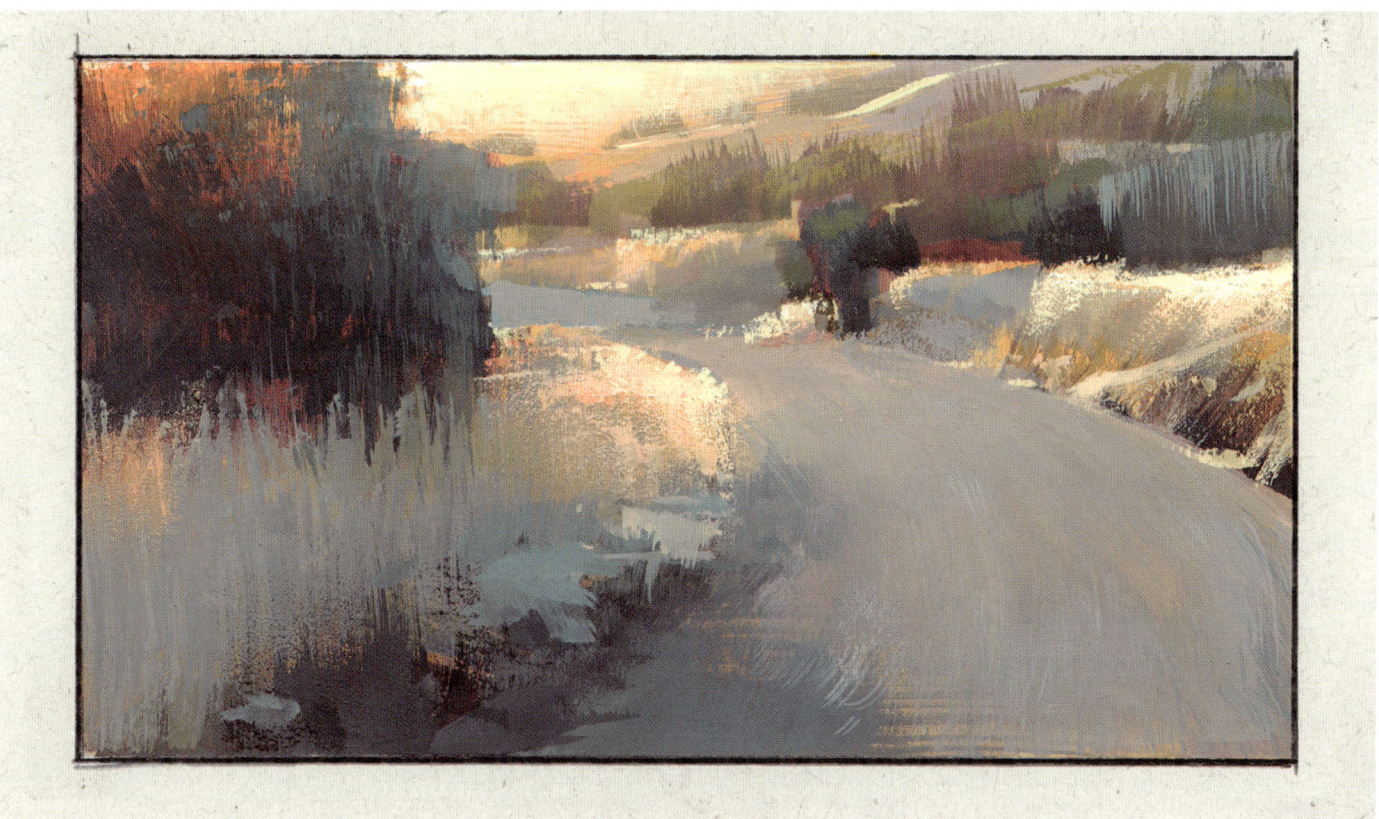

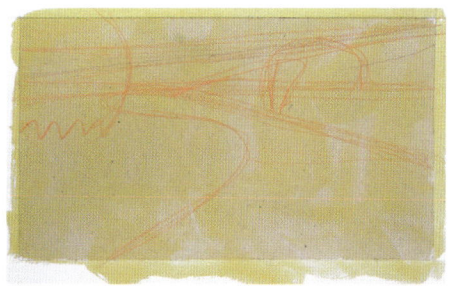
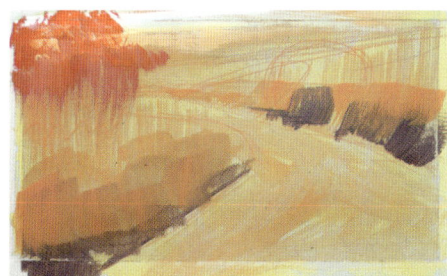
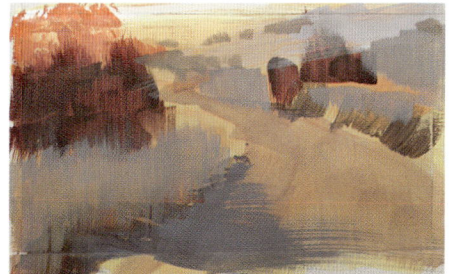
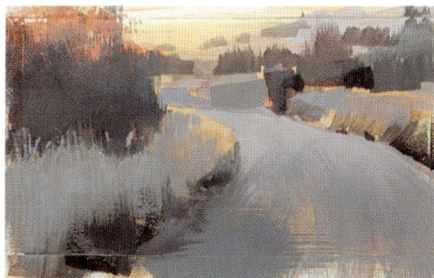

It's About the Road...

Toned mixed-media sketchbook, 4 x 6 inches

Here's yet another scene filled with complexities, and the sun is setting fast. What to emphasize in all of this? Personally, I liked the way the road wrapped around the corner heading toward the sunset; it seemed to me that the connection of the light source and the road was the big moment here.

You can see that my initial sketch and lay-in focus on that simple relationship. After the warm underpainting is set up, I block in the simple shape of the road, and lastly, add the cool of the shadows and the lightest highlights. Time to peel the tape off and see what I have in the quickly dimming light! Because some of my values are similar to the paper, I use a B hardness graphite pencil for a border to give the painting a clear boundary.

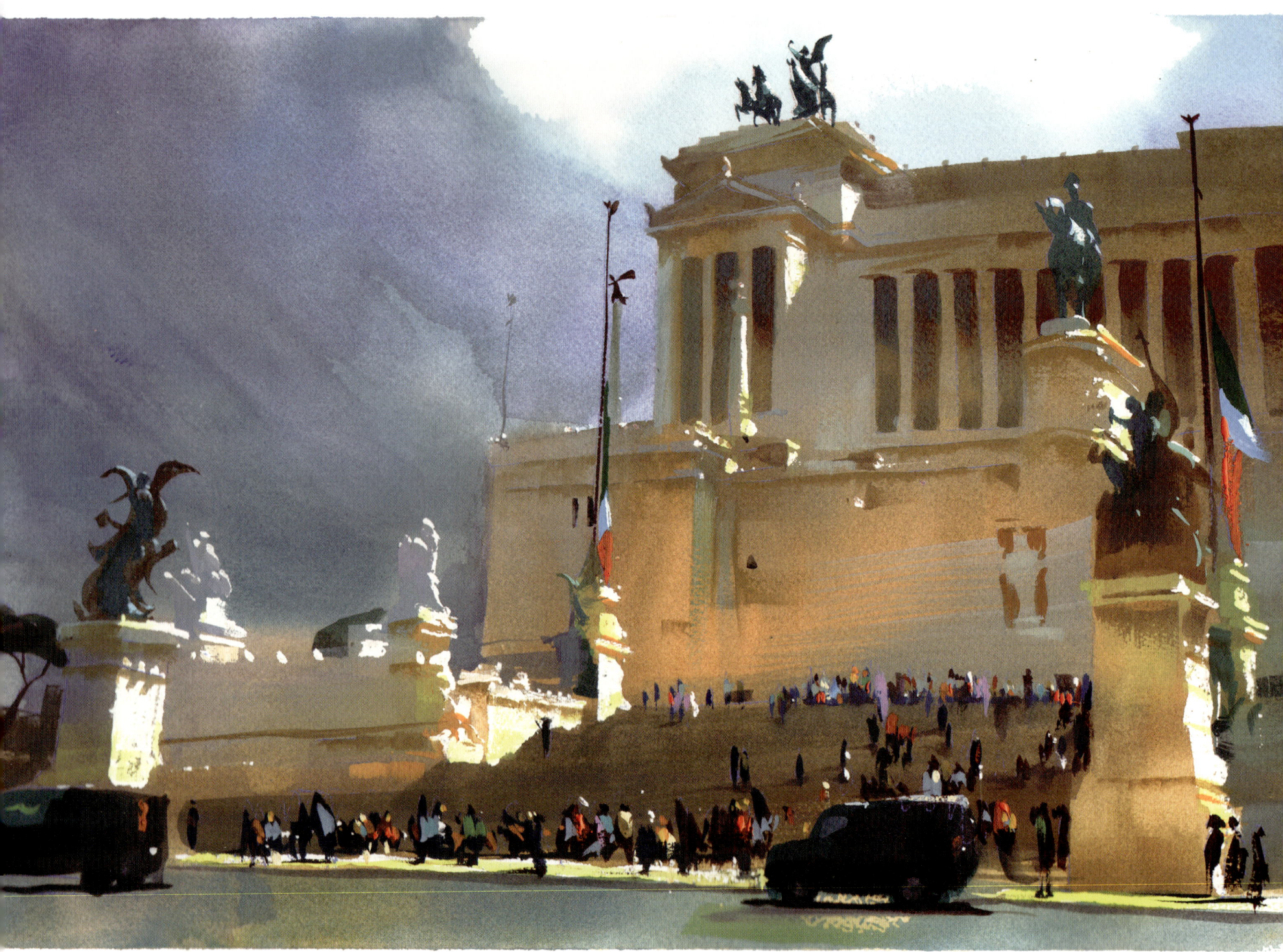

Altare della Patria Rome

N. Fowler '17

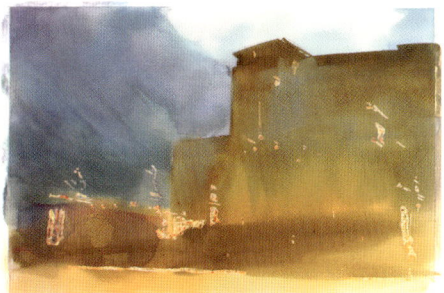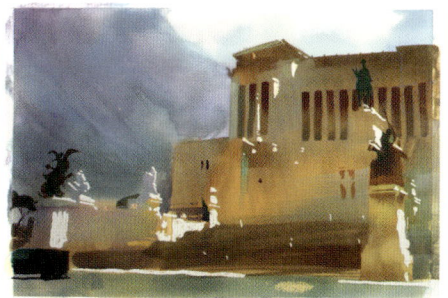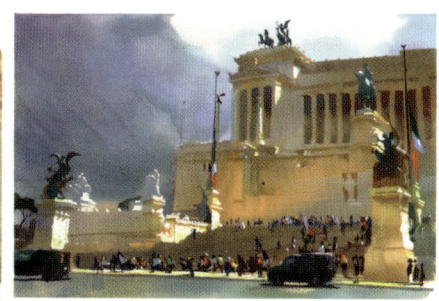

Chapter 10

Putting It All Together

Take a look at step two in the demonstration images above. It represents what is possibly the most important thing I know about landscape painting: finding unity of purpose in each image. In this case, the values of the land and sky are pretty much identical. This simple grouping allows me to then choose the contrasts that I believe will make the best representation of this place, a place of grandeur and history, the Altare della Patria (Altar of the Fatherland) in Rome, Italy.

So let's review the foundational idea of why landscape painting is so difficult: we must learn to work in a way that is unnatural to us. Our eyes don't look for unity, they go for the gold, the areas where the most information is present, which is the contrasts! So we tend to paint that way, emphasizing the contrasts, but not the unifying elements, and our paintings come out as a bunch of wretched parts that don't feel like they belong together. And the harder we try to accurately observe what we see, the more we focus on the contrasts, and our paintings get worse and worse. And with failure after failure, we throw our arms in the air and give up, believing that we just don't have any natural talent. This doesn't have to happen. We just need to recognize the critical importance of emphasizing the unifying elements of our paintings. So in this chapter we make absolutely certain that we know how to overcome our own nature and meaningfully bring together all the elements that make up our paintings.

"The harder we try to accurately observe what we see, the more we tend to focus only on the contrasts, and our paintings get worse and worse. This doesn't have to happen. We just need to recognize the critical importance of focusing on what unifies our paintings."

Review of Concepts

Strathmore 400 Series Toned Tan Mixed Media paper, 12 x 9 inches

This is the Sagrada Família basilica in Barcelona, Spain, the masterpiece of the great architect Antoni Gaudí (1852–1926). If you've ever had a chance to visit, you know of its extraordinary complexity. It's a daunting landmark to paint, which means it's perfect for a review of our "simple statement" ideas.

 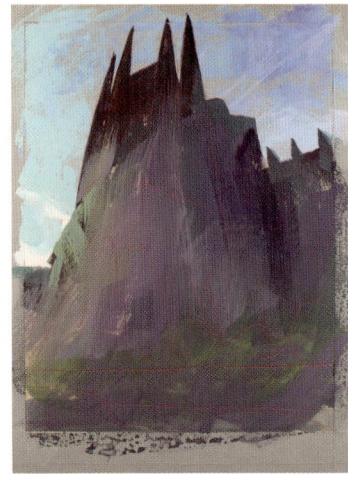 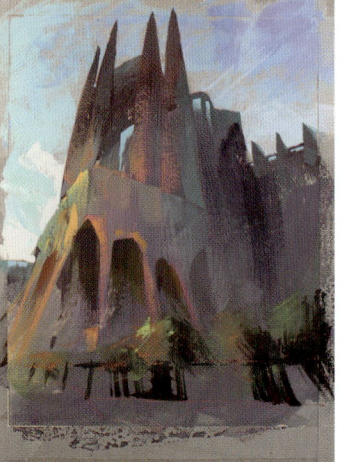 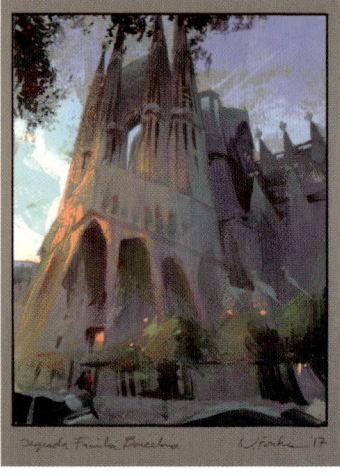

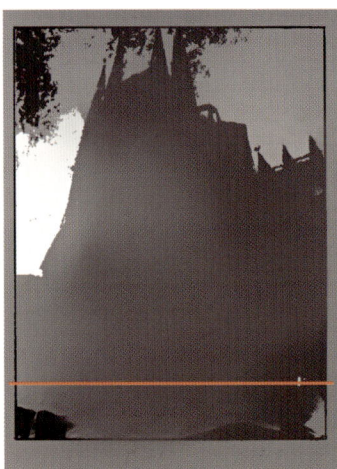 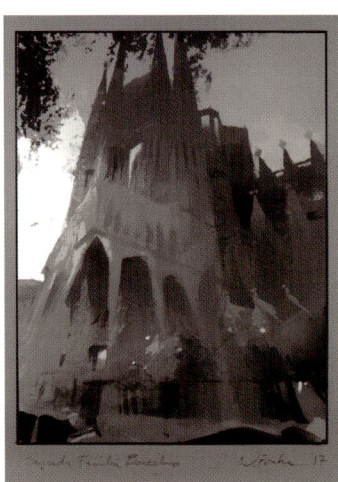 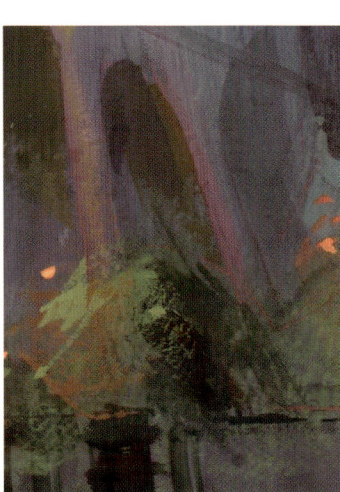 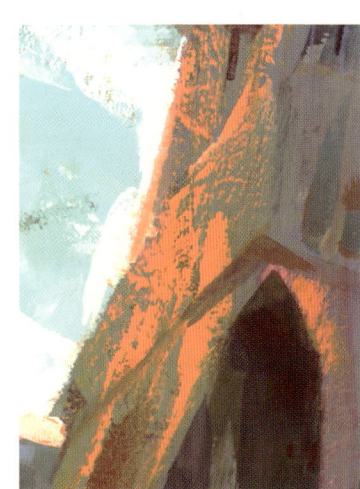

(1) Silhouette, eye level, framing. These are the most basic qualities of the painting; they are the foundation on which everything that comes after is built. I chose a framing that would emphasize the majestic, vertical quality of the building with a low eye level for the feeling of looking upward. The silhouette carries a great deal of authority and impact, so this quality was emphasized throughout the painting process.

(2) Value, shape, rhythm. I carefully avoided individual patches of value, instead, looking for big transitions such as the darker crest of the building that gradates to the lighter front area. The rhythmic repetition of shapes is clearly an important aspect of the architecture, so this quality was emphasized as well.

(3) Edge, texture. The front arches of the building are a major focal area, so I maintained the harder edges there, while allowing a softness throughout the rest of the building. The foliage in front contributed to the sense of rhythm and depth, so texture was emphasized in that area especially. But I was careful it didn't become too important, so there's plenty of "lost and found" in the texture and edges of the landscaping.

(4) Color hue, color saturation. This is the area of primary visual interest, so it's treated as the intersection of many forms of contrast. It has contrast of color hue, color saturation, texture, value, and edge.

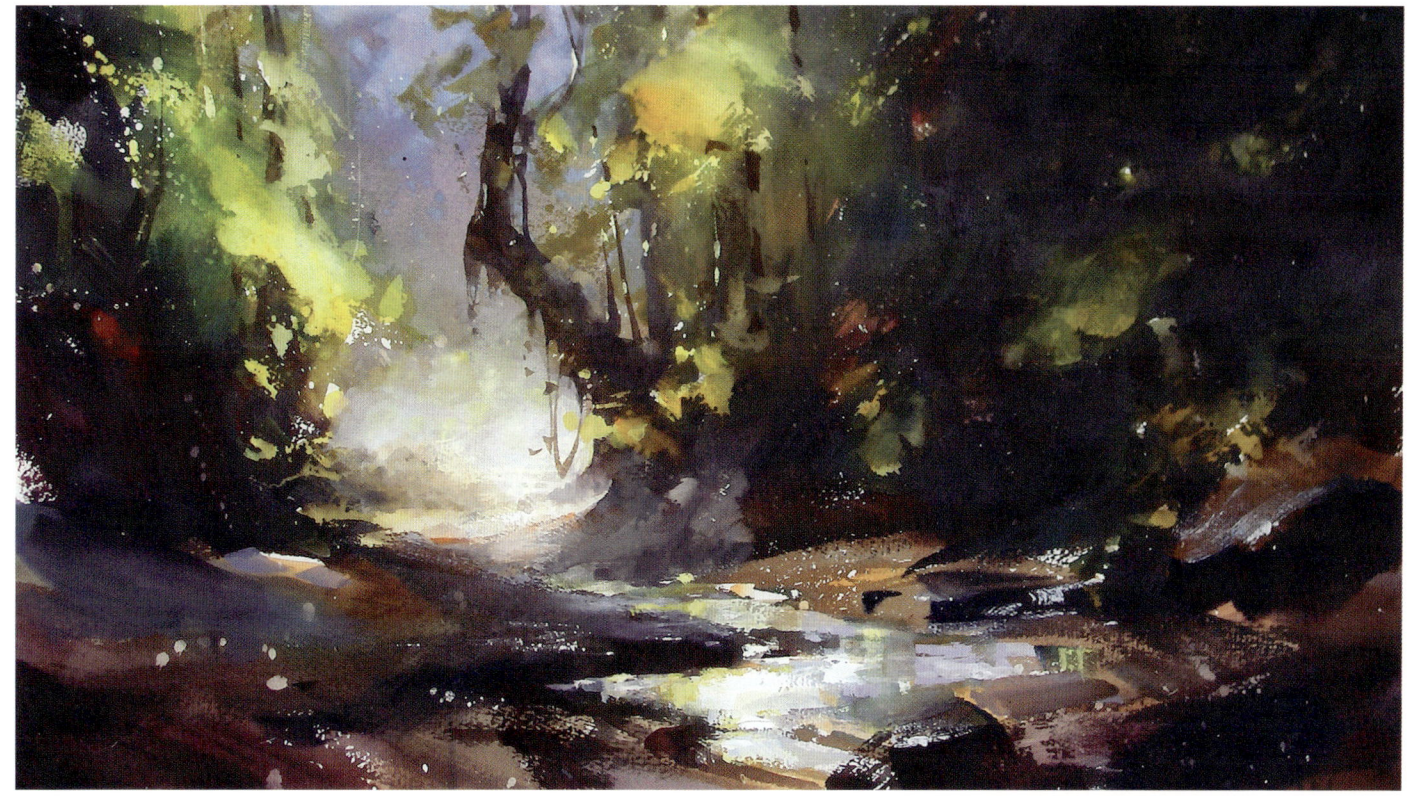

Arches cold-pressed paper, 12 x 18 inches

This Corcovado rainforest watercolor is from a painting trip to Costa Rica. Dealing with the complexities of the location was nearly as difficult as dealing with the mosquitoes!

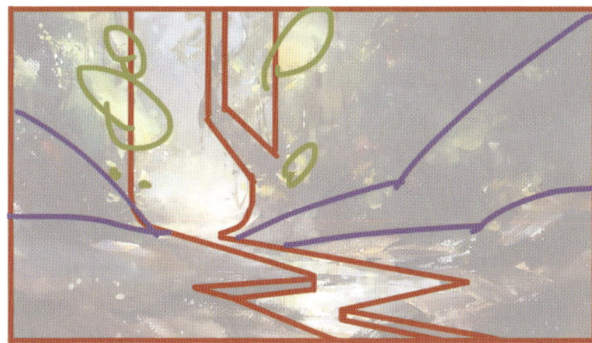

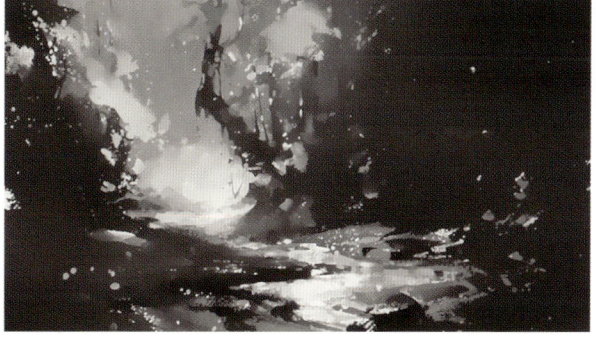

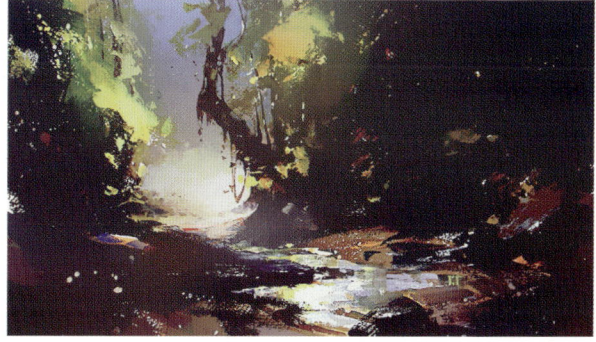

① **Simple design structure.** There's a lot going on in a jungle setting, but what's emphasized here is the sense of a destination, the feeling that we can hike through the gap in the jungle and find out what's around the corner!

② **Simple value statement, active vs. passive.** Although there's a suggestion of detail sprinkled everywhere, the strongest contrasts are kept to the light areas. And the light areas emphasize our concept of a destination.

③ **Color design.** Color contributes to the lush, atmospheric beauty of the place. The contrast of reds and greens, plus the distant atmospheric purples work to create unique color contrast where needed. But note that color contrast is limited to the same areas of visual interest as the design structure and value statement.

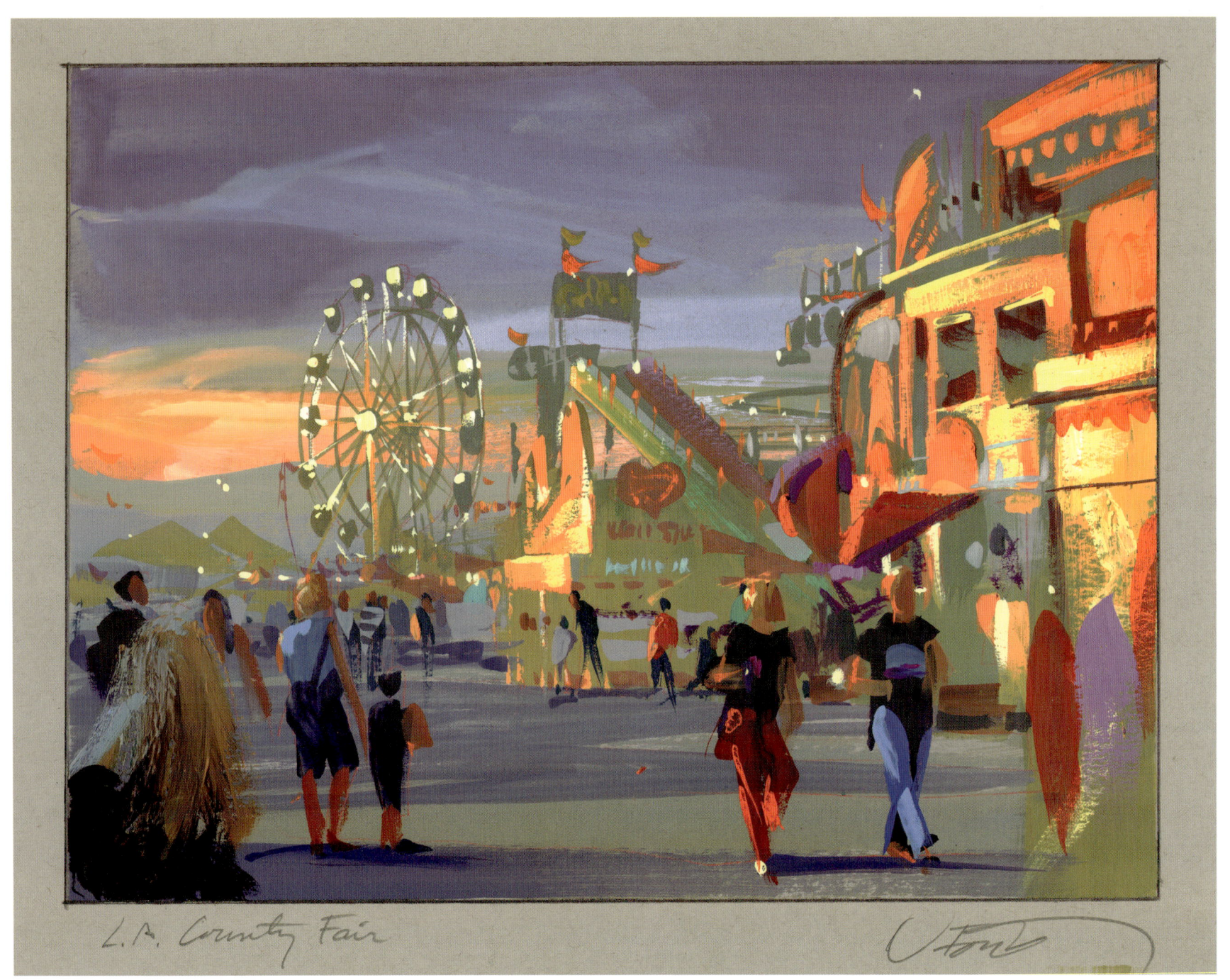

L.A. County Fair

Organizing Complexities: The County Fair

Strathmore 400 Series Toned Gray Mixed Media paper, 9 x 12 inches

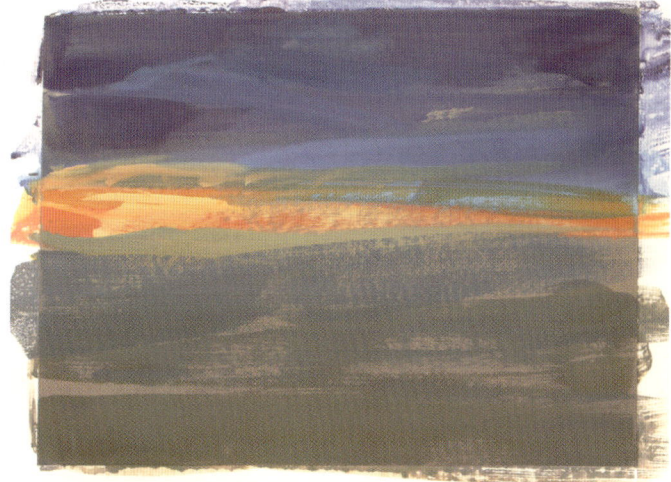

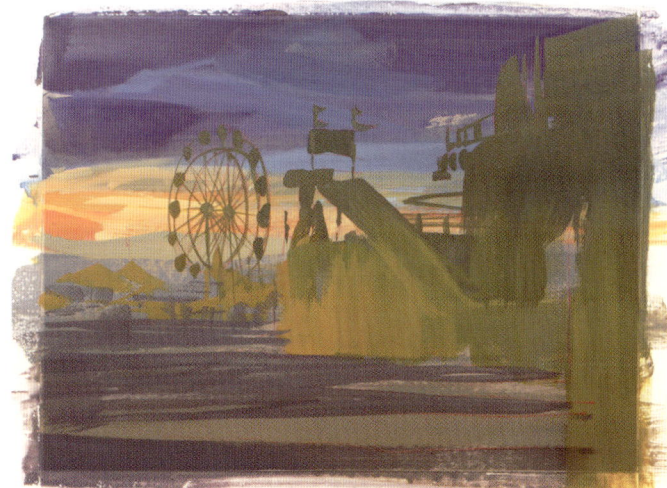

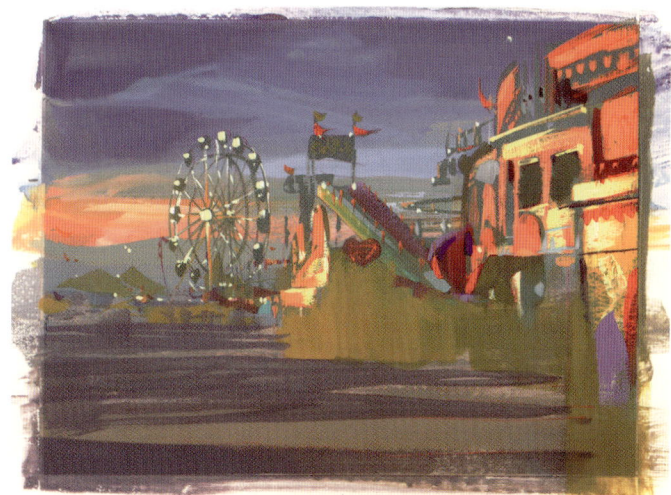

I've included several sketches of our L.A. County Fair in this book because not only is it an exciting subject, it's also an exercise in restraint. To begin the painting, the question to myself was "What's the least amount of information I can use that will create the most visual excitement, without losing the clarity of the place?"

1. **Simplest idea first!** The blues and grays of the background, plus the warm horizon where land meets sky, are a simple value, color, and line statement that I can build on.

2. **Simple silhouette.** Frankly, I was worried about the complexities of the rides and buildings, but found they were quite easy when blocked in as a silhouette. The only change of value is the gradual transition from darker at top to lighter at bottom. The long cast shadows are also important for the quality of sunset light.

3. **Emphasis on the light.** All the simplicity of underlying elements allows me to emphasize the vibrant local colors in the light, and the people are made to pop from local value and local color contrast.

"For this painting, the question was
'What's the least amount of information I can use,
that will create the most visual excitement without
losing the clarity of the place?'"

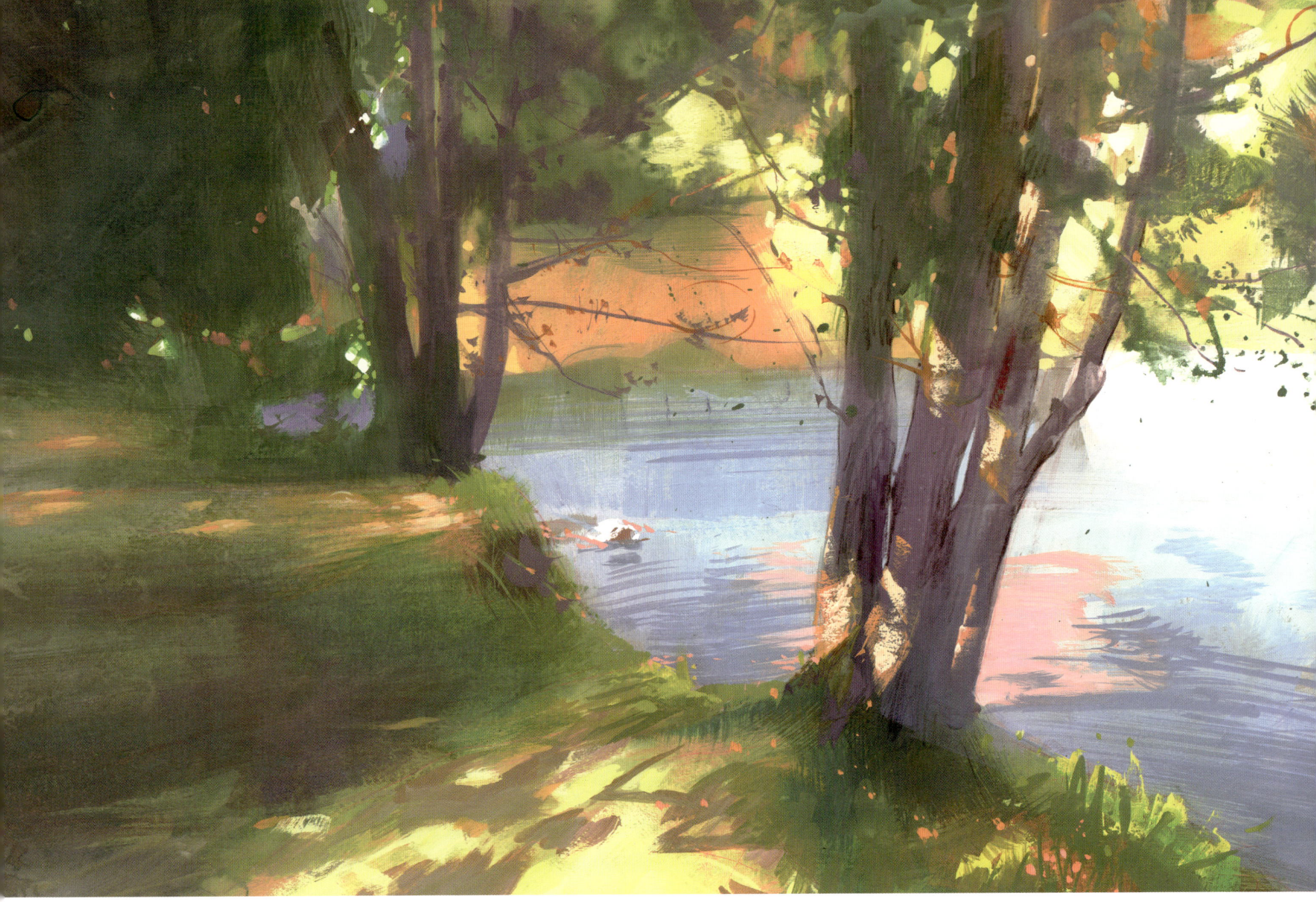

Patterns of Light and Shadow

Strathmore 400 Series Toned Gray Mixed Media paper, 16 x 20 inches

This painting is inspired by a business trip to Trollhättan, Sweden. Unfortunately, I didn't have time to stop and paint, but during a brief walk along the river by my hotel, I came across this particular scene.

I was struck by the patterns of light and shadow, and took a few photos, hoping to translate it into a painting back home in the studio. This is the result.

The challenge was to stick to the concept that made me want to paint this location in the first place, the remarkable patterns of light and shadow. Even though there were leaves and grasses by the thousands, I believed that if they were simplified in value, shape, and edge, the light and shadow would be emphasized as the engaging element in the painting. The steps that follow are my attempt to reach this goal.

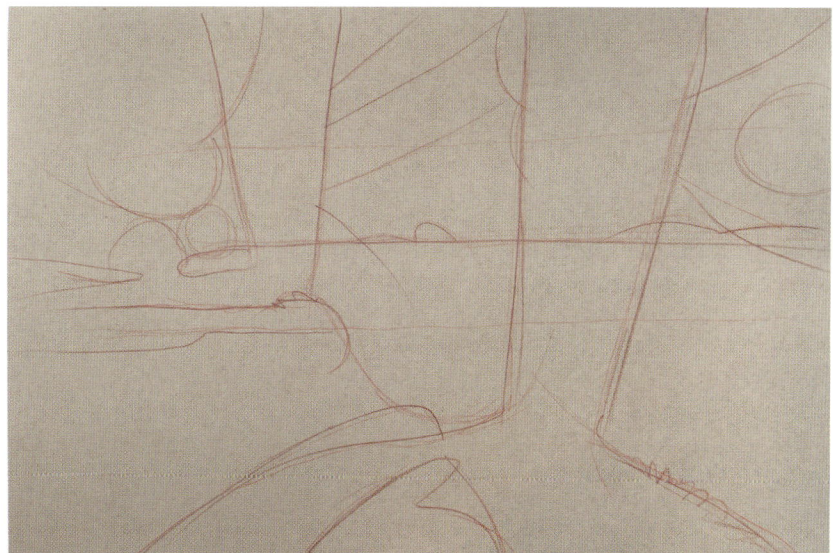

① I take my time on this step to carefully figure out the placement of the big simple shapes and place the shoreline and the horizon.

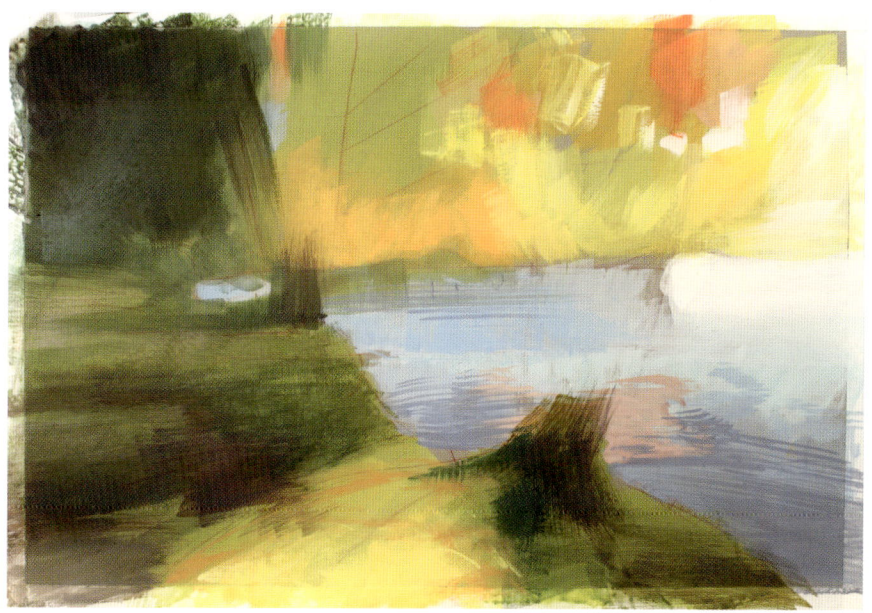

② Now it's time to emphasize my idea of big, simple masses. I'm identifying what's in light and shadow, then scumbling in the appropriate color and value. The cool reflections of sky in the water will be a major color contrast to help emphasize the warm light areas.

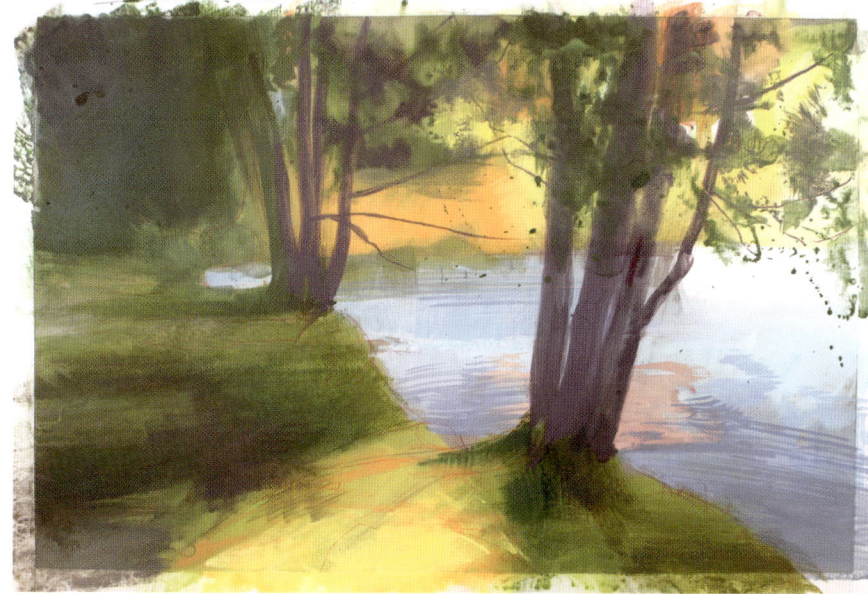

③ I'm ready to take advantage of the underpainting by adding the trees and foreground foliage over top. I avoid rendering individual leaves by spattering paint and using the bristles of my brush to stamp random shapes to suggest the visual activity of the foliage.

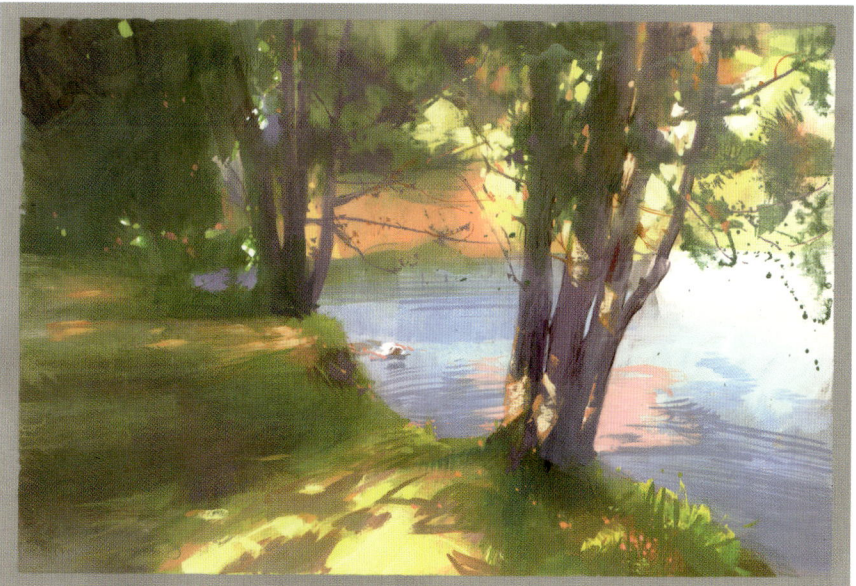

④ The final step is to give strong emphasis to the quality of light that made me want to paint this in the first place. I use opaque white with some yellow to strengthen the backlit quality of the tree and the dappled light falling across the ground. To bring the painting to completion, I add a sprinkling of light in the background, plus visual activity of grasses in the foreground, and it's a wrap!

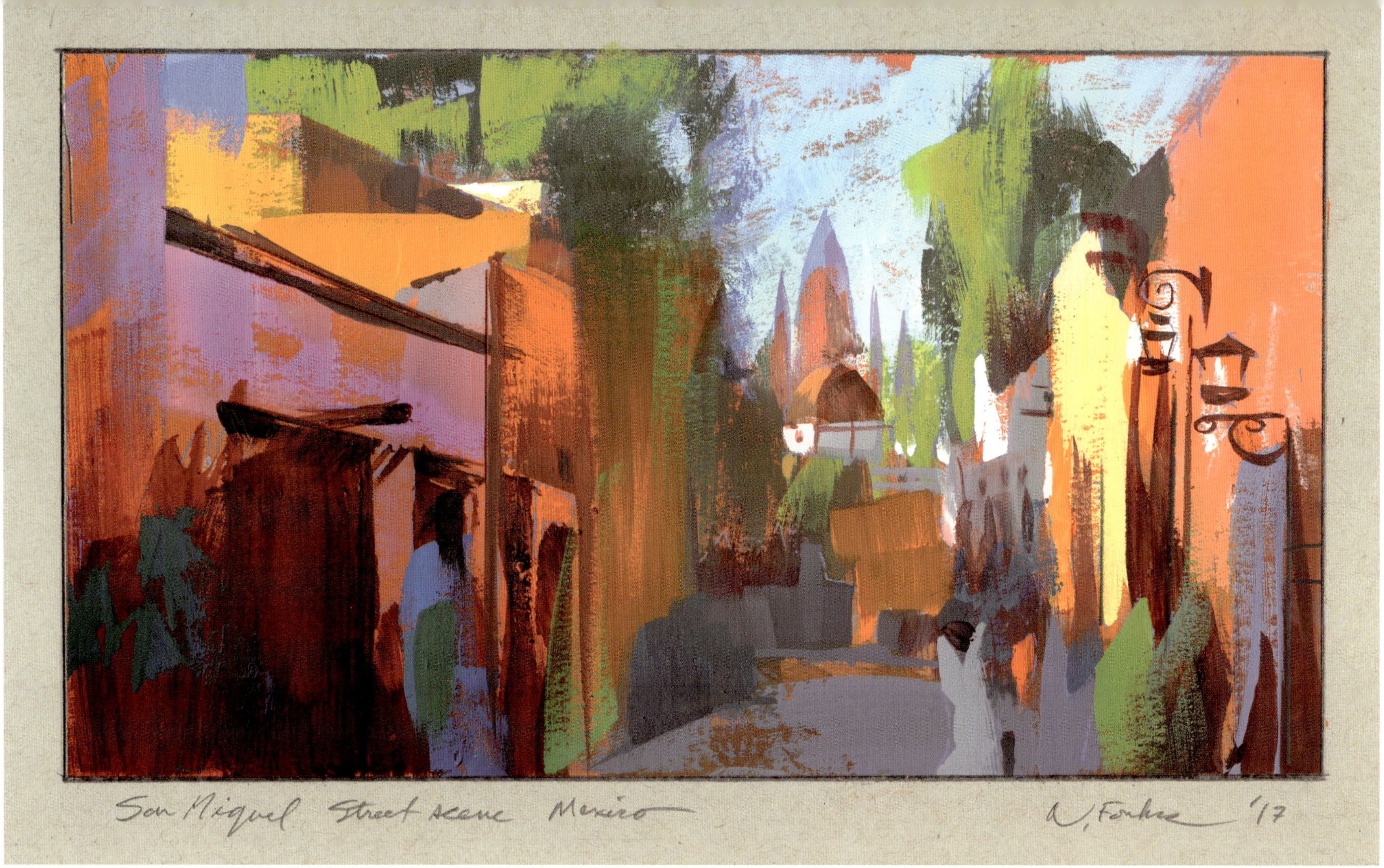

![San Miguel Street Scene painting]

San Miguel Street Scene Mexico   A. Forbes '17

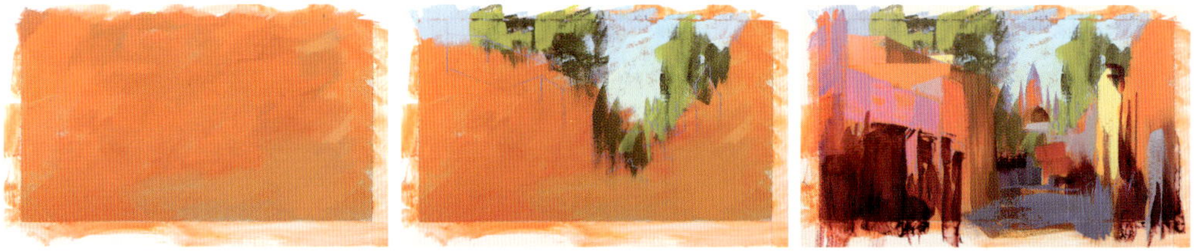

Finding Unity

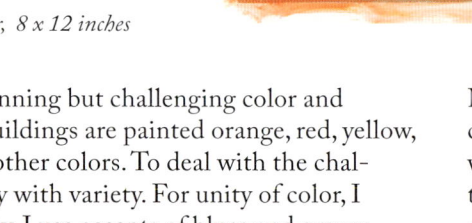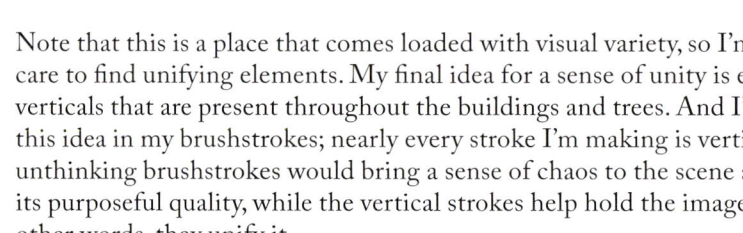

Strathmore 400 Series Toned Tan Mixed Media paper, 8 x 12 inches

Back to San Miguel de Allende for some stunning but challenging color and contrast. This is a town where many of the buildings are painted orange, red, yellow, and magenta and accented with a variety of other colors. To deal with the challenge, I look to the foundational idea of unity with variety. For unity of color, I focus on warms and reds, and for color variety, I use accents of blues and greens. But because the scene largely groups in a mid-value, I made a point to emphasize the lighter buildings in a way that created balance and rhythm, sprinkling them through the center of the image.

Note that this is a place that comes loaded with visual variety, so I'm taking great care to find unifying elements. My final idea for a sense of unity is emphasizing the verticals that are present throughout the buildings and trees. And I'm reinforcing this idea in my brushstrokes; nearly every stroke I'm making is vertical. Random, unthinking brushstrokes would bring a sense of chaos to the scene and disturb its purposeful quality, while the vertical strokes help hold the image together—in other words, they unify it.

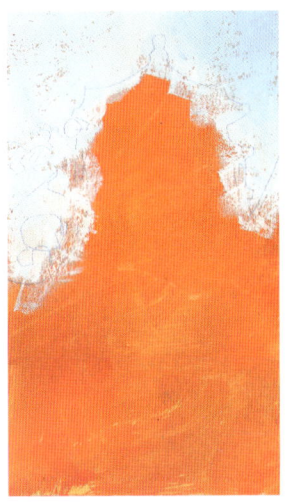

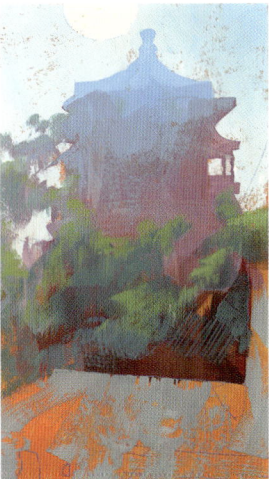

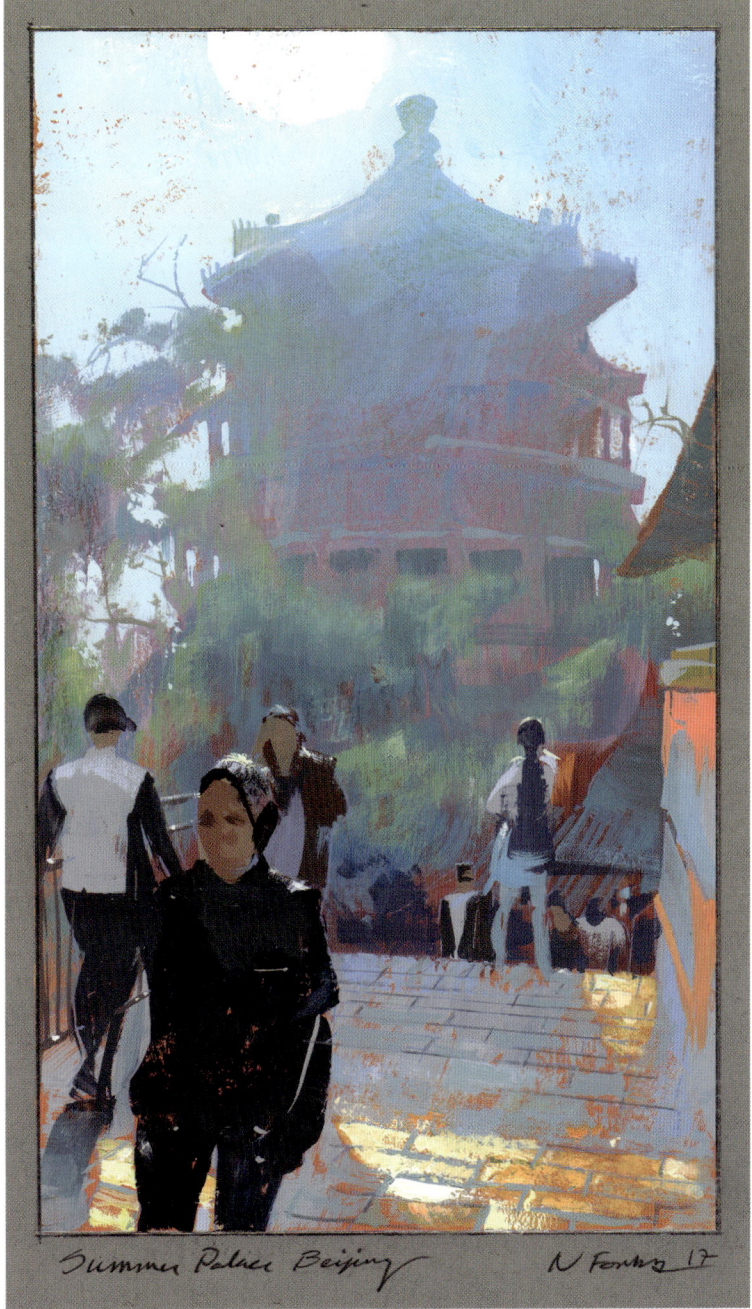

Summer Palace Beijing

Using Atmosphere

Strathmore 400 Series Toned Tan Mixed Media paper, 12 x 8 inches

Atmosphere, especially when it's backlit by the sun, can be a powerful unifying element in a painting, and this trip to Beijing, China came with lots of built-in "atmosphere." This is the stunning Summer Palace, full of history and visual interest. Its local color is primarily red and is surrounded by contrasting green foliage. These colors demand much attention when side by side, but I was much more interested in the atmospheric silhouette. So the thick atmosphere created three unifying qualities: it grouped the background in value, it desaturated the contrasting colors, and it created a unifying cool temperature.

The background still has some interesting color hue contrast, but its unified quality complements the strong value and saturation contrasts in the foreground. The final result is an elegant unity radiating out from the sun, gradually moving to more and more contrast in the foreground to create an image that has an engaging sense of unity with variety.

"The world around us comes loaded with visual variety, so we must take care to find unifying elements. Random, unthinking brush strokes can bring a sense of chaos to a painting and disturb its purposeful quality. Designed strokes help hold the image together—in other words, they unify it."

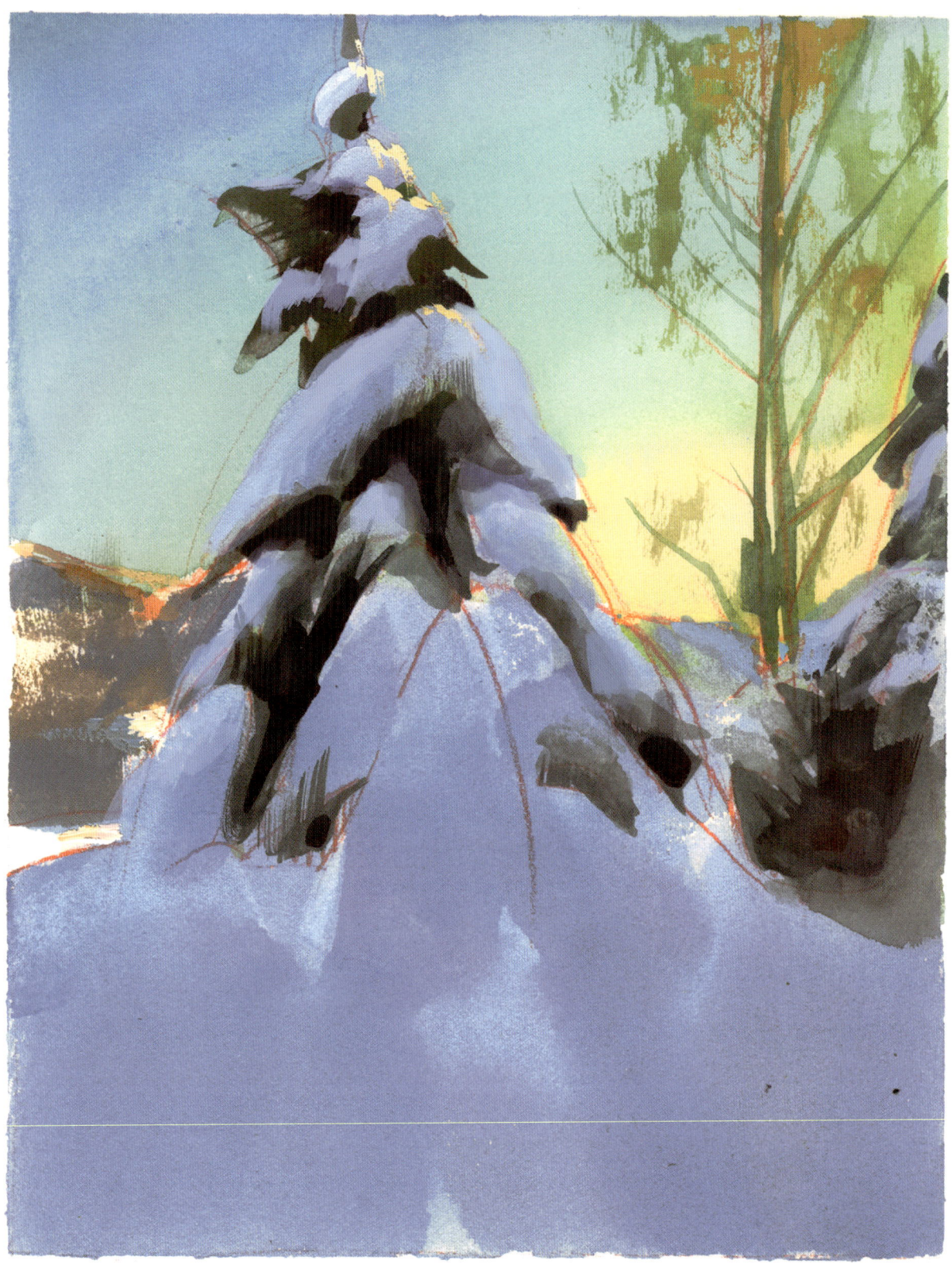

A Change of Weather

We've had a chance to discuss the importance of weather in our landscapes, but snow has been conspicuously absent thus far. There are two reasons for this. One is that I live in Southern California, but it's no excuse because you've seen sketches from a great variety of places. So the other reason is the truer one, which is that I don't much like being cold.

So here's what I recommend; make sure you get out and paint in the snow at least one time so that you can brag to everyone that you're a very serious and hard-core painter. But after that, do what I do on a winter-time trip. Find a spot with a nice snowy vista where you can pull over in your car, then crank up the heater, turn on some nice background music, and sketch away sitting in your car.

But in all seriousness, remember what I said from the beginning of this book: if we are to paint every day, we must take steps to enjoy the process at some level so that we'll be willing to come back to it again and again.

> *"If we are to paint every day, we must take steps to enjoy the process at some level so that we'll be willing to come back to it again and again."*

You can see a reference photo of this location on page 178/179.

Crescent 100 illustration board, 8 x 6 inches

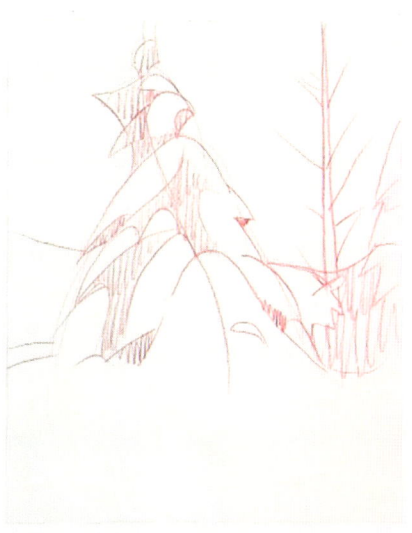 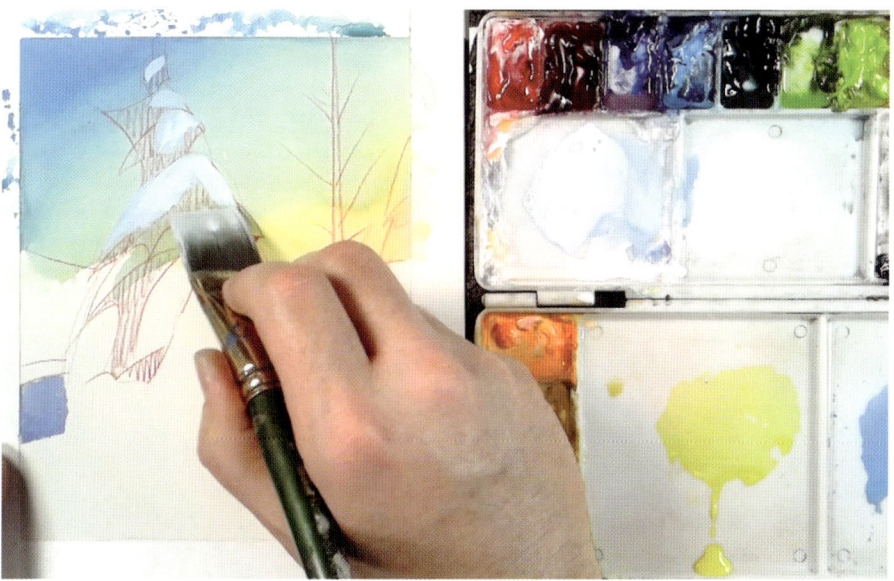

(1) The gesture and shape of the tree is important, so I begin with a drawing that emphasizes that quality with red Prismacolor pencil. I plan to begin my painting with transparent washes so that the drawing will remain visible.

(2) I lay down a wash for the sky, beginning with clean yellow and transitioning into cyans and blues to create a quality of glowing warm light. The opaquely painted snow on the tree is about the same value as the sky, so I've carefully set up a color contrast to be sure the snow reads clearly; the background sky has a greenish quality and the snow has an ultramarine blue quality.

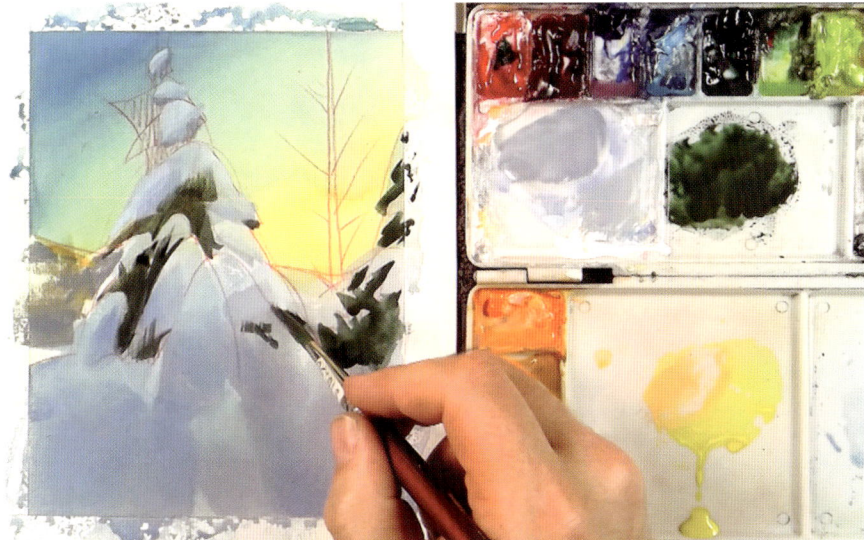 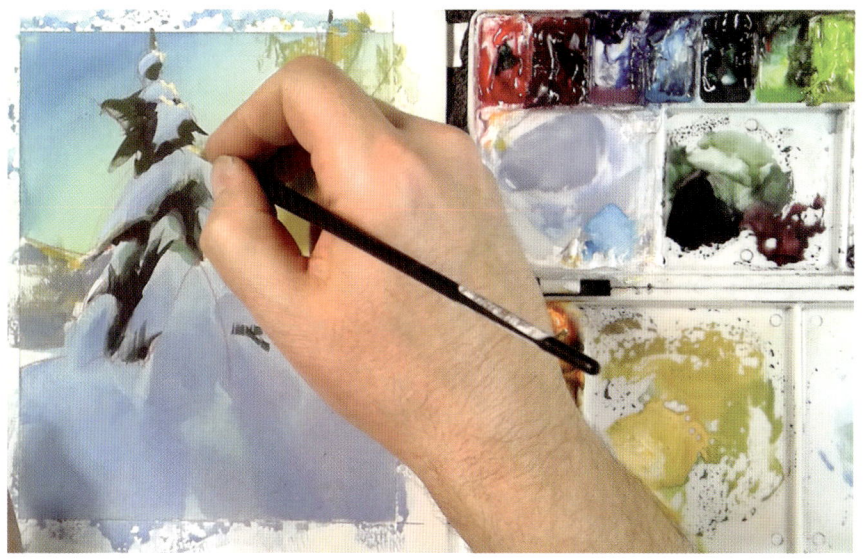

(3) I finish off the snow, then scumble in a suggestion of the hillside and trees behind it. The dark accents are the critical elements to get this image to pop, so I establish those as well.

(4) The sunrise highlights on the tree are the "frosting on the cake," so I wrap up with those. I'm using thick white gouache with yellow added, and I'm dragging my brush for some engaging color and texture contrast.

Don't Forget Interiors!

When I started teaching painting classes, I asked my students to do a daily sketch of any place that interested them to bring in as homework. I noticed that, almost without exception, the work was of outdoor subjects, there were no interiors. It's understandable, after all, we call it landscape painting, which often makes us think of dramatic sweeping vistas, but paintings of interiors can have their own emotional poignancy and should not be forgotten or avoided. An interior can have a kind of intimacy, it can tell the story of the people who live there, or the purpose the building serves.

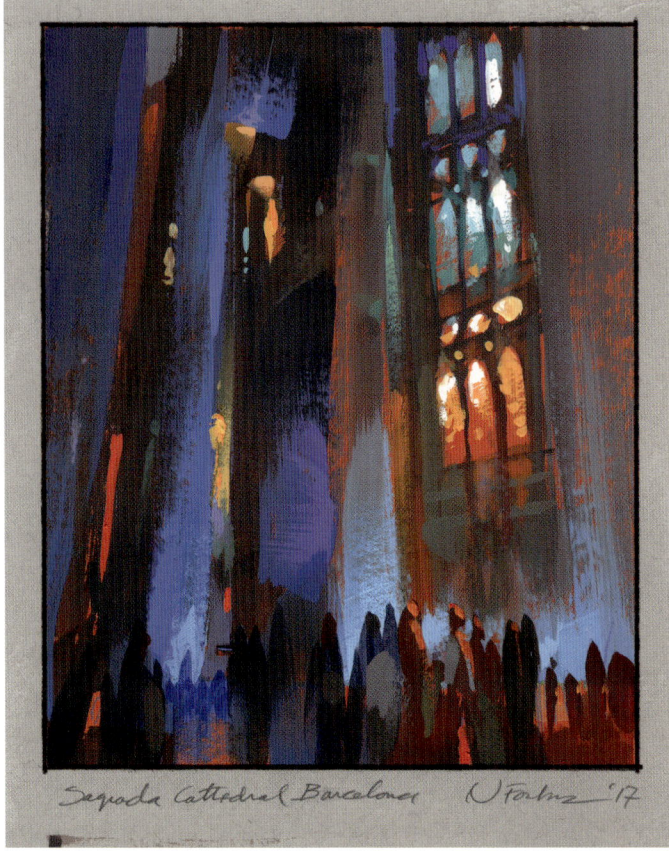

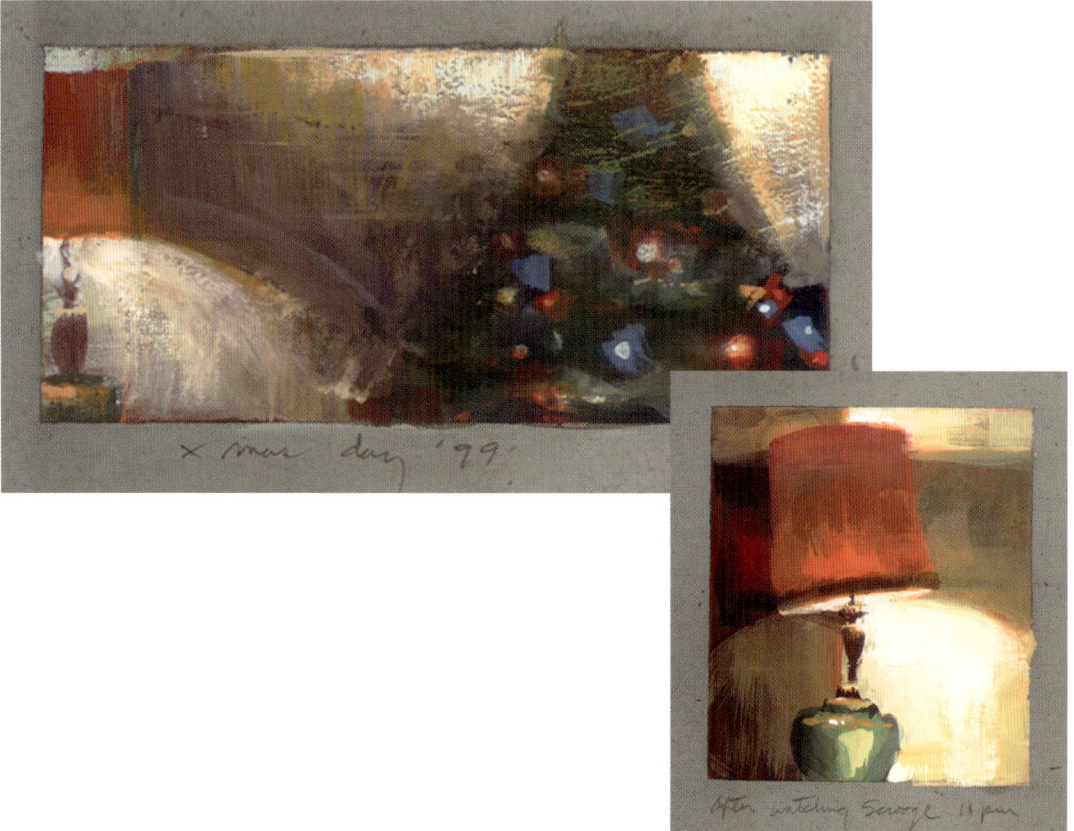

The above is a sketch of the interior of the Sagrada Família cathedral in Barcelona Spain. It's the same building we looked at a few pages back, and the interior is even more stunning than the outside, especially with the illumination of the multicolored stained-glass windows. As you can imagine, no paint was allowed inside, so I stuck to drawings on location, but I just had to capture the lighting affect in paint. I used photos taken on site as references to complete the painting at home.

Here's a sketchbook page from Christmas back in 1999. It was so nice to go back and thumb through this sketchbook that was full of memories! I was home visiting for the holidays and of course had my pocket sketch kit with me, so these quick sketches in the living room were the result. It's fantastic to get outside and paint, but we spend much of our lives and make many of our memories indoors.

"An interior can have a kind of intimacy, it can tell the story of the people who live there, or the purpose the building serves. We all know it's great to get outside and paint, but we spend much of our lives and make many of our memories indoors."

Let's do a quick sketch of an interior, we'll stick with our subject of the Sagrada Família cathedral.

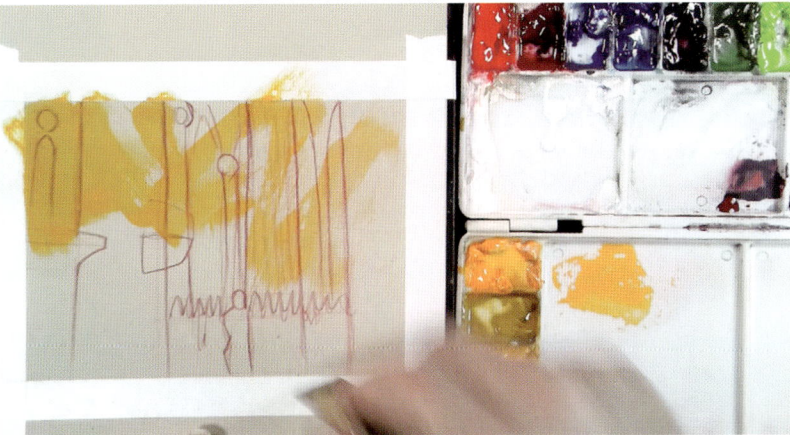

1 I'm using a dark red Prismacolor pencil to sketch in the position of the columns. The background golden glow is the key to this image so I begin by brushing in that color, following up with some reds.

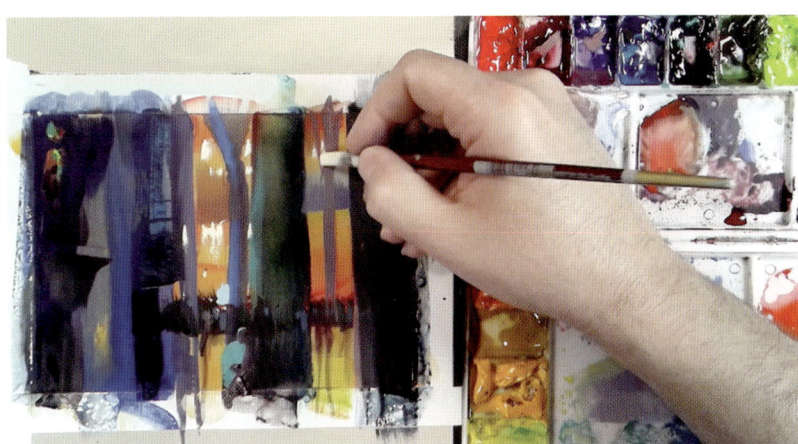

3 There were crowds of people standing toward the far wall, and a few in the fore-ground, so I rough a suggestion of them into the image, then go for the final lights. Don't forget that brilliant highlights need a good amount of thickness and opac-ity. Thin, watery paints can look light when initially laid in but sometimes they dry looking even darker than their surroundings! So I load my brush with thick white gouache and a little yellow and drag the brush through the areas of greatest illumination. The texture of the stroke creates a substantive glow and gives a more finished quality to an otherwise very loose impression of the moment.

The stained-glass windows here are designed to create a unique color contrast; blue and green light illuminates the interior columns, with red and yellow to the back. The result is a brilliant contrast of color and value, and so the sketch just has to focus on that idea.

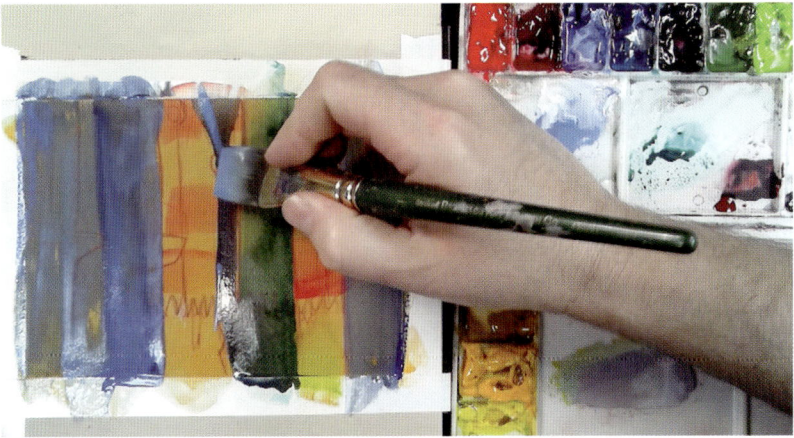

2 I block in the cooler, darker columns over top, making sure to do them in a single stroke with a large brush so the under color does not lift up. Then I mix a little white into my blues and greens and paint in a suggestion of cool, colored light, coming in from the left.

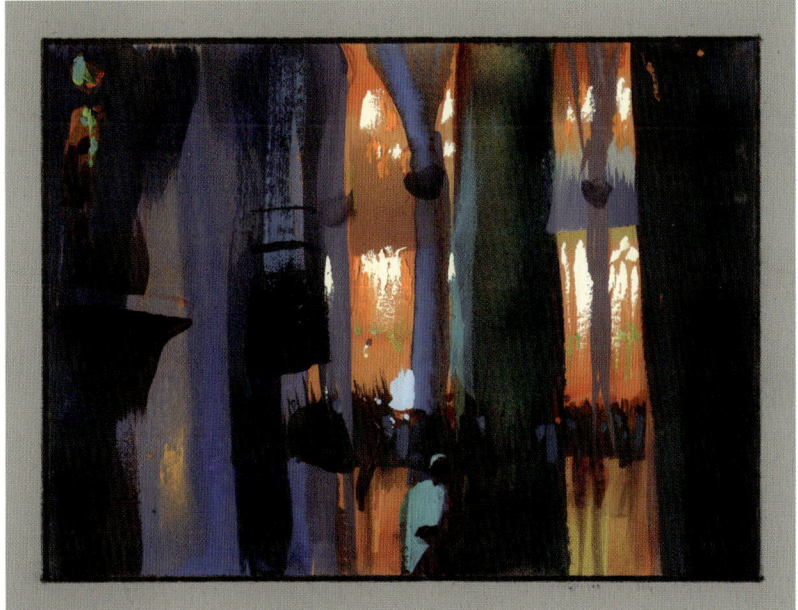

4 To wrap up, I peel the tape off and using a ruler, I pencil in a border for the image. This is yet another example of our simple statement approach; clear decisions up front allowed for a speedy sketch that I think captures the feeling of the place.

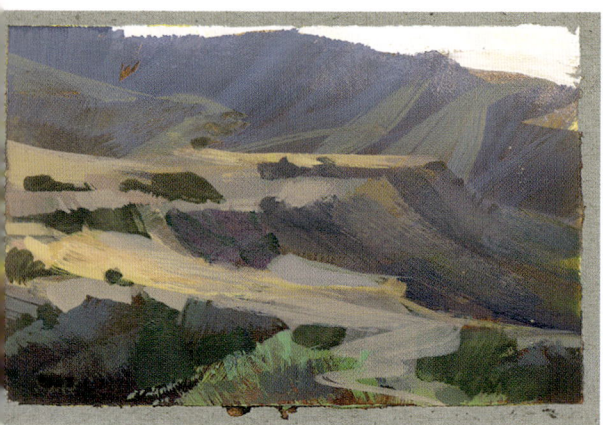
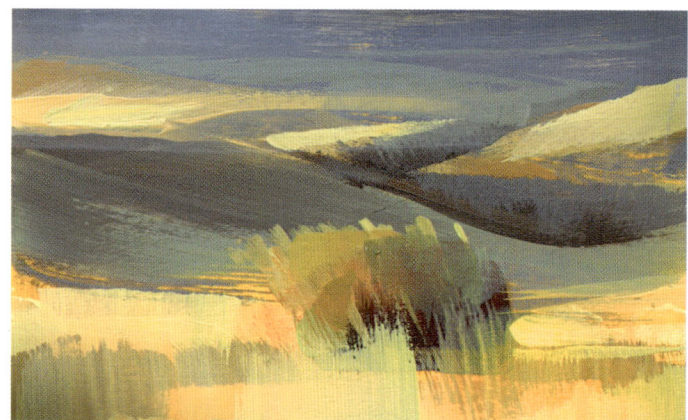
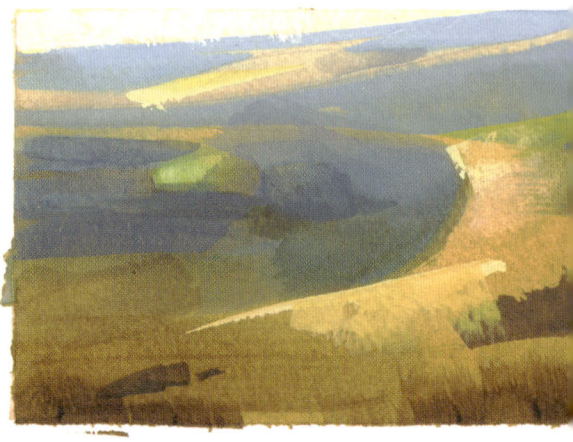

Story of the Place

If you've ever been out to California and made the drive on Interstate 5 between Los Angeles and San Francisco, you've passed through the area where I grew up. It was on 20 acres of property outside the town of Coalinga, right where the flat plains of the San Joaquin Valley meet the rolling hills and canyons that eventually lead to the ocean.

As a kid, I hiked all around that landscape and absolutely loved it, so I was surprised to hear that not everyone felt the same way. Back then, a friend of the family told us about his first time visiting. He had received an offer to work for the city, so he drove out to have a look around, feeling quite unsure of moving his family to this little, rural California town. But as he drove, the local hills were covered with lush springtime green grasses and ornamented with brilliant patches of wildflowers of all colors, especially the golden California poppy. The area was much more attractive than he expected, and as he drove, he said to himself, I can do this, this is beautiful! And he ended up accepting the job.

The punchline of the story is that by the time he sold his house and drove back out with his family to relocate, it was summer, and all that beautiful growth had turned to dry yellow straw. The wildflowers had long since wilted away under that blazing California sun. He said that he wanted to turn around and drive back.

I was a teenager at that time, already a hopeful artist, and was surprised at this critique of our native landscape. To me, even in summer, those hills were magical. In the evening, the red light of sunset would create amazing patterns of shadow across the hills, and the dry grasses would turn blazing red where they were illuminated. In the shadows, the bluish skylight would turn the yellow fields to a shimmering green. I didn't know about simultaneous contrast of color yet, but I knew that those patterns of shimmering color were something special, and I swore that once I was a real artist I would come back and put that experience down in paint.

I've now gone back many times with my sketchbook, and on these pages are examples. They're mostly quick, on-the-spot impressions, but they mean a great deal to me personally, because they try to capture and hold onto that childhood experience. They're an intense reminder about why we do this; our sketchbooks are a visual journal of where we've been and what we've done. For me, opening an old sketchbook brings memories rushing back that might otherwise be lost. I keep them all on a bookshelf in my studio and thumb through them from time to time.

"Our sketchbooks are a visual journal of where we've been and what we've done, opening an old sketchbook brings memories rushing back that might otherwise be lost to us."

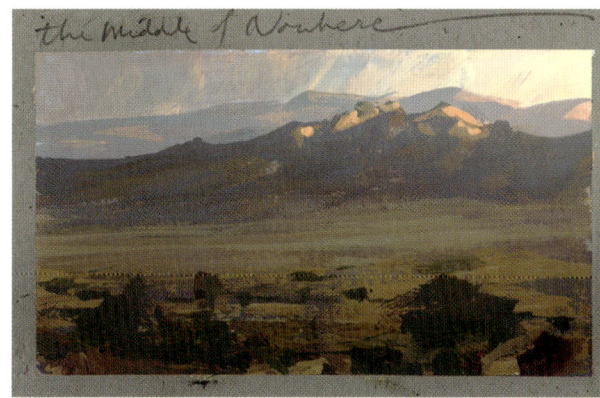

the middle of Nowhere

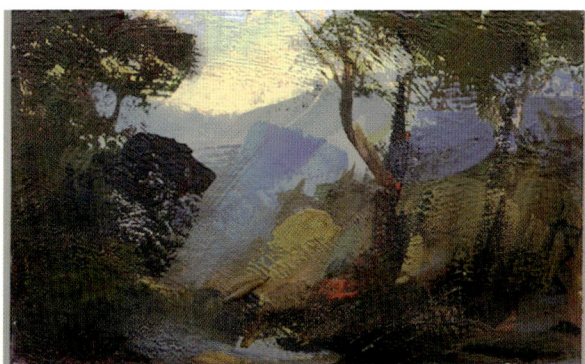

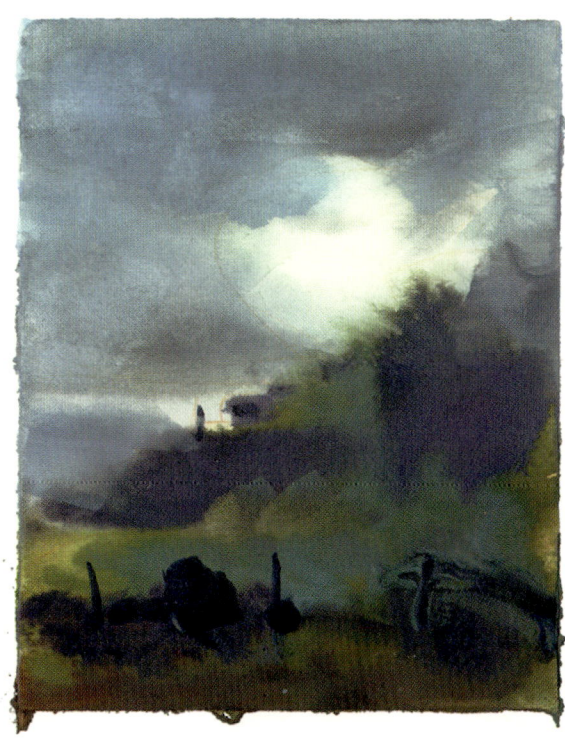

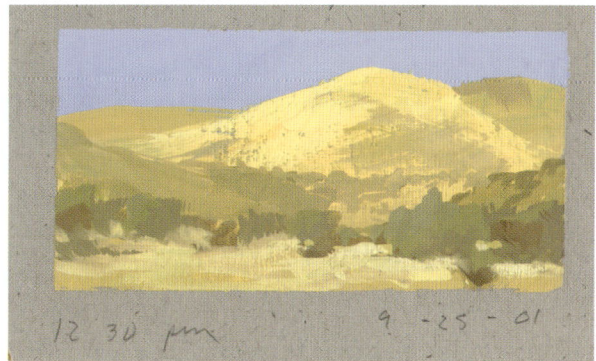

12 30 pm   9 -25 - 01

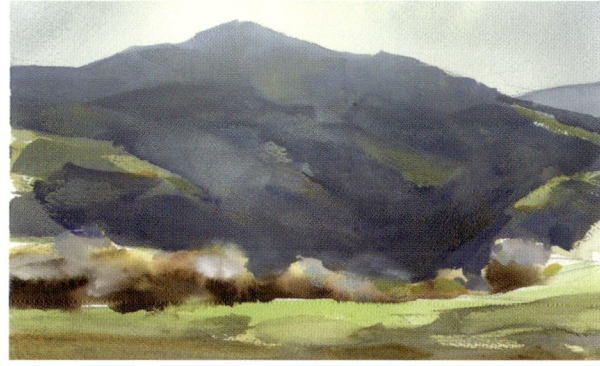

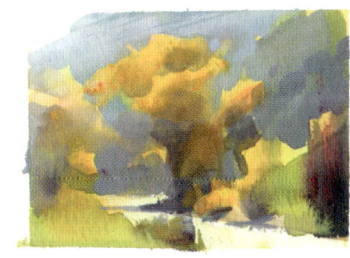

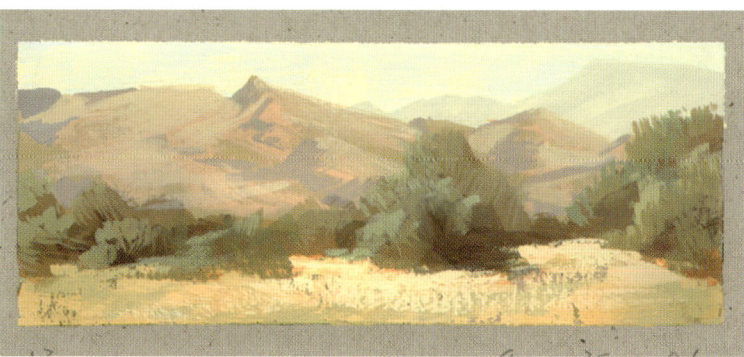

Highway 33 outside of Coalinga

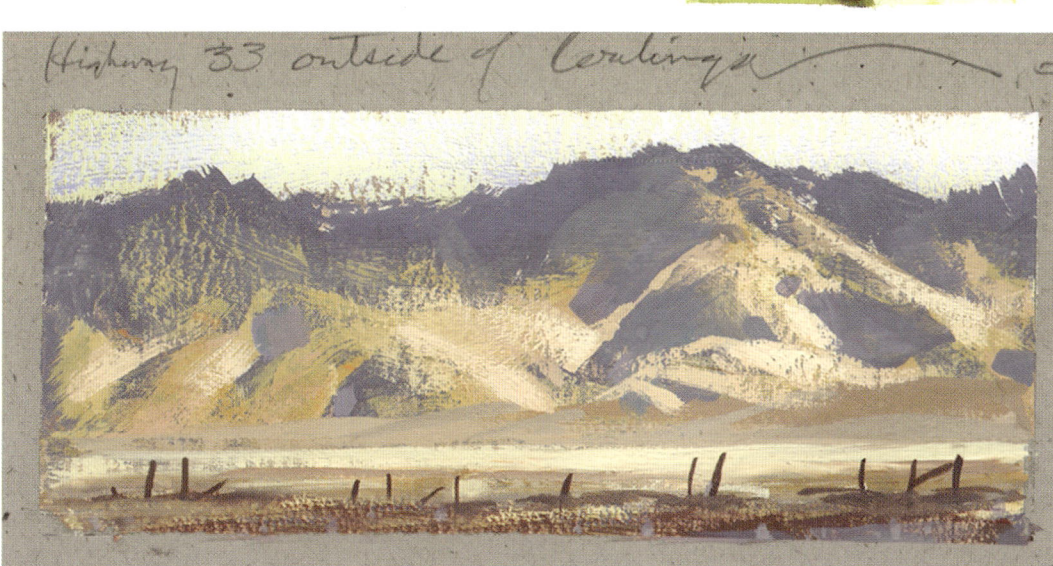

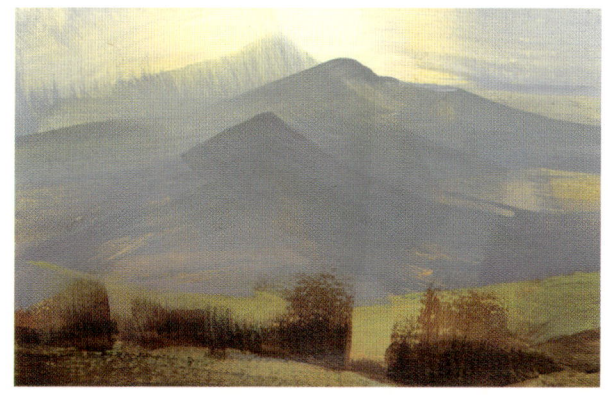

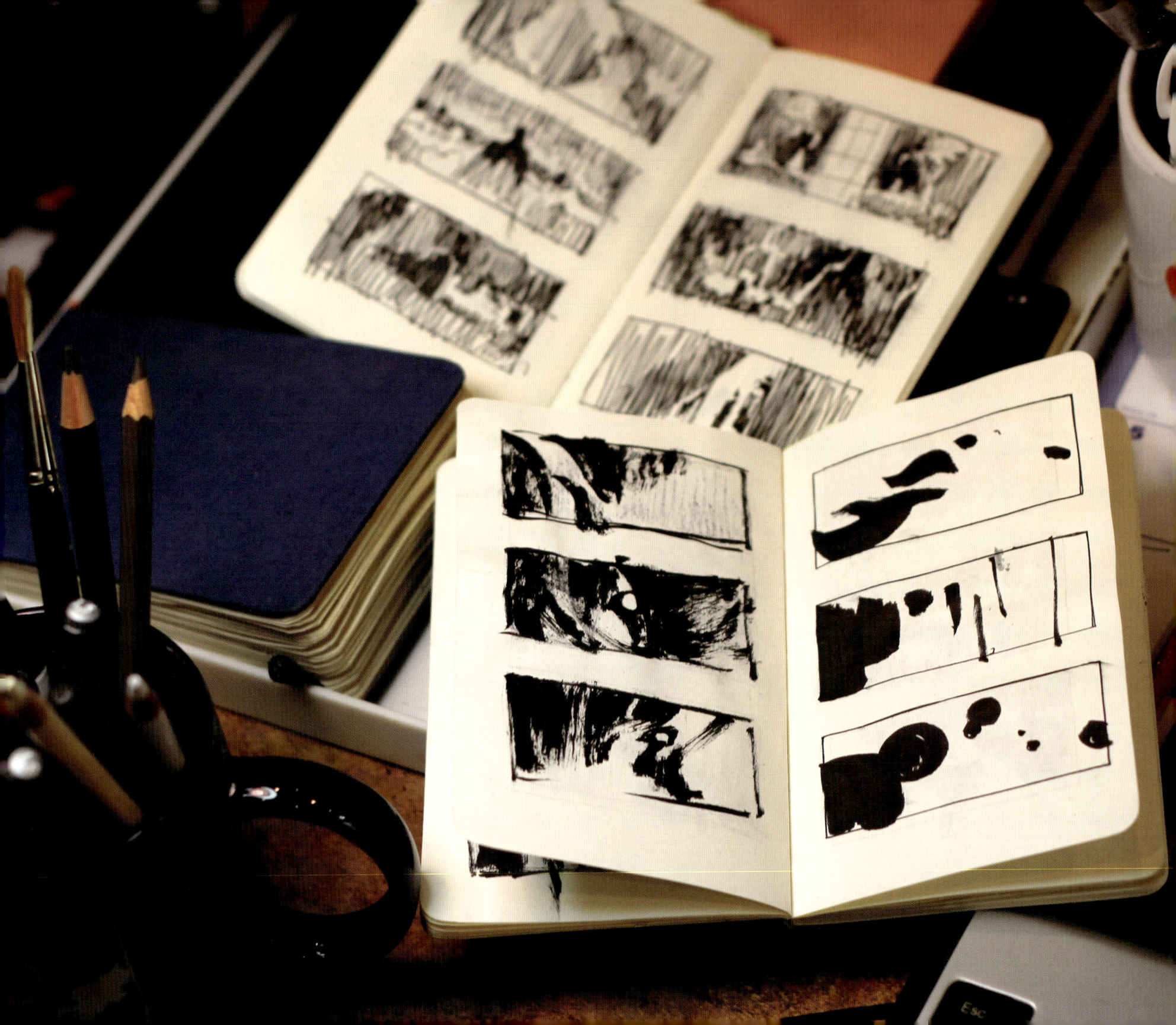

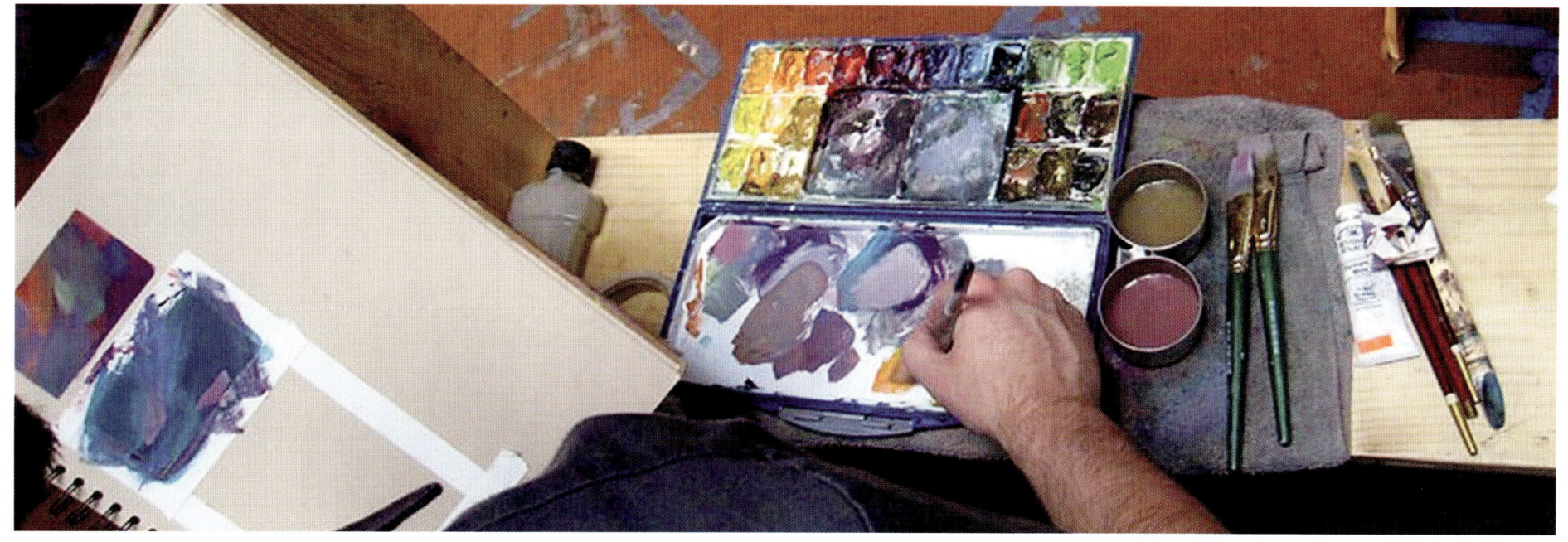

Chapter 11

Recommended Exercises

For me, painting has never come easy, nor has it come naturally; it's been a process of finding good ideas and applying them in sketch after sketch, study after study, painting after painting.

My hope is that this book has identified useful ideas and approaches for YOU, and now it's time to be sure those ideas are put into practice. This chapter is meant to refine your abilities, which will ultimately lead you to mastery. I invite you to take advantage of each of the exercises presented, they're meant to reinforce the essential principles and skills of landscape painting.

The ultimate goal is to be able to capture the immediate effects of light and atmosphere anywhere, anytime, in our sketchbooks, and that takes practice!

And don't forget the importance of organizing your tools! We've got to do whatever it takes to make the process so convenient and so enjoyable that we'll look forward to doing it in every spare moment. No excuses. Daily practice will be the thing that gives mere mortals like you and me the chance to find success as landscape painters.

"This never comes easy, or naturally, it's a process of finding good ideas and applying them in sketch after sketch, study after study, painting after painting."

Value Exercises

These value studies are based on a landscape by the artist Edgar Payne. I recommend you try this kind of exercise by doing master copies of work by artists you admire, and going out on location to do limited value studies of real places.

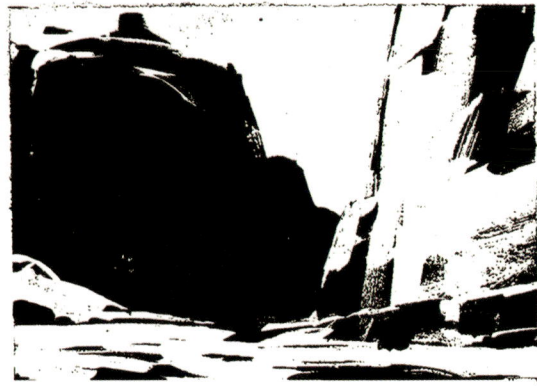

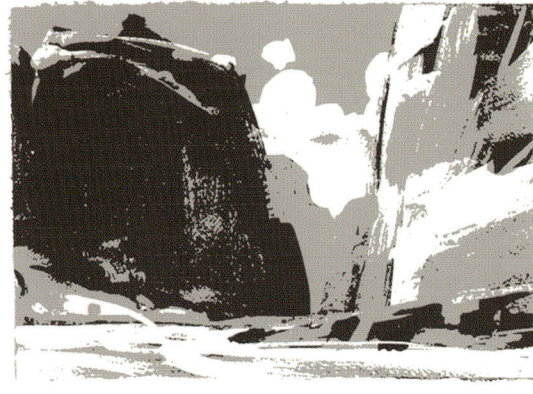

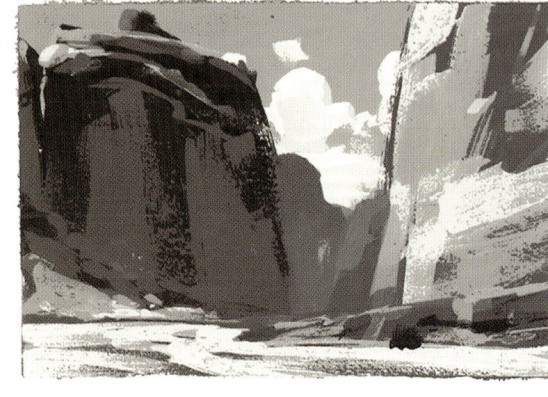

Two Values

Try doing landscape studies in two values only! You can do this with paint, but the simplicity of a black marker on paper might be even better. The exercise forces you to clearly separate light and shadow and to design shapes in an understandable way. You just might find that your full color paintings fall into place more easily after developing the discipline demanded by this two-value exercise.

Three Values

I find three-value studies even more difficult than two-value. Because, what do you do with the middle value? Is it light or is it shadow? This exercise forces us to make those difficult decisions; we can't just mindlessly render details. Keep in mind that you're not limited to black, white, and middle gray; choose which three values will best suit your subject. This is an excellent exercise, and I hope you accept the challenge, but it's an exercise only. I don't recommend it for naturalistic painting.

Four Values

You may have heard that using four values is a useful way to approach painting from life. But why would we do that? Why would we limit ourselves when nature is so beautifully complex? It's useful because it's a simple way to deal with the value limitations of our medium. Remember, our medium is not capable of reproducing the value range that we see, so the limit of four values forces us to think in terms of simple value relationships. Otherwise, it's easy to get lost in the moving target of trying to paint what we see with a medium that cannot do it.

The Simple "Why" of It

It takes a surprising amount of practice and discipline to effectively leave information out of our paintings. But to create paintings with a clear sense of purpose, it's something we must get comfortable with. For this exercise, identify what you believe to be the strongest or most interesting characteristic of a location, then do quick value studies emphasizing only that.

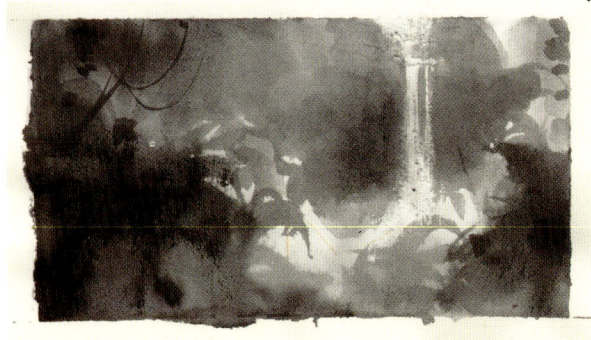

In the case of the waterfall image, I wanted the waterfall itself to stand out most prominently, then the suggestion of jungle foliage in the foreground. Notice that contrast is limited to those two areas, everything else is quite simple, and grouped in value.

In this sketch of a creek at sunset, it was the light reflecting on the water that I found most engaging. Even though the sketch suggests many layers of landscape to create the depth of the place, all those areas are simply grouped in value so the light reflections will pop in contrast to the land.

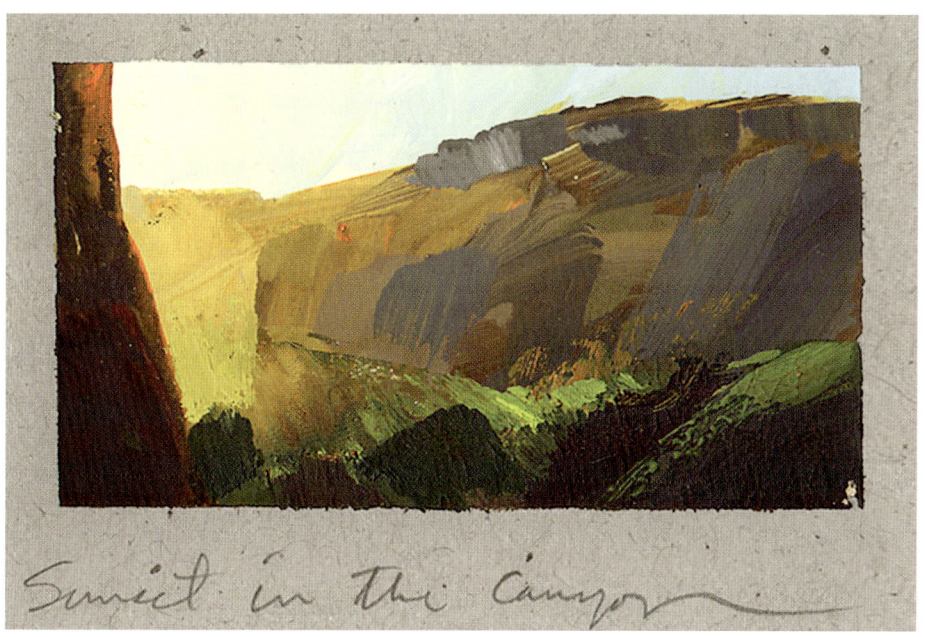

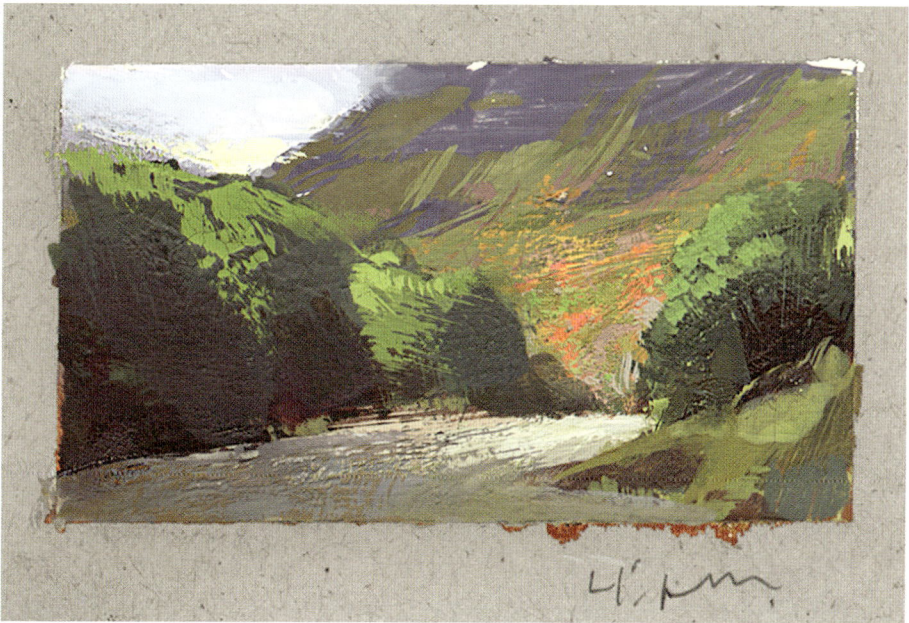

Finding Texture and Losing Edges

We have a real tendency to render landscapes as a bunch of individual objects, but if you study the great landscape painters, they are very much in the habit of using "lost and found" to give a purposeful quality to their paintings. They refine their subject by using texture to create contrast where needed, and lost edges to reduce it elsewhere.

Take a look at the two quick sketches above and notice how often one shape disappears into another; this allows the areas of greater texture and contrast to become even more special. Give this a try! In fact, practice doing it over and over. You'll find that the common saying of "less is more" can really be true!

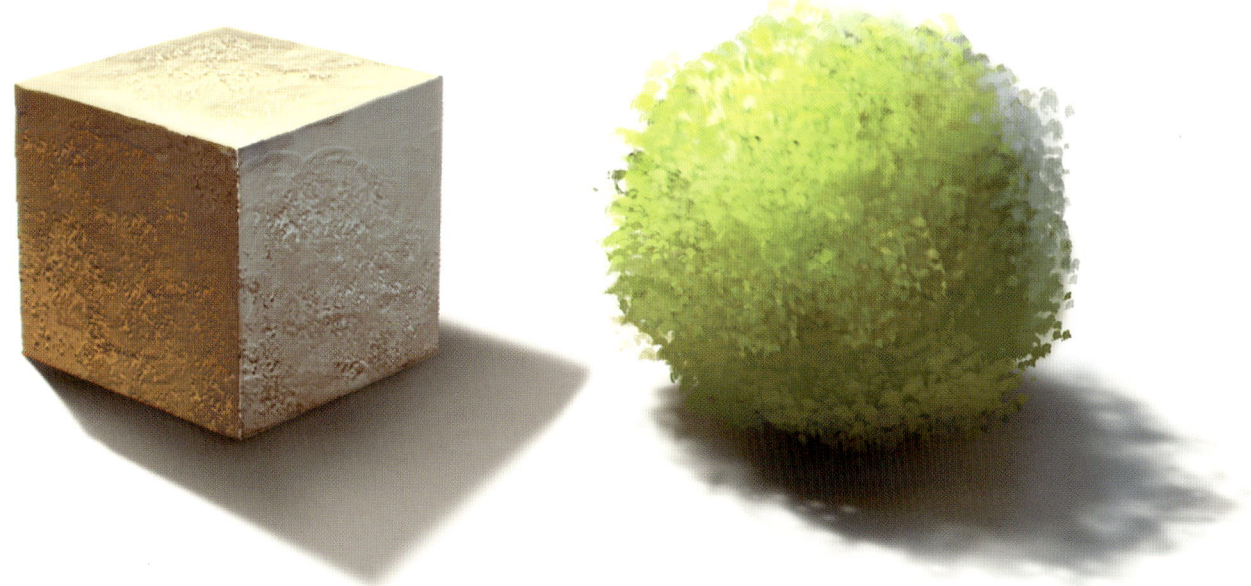

Emphasizing Form

Our flat sketchbook page has no form, but our subject does. To compensate, we often need to emphasize and even exaggerate the three-dimensional nature of our subject. Get outside and paint a tree or a bush and treat it as a simple sphere. Find a rocky outcropping and carefully treat it three-dimensionally, with a top plane, front plane, and side plane. You may be surprised at how your sketches leap off the page!

Color Exercises

Color is complicated, but we can learn to manage it. For this exercise, pick three colors that are equally distant from each other on the color wheel. In the example here I'm using green, purple, and orange. Go ahead and put the colors side by side and notice how "loud" and contrasting they are. Next, mix all three together to get a gray green, gray purple, and a brown.

They become quite dull, but if you put them side by side, they bring each other to life, becoming rich and vibrant without becoming sugary and loud. (Some white is also used to mix colors in the abstract image.) Consider putting down a single stroke of a more saturated color for a unique bit of contrast. This is the effect of unity with variety; much of nature is a rich combination of neutral hues with occasional accents of saturation.

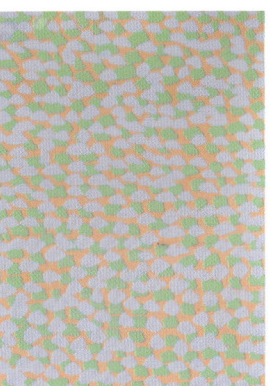

Optical Gray

Now take the original three colors and add white to each until they are all the same value, then dot them side by side so they are evenly and equally represented. The goal here is that when you step back, they optically mix to become a gray. But it's much more than a flat gray can ever be, it vibrates with luminosity and can mimic the vibrancy of light and atmosphere. This simultaneous contrast of color was the breakthrough of the Impressionists, so congratulations, you are now an Impressionist!

Hue and Saturation

I've noticed that students most frequently default to using value for contrast, but that's only one third of our palette, hue and saturation are not to be left out. So try this exercise: blend together colors that have contrast of hue and saturation in any way that you find interesting. As you work, make sure that your pigments have very little value contrast. This will help you get comfortable with the full possibilities of your pigments. With practice, these little abstractions can help give you a big mastery of hue and saturation relationships.

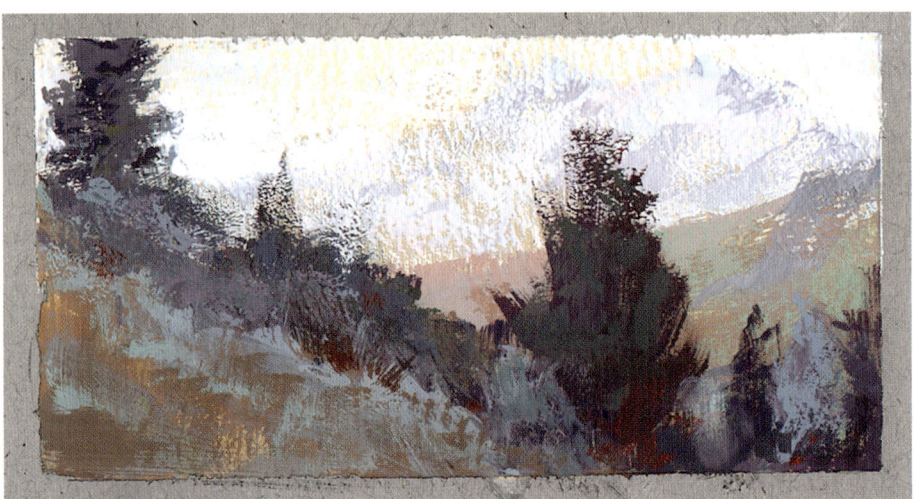

Putting It into Practice

Here's a quick sketch in the mountains of Utah. The place was colorful, luminous, and atmospheric. To meet the challenge in the time available, I used all of the ideas mentioned on this page with the technique of drybrushing. Colors are laid over the top of each other to create the optical effect of luminous atmosphere, and the colorful variety of earth and foliage in the foreground.

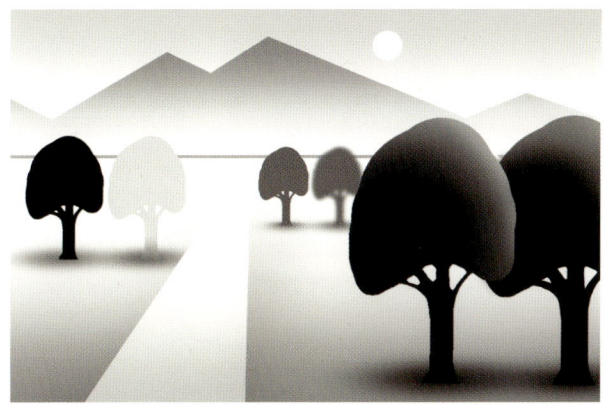

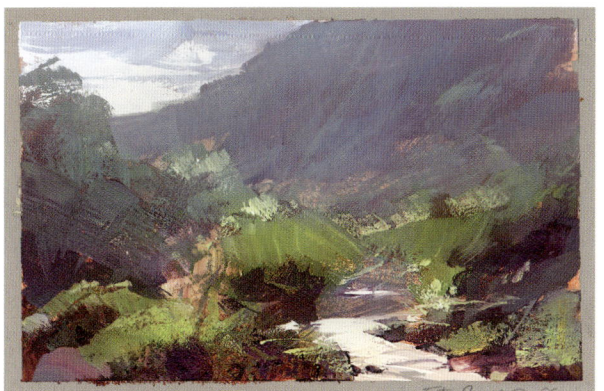

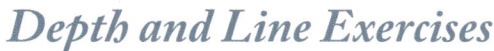

Depth and Line Exercises

We've learned that one of the great challenges of landscape sketching is representing the vast, three-dimensional depth of a landscape on a two-dimensional sketchbook page. To meet the challenge, we need to emphasize and even exaggerate depth cues in our paintings. In the above image, depth is created by basic graphic devices, including perspective, overlap, value contrast, edge contrast, and shadows. Go out and find yourself a wide-open stretch of landscape and practice emphasizing these ideas!

Here's a painterly approach that uses many of the same ideas, with the addition of color temperature and texture. Notice that I have much warmer colors in the foreground, and cooler, more neutral colors in the background. Textures are also dramatized in the foreground and ignored in the distant background. These elements really existed on location but are highly exaggerated in the sketch; it's another case of telling a few white lies to get to a greater truth.

I'm always jotting down little landscapes and ideas. Despite the simplicity of these sketches, I hope for them to carry some emotion. I know I can always count on the simple design of line— calm horizontals, stable verticals, and dynamic diagonals—to do the job.

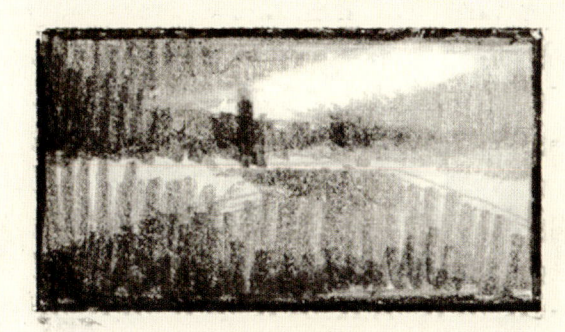

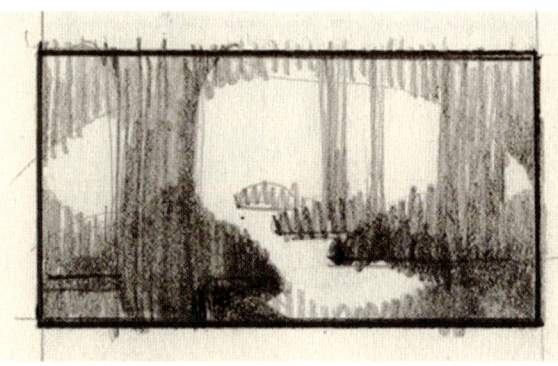

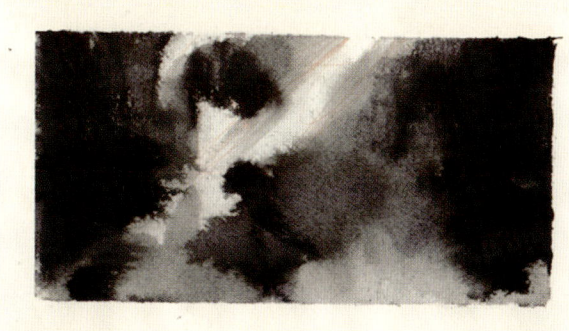

"A sketch a day, five or six days a week, adds up to nearly 300 paintings a year. And if you take a little extra time to find solutions for the paintings that went badly, think of how skillful you'll become after just one year!"

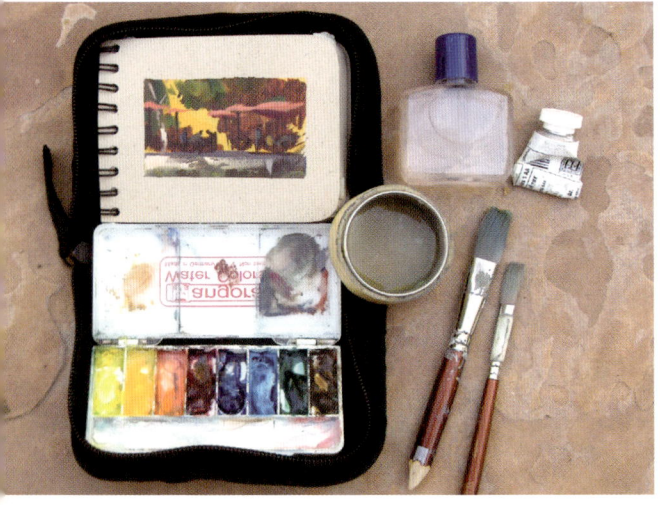
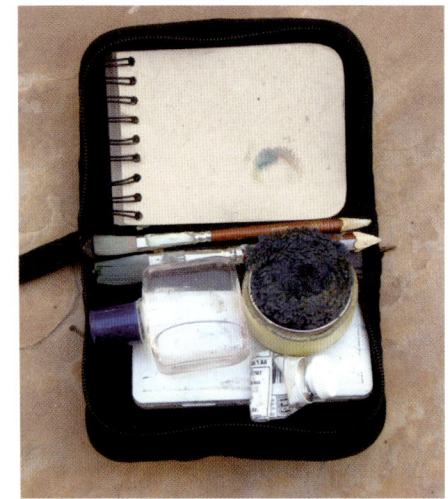
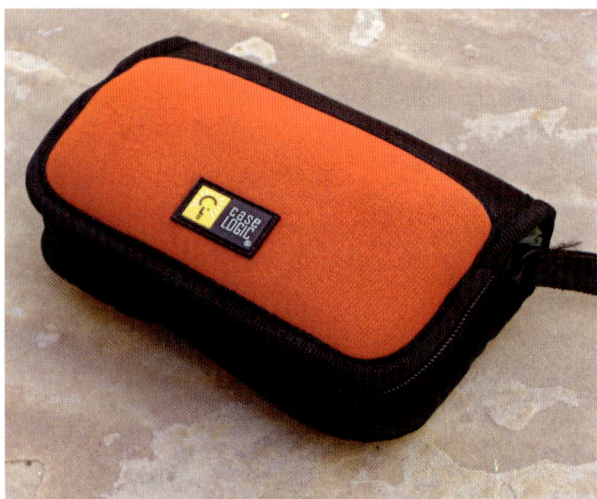

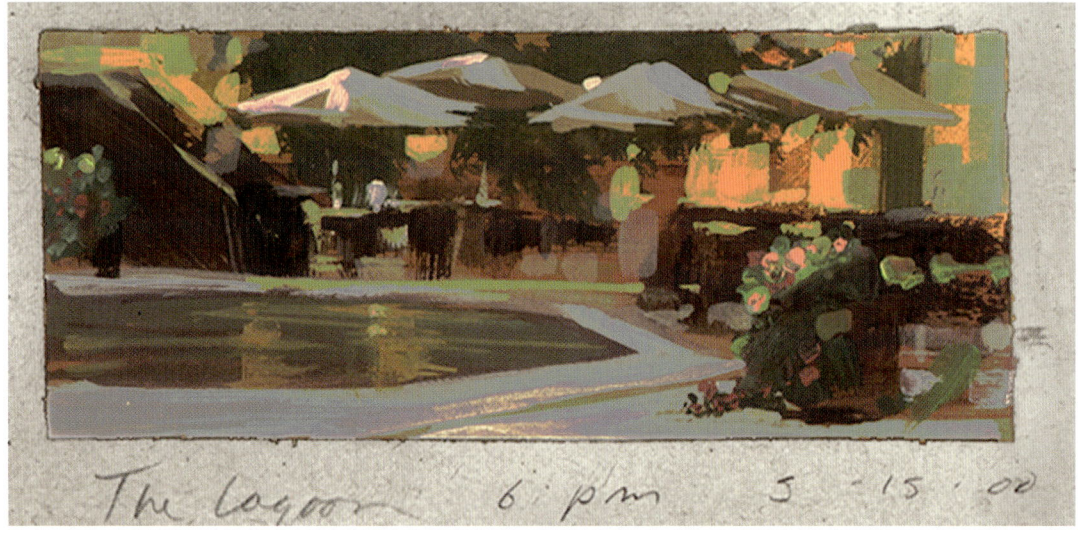

The Lagoon   6 pm   J - 15 - 00

The Lunchtime Challenge!

No doubt you're very busy. You have a job, family obligations, and innumerable other responsibilities, it's tough to get out and paint! Can you put together a handy little kit like this and get a sketch in every day at lunchtime? I know that you can! A sketch a day, five or six days a week, adds up to nearly 300 paintings a year. And if you take a little time in the evening to find solutions for the paintings that went badly, think of how skillful you'll become after just one year!

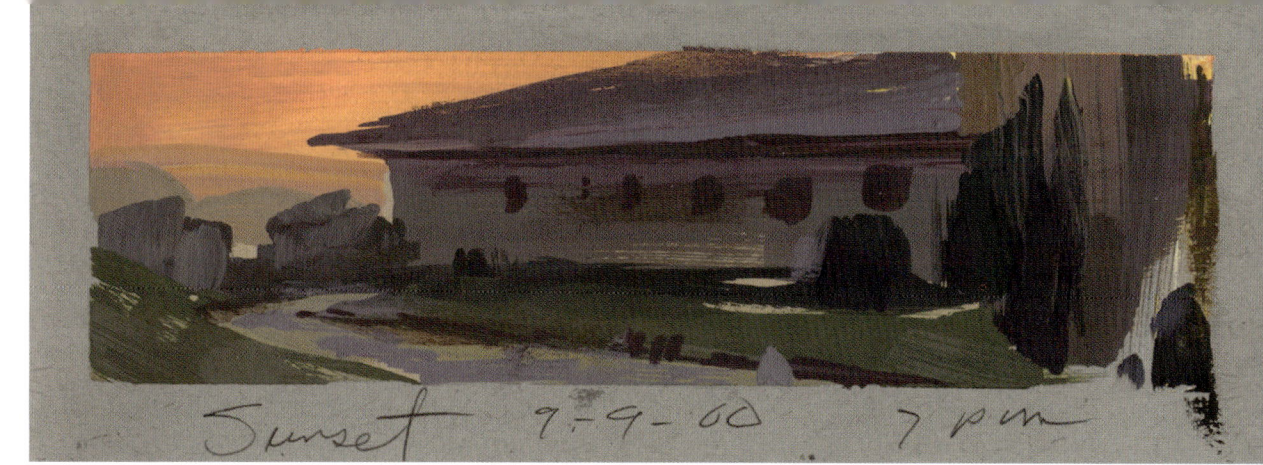

Sunset 9-9-00 7 pm

End-of-Day Challenge

If you miss your lunchtime sketch, no worries, sunset just might be the best time of all for a sketch! It has a built-in time limit, and forces you to make the tough, on-the-go decisions that a good landscape painter must. And sunset often has beautiful color and value contrast; so lots of practice with color and value relationships means that you're a master artist in training!

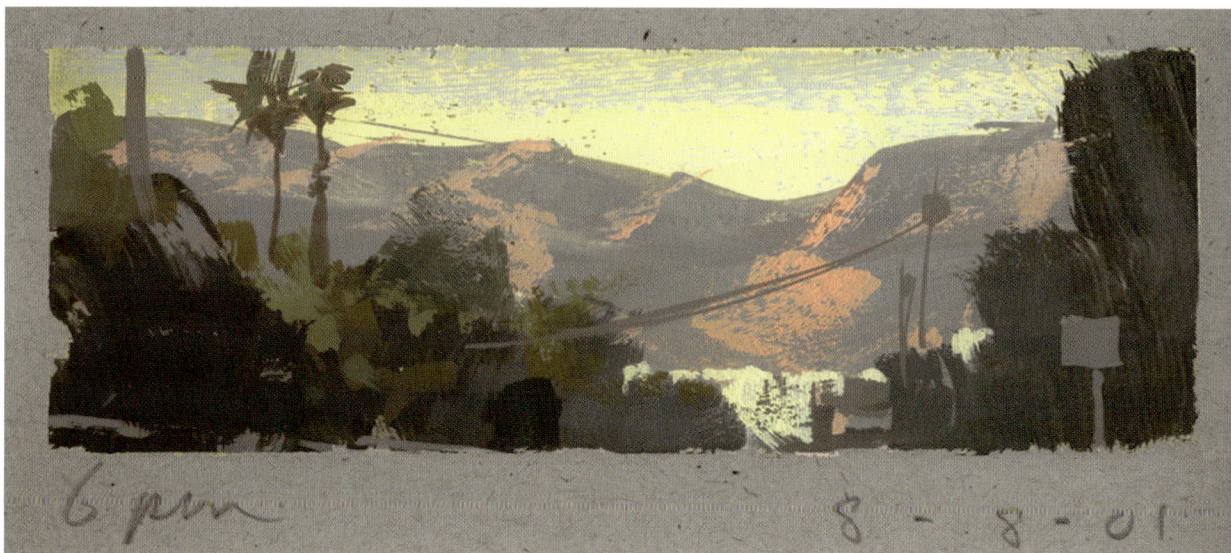

6 pm   8 - 8 - 01

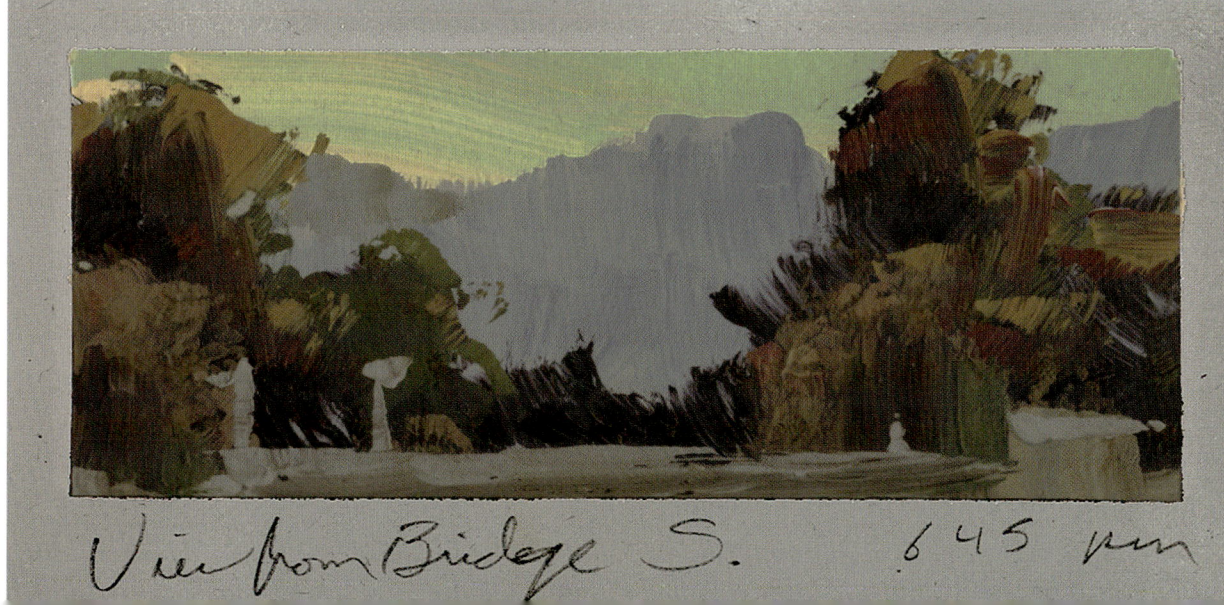

View from Bridge S.   6 45 pm

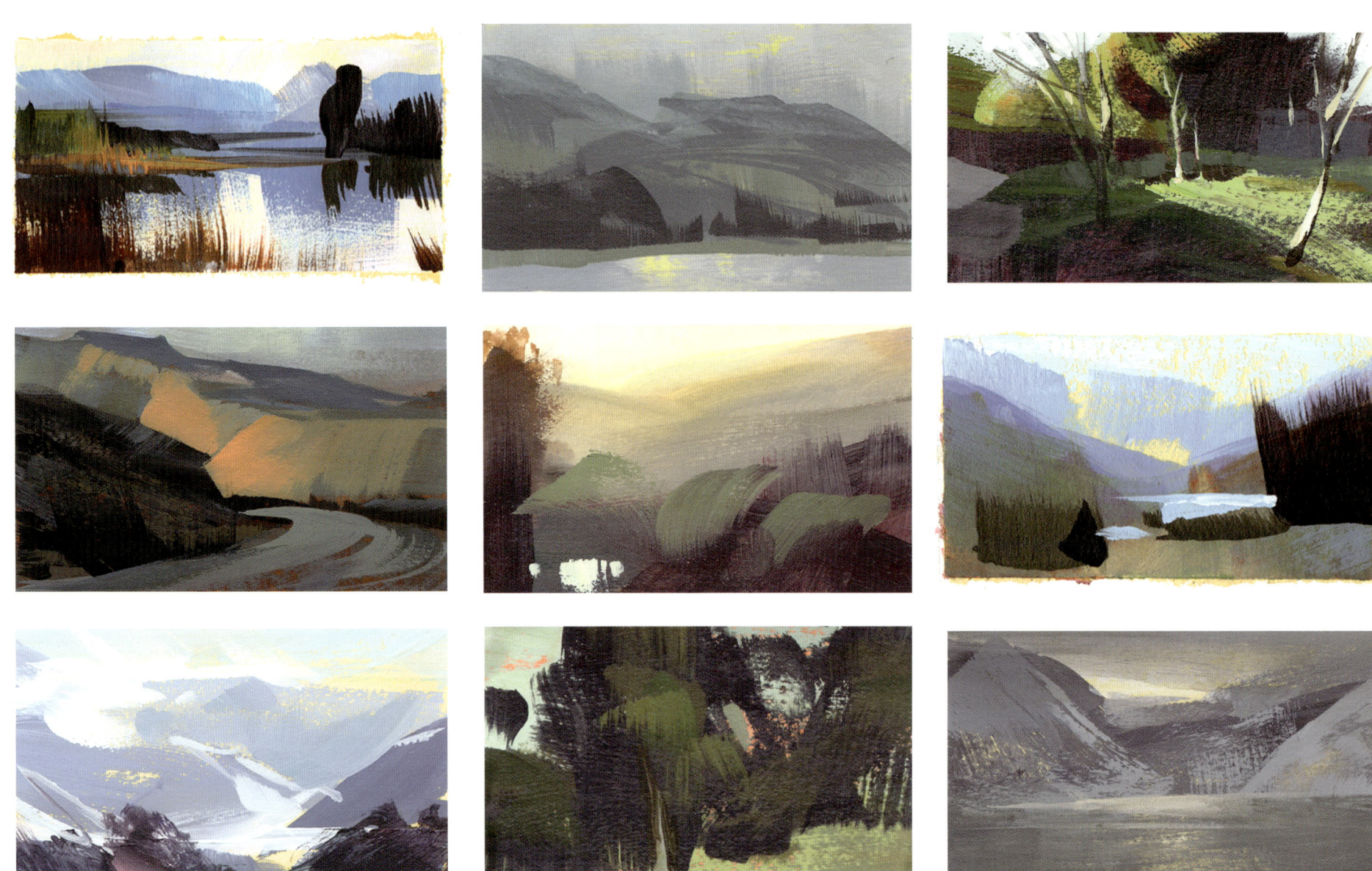

The 20-Stroke Challenge

Most everyone is familiar with the idea of quick, gestural drawings of the human figure as an exercise, so I'm surprised that few art students practice landscape painting the same way. I encourage my students to take on the 20-stroke challenge as an exercise.

Each of the sketches here is limited to roughly 20 strokes; every stroke must be carefully designed to contribute to the overall simple statement. Each must have the right value, hue, saturation, shape, and edge. It's an exercise that is challenging and instructive for the on-location painter.

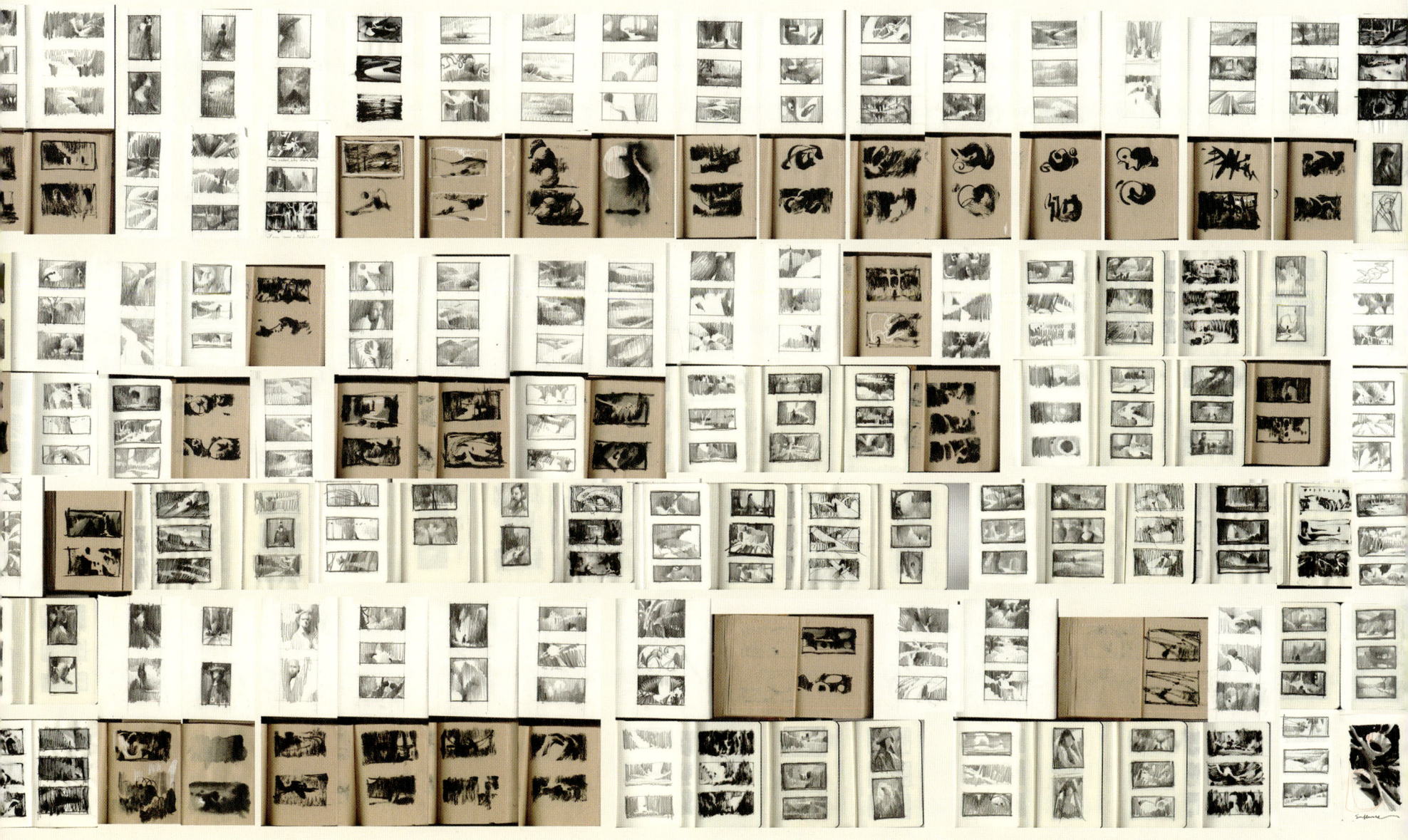

Sketch, Sketch, Sketch!

I keep insisting on a great deal of practice, at the same time, I understand that constantly setting up and taking down a paint kit is not always feasible. But a slim, soft-cover sketchbook and a pencil is! I usually have one in my pocket, in my car, at my desk; anywhere I spend time, I have a sketchbook sitting there.

The sketches shown here are done from life, from imagination, and from images I admire. I consider these kinds of five-minute sketches a great luxury, the stakes are not so high that any one of them can turn into a devastating failure. When all else fails, even one such sketch a day is valuable. They may not be significant works, but the habit of daily sketching is reinforced and the dream lives on!

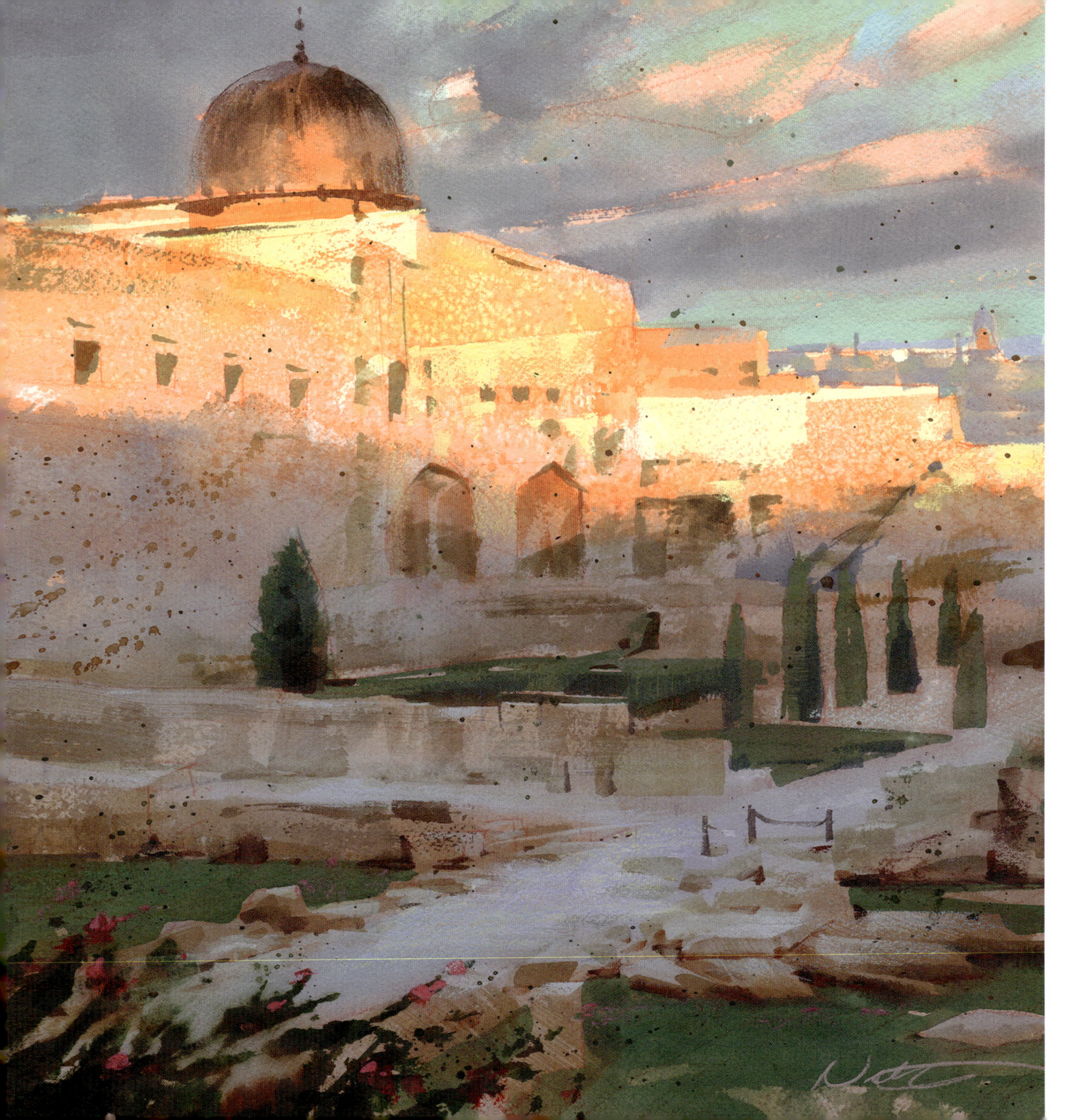

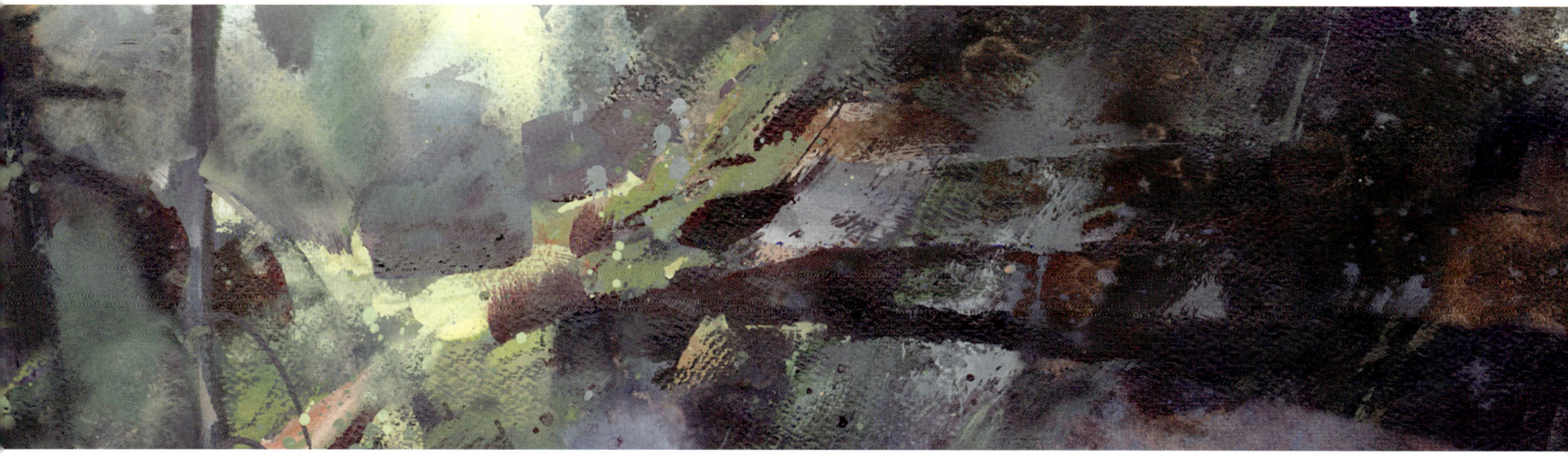

Chapter 12

Gallery of Paintings

Our sketches and paintings attempt to make permanent the meaningful but transitional quality of each place we visit, and we can take great pride in the undertaking of this endeavor. For me, a simple painting kit and a handful of simple principles has turned every place I visit into a potential painting. On these final pages, I'd like to share with you the rest of the places I've had a chance to visit and my attempts to capture them in paint.

"Our sketches and paintings attempt to make permanent the meaningful but transitional quality of each place we visit; and we can take great pride in the undertaking of this very difficult endeavor."

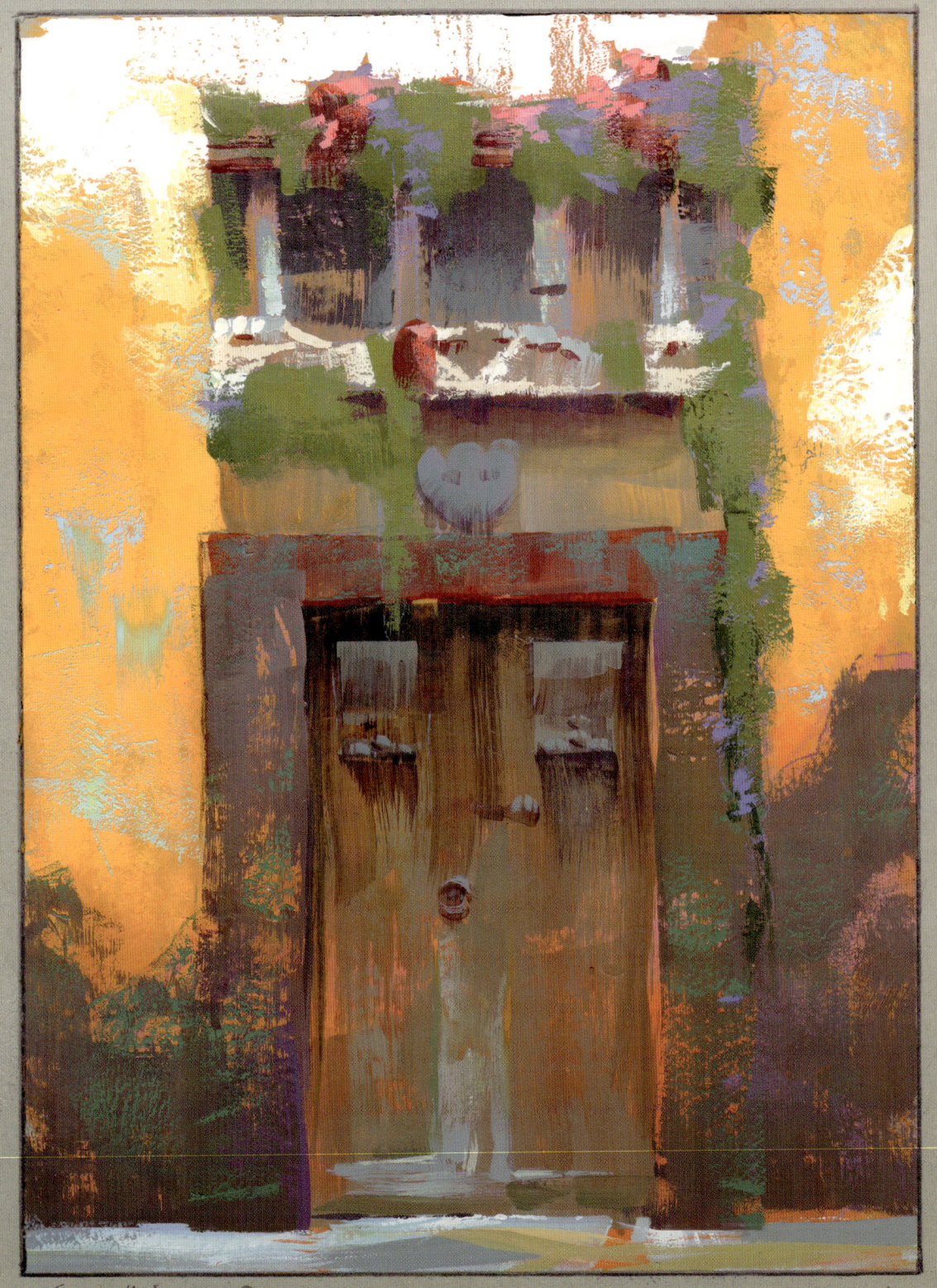

San Miguel Doorway, Mexico

N. Forbes '17

San Miguel de Allende, Mexico; watercolor and white gouache on toned mixed-media paper, 16 x 12 inches

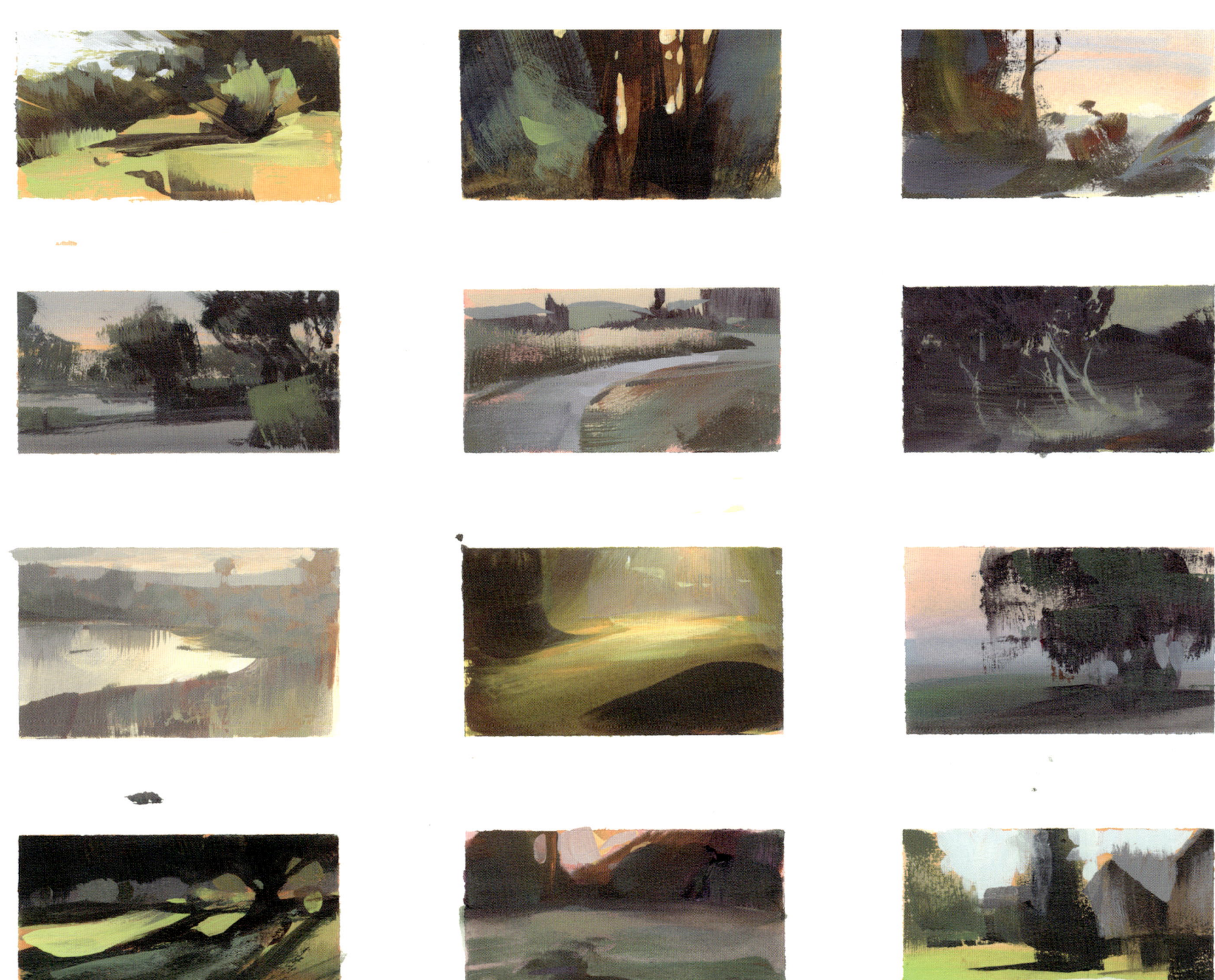

Northern California sketches; watercolor and white gouache on a single page of Crescent No. 100 illustration board, 15 x 20 inches

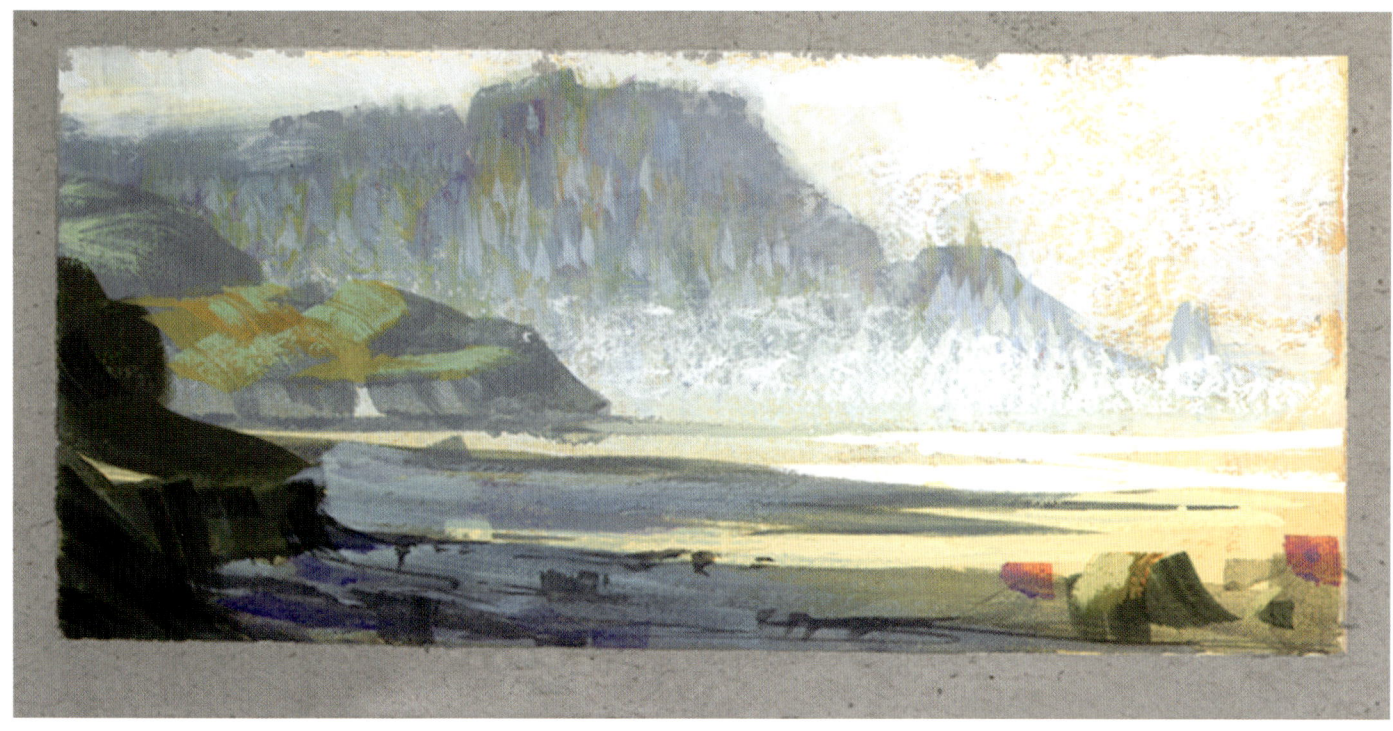

Central California coastline; water-color and white gouache on toned mixed-media paper, 4 x 7 inches

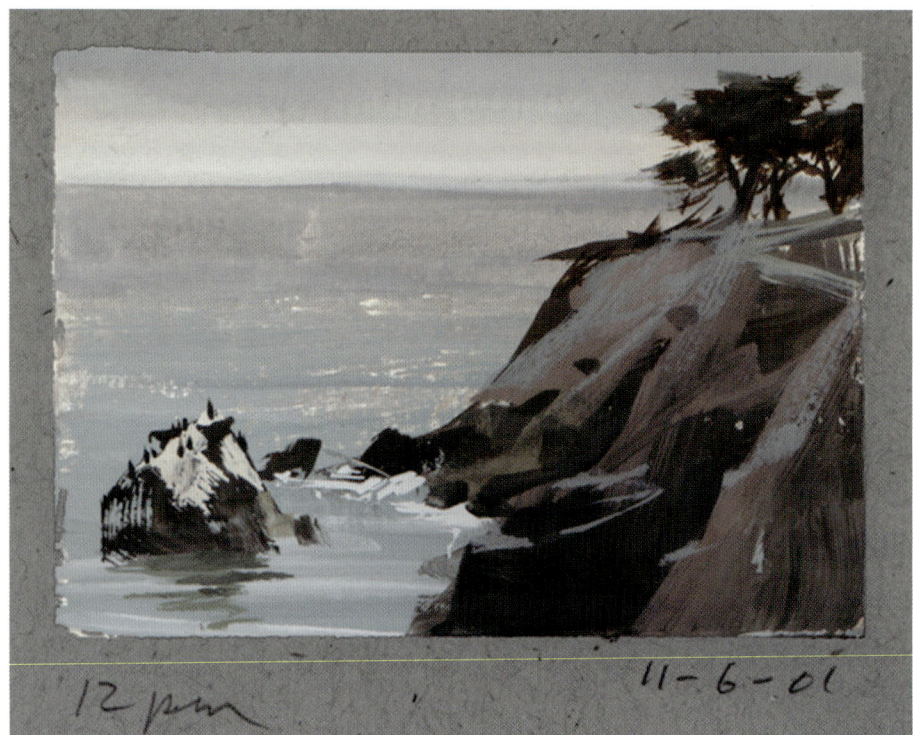

San Simeon, California; watercolor and white gouache on toned mixed-media paper, 4 x 6 inches

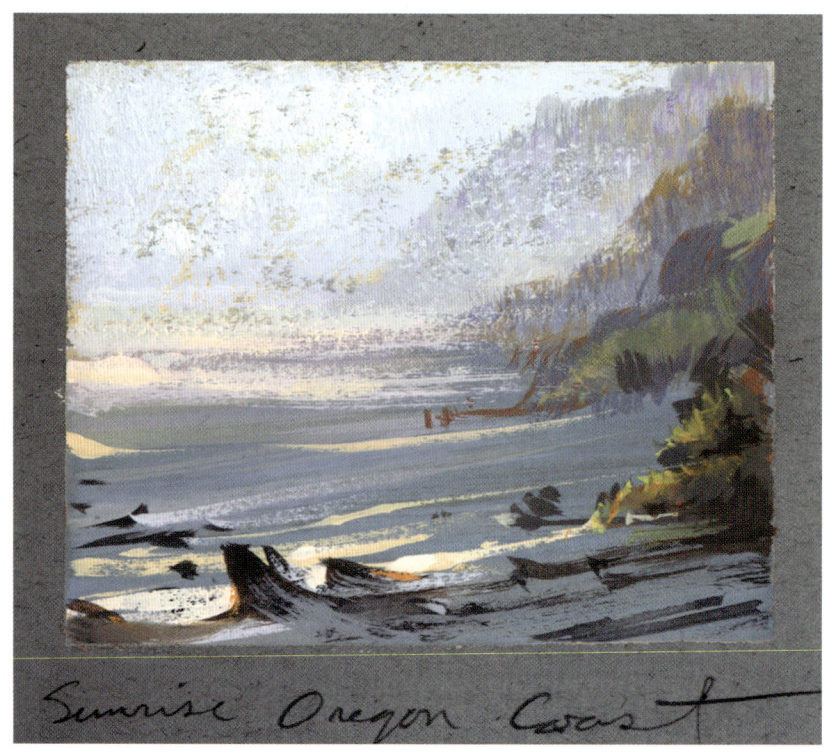

Oregon coast; watercolor and white gouache on toned mixed-media paper, 4 x 5 inches

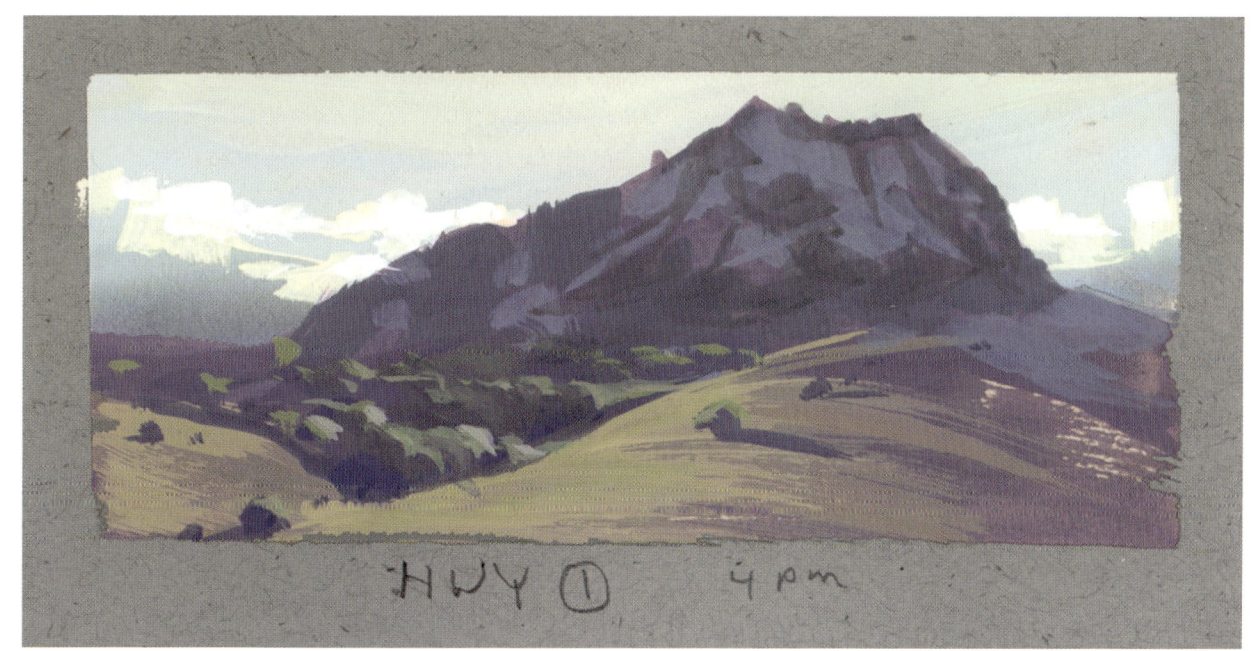

Highway 1, Central California coast; watercolor and white gouache on toned mixed-media paper, 3 x 6 inches

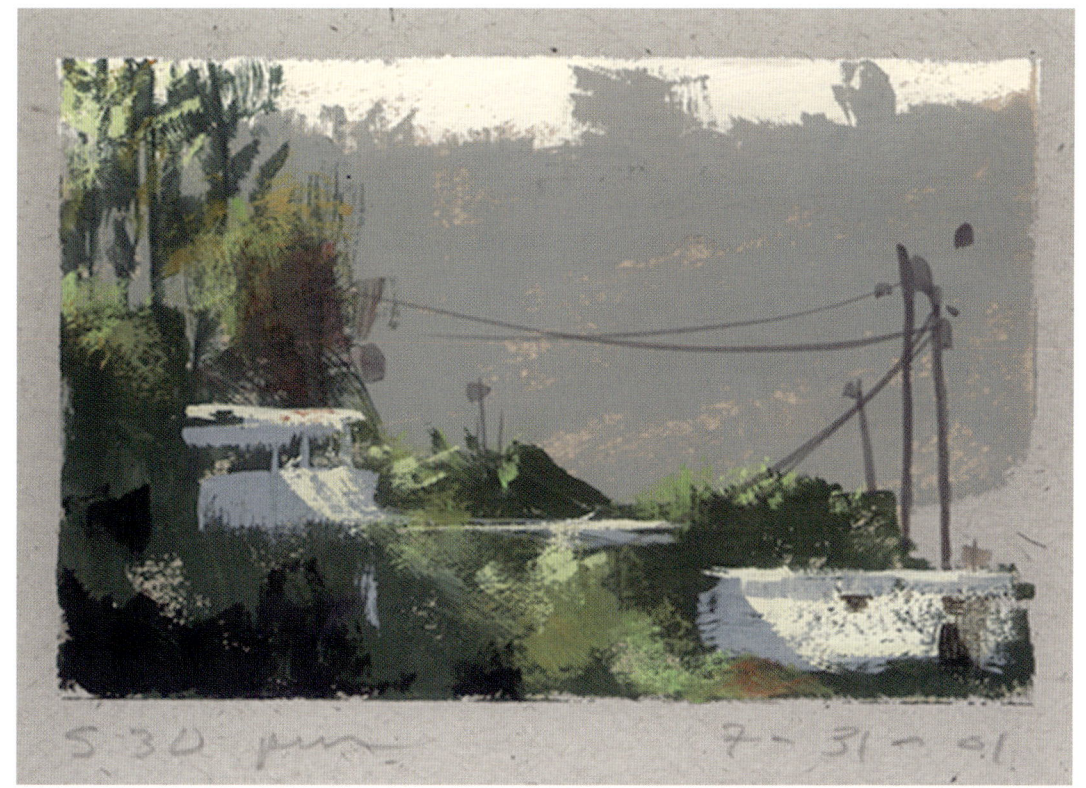

Hollywood Hills, California; watercolor and white gouache on toned mixed-media paper, 3 x 5 inches

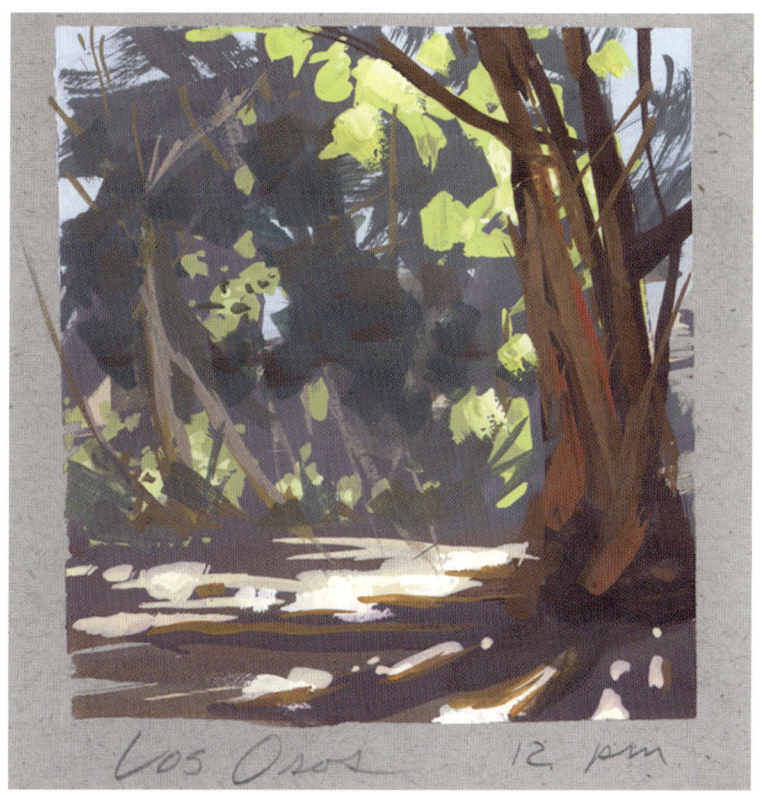

Los Osos tree, California; watercolor and white gouache on toned mixed-media paper, 5 x 3 inches

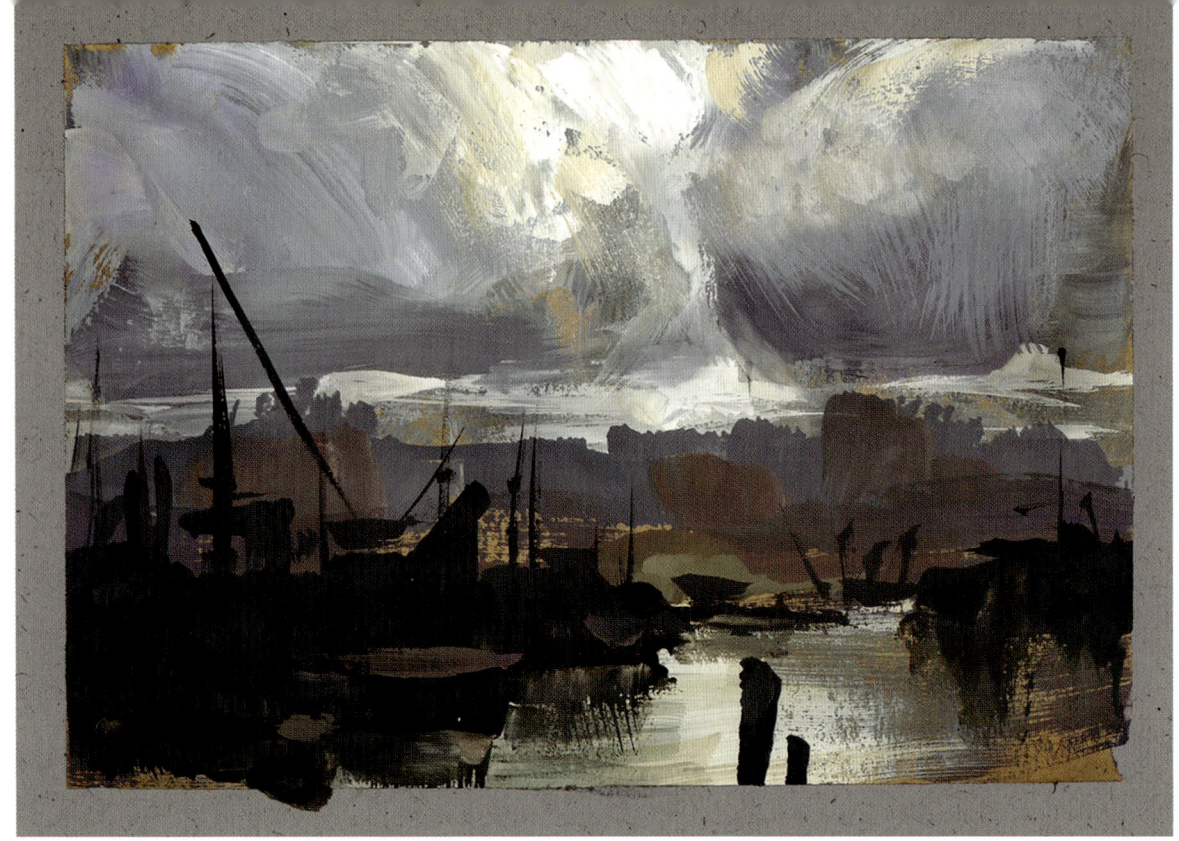

San Francisco harbor, San Francisco County, California; watercolor and white gouache on toned mixed-media paper, 3 x 5 inches

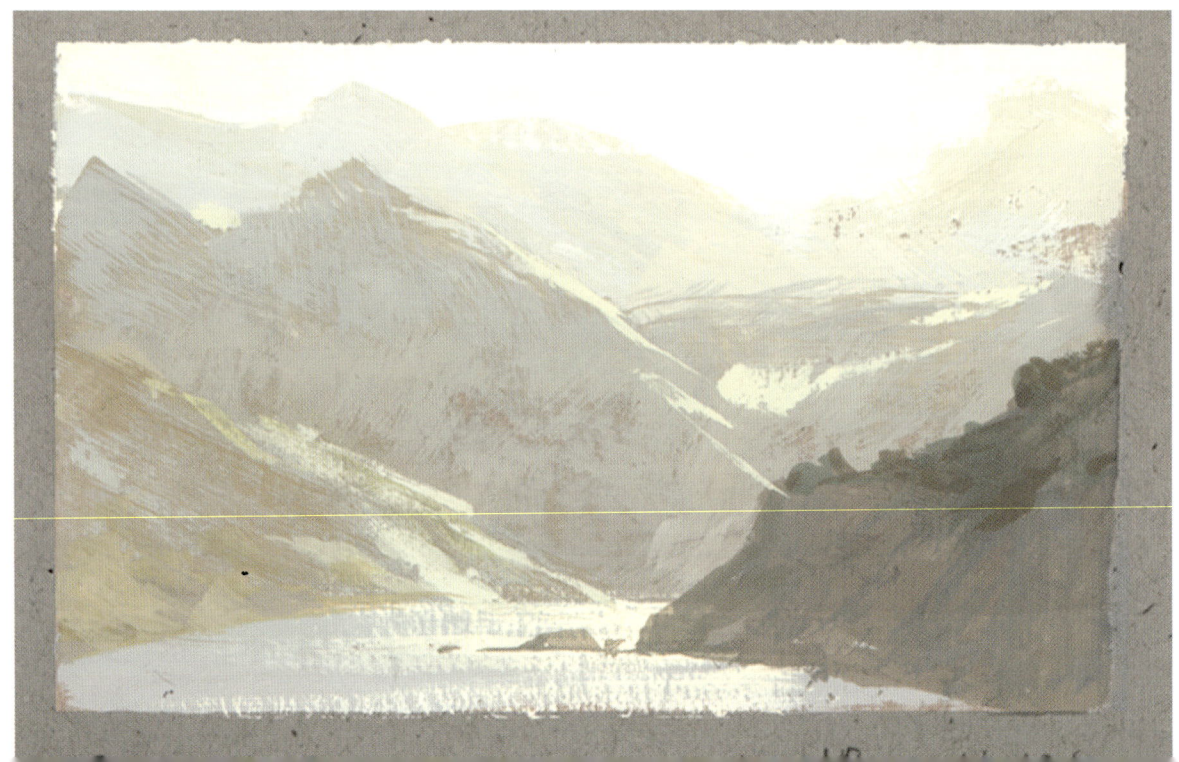

Pyramid Lake, Los Angeles County, California; watercolor and white gouache on toned mixed-media paper, 3 x 5 inches

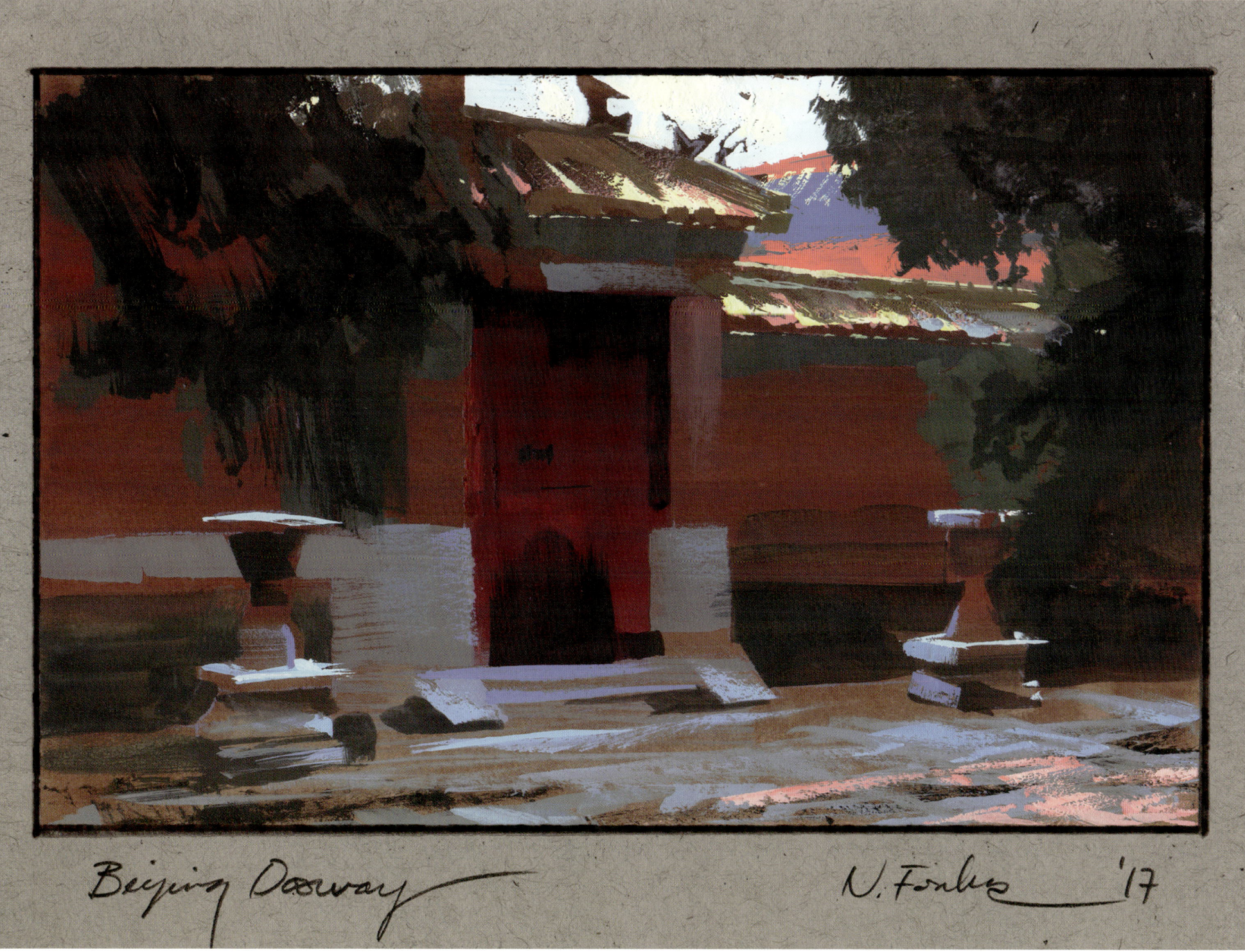

Beijing doorway, China; watercolor and white gouache on toned mixed-media paper, 9 x 12 inches

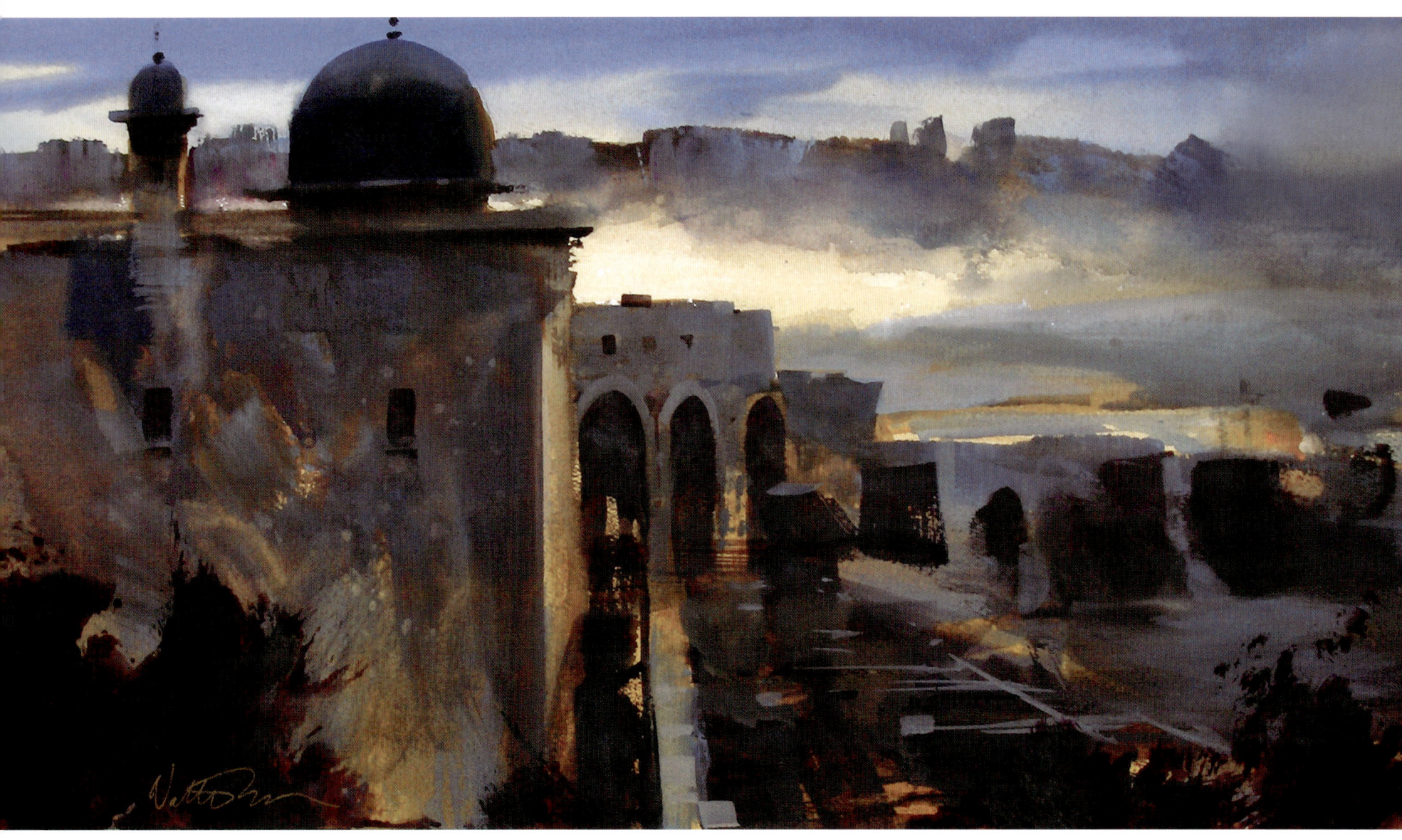

Old City, Jerusalem, Israel; watercolor on Arches cold-pressed paper, 12 x 18 inches

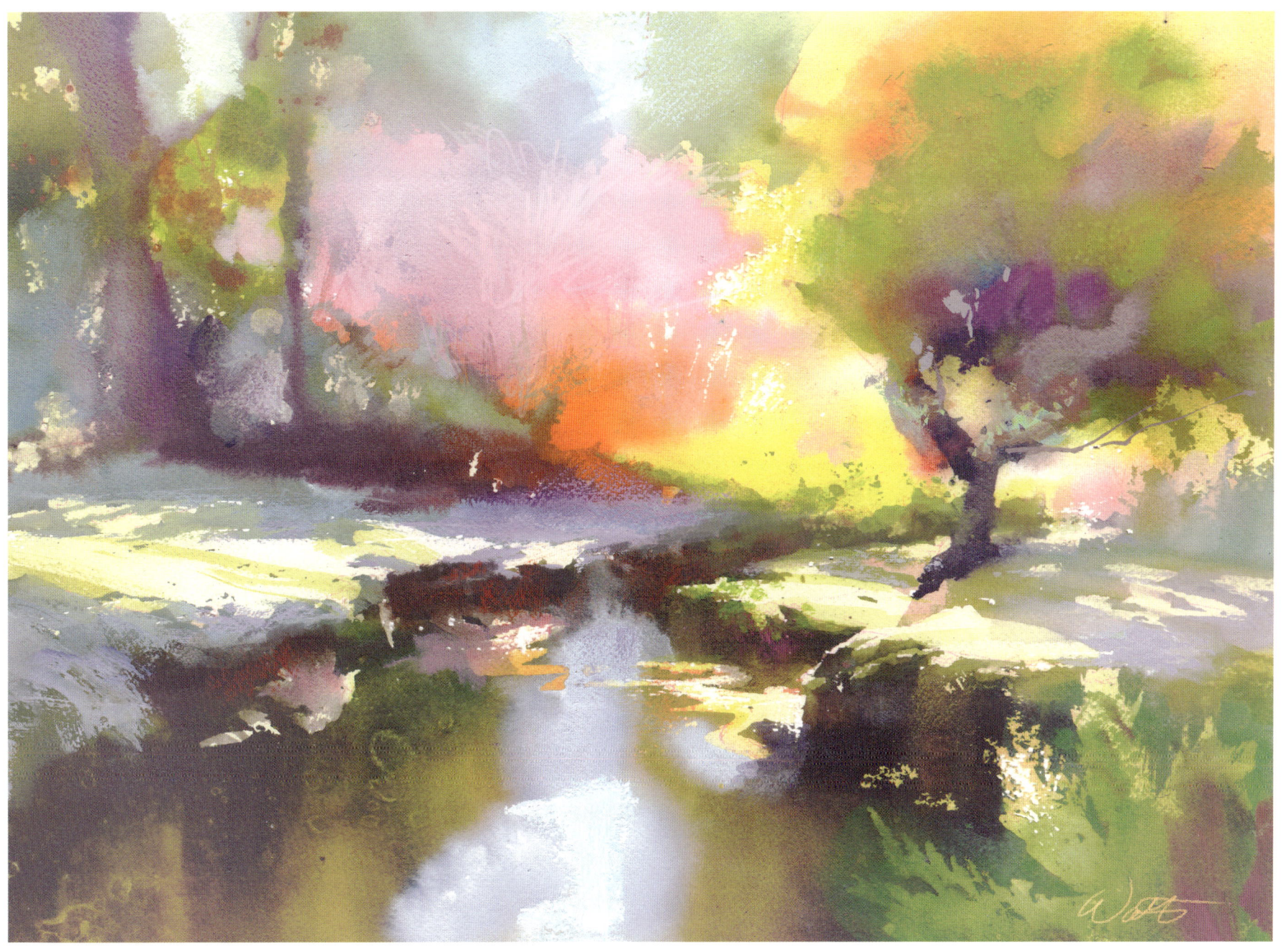

Descanso Gardens Stream, La Cañada, California; watercolor and white gouache on Arches cold pressed paper, 12 x 16 inches

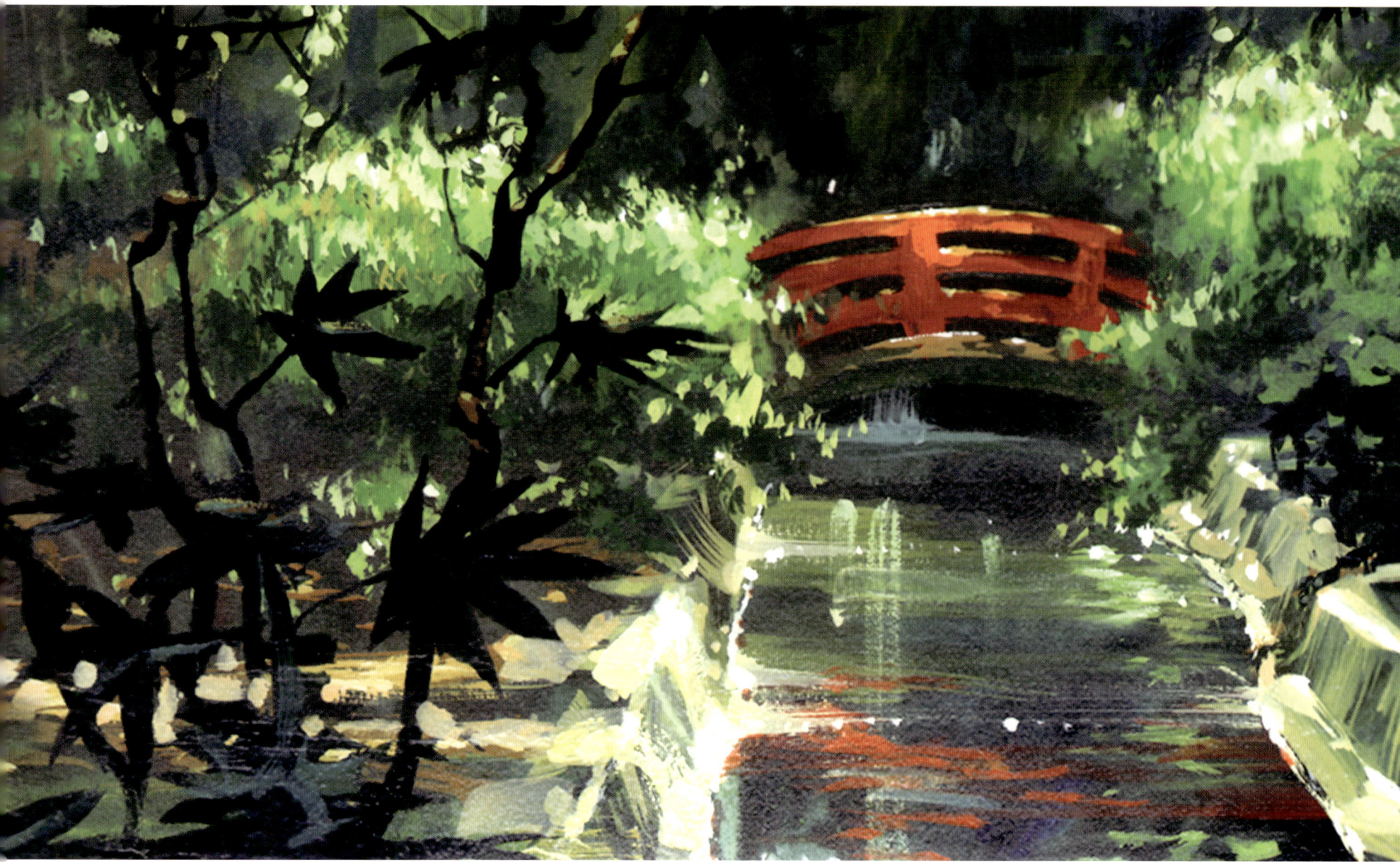

Descanso Gardens, La Cañada Flintridge, California; watercolor and white gouache on Crescent No. 100 illustration board, 6 x 9 inches

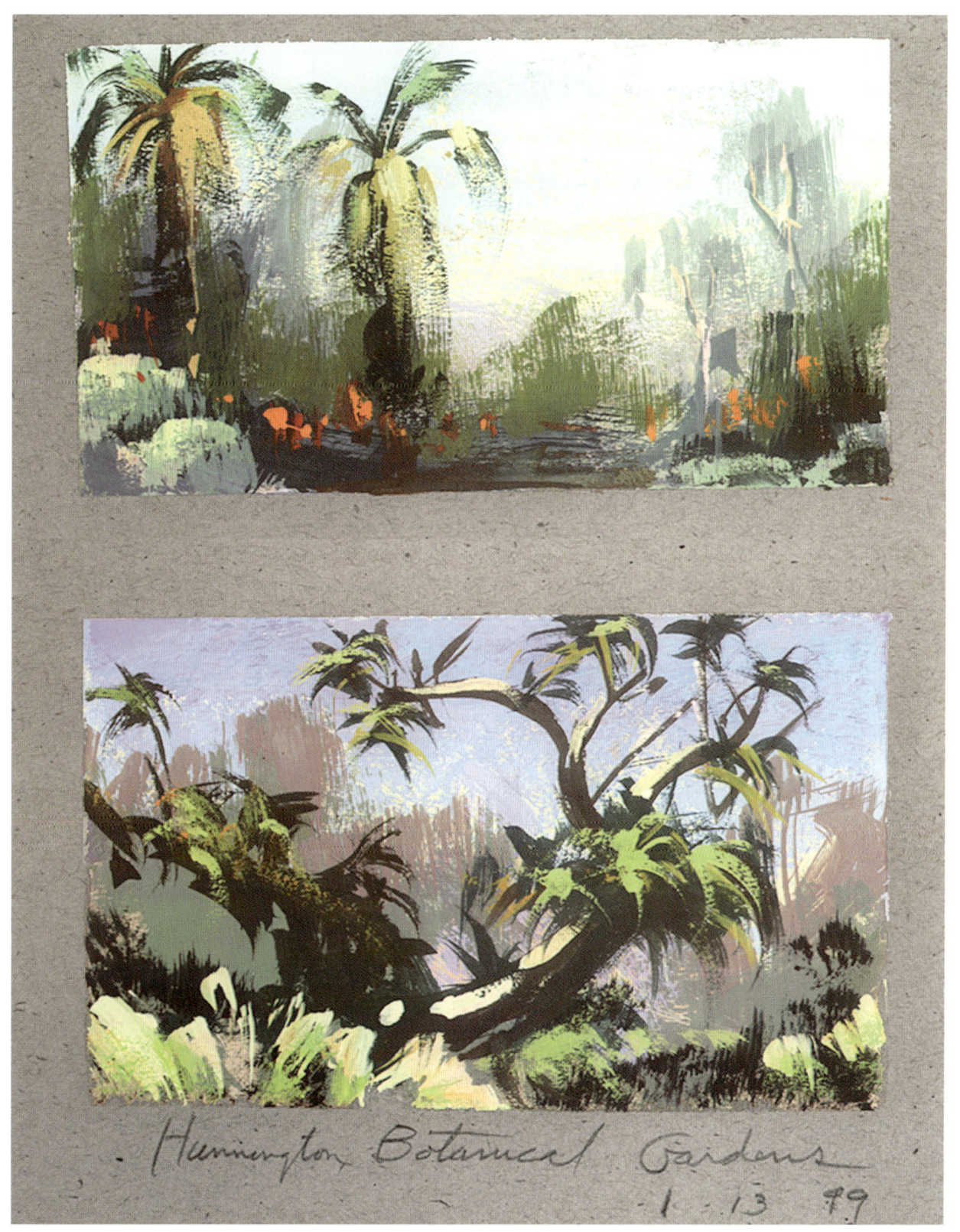

The Huntington Gardens, San Marino, California; sketchbook page, watercolor and white gouache on toned mixed-media paper, 9 x 5 inches

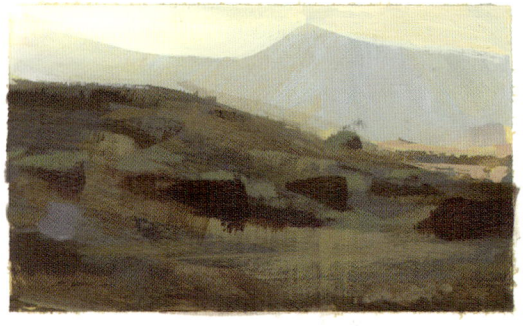
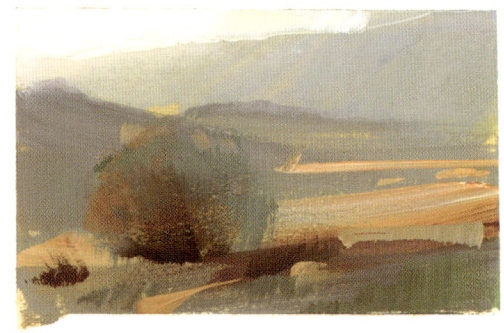
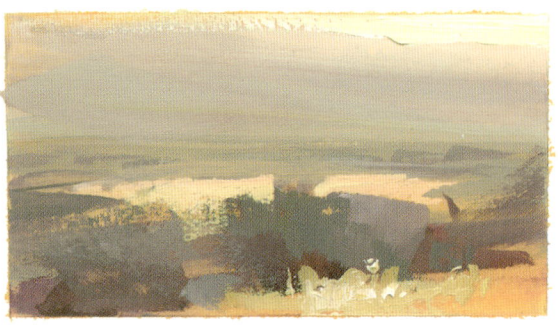
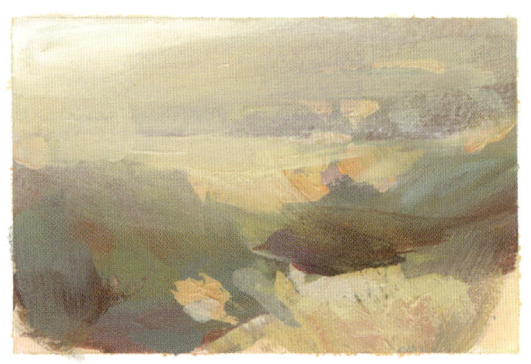
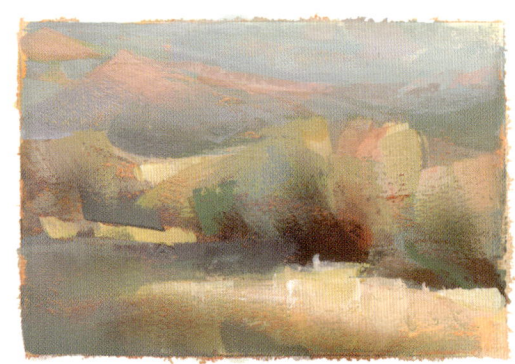

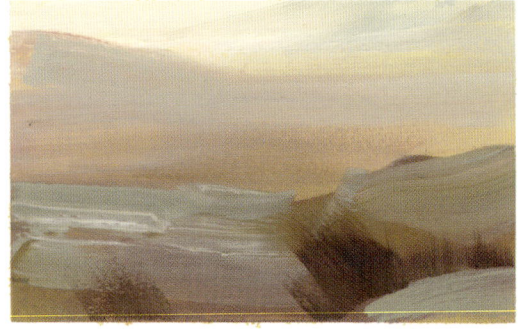
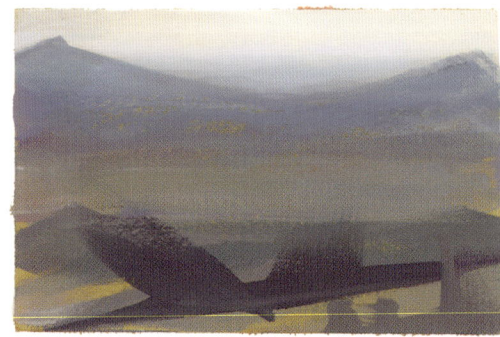
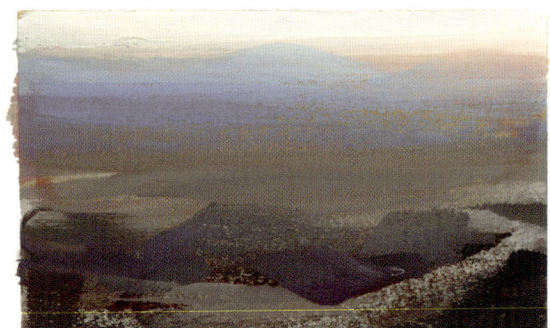

Central California sketches; painted on a single page of Crescent No. 100 illustration board, 15 x 20 inches

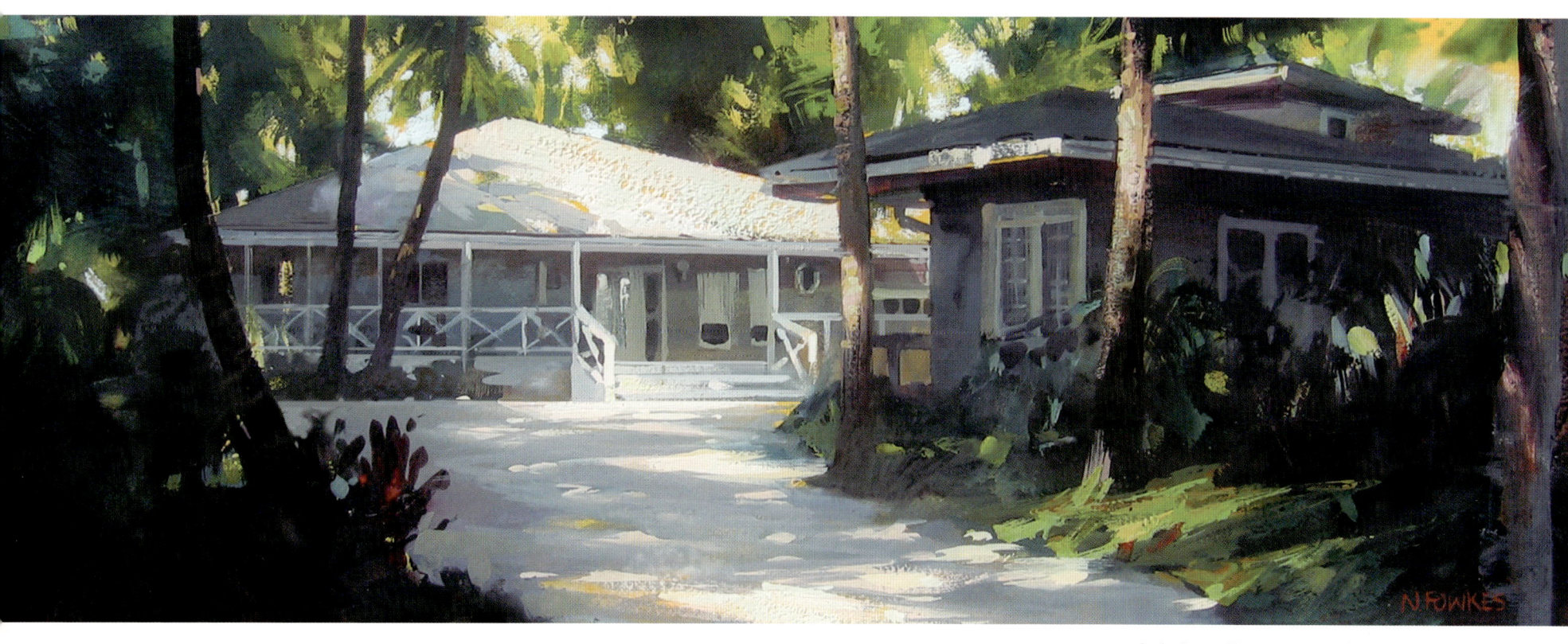

Oahu house, Hawaii; watercolor and white gouache on Crescent No. 100 illustration board, 8 x 18 inches

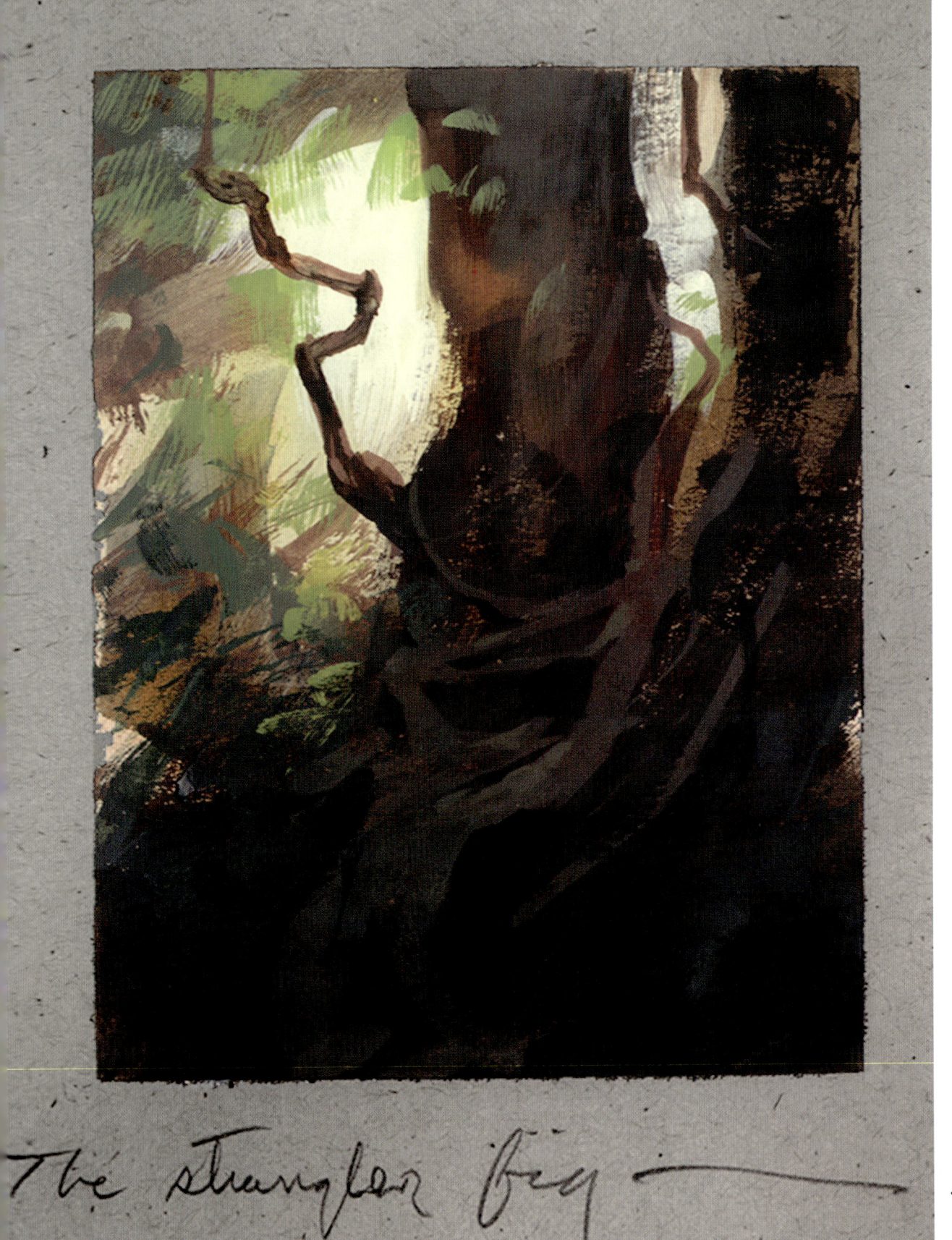

The strangler fig

Strangler fig, Costa Rica; watercolor and white gouache on toned mixed–media paper, 6 x 4 inches

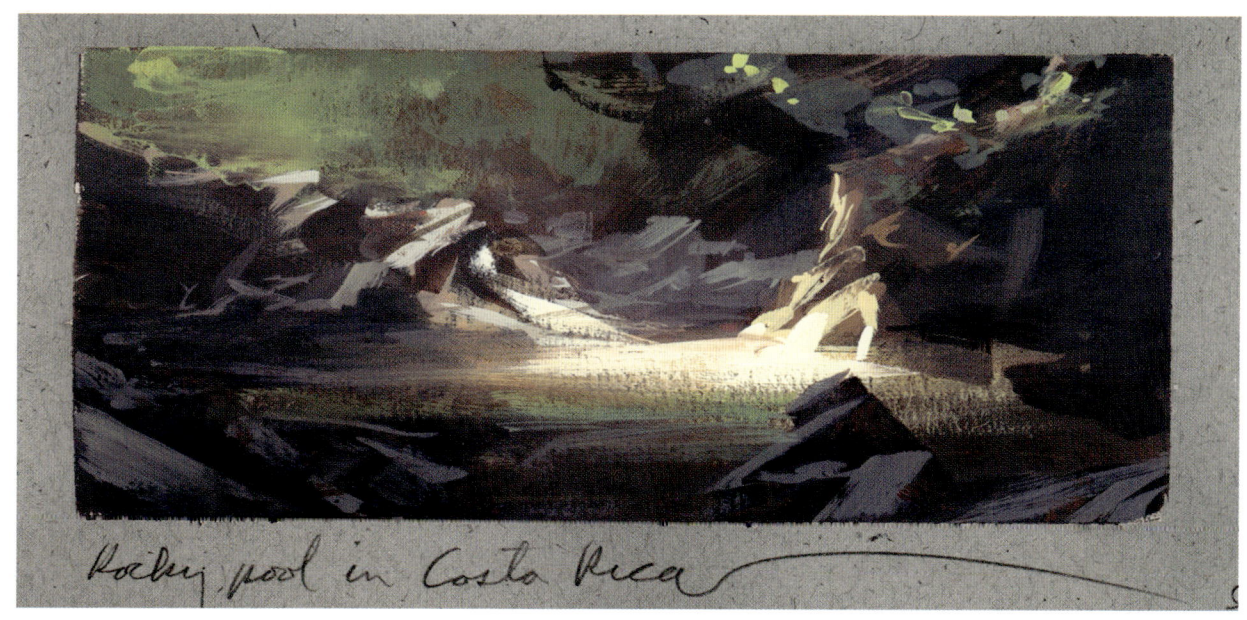

Rocky pool, Costa Rica; watercolor and white gouache on toned mixed-media paper, 3 x 6 inches

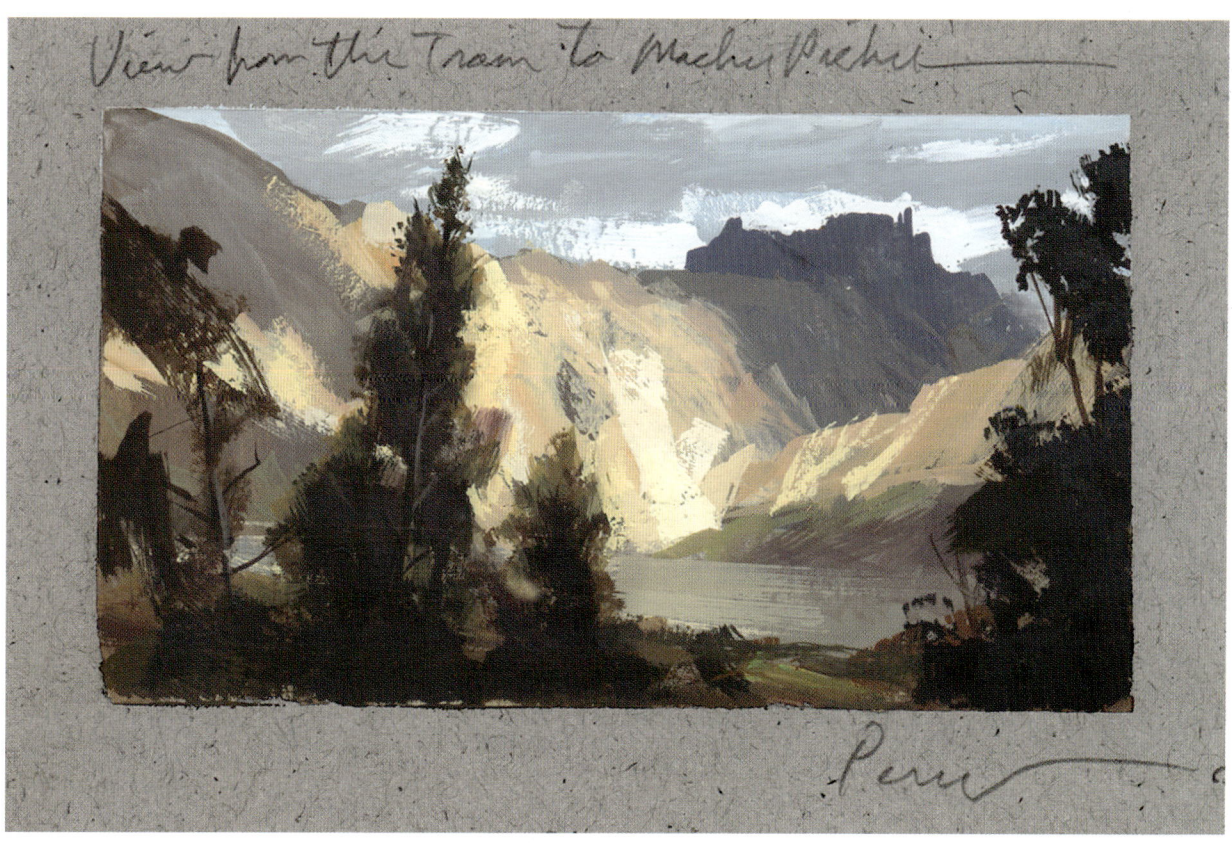

Mountain valley, Peru; watercolor and white gouache on toned mixed-media paper, 3 x 5 inches

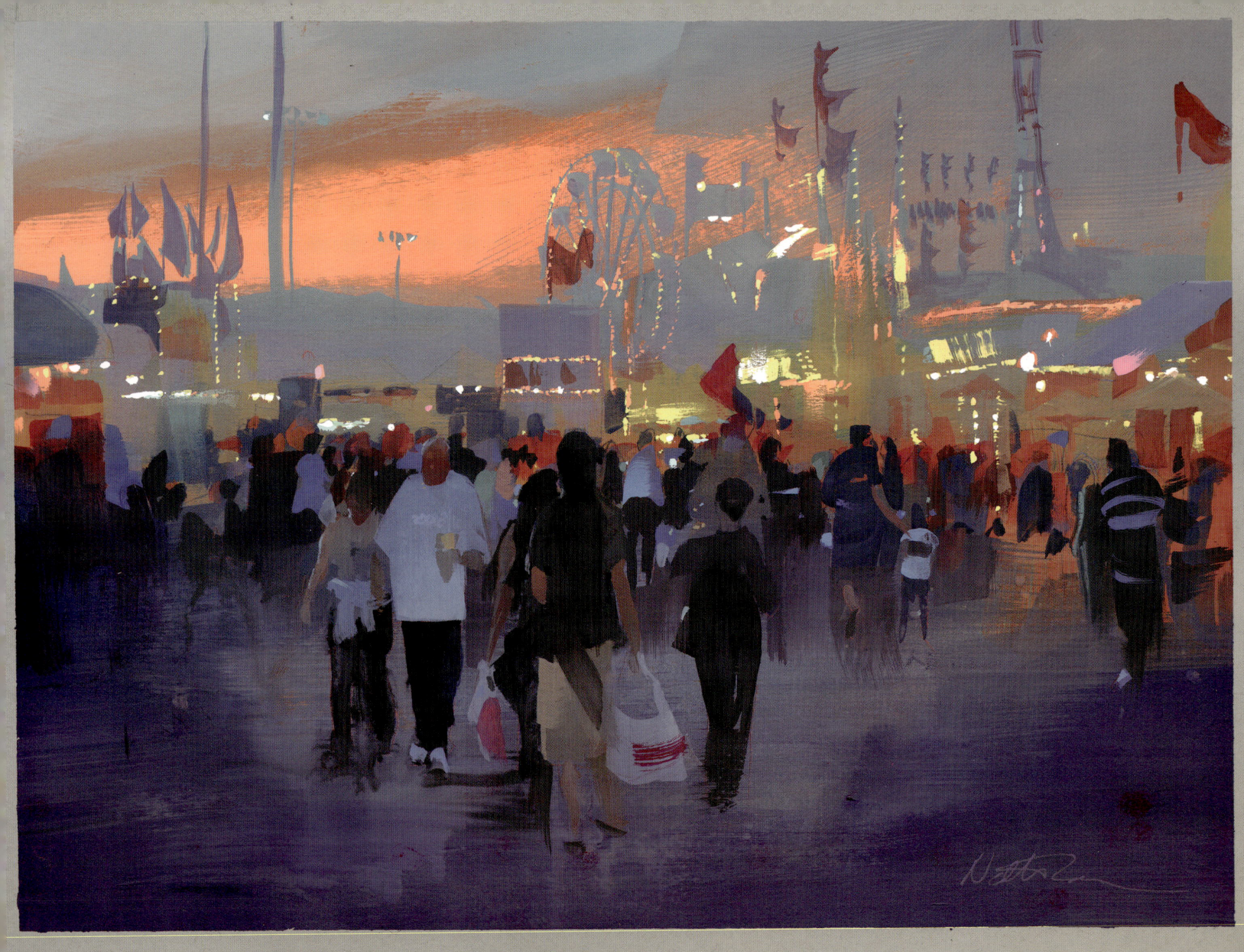

*The Los Angeles County Fair, Pomona, California; watercolor and
white gouache on toned mixed-media paper, 12 x 16 inches*

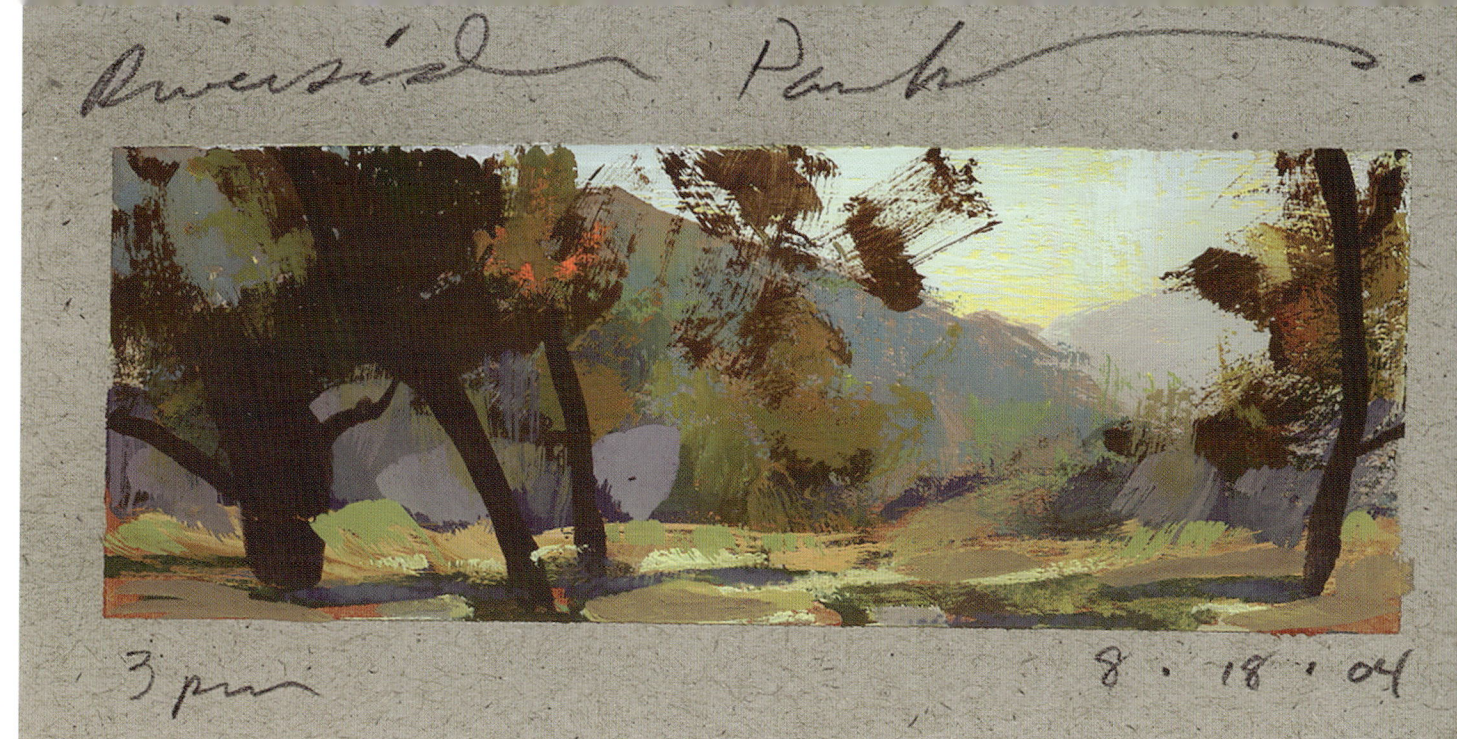

Riverside Park, Humboldt County, California; watercolor and white gouache on toned mixed-media paper, 2 x 5 inches

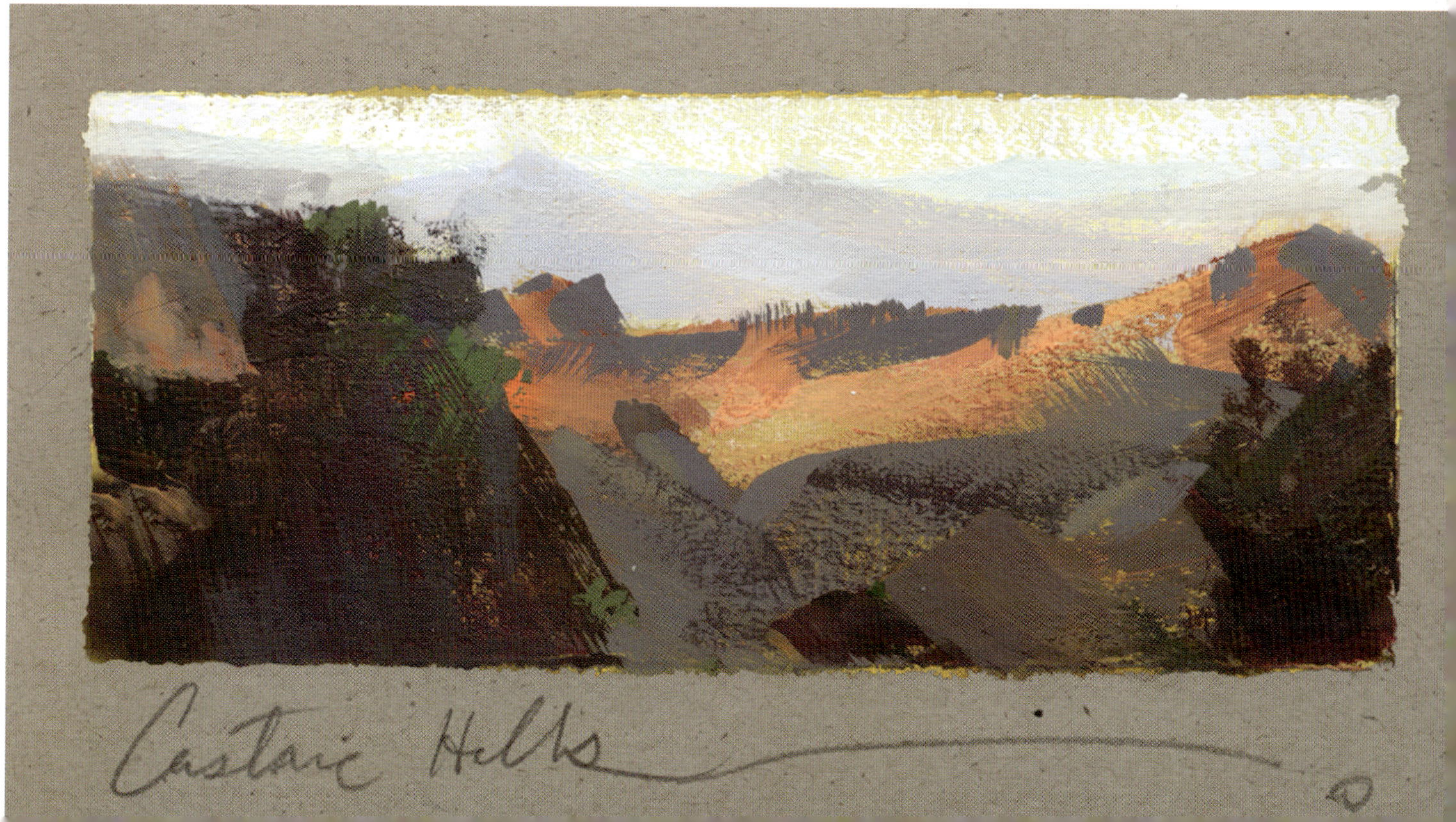

Castaic hills, Los Angeles County, California; watercolor and white gouache on toned mixed-media paper, 3 x 6 inches

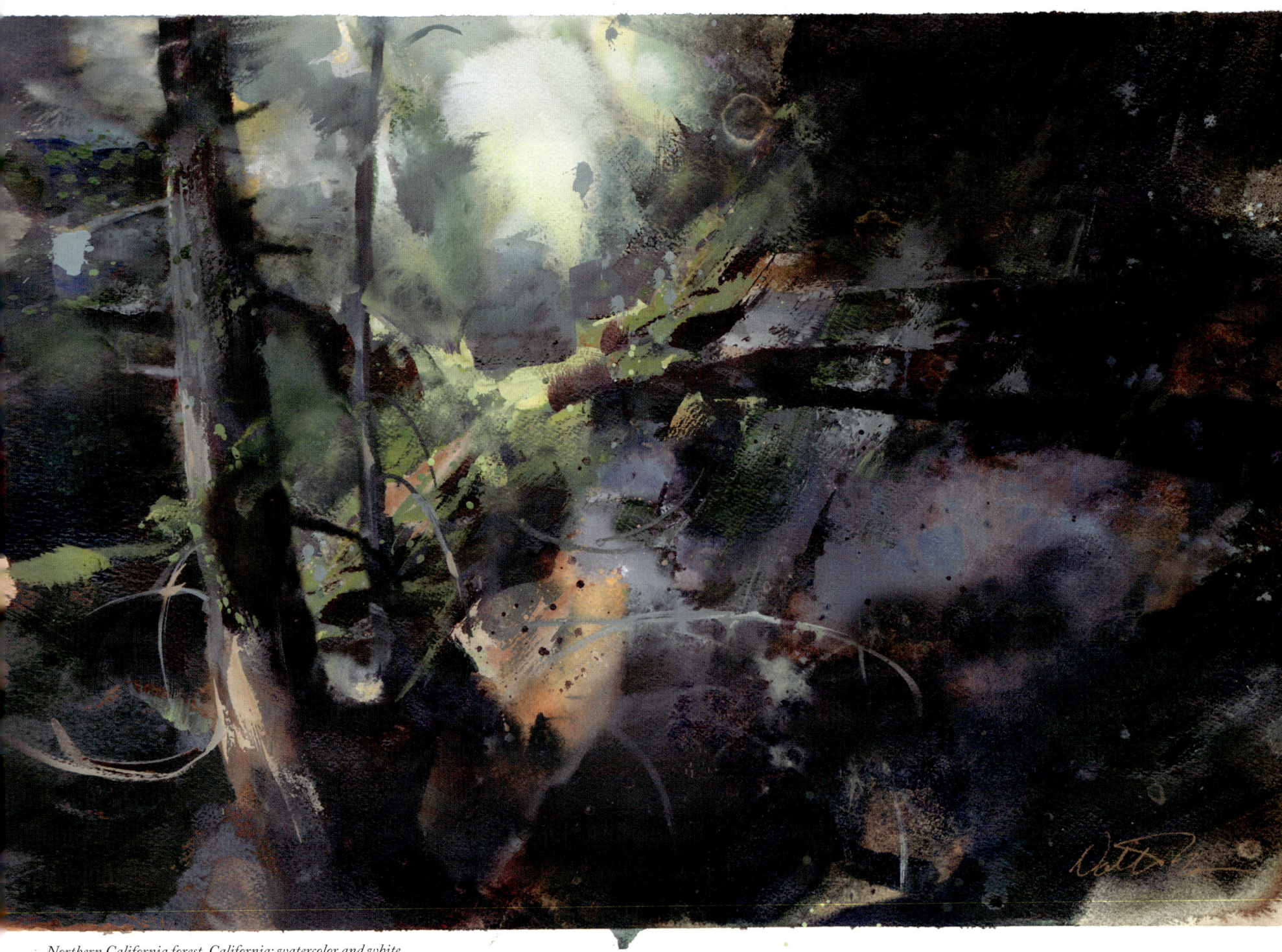

Northern California forest, California; watercolor and white
gouache on Arches cold-pressed paper, 14 x 20 inches

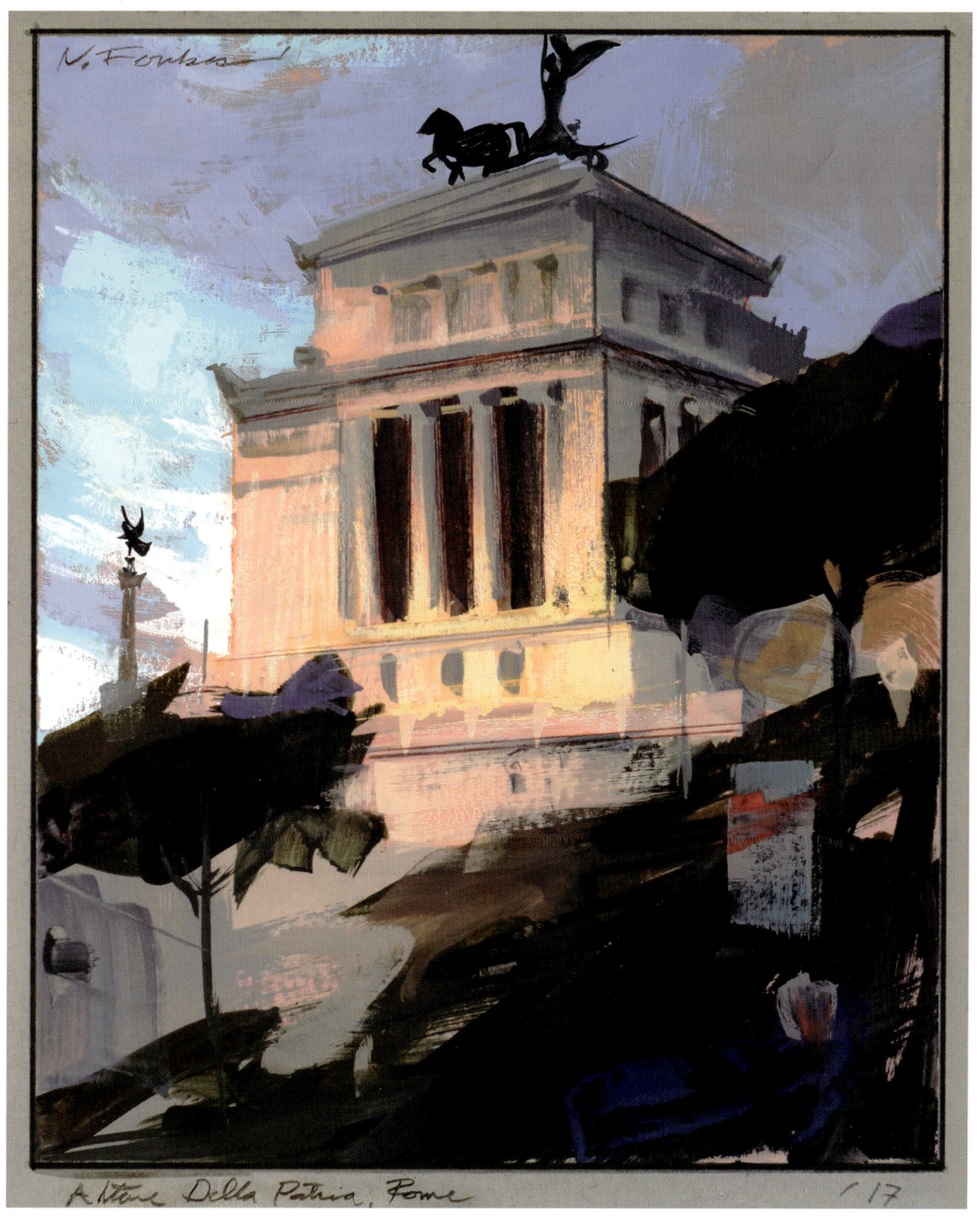

Altare della Patria, Rome, Italy; watercolor and white gouache on toned mixed-media paper, 12 x 9 inches

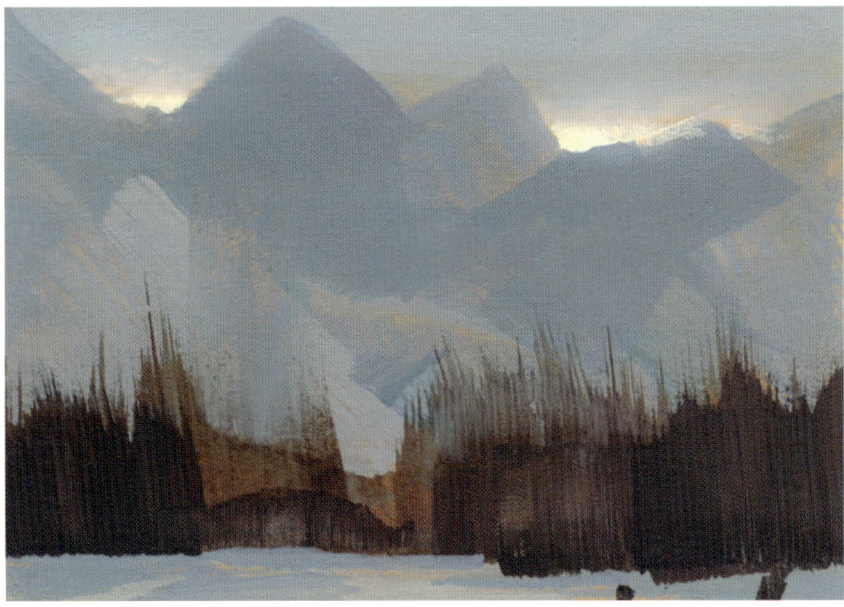

Wasatch Mountains, Utah; watercolor and white gouache on Crescent No. 100 illustration board, 2 x 3 inches

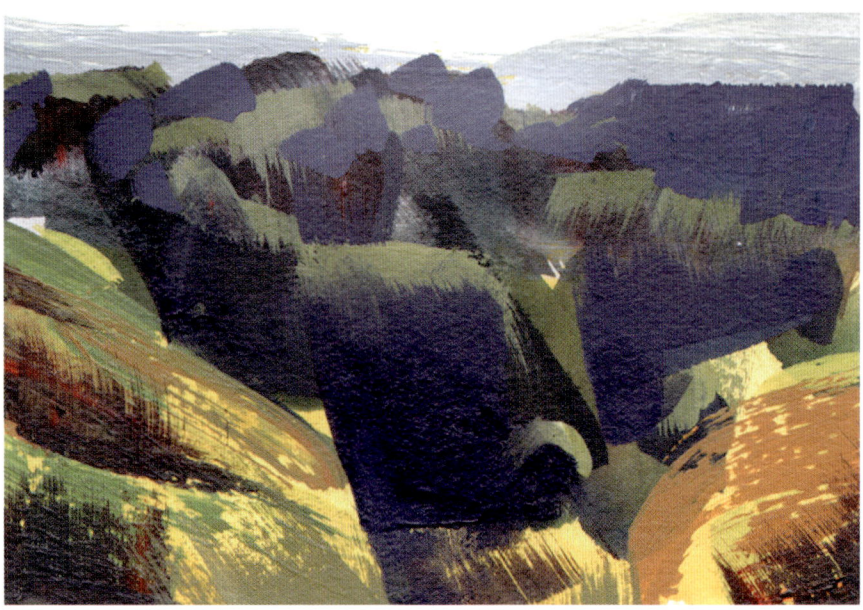

Griffith Park, Los Angeles, California; watercolor and white gouache on Crescent No. 100 illustration board, 2 x 3 inches

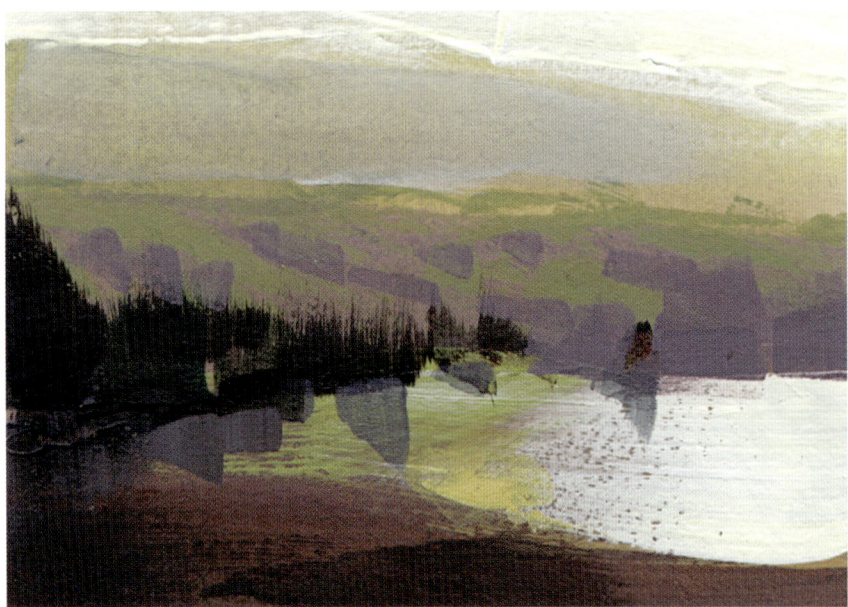

Crystal Springs Reservoir, San Mateo County, California; watercolor and white gouache on Crescent 100 illustration board, 2 x 3 inches

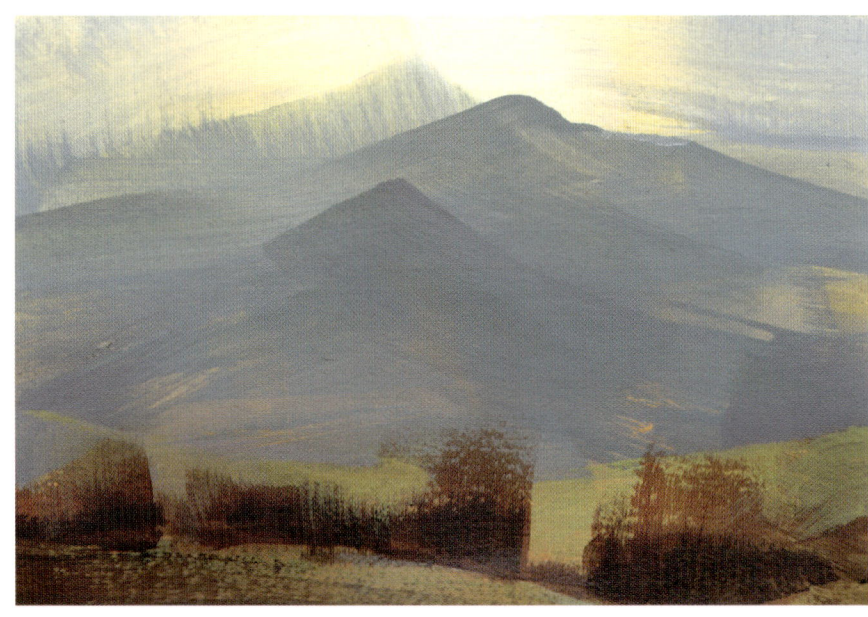

Los Gatos Mountains, Los Gatos, California; watercolor and white gouache on Crescent No. 100 illustration board, 2 x 3 inches

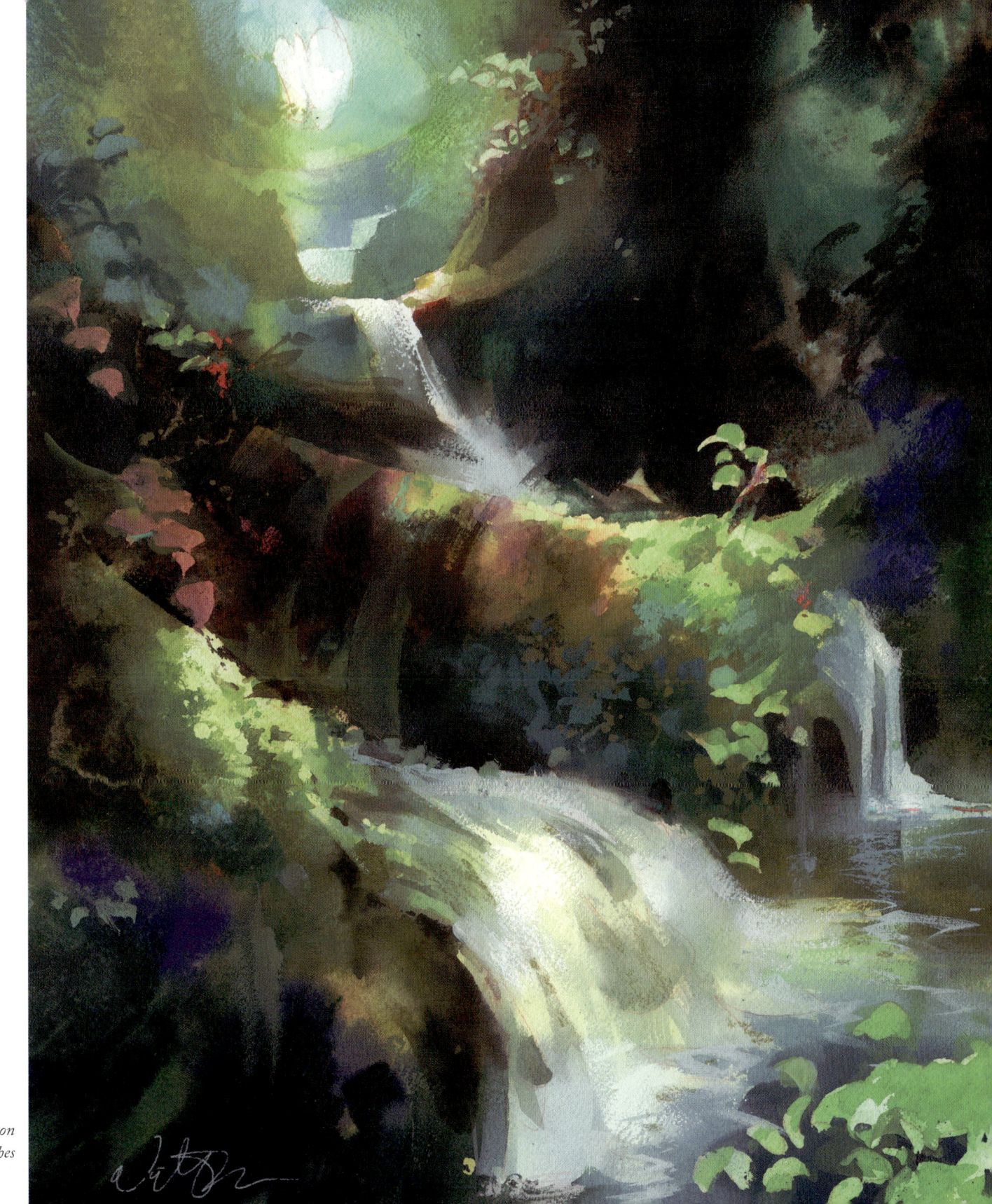

*Jungle falls, Kauai, Hawaii; watercolor on
Arches cold-pressed paper, 16 x 12 inches*

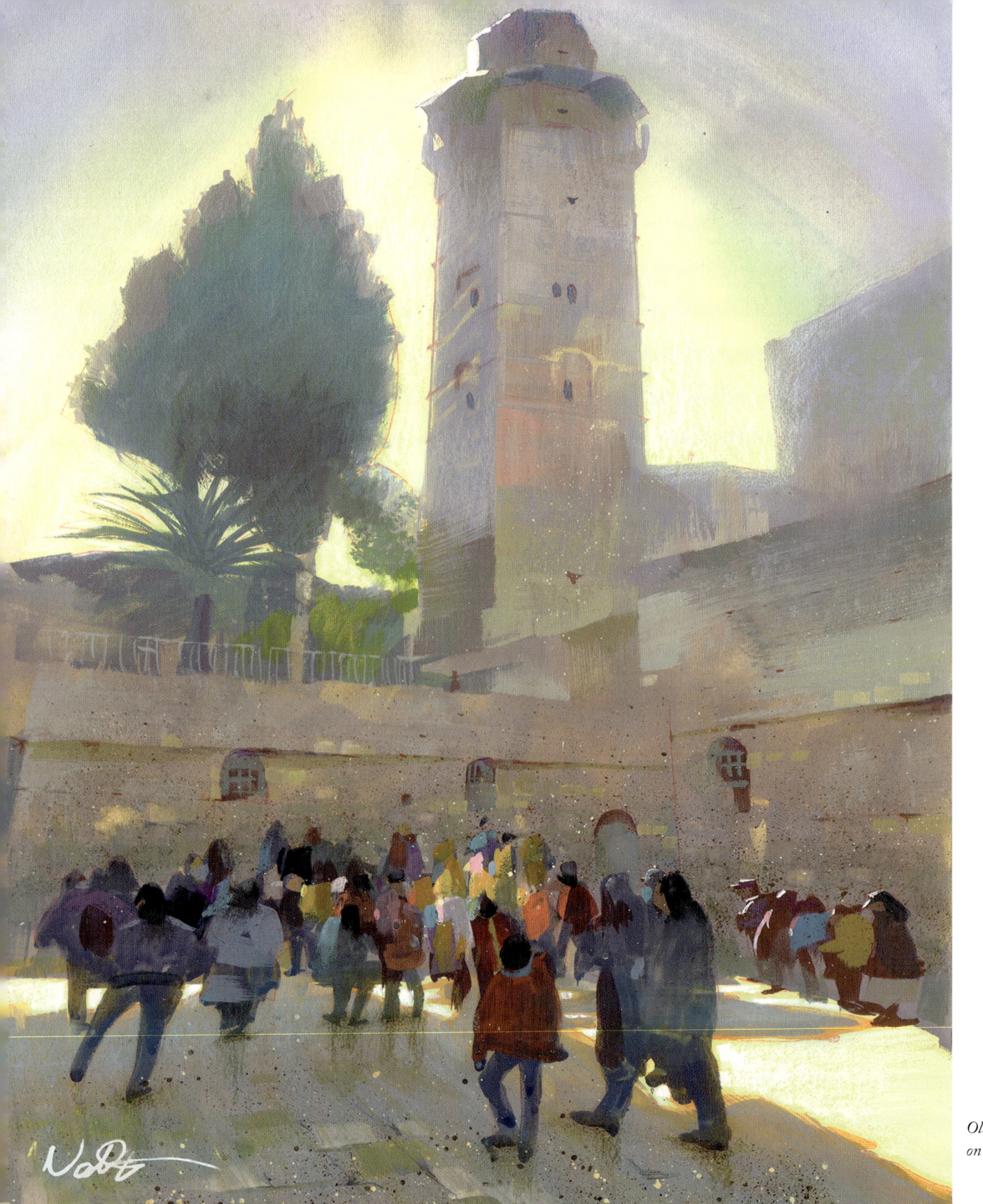

Old City, Jerusalem, Israel; watercolor and white gouache on Crescent No. 100 illustration board, 18 x 14 inches

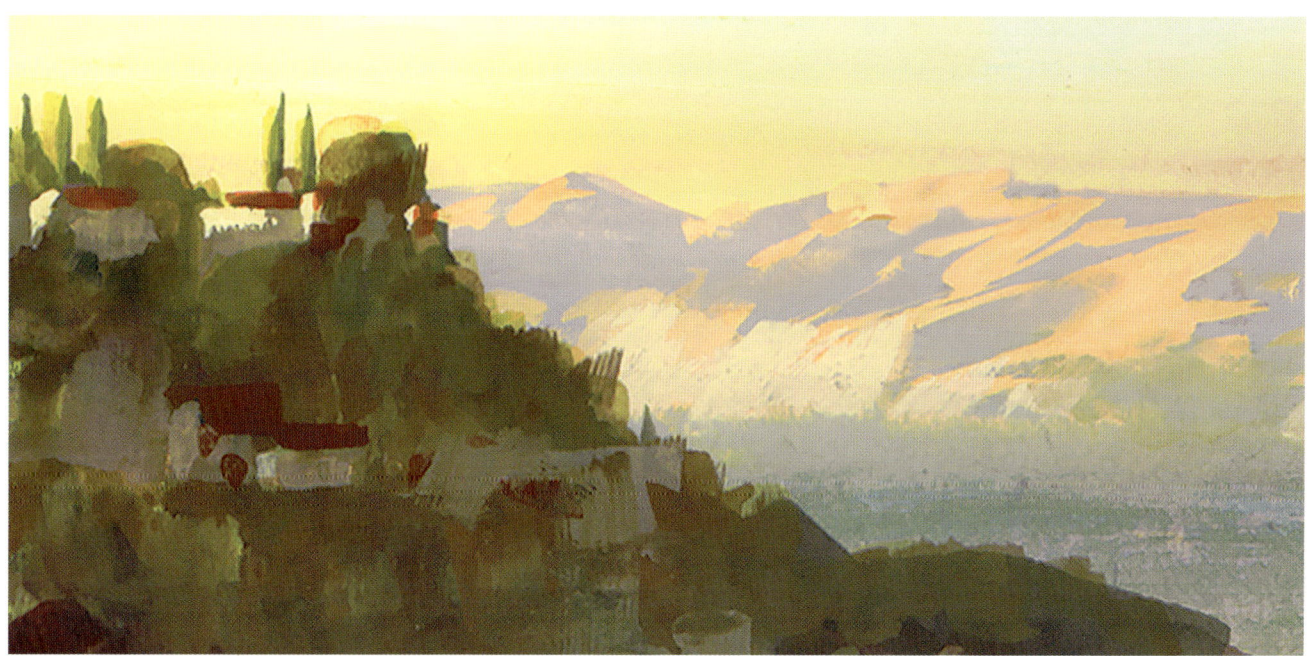

Hollywood Hills, Los Angeles, California; watercolor and white gouache on toned mixed-media paper, 3 x 6 inches

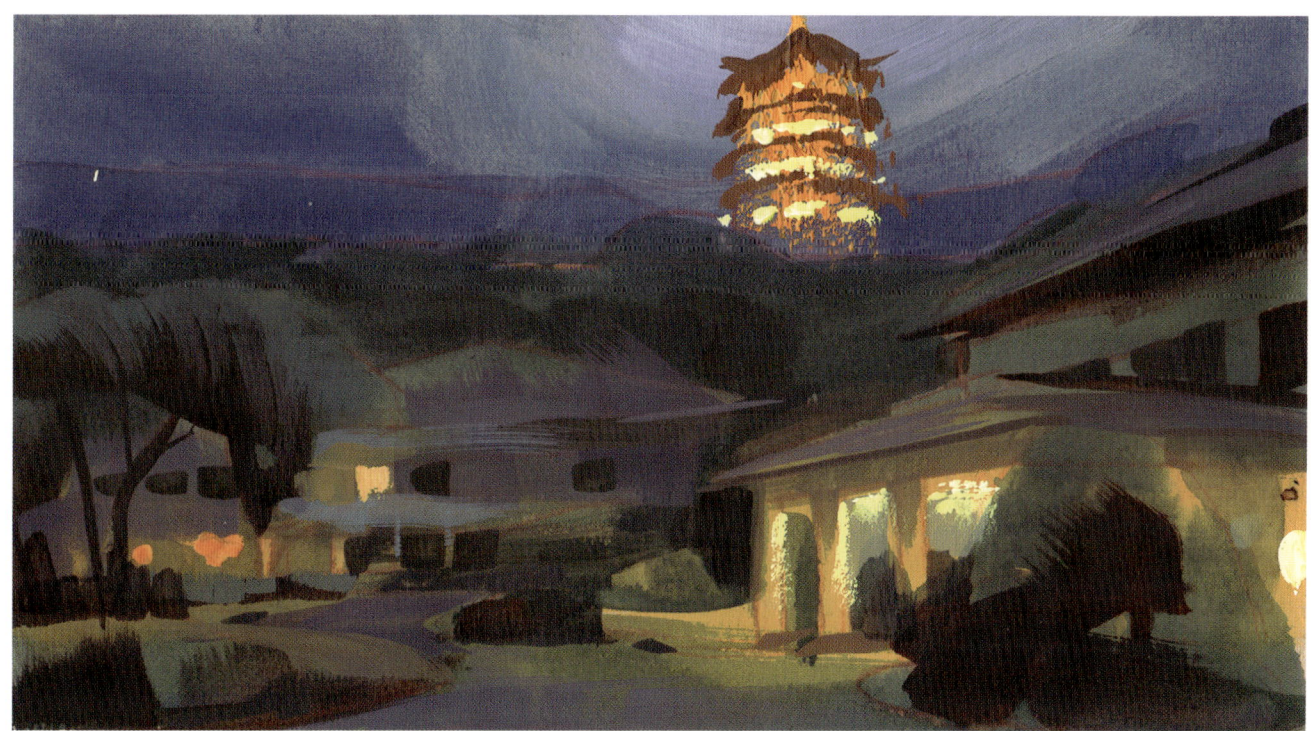

Beijing pagoda, China; watercolor and white gouache on toned mixed-media paper, 4 x 7 inches

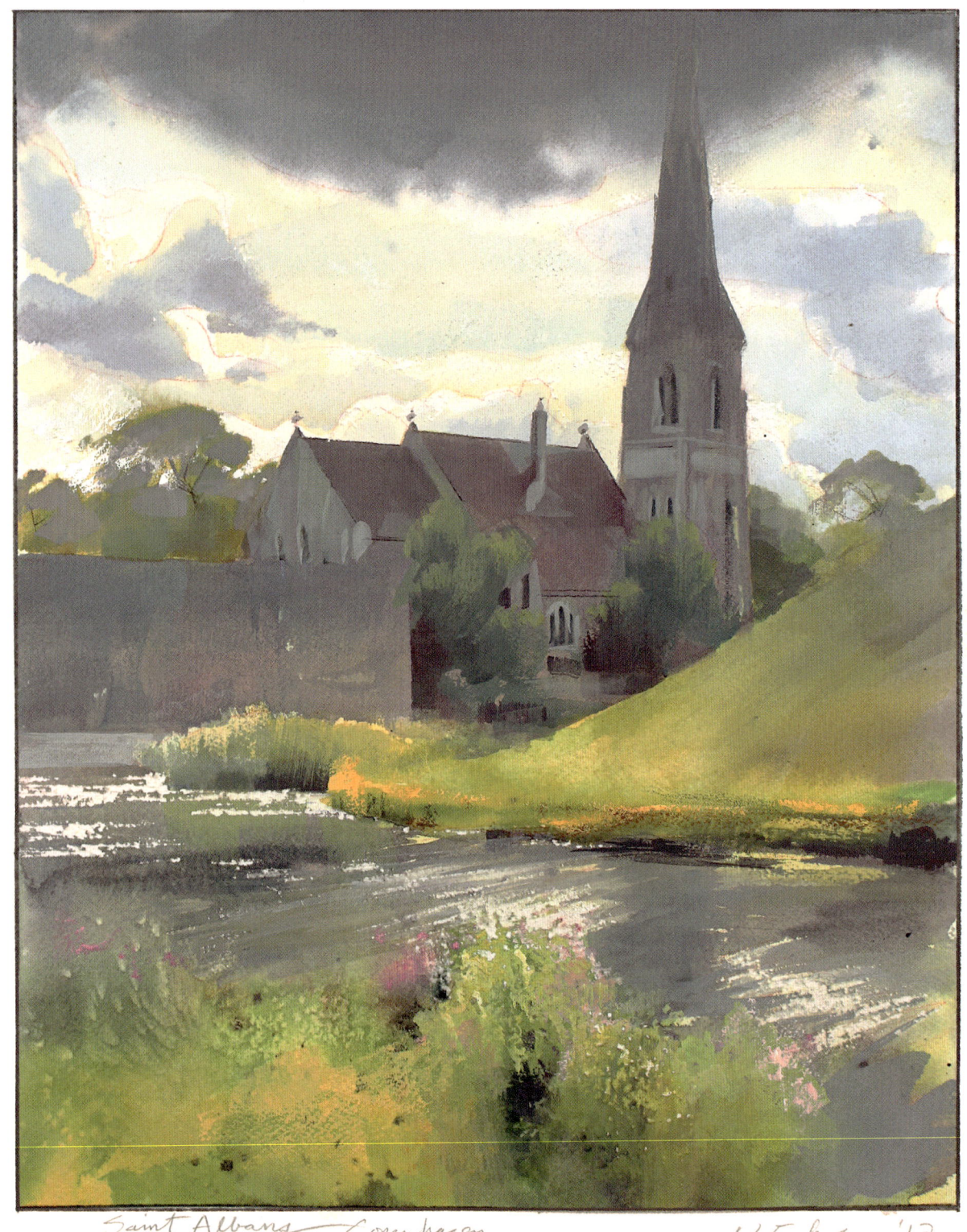

Saint Albans Copenhagen *N. Forbes '17*

St. Alban's church, Copenhagen, Denmark; watercolor on Arches cold pressed paper, 18 x 12 inches

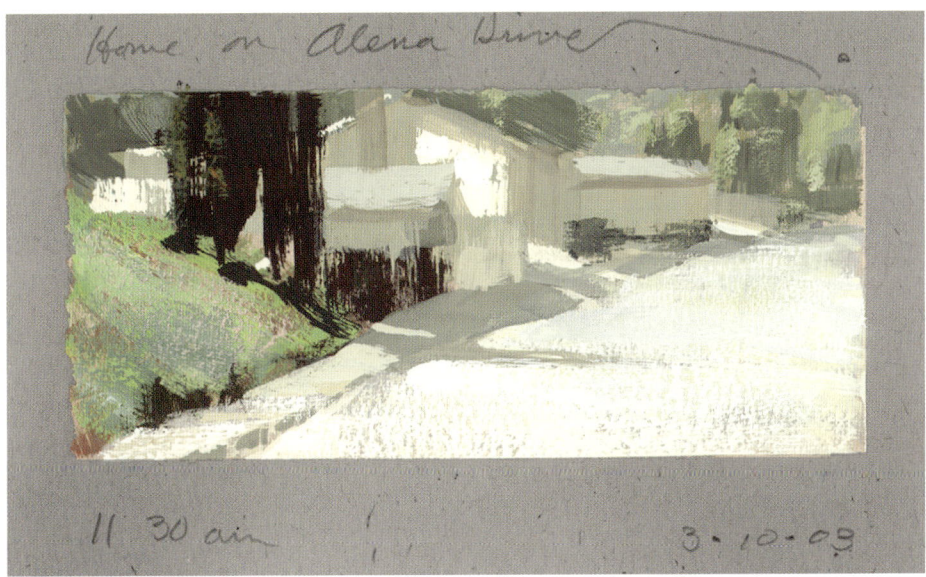

*Los Angeles, California; watercolor and white gouache
on toned mixed-media paper, 2 x 4 inches*

*Glendale, California; watercolor and white gouache
on toned mixed-media paper, 4 x 6 inches*

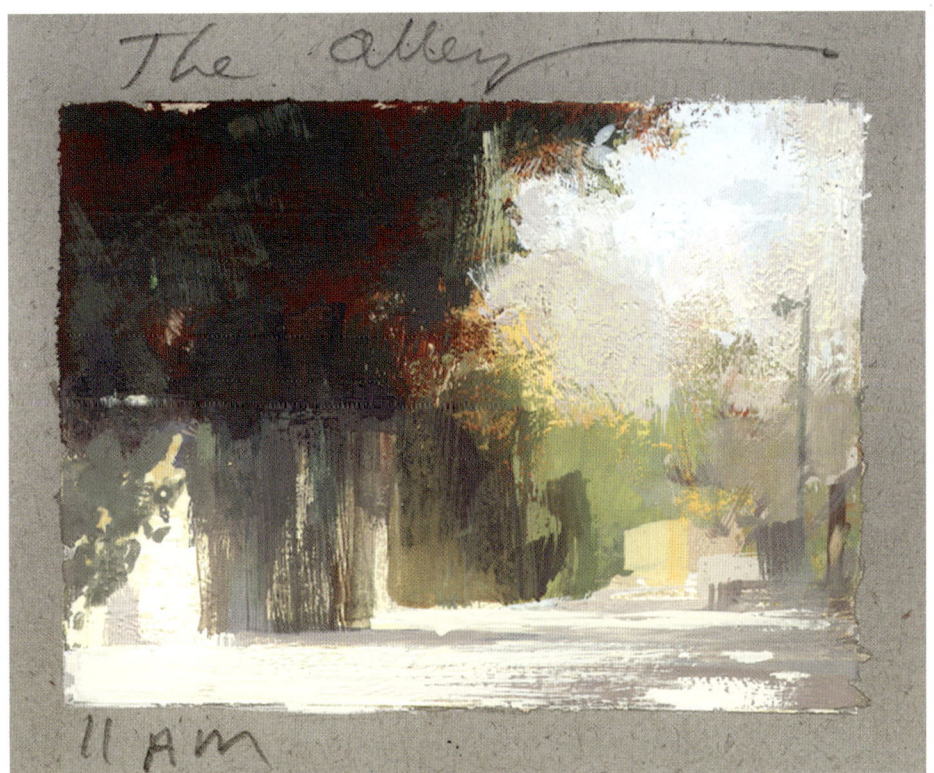

*San Fernando Valley, California; watercolor and white
gouache on toned mixed-media paper, 5 x 6 inches*

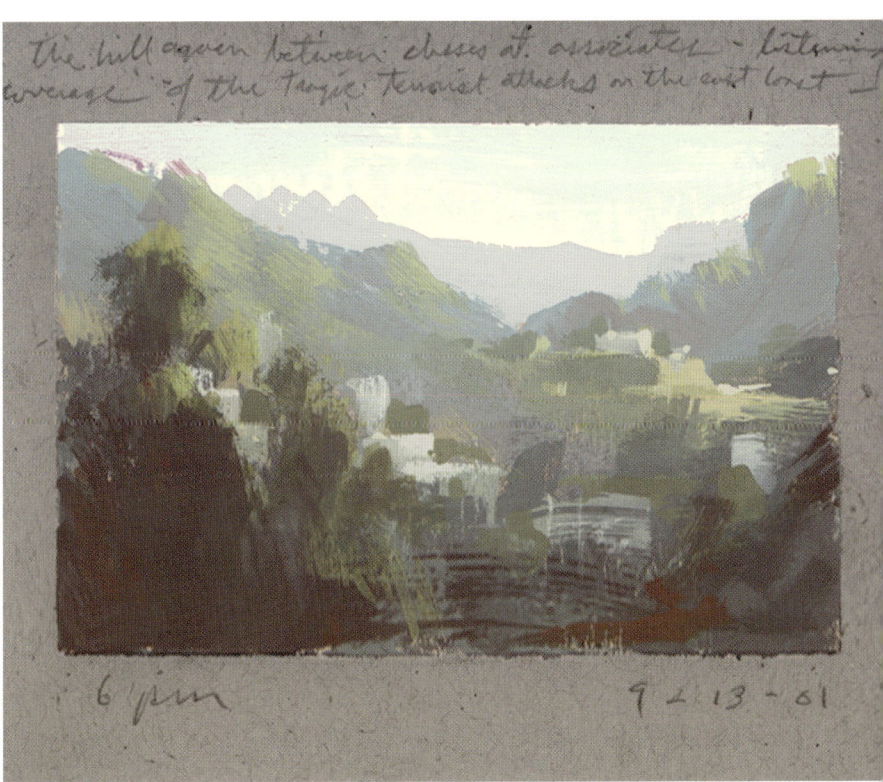

*Hollywood Hills, Los Angeles, California; watercolor and
white gouache on toned mixed-media paper, 5 x 6 inches*

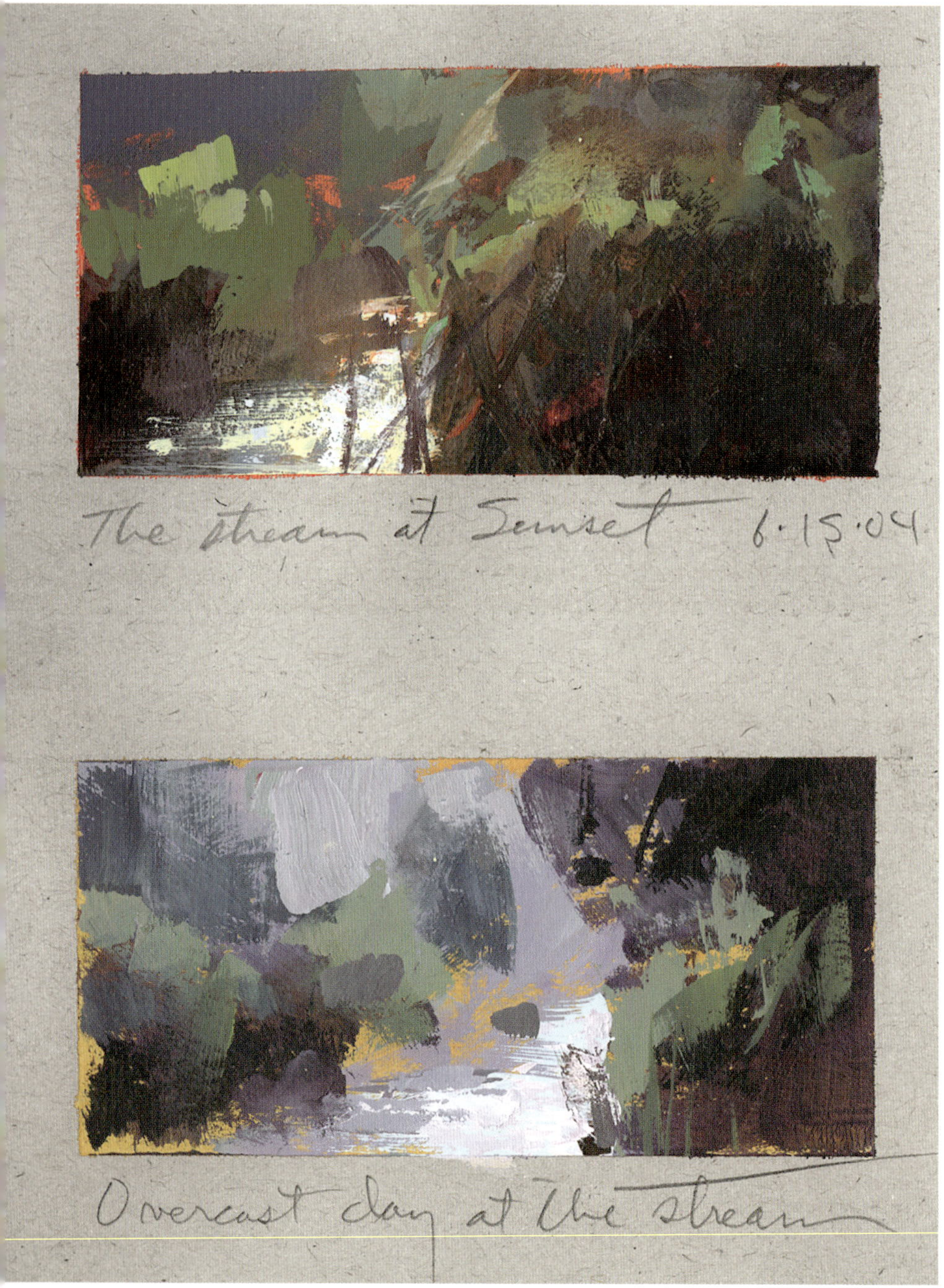

The stream at Sunset   6·15·04

Overcast day at the stream

outside the Corcovado Rain forest Costa Rica

DreamWorks Animation campus stream, Glendale, California; watercolor and white gouache on toned mixed-media paper, 9 x 5 inches

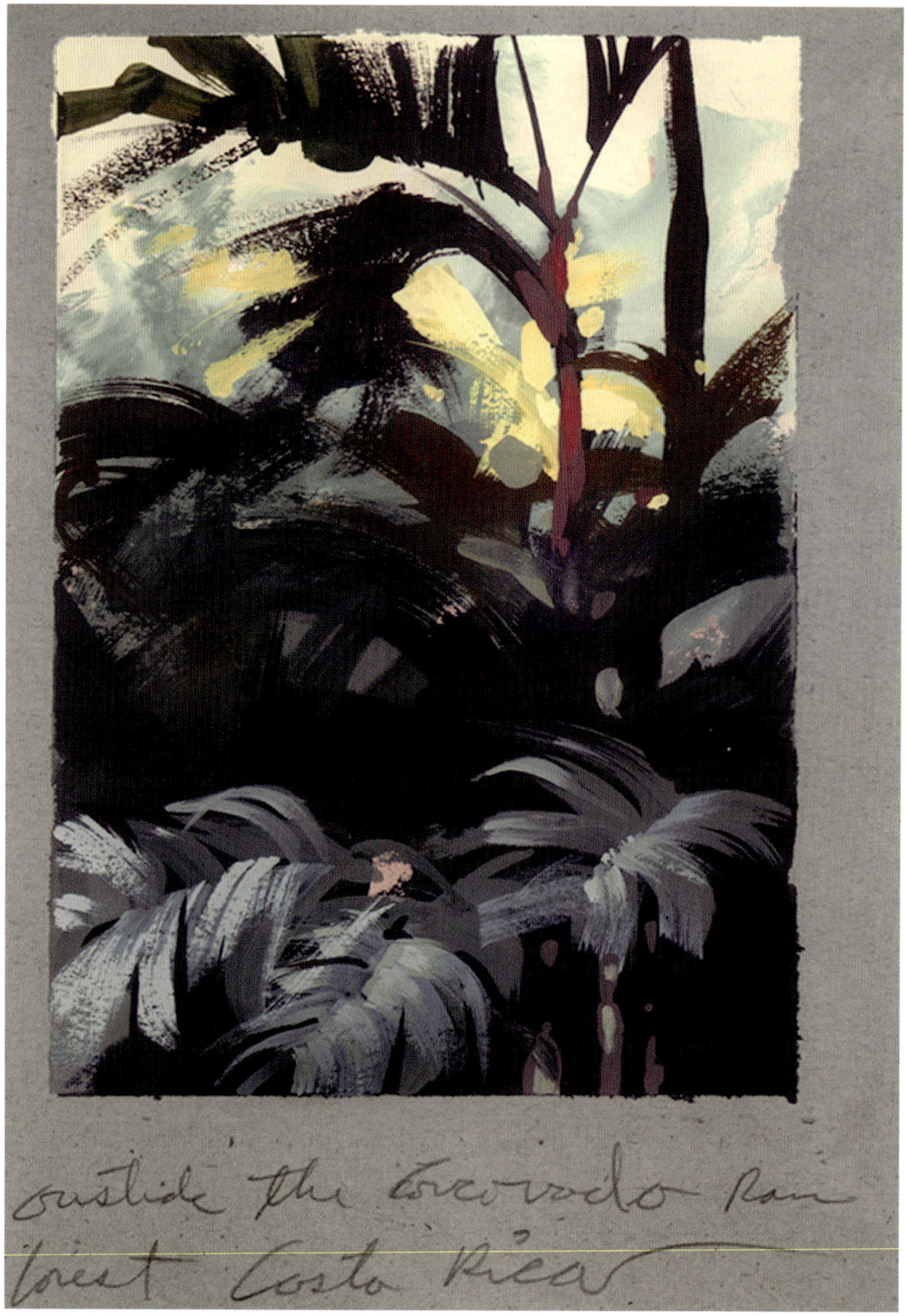

Jungle palm, Costa Rica; watercolor and white gouache on toned mixed-media paper, 6 x 4 inches

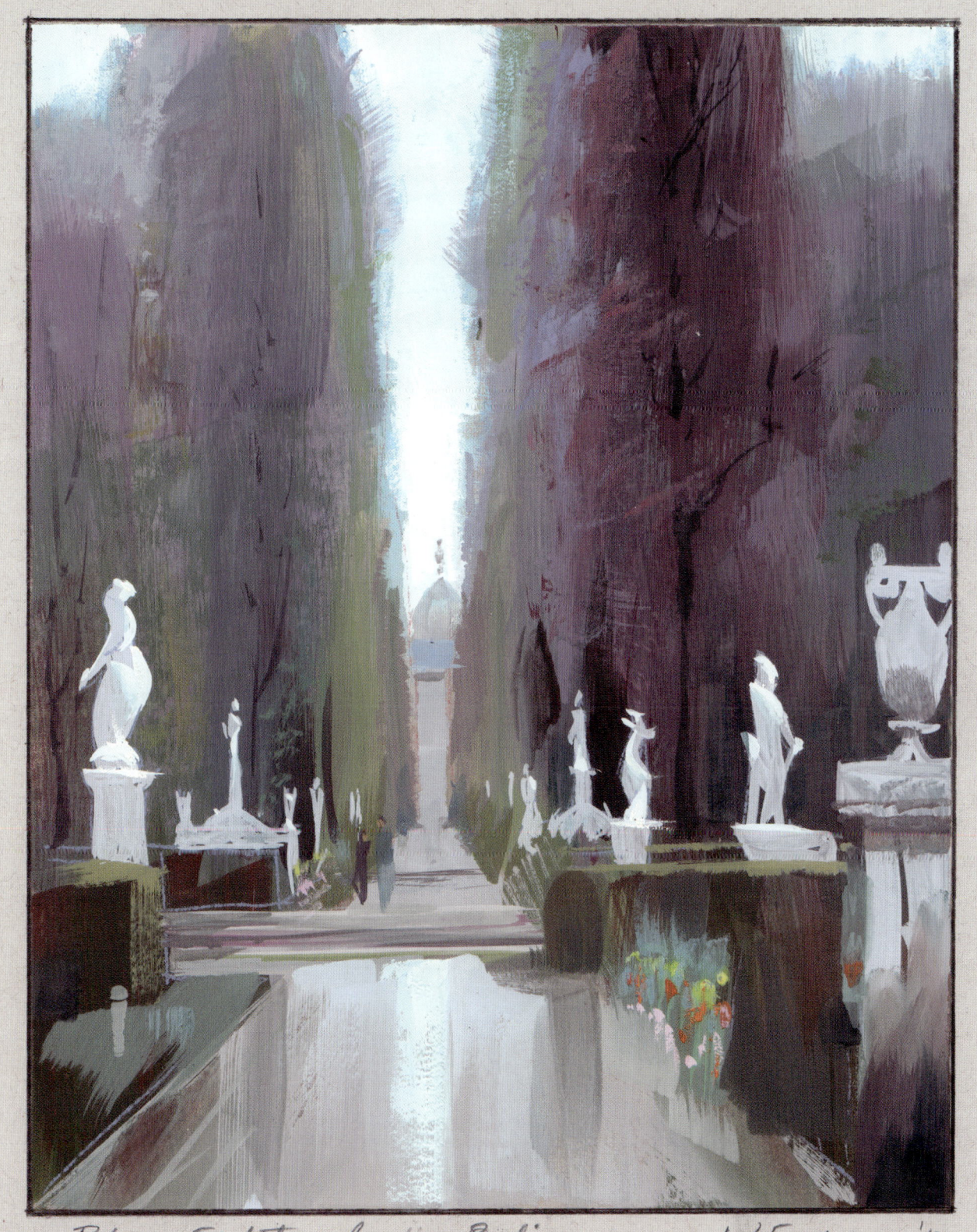

Palace Sculpture Garden, Berlin, Germany;
watercolor and white gouache on toned
mixed-media paper, 14 x 11 inches

Palace Sculpture Garden Berlin   N. Fortes '17

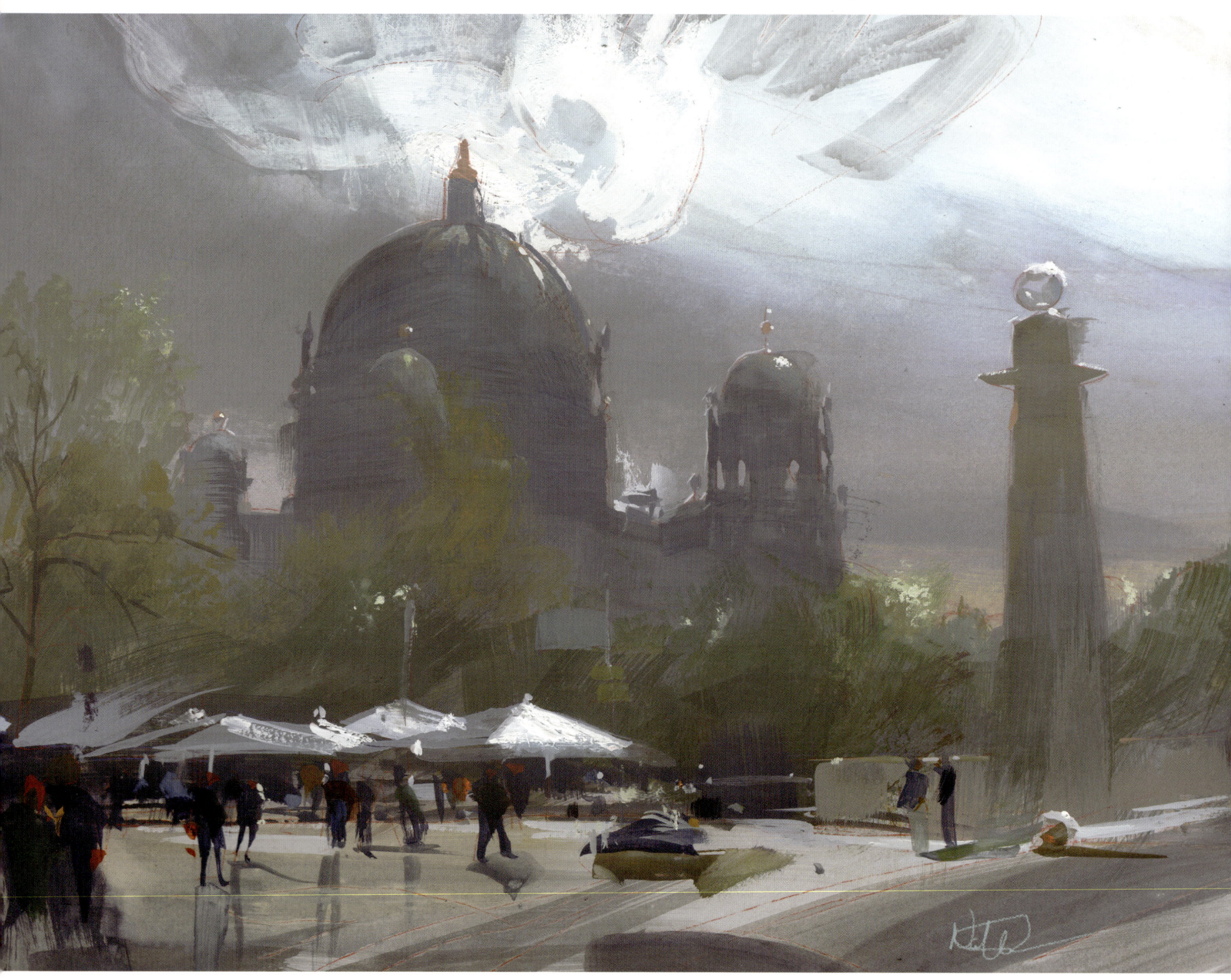

Berlin Cathedral, Germany; watercolor and white gouache on toned mixed-media paper, 12 x 18 inches

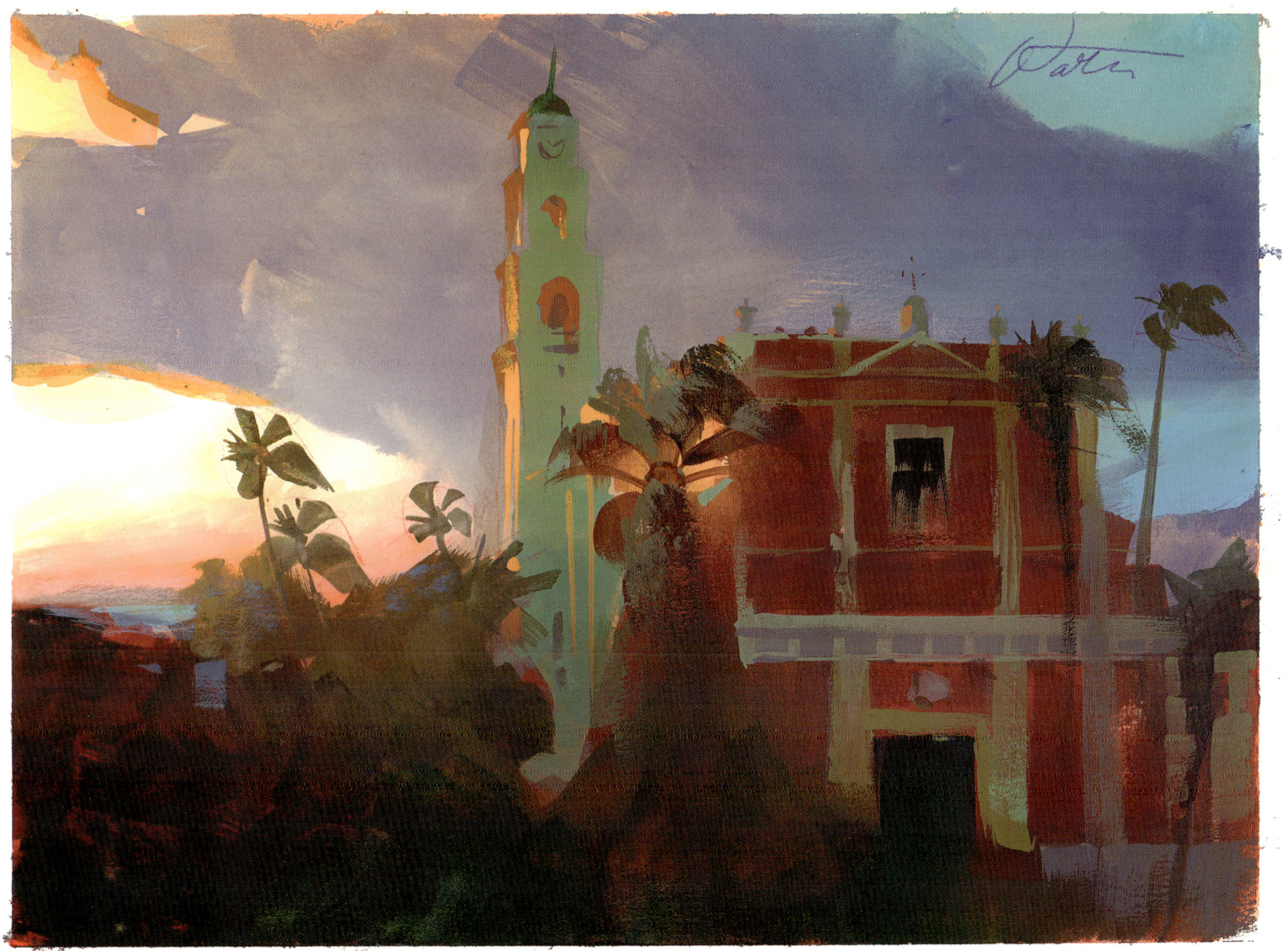

St. Peters Church, Jafa, Israel; watercolor on Crescent No. 100 illustration board, 8 x 12 inches

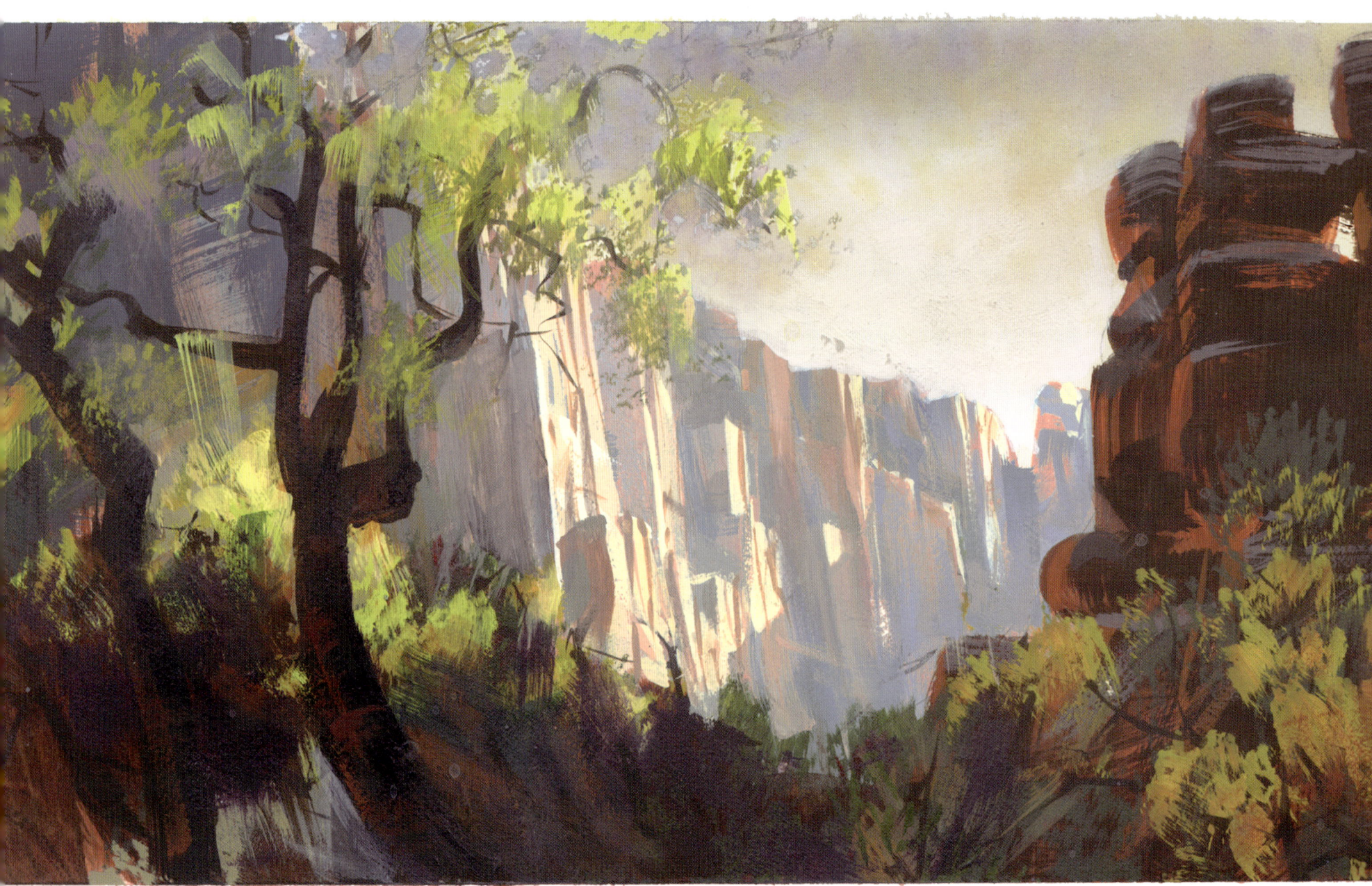

Zion National Park, Utah; watercolor and white gouache on
Crescent No. 100 illustration board, 6 x 10 inches

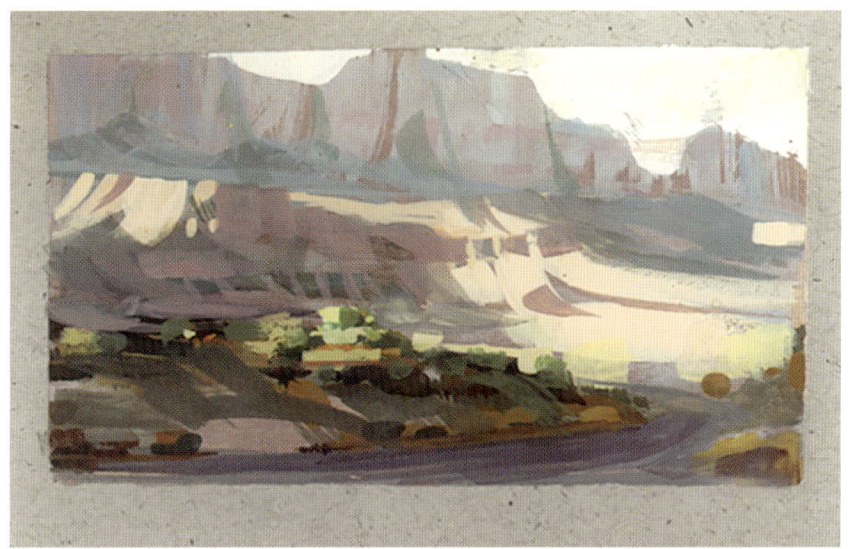

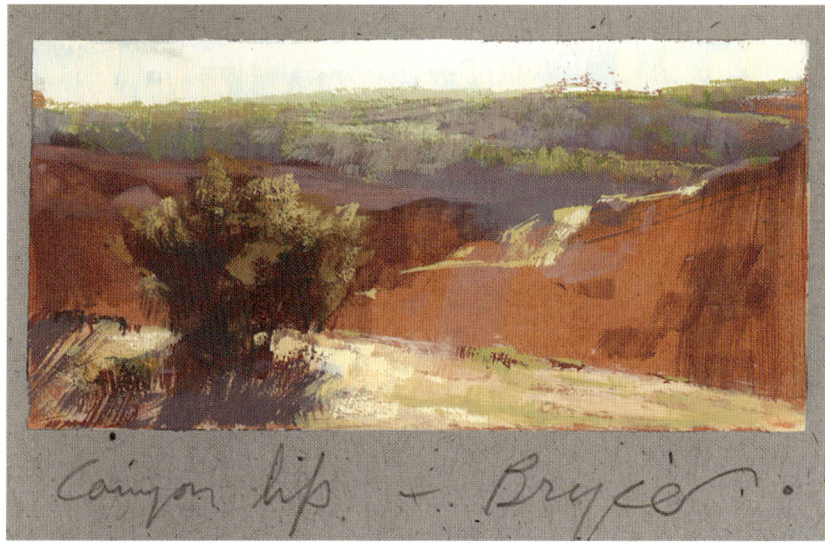

Canyon lip + Bryce

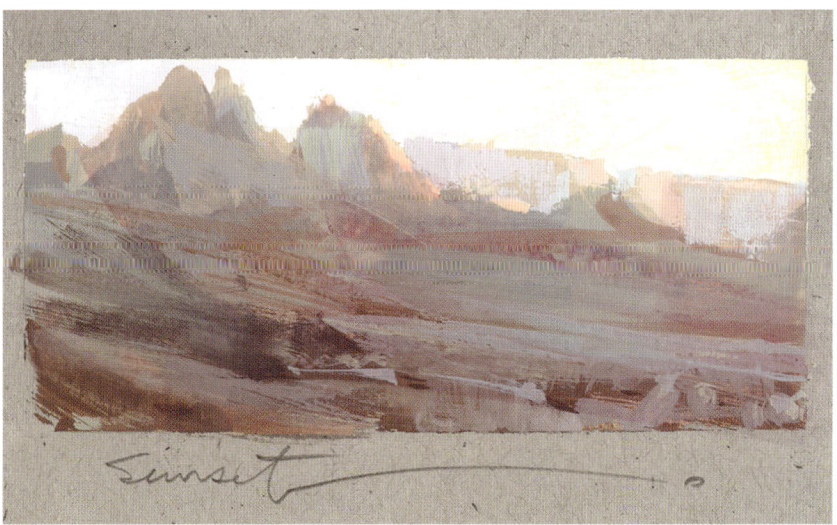

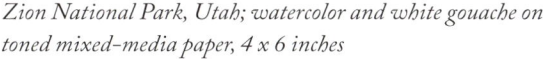
Sunset

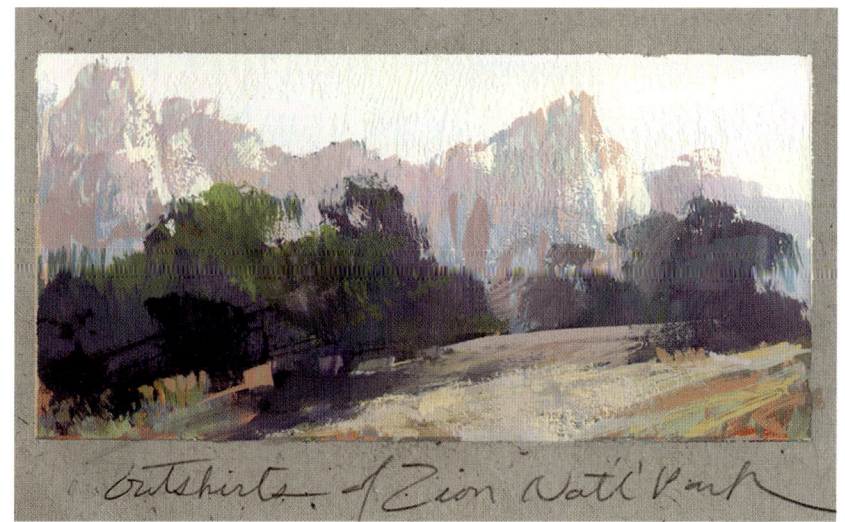

outskirts of Zion Nat'l Park

_Zion National Park, Utah; watercolor and white gouache on
toned mixed-media paper, 4 x 6 inches_

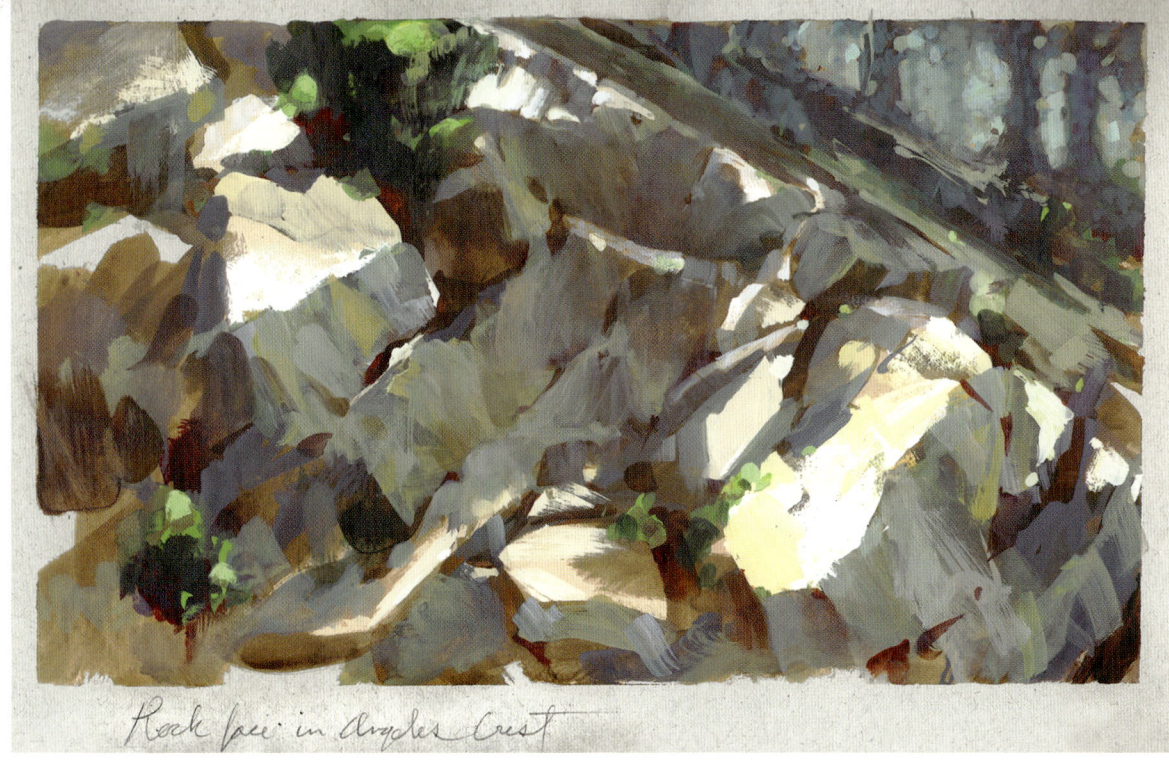

Rock face in Angeles Crest

Rock face, Angeles National Forest, Los Angeles County, California; watercolor and white gouache on toned mixed-media paper, 6 x 10 inches

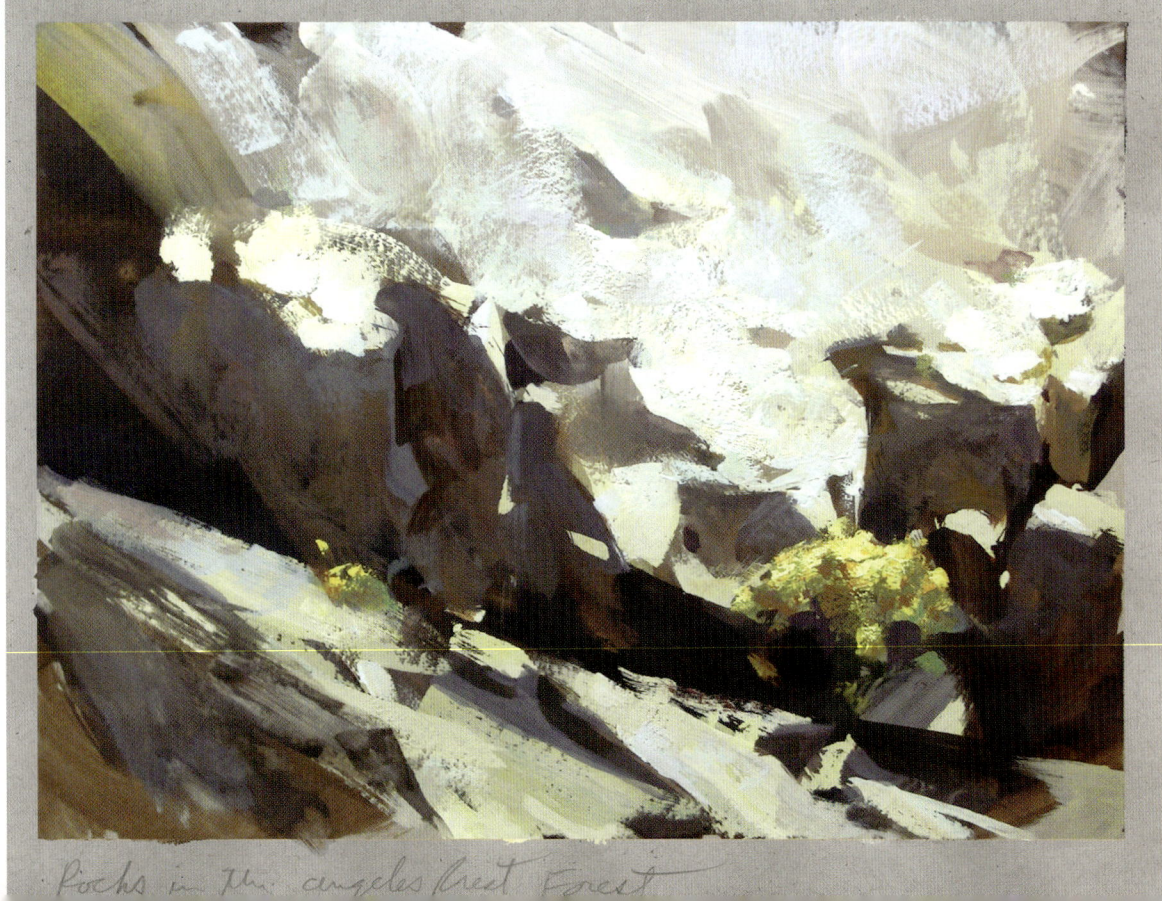

Rocks in the angeles Crest Forest

Canyon rocks, Angeles National Forest, Los Angeles County, California; watercolor and white gouache on toned mixed-media paper, 8 x 10 inches

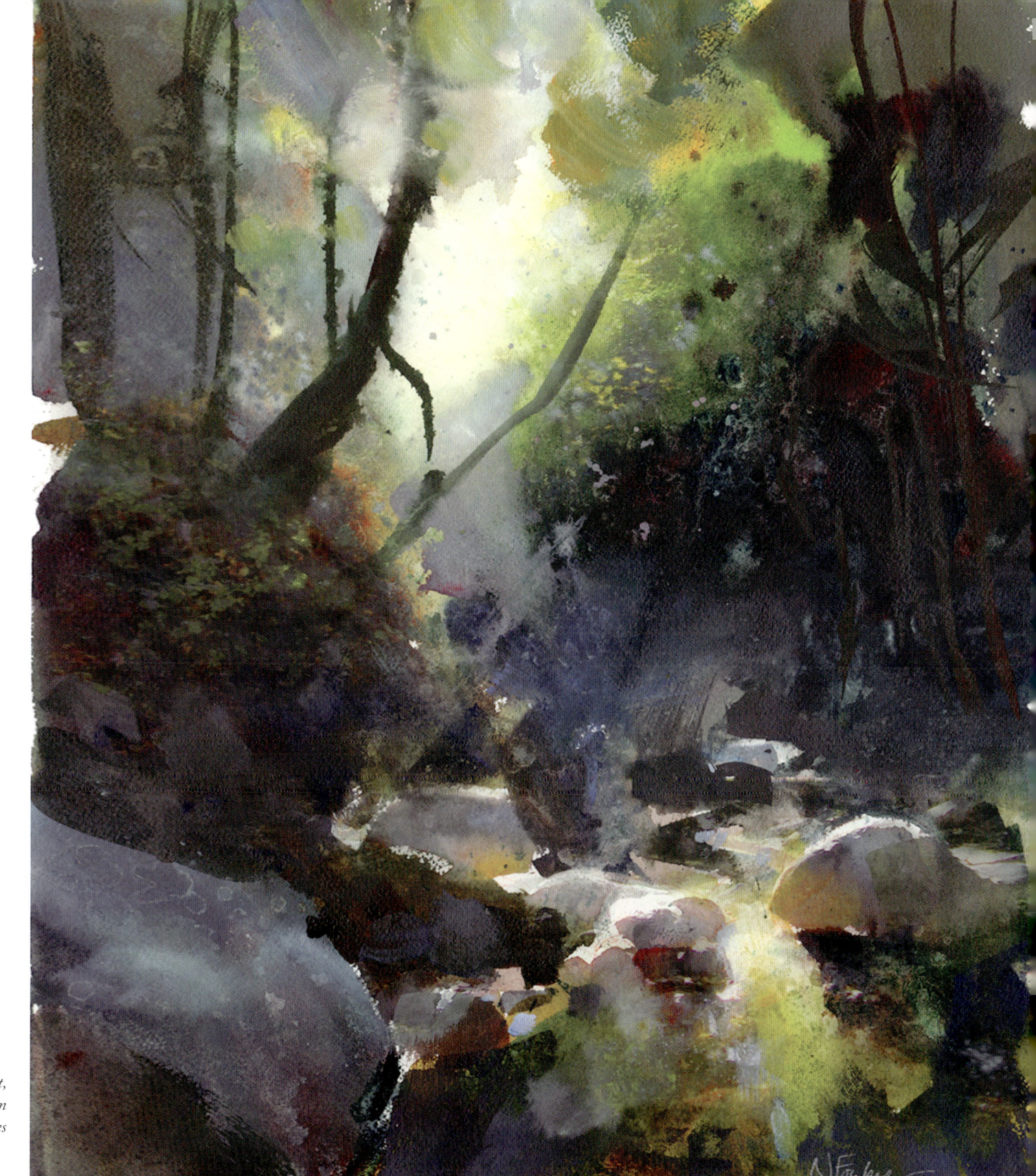

*Rocky creek, Angeles National Forest,
Los Angeles County, California; watercolor on
Arches cold-pressed paper, 14 x 11 inches*

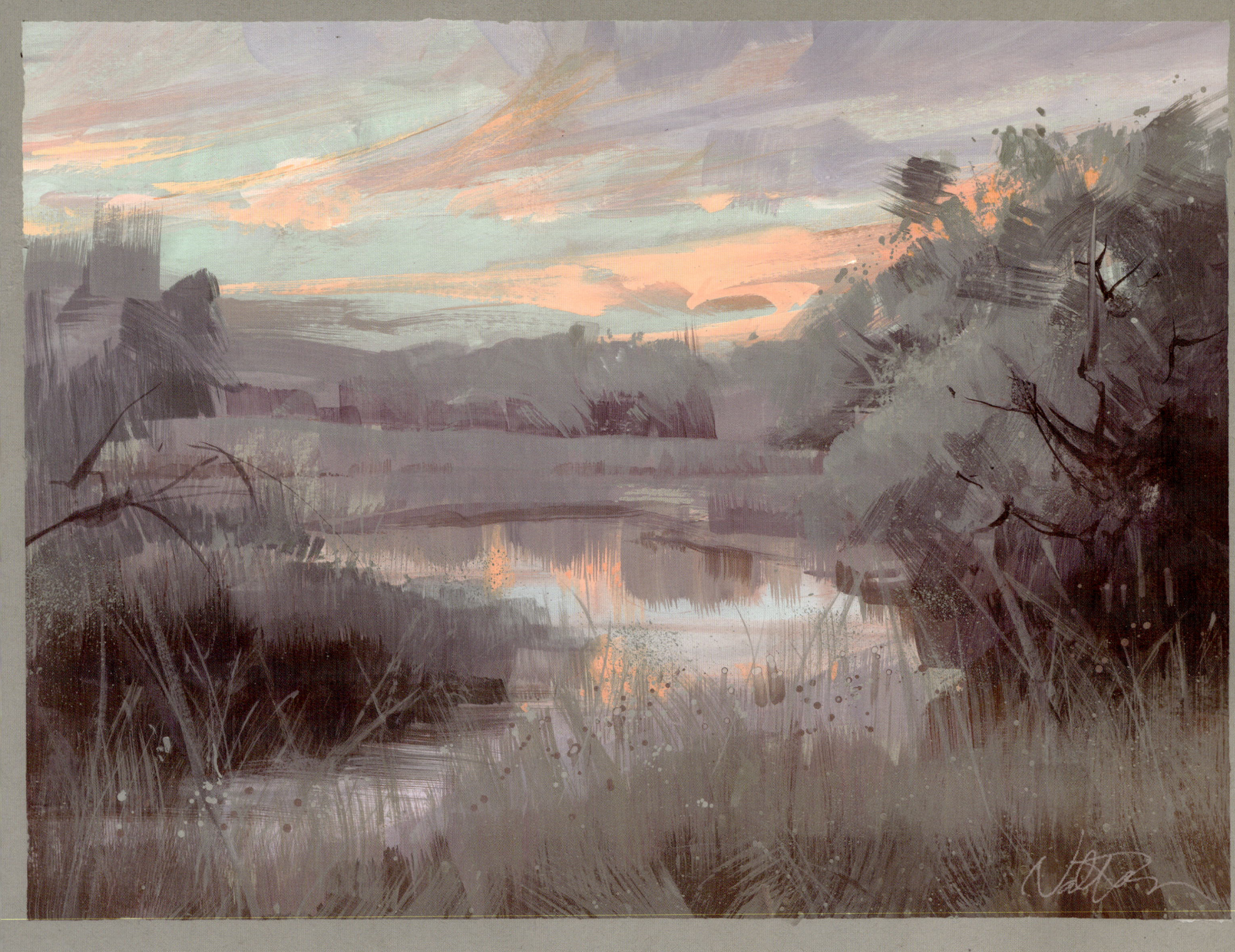

*Santaquin pond, Utah; watercolor and white gouache
on toned mixed-media paper, 11 x 14 inches*

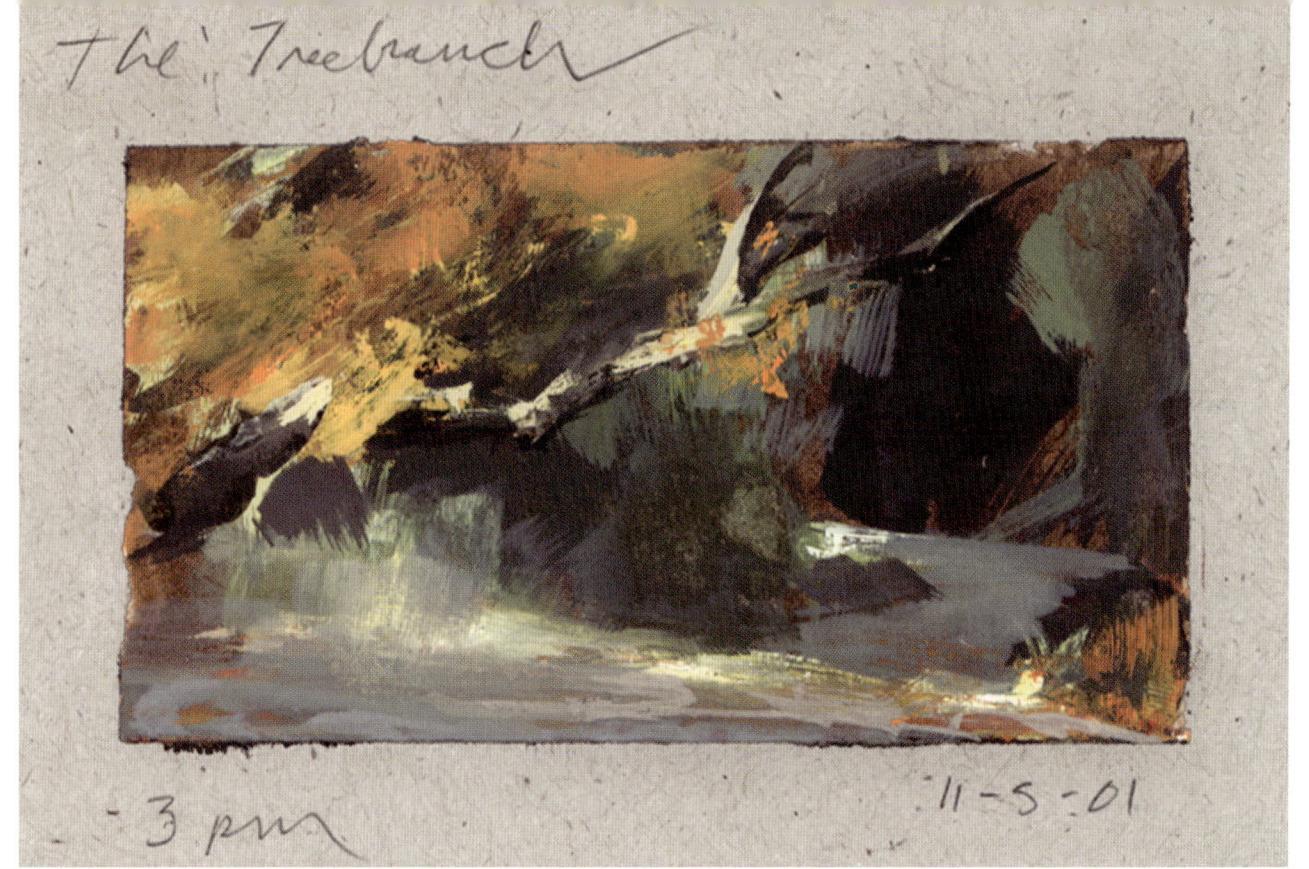

Central California forest, California; watercolor and white gouache on toned mixed-media paper, 3 x 5 inches

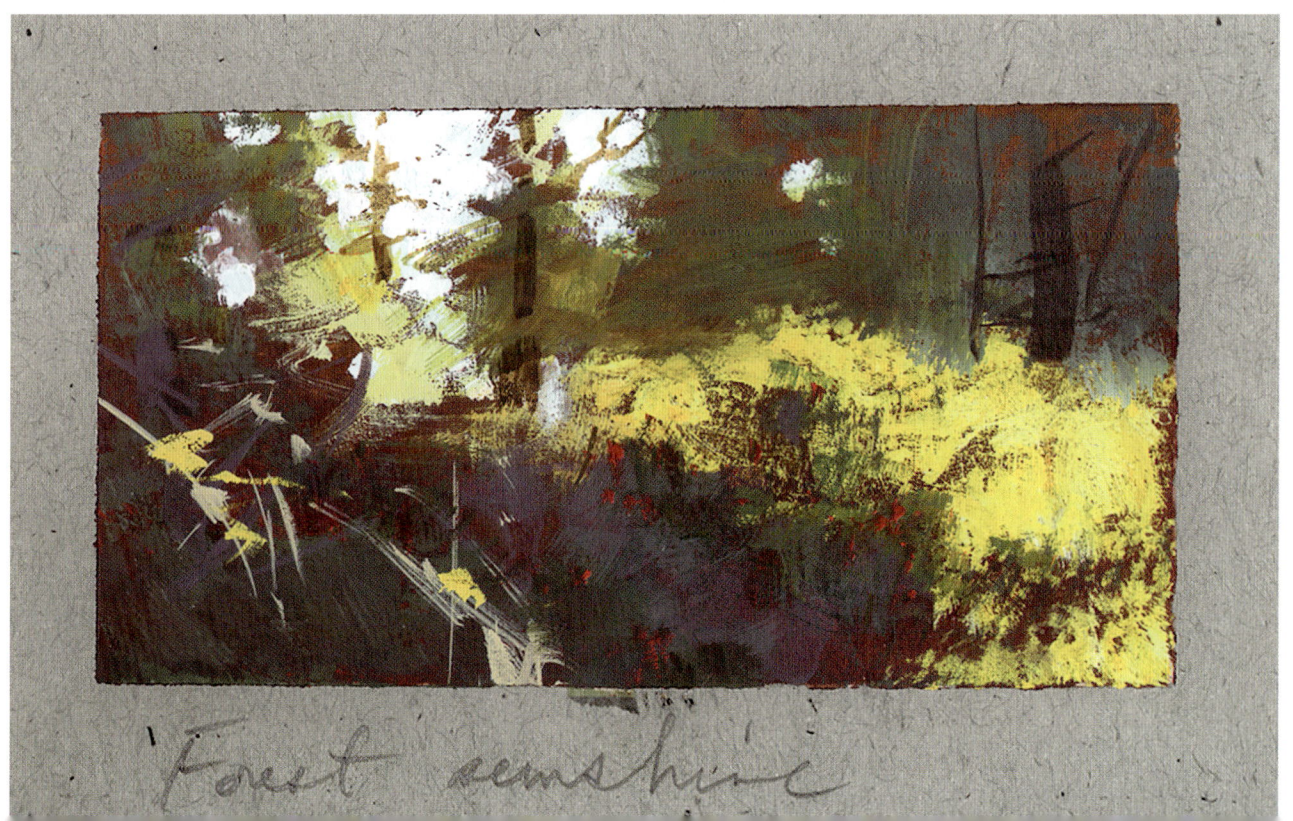

Northern California forest, California; watercolor and white gouache on toned mixed-media paper, 3 x 5 inches

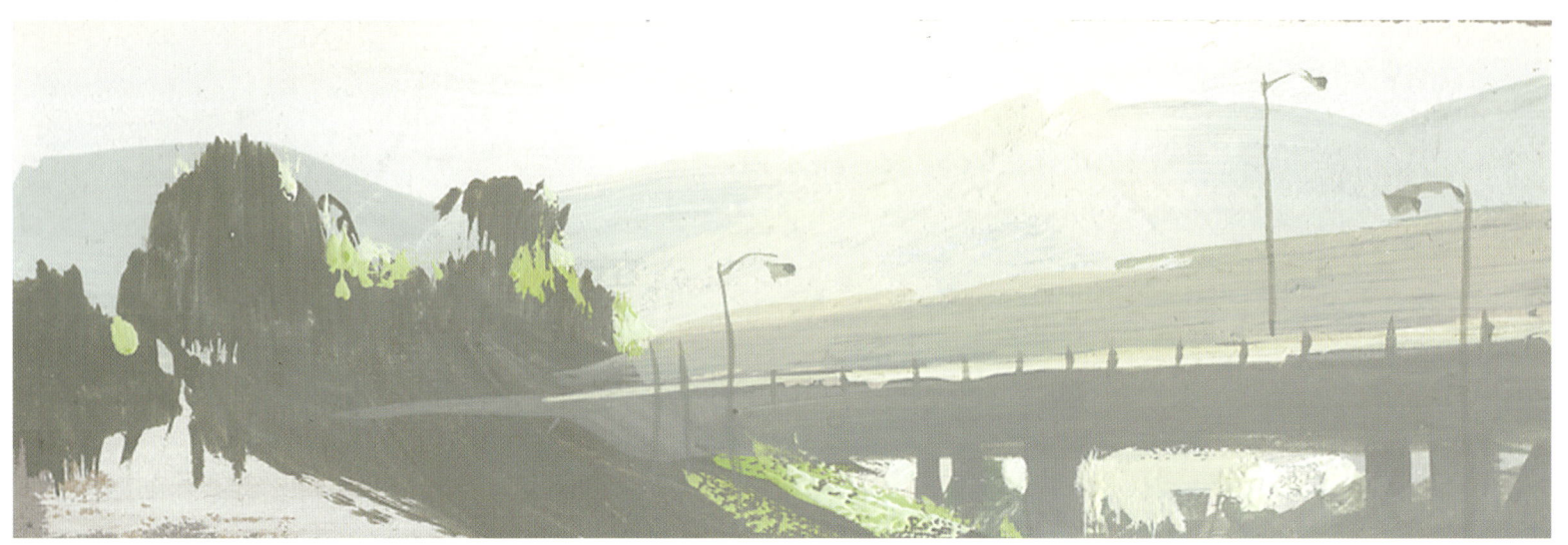

Freeway overpass,
Los Angeles, California;
watercolor and white gouache
on toned mixed-media paper,
2 x 5 inches

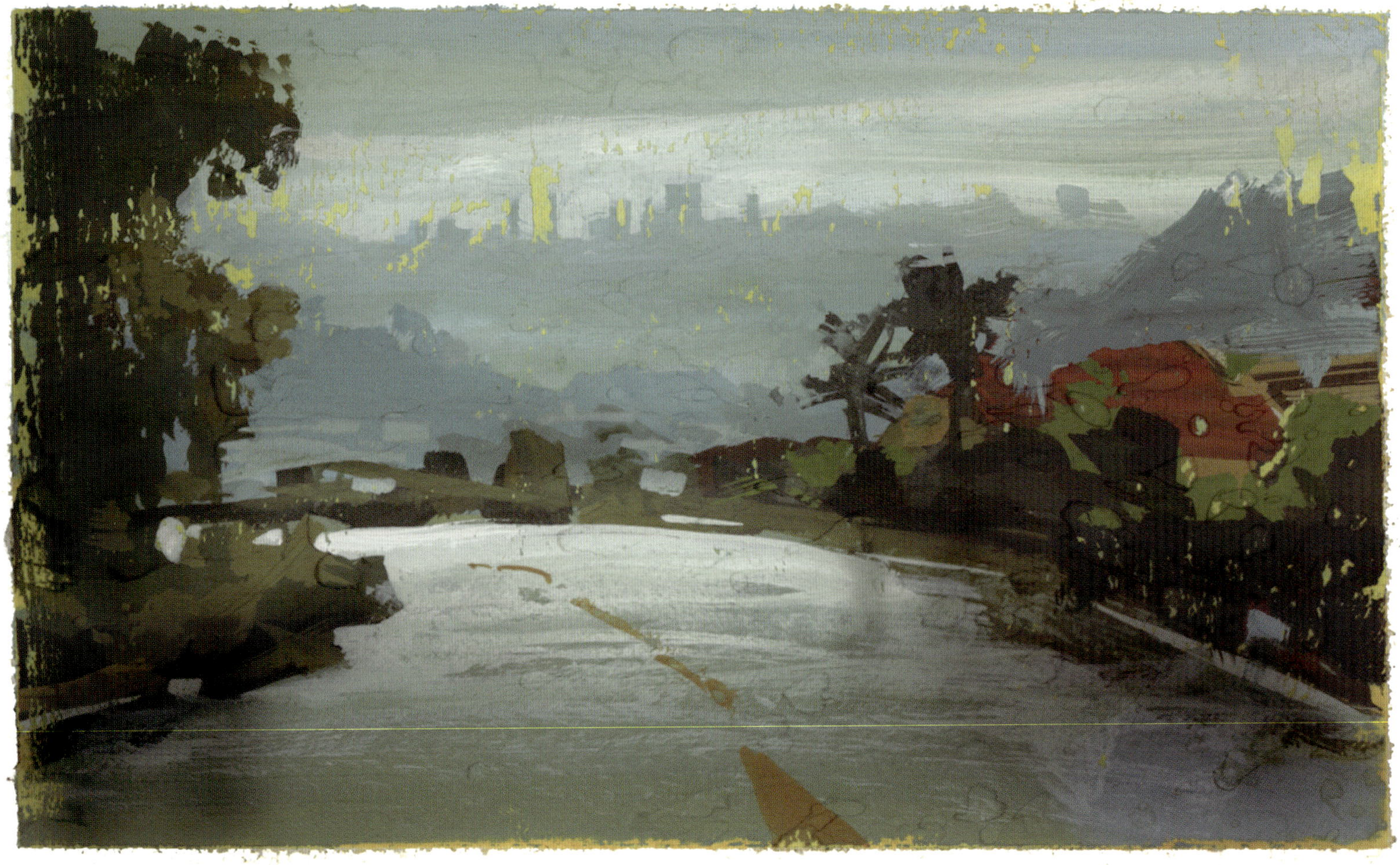

Los Angeles, California;
watercolor and white gouache
on Crescent No. 100 illustra-
tion board, 5 x 7 inches

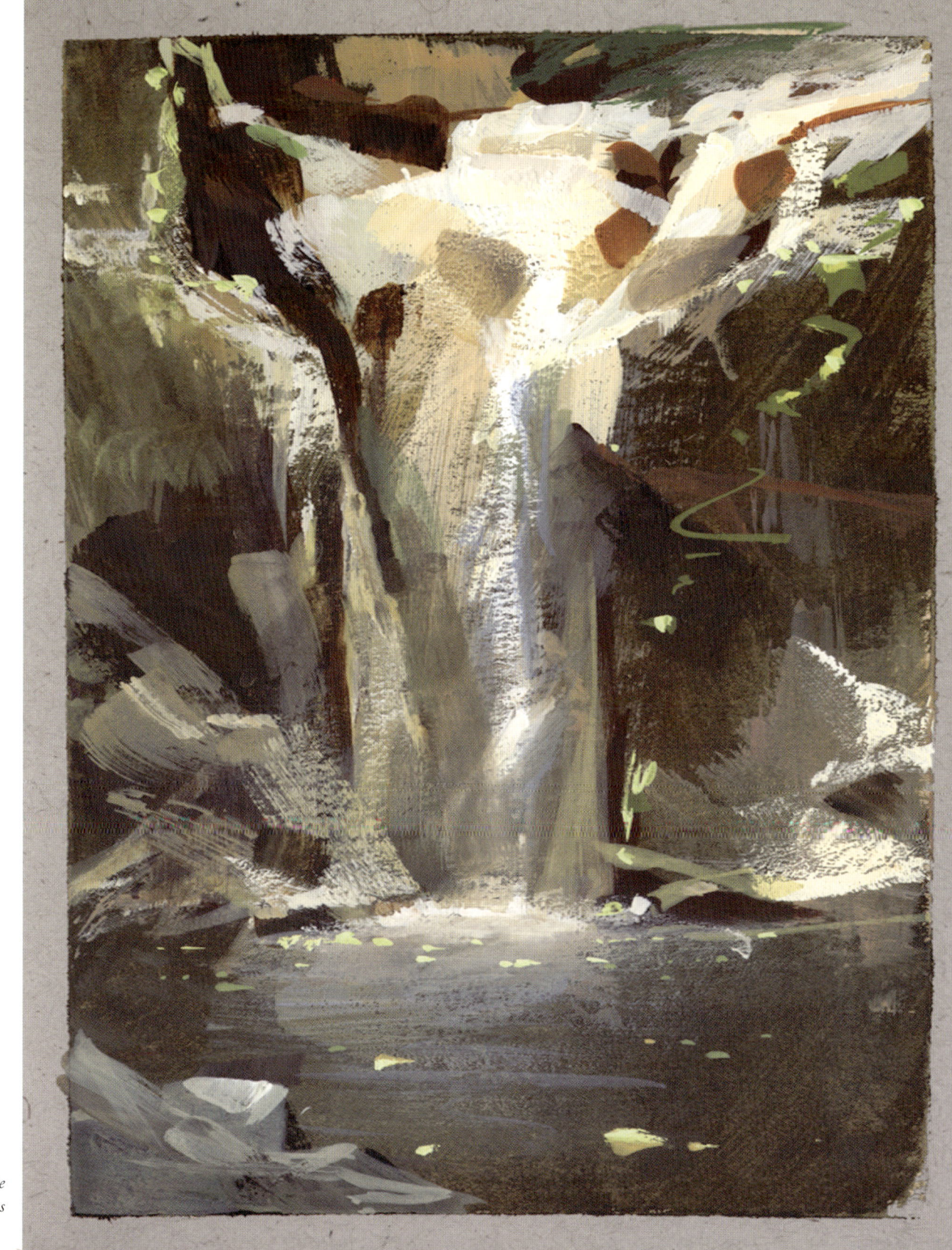

Jungle falls, Costa Rica; watercolor and white gouache on toned mixed-media paper, 6 x 4 inches

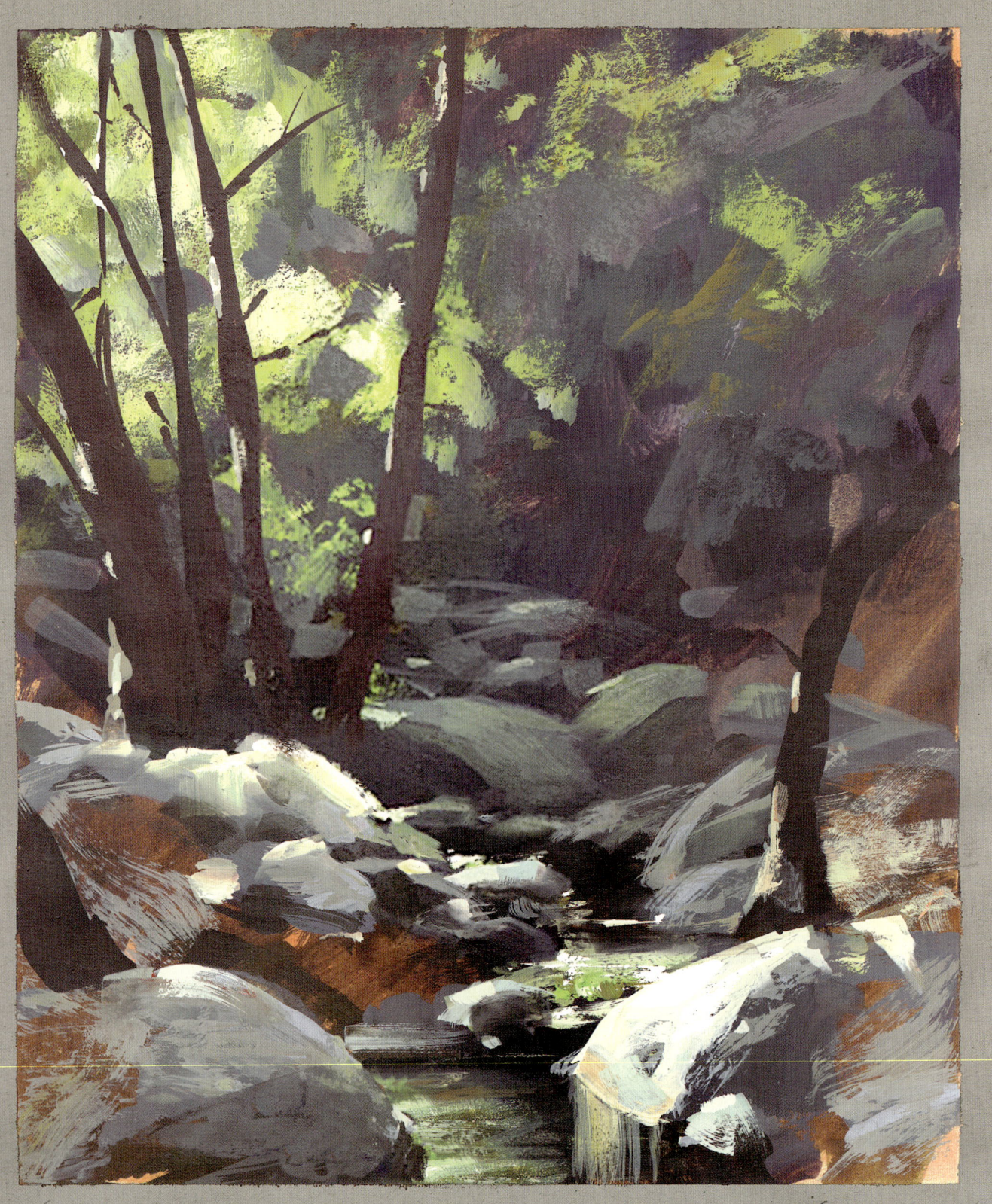

Switzer canyon creek

9·23·04

Switzer Canyon creek, San Diego, California;
watercolor and white gouache on toned
mixed-media paper, 10 x 7 inches

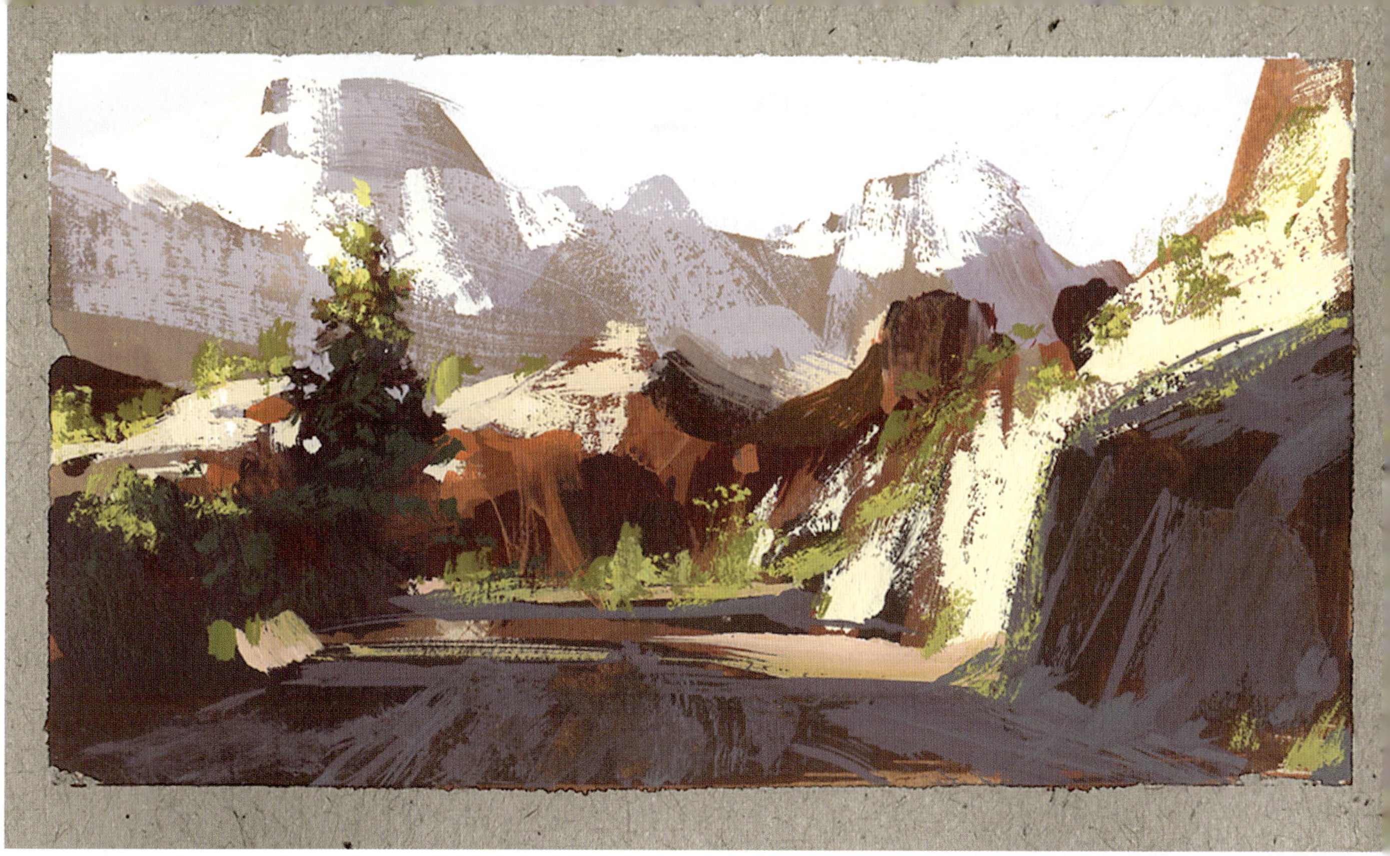

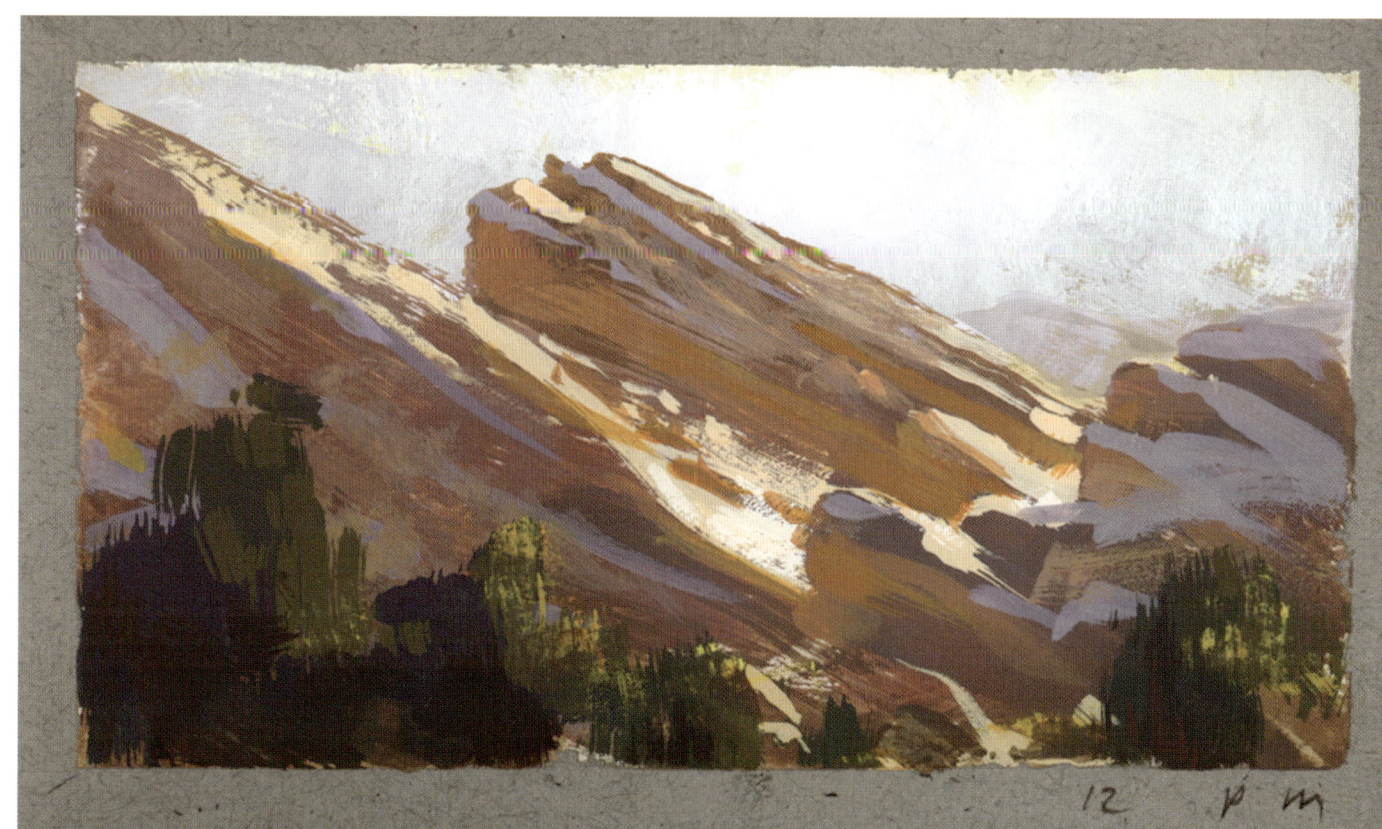

*Zion National Park, Utah; water-
color and white gouache on toned
mixed-media paper, 3 x 5 inches*

*Vasquez Rocks, Los Angeles County,
California; watercolor and white gouache on
toned mixed-media paper, 3 x 5 inches*

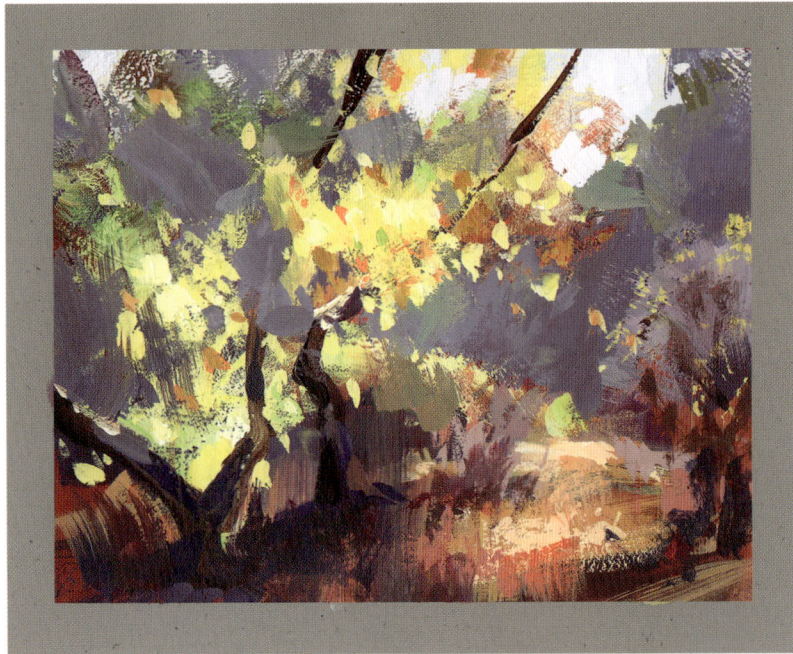

Eaton Canyon tree, Pasadena, California; watercolor and white gouache on toned mixed-media paper, 5 x 7 inches

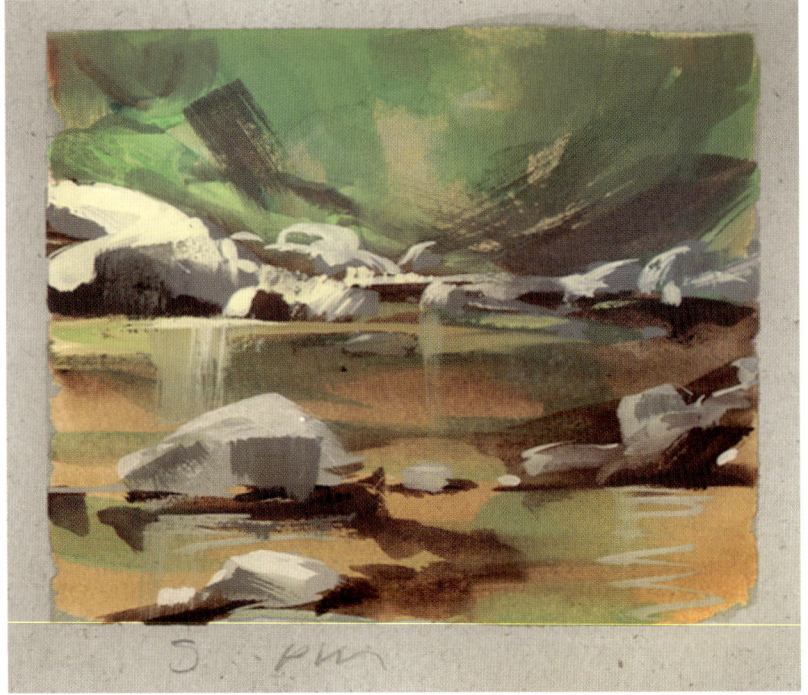

Big Tujunga Creek, Los Angeles County, California; watercolor and white gouache on toned mixed-media paper, 4 x 5 inches

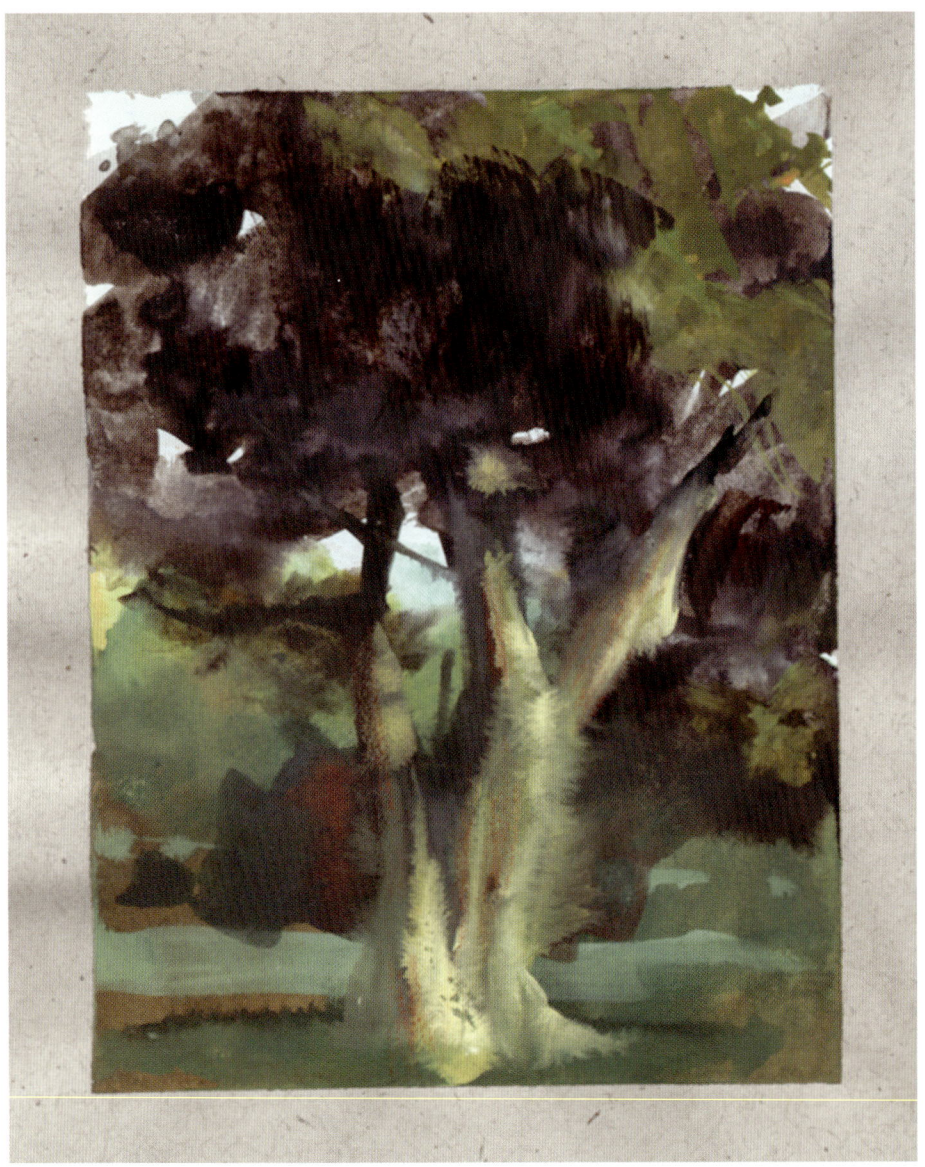

Griffith Park tree, Los Angeles, California; watercolor and white gouache on toned mixed-media paper, 7 x 4 inches

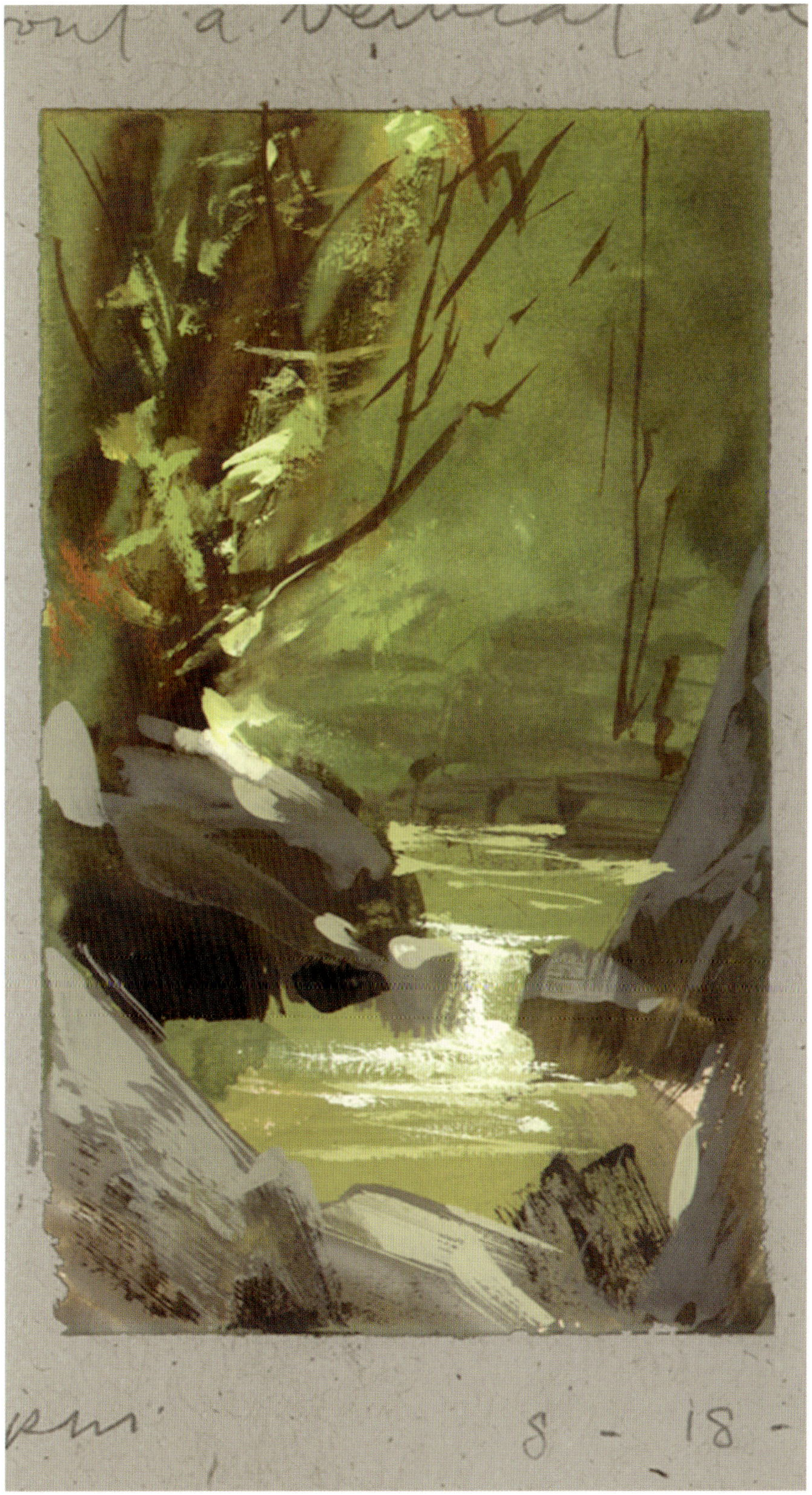

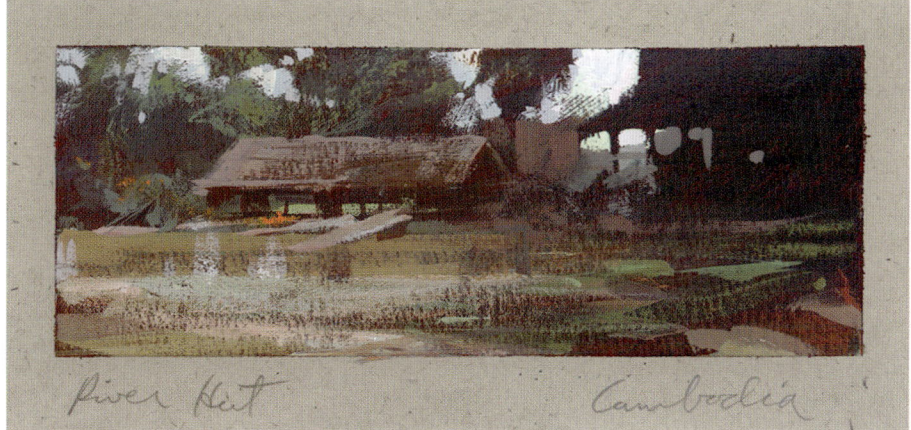

River hut, Cambodia; watercolor and white gouache on toned mixed-media paper, 3 x 6 inches

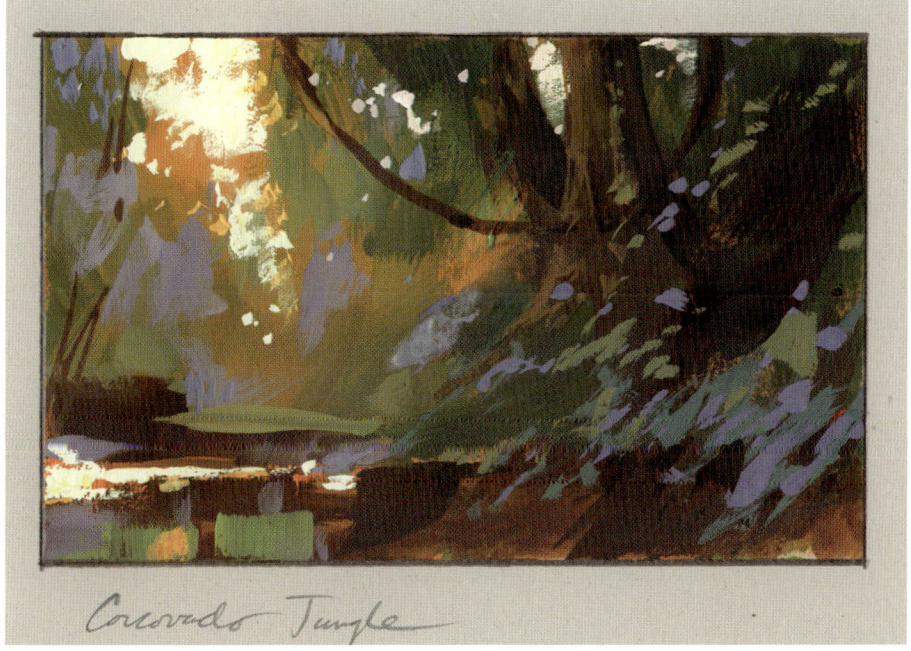

Corcovado National Park, Costa Rica; watercolor and white gouache on toned mixed-media paper, 5 x 7 inches

Big Tujunga Creek, Los Angeles County, California; watercolor and white gouache on toned mixed-media paper, 8 x 4 inches

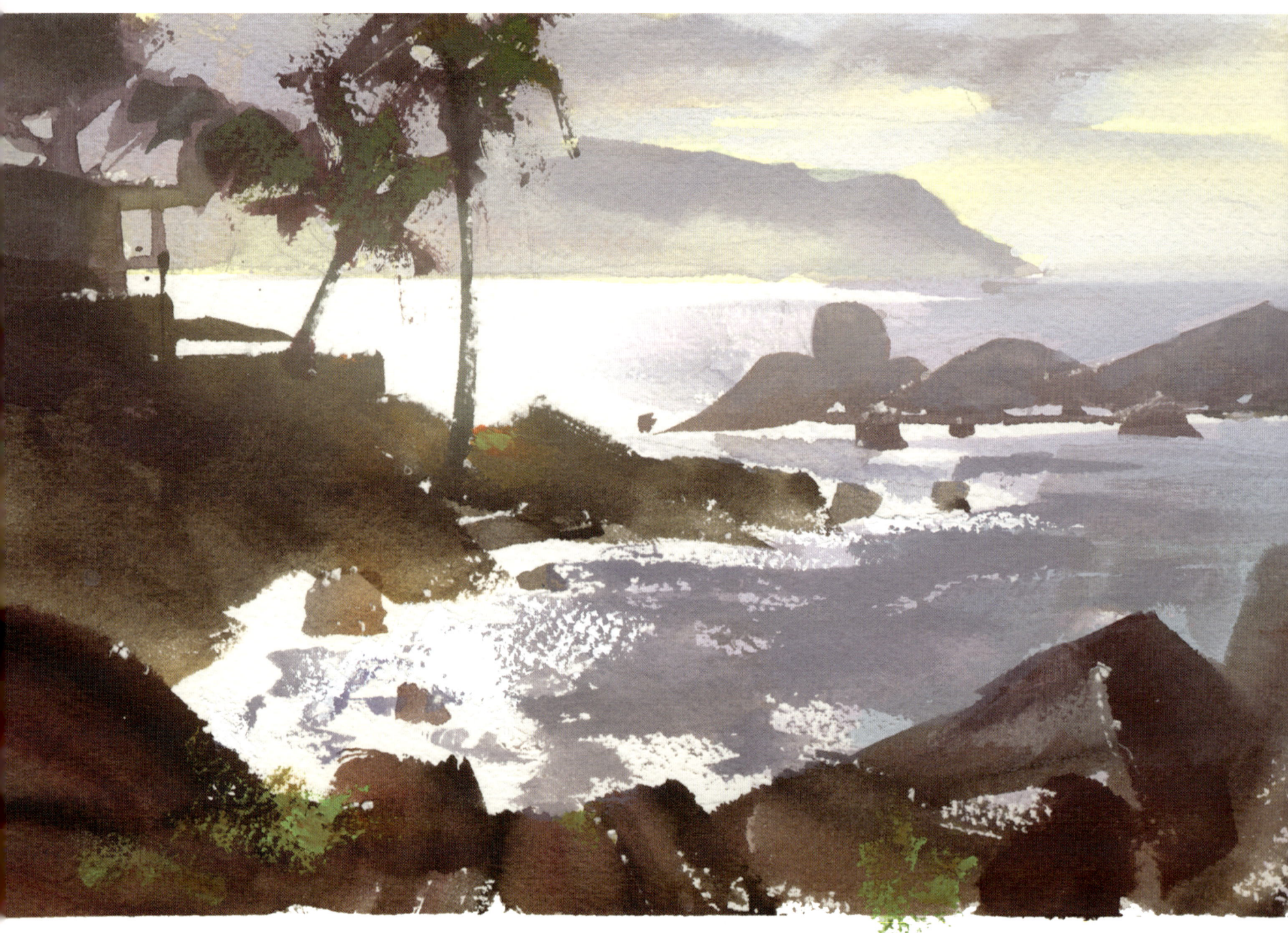

North Shore, Oahu, Hawaii; watercolor on
Arches cold-pressed paper, 7 x 10 inches

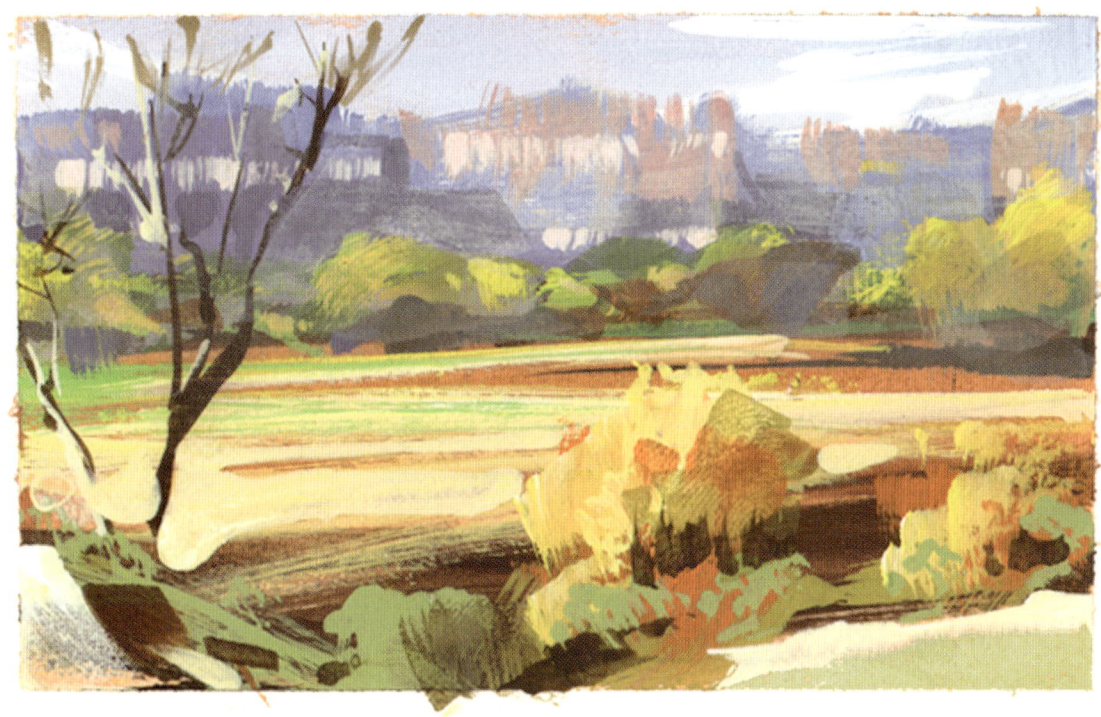

Hurricane, Utah; watercolor and white gouache on Crescent No. 100 illustration board, 5 x 7 inches

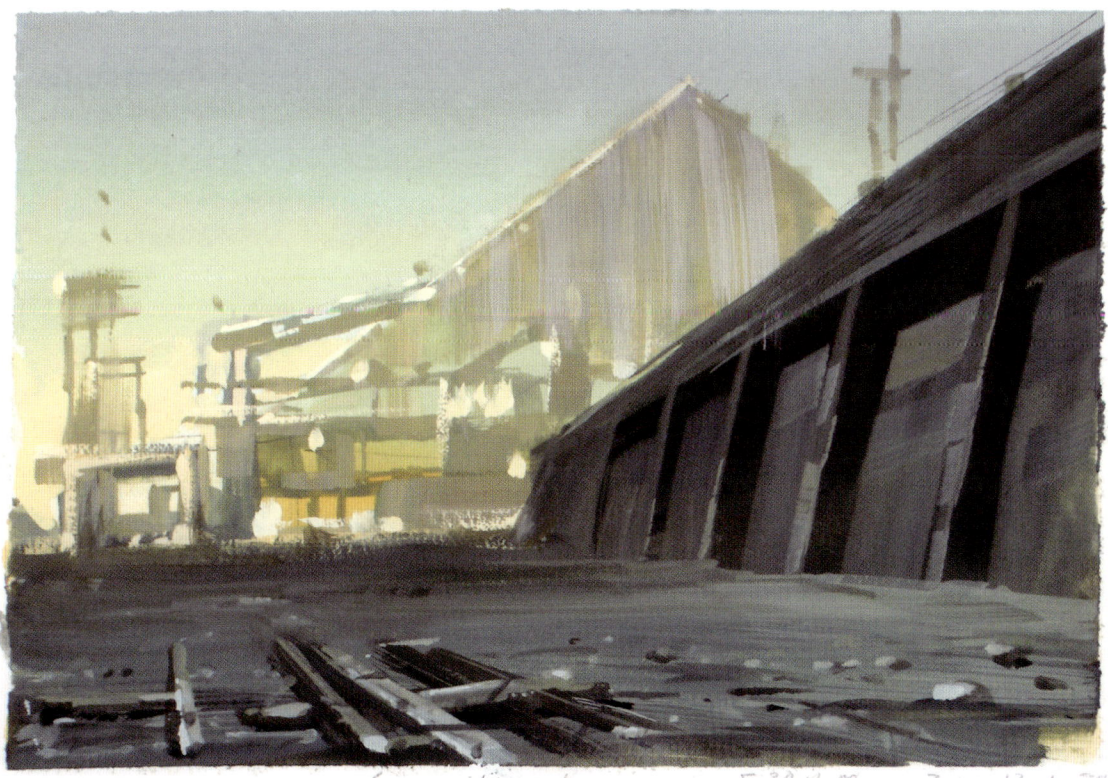

Industrial docks, San Pedro, California; watercolor and white gouache on Crescent No. 100 illustration board, 6 x 8 inches

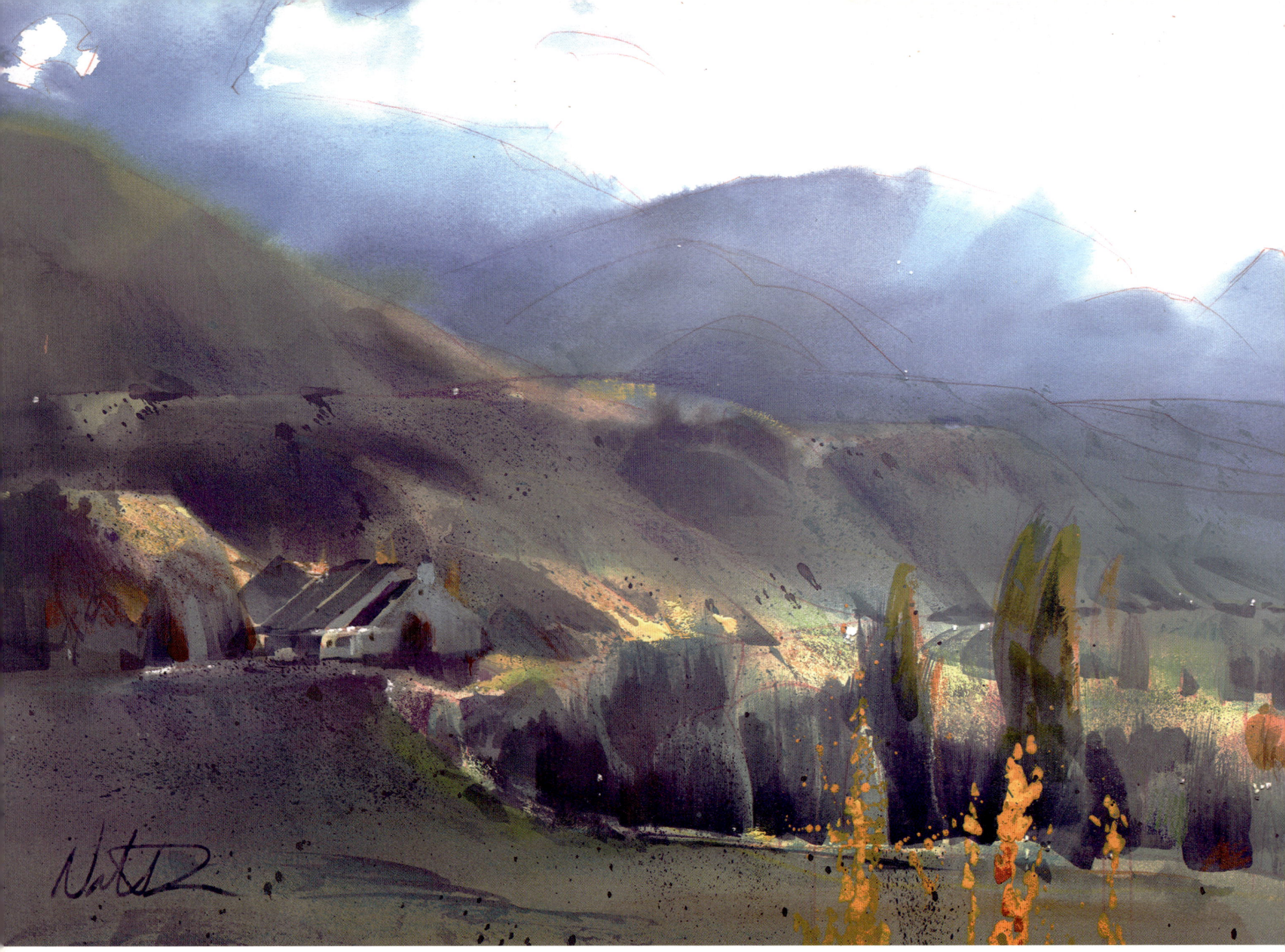

*Springville, Utah; watercolor on Crescent No.
100 illustration board, 11 x 14 inches*

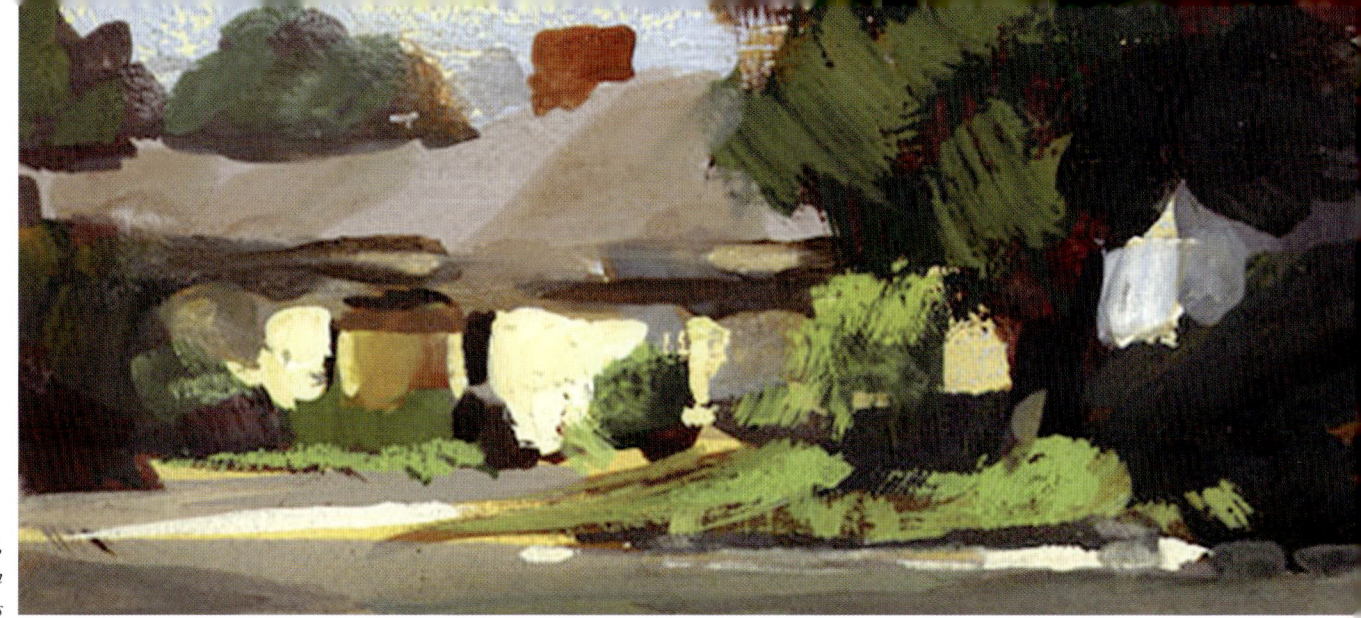

Neighborhood home, Glendale, California; watercolor and white gouache on toned mixed-media paper, 2 x 4 inches

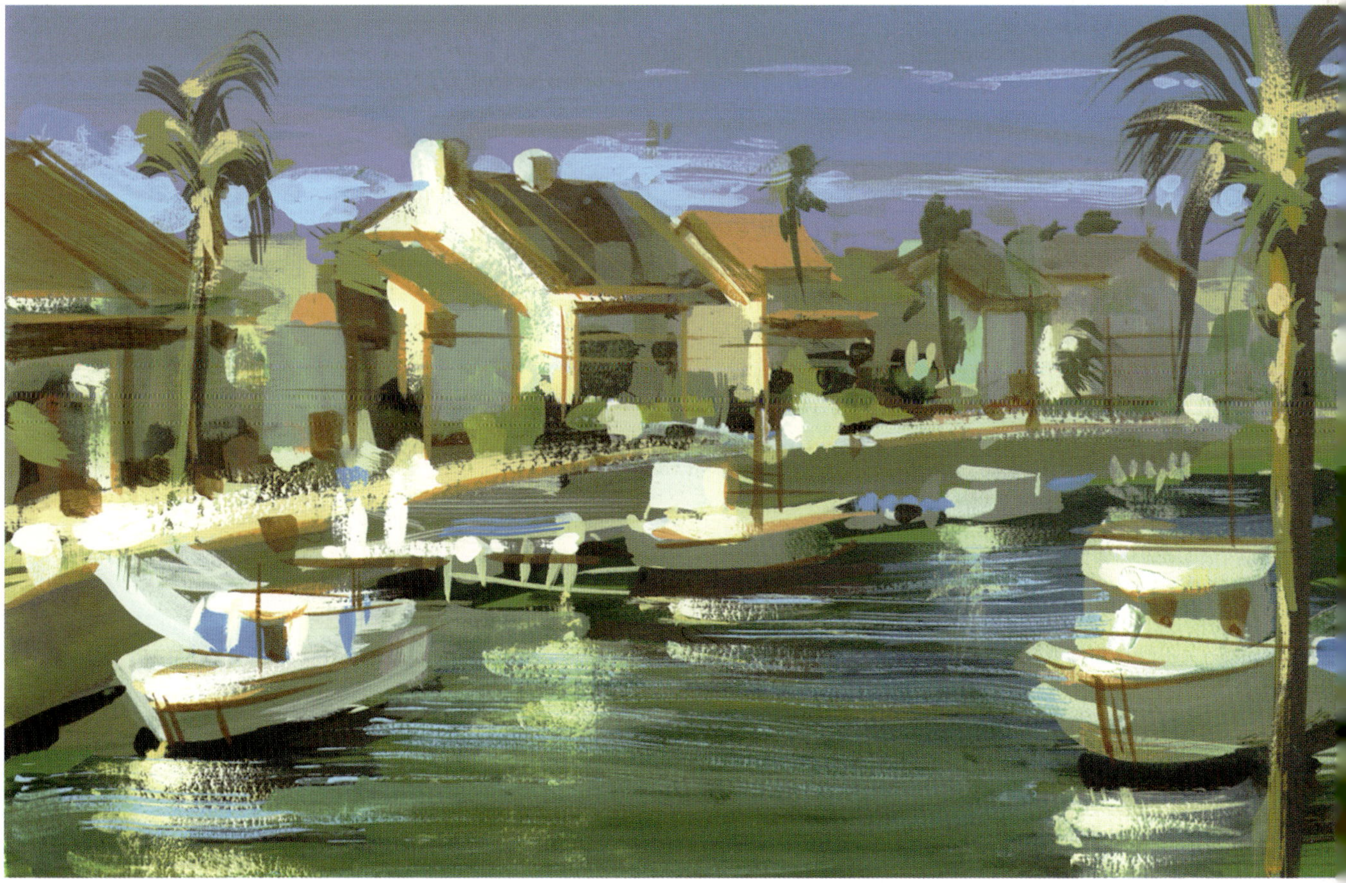

Belmont Shore, Long Beach, California; watercolor and white gouache on Crescent No. 100 illustration board, 5 x 7 inches

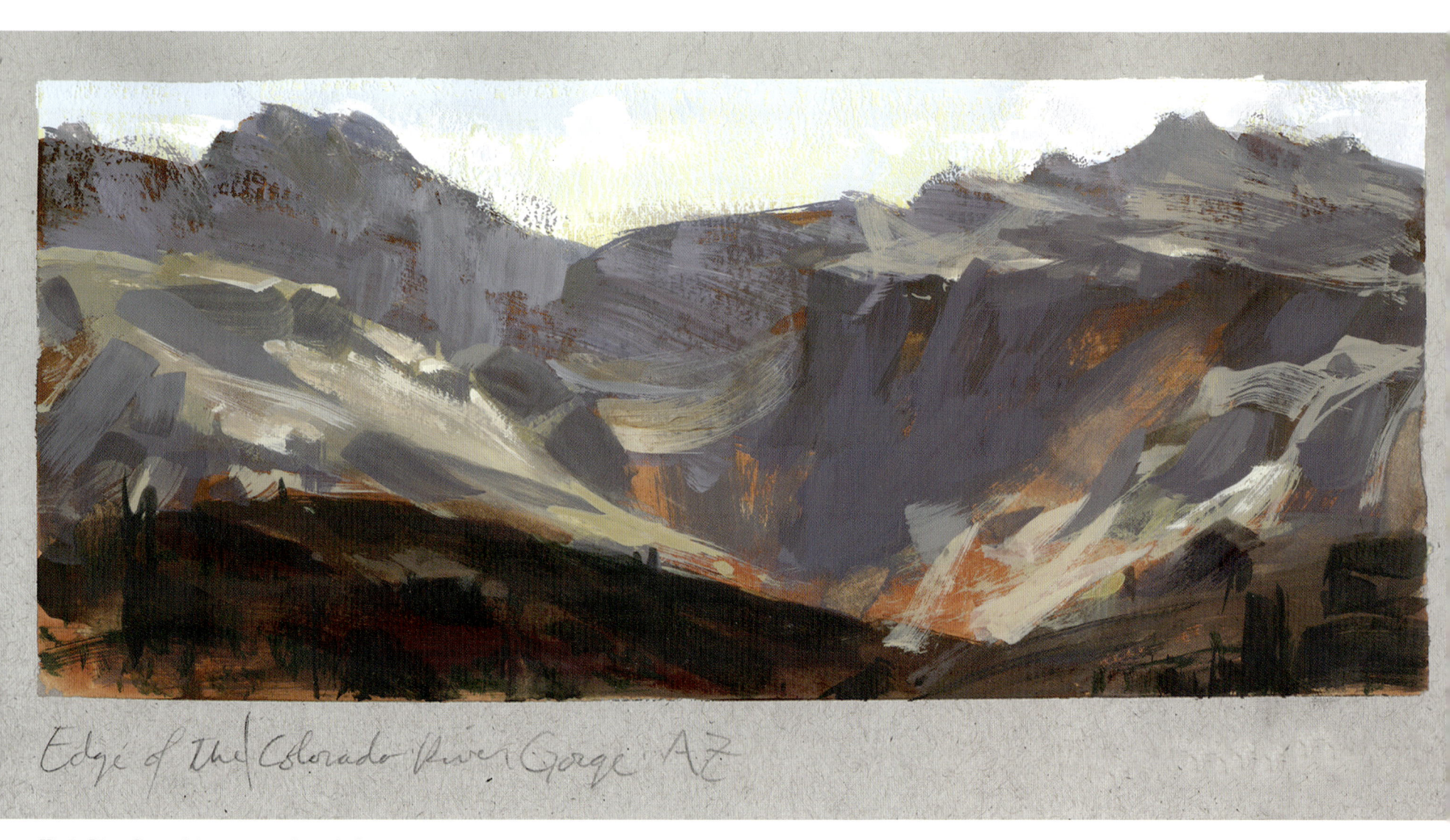

Edge of the Colorado River Gorge · AZ

Virgin River Gorge, Arizona; watercolor and white
gouache on toned mixed-media paper, 7 x 12 inches

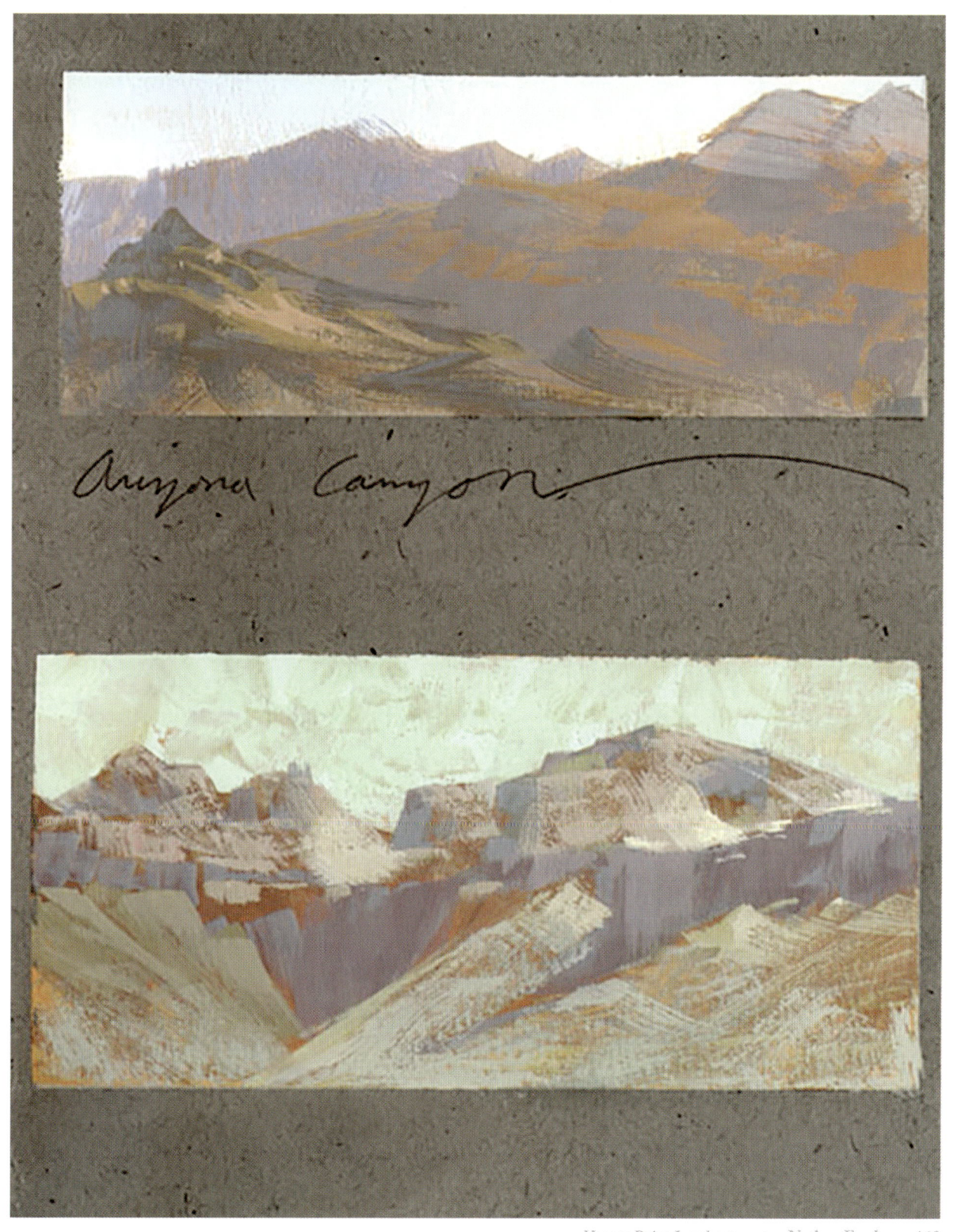

Arizona canyons, Arizona; watercolor and white gouache on toned mixed-media paper, 9 x 5 inches

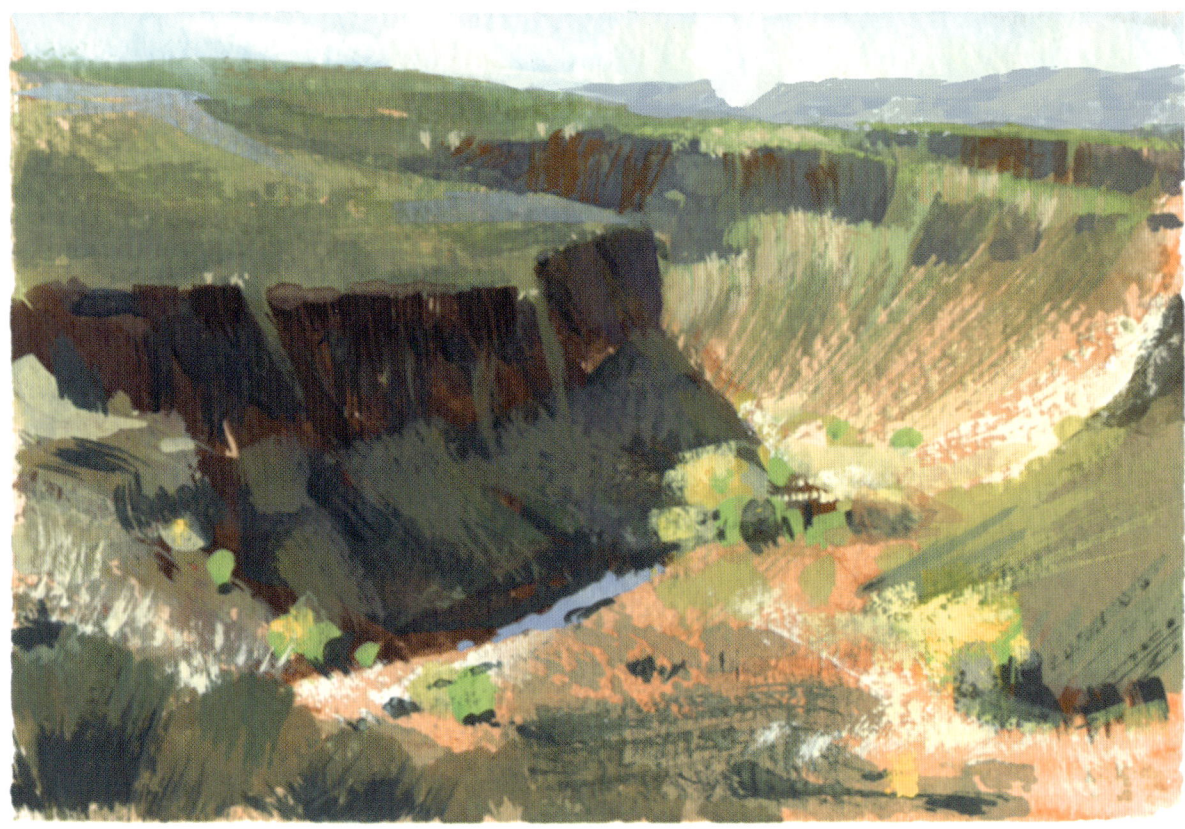

*Hurricane canyon, Utah; watercolor and white gouache
on Arches cold-pressed paper, 5 x 7 inches*

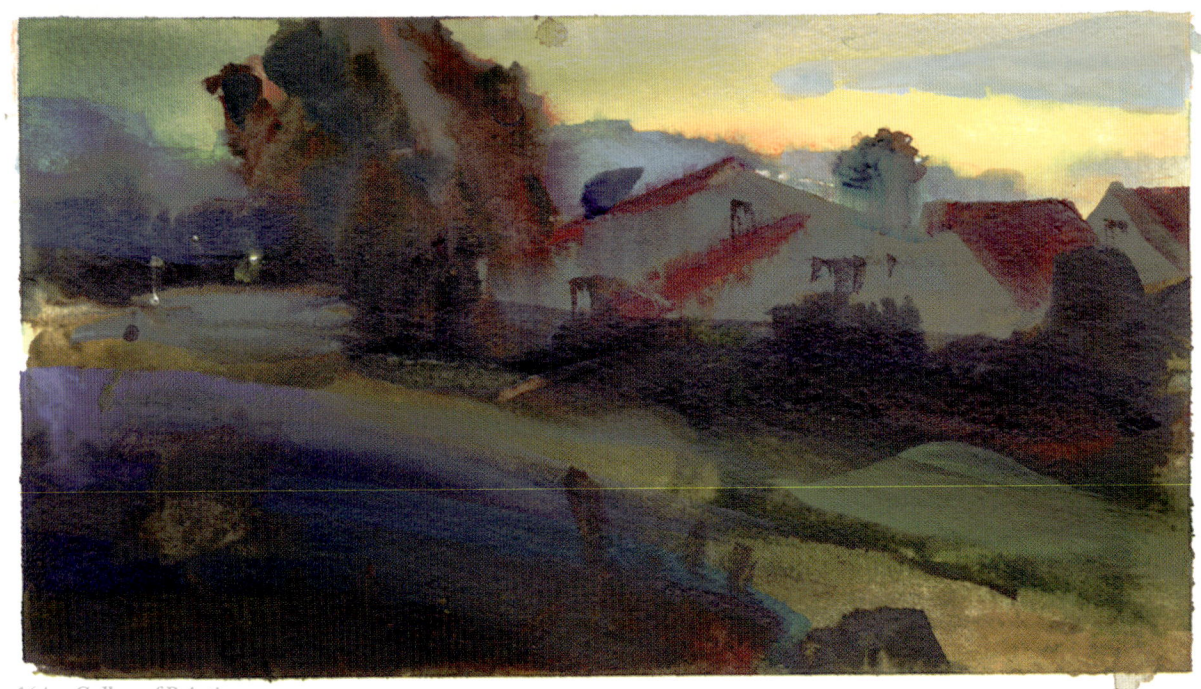

*Redwood Shores, Redwood City, California; Moleskine
watercolor and white gouache sketchbook, 4 x 7 inches*

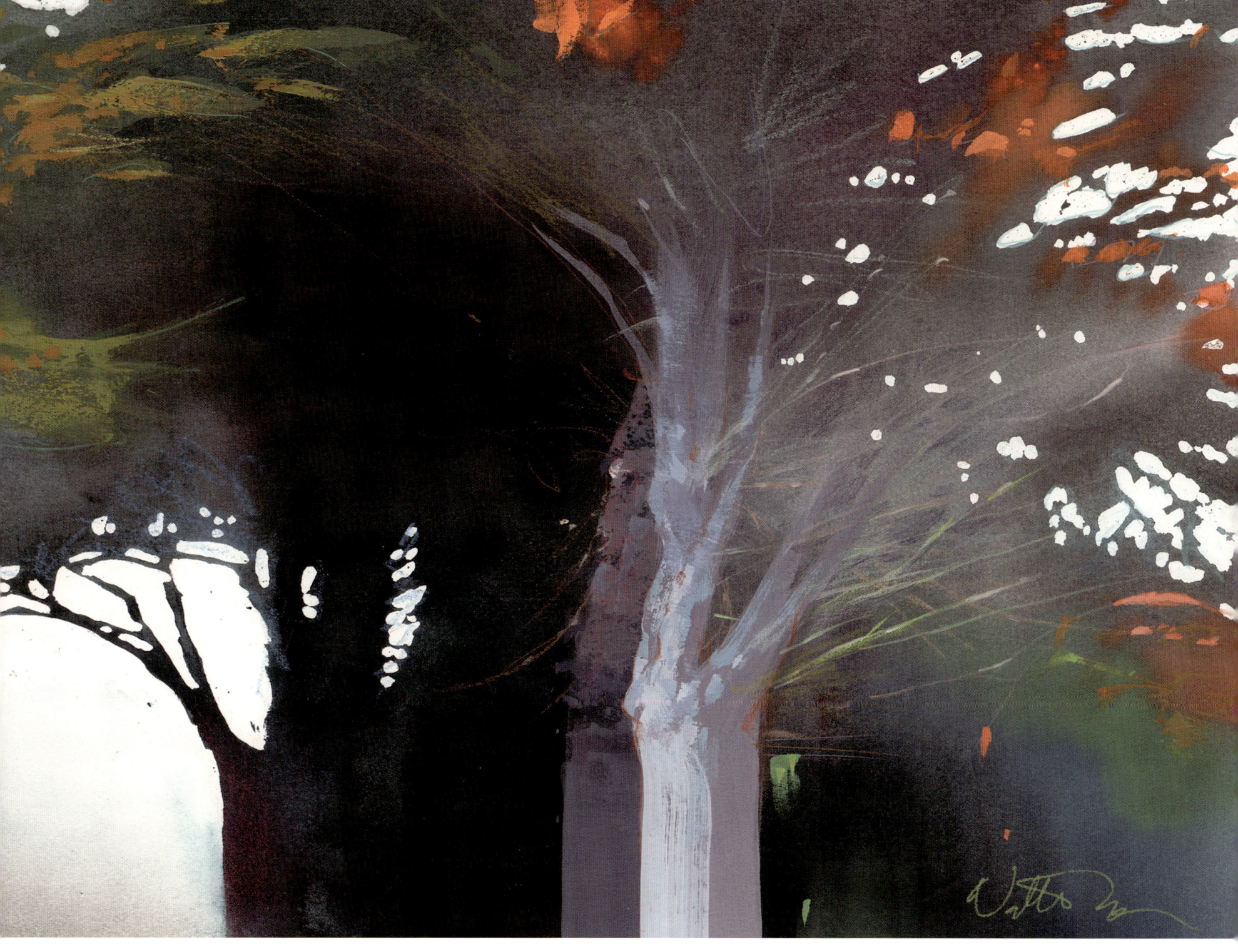

Coastal trees, San Francisco Bay Area, California; watercolor and white gouache on Crescent No. 100 illustration board, 11 x 14 inches

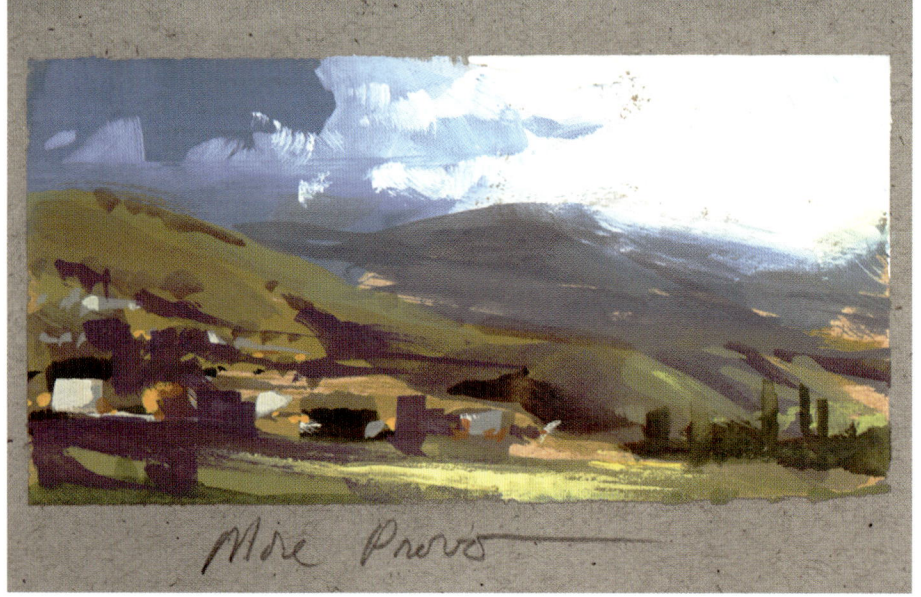

More Provo

Provo, Utah; watercolor and white gouache on toned mixed-media paper, 4 x 6 inches

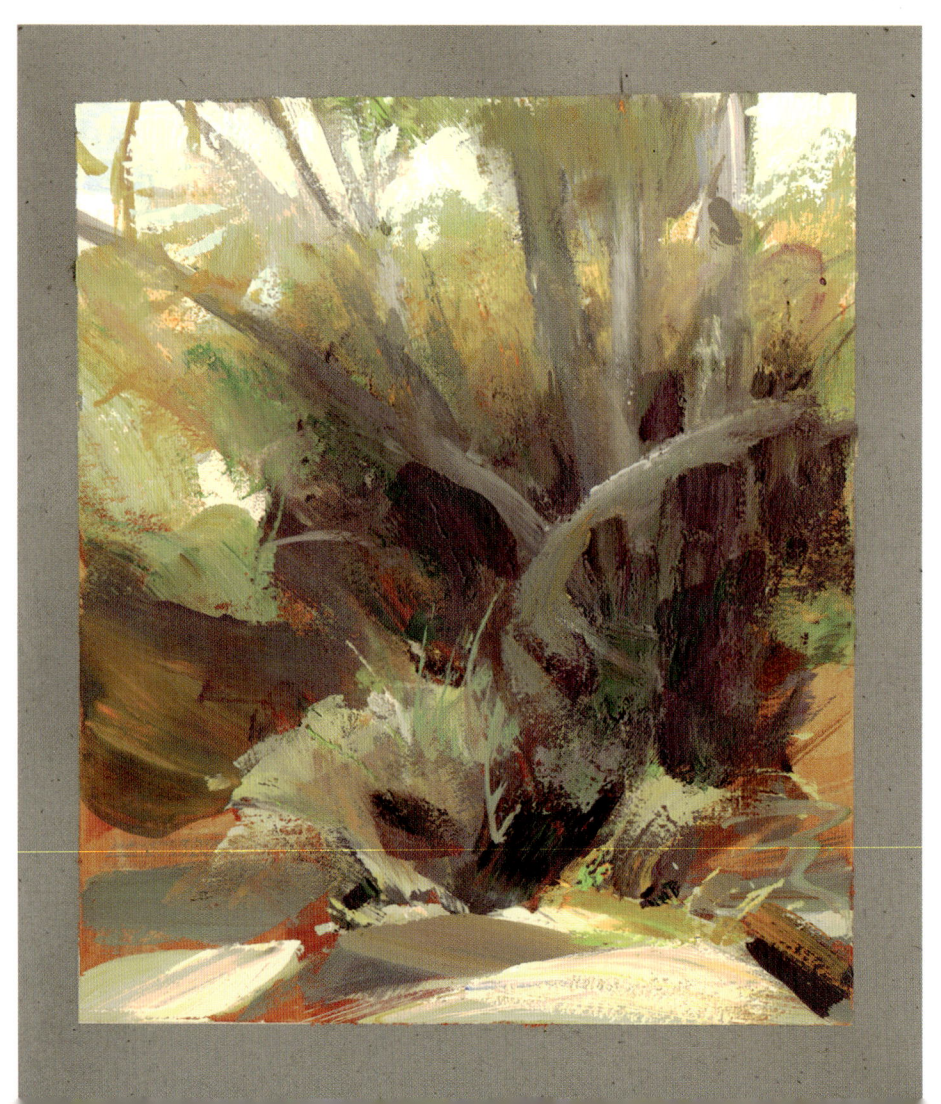

Eaton Canyon, Pasadena, California; watercolor and white gouache on toned mixed-media paper, 8 x 6 inches

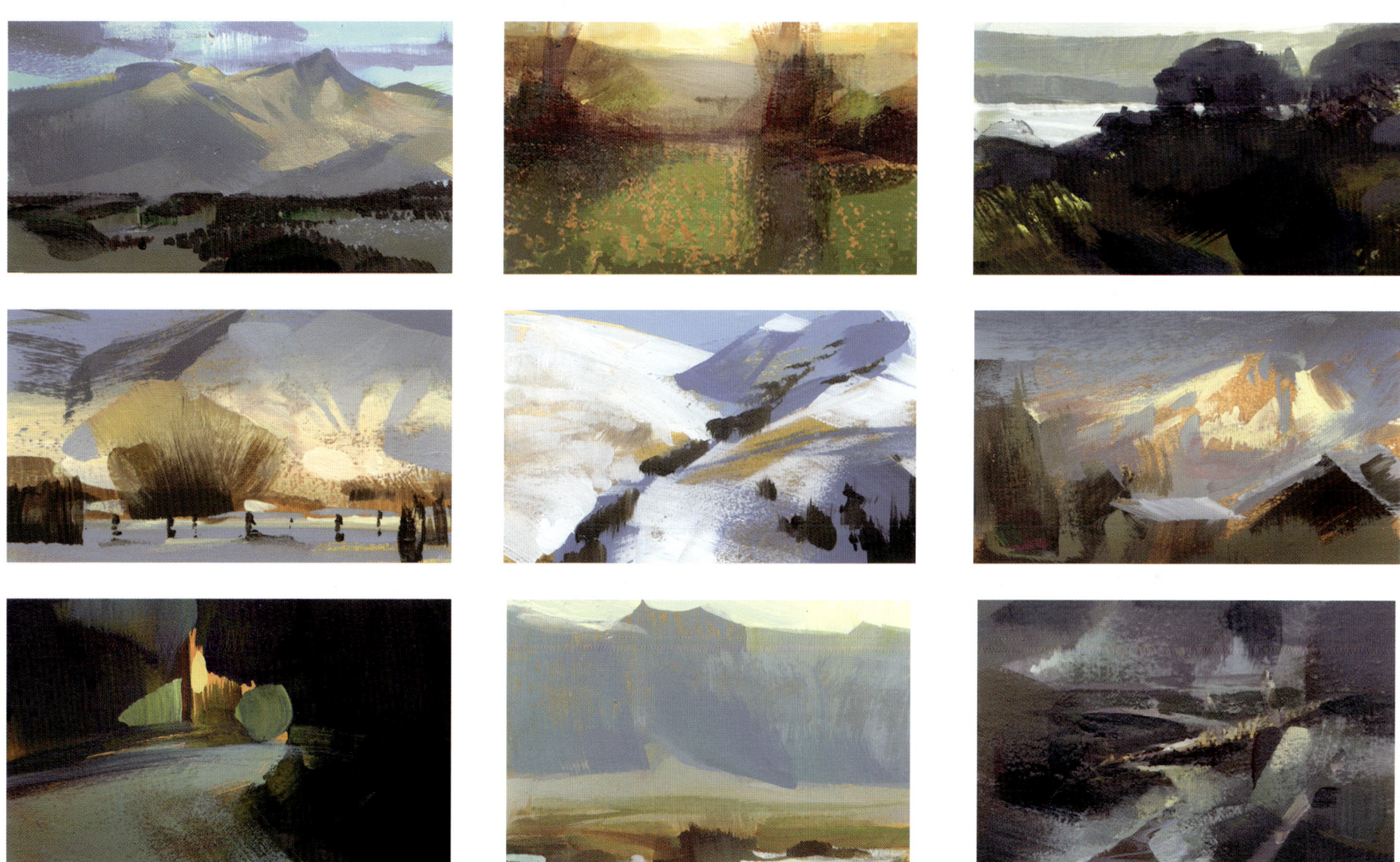

Central Utah studies, Utah; Crescent No. 100
illustration board, 15 x 20 inches

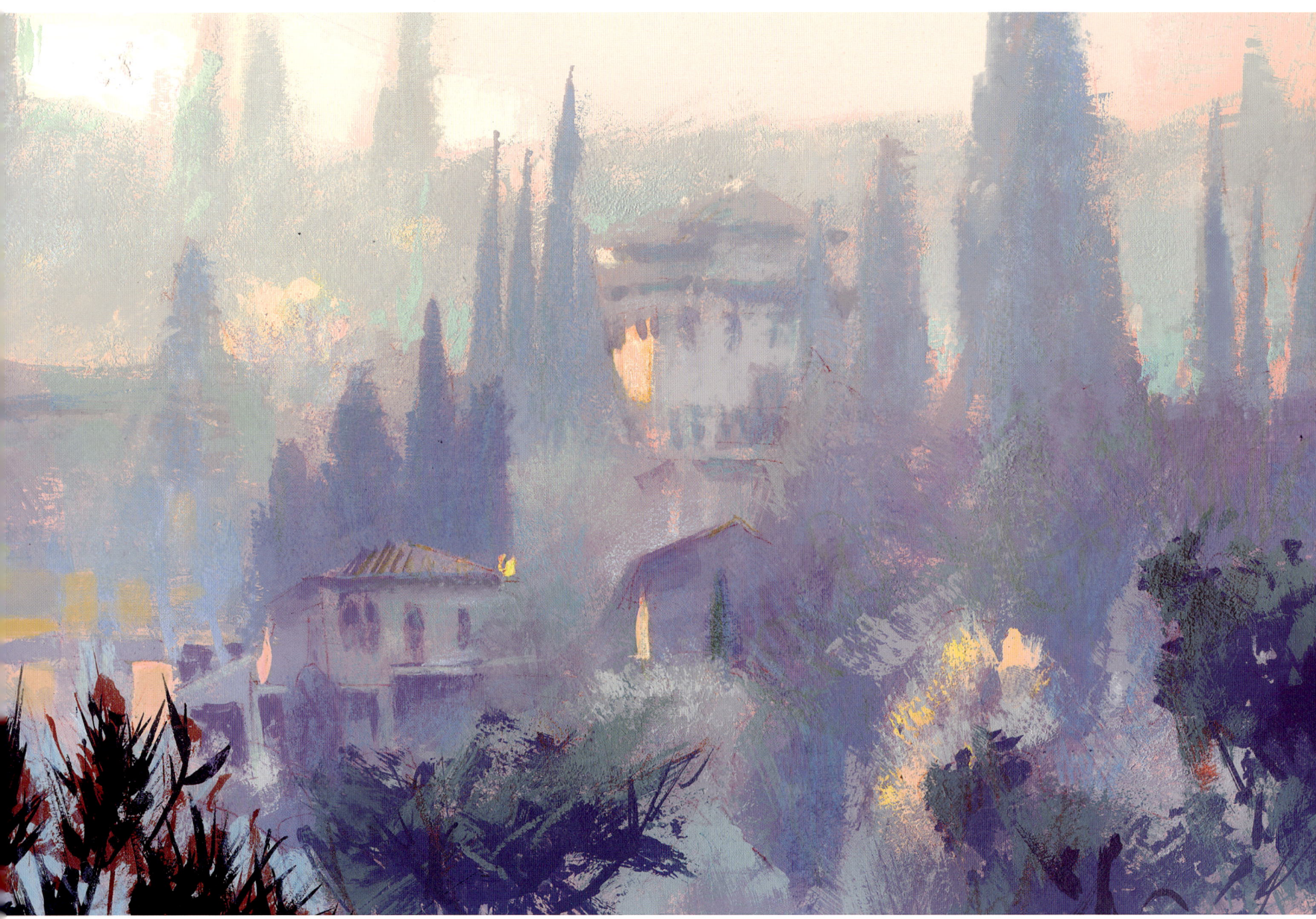

Florence Hillside, Italy; watercolor and white gouache on toned mixed-media paper, 12 x 16 inches

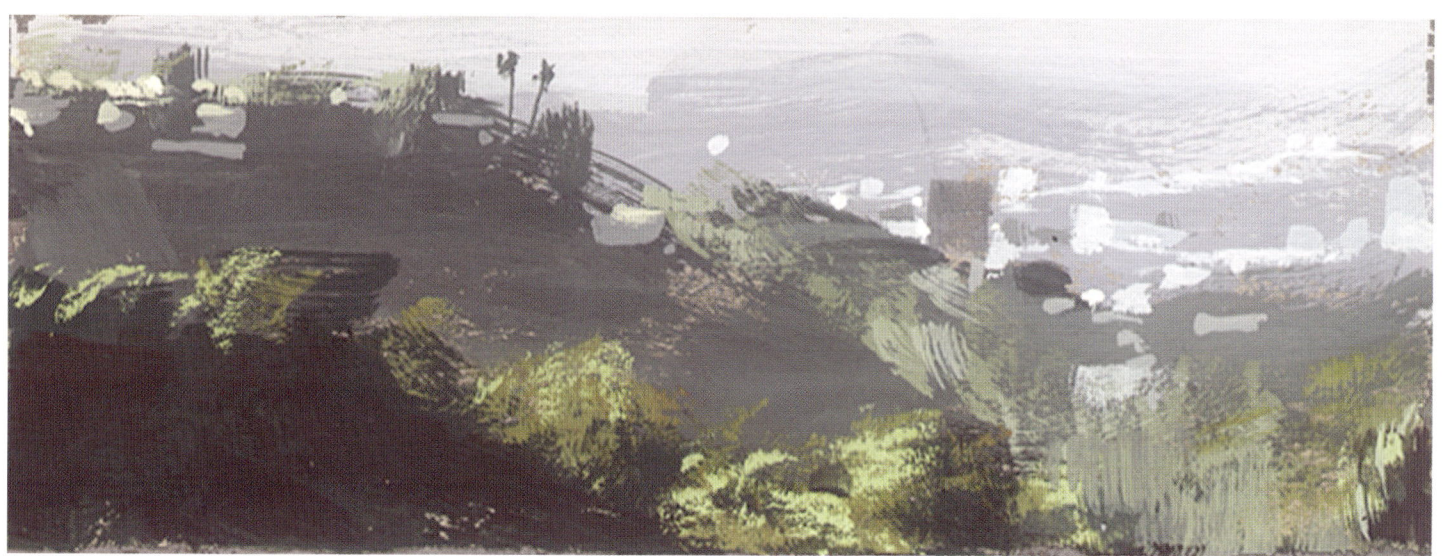

Mulholland Drive,
Los Angeles, California;
watercolor and white gouache
on toned mixed-media paper,
3 x 8 inches

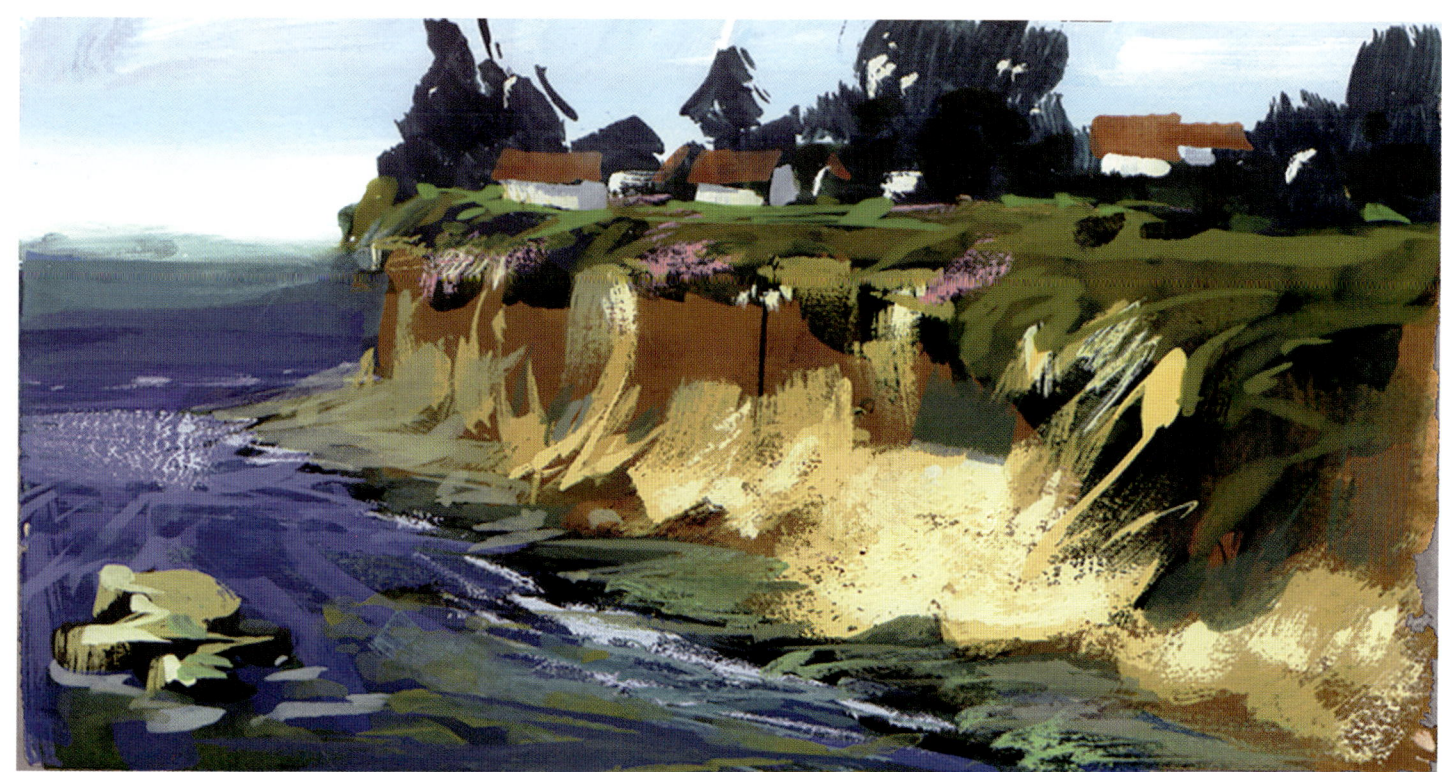

Shell Beach, Pismo Beach,
California; watercolor
and white gouache on
toned mixed-media paper,
4 x 6 inches

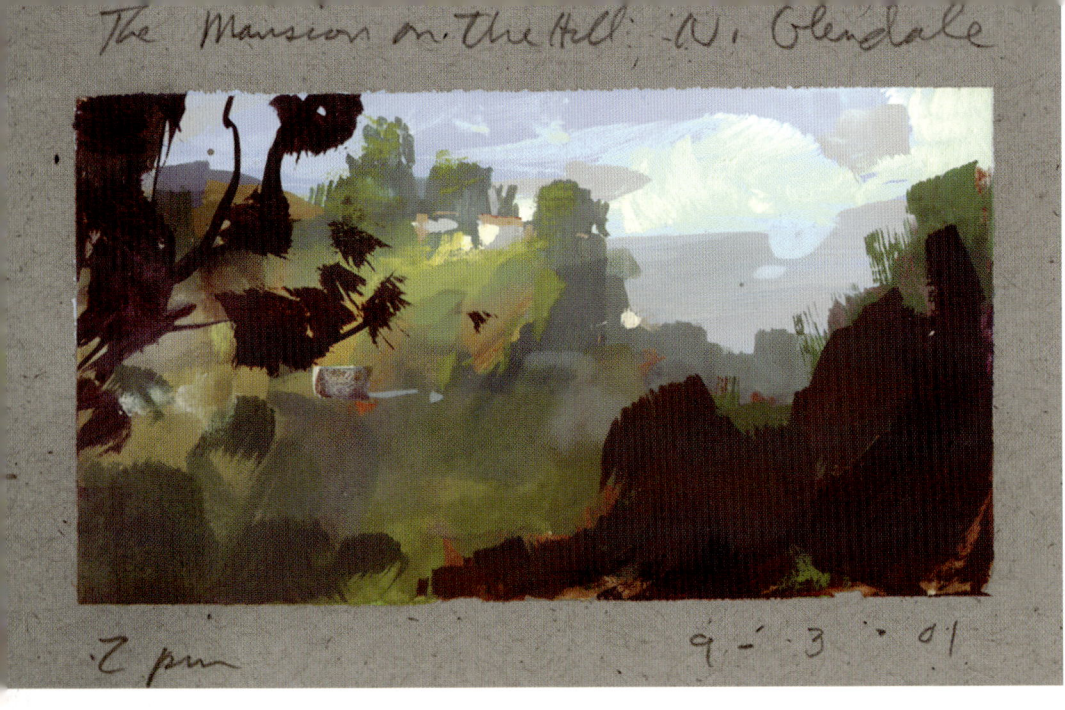

The Mansion on the Hill; N. Glendale

2 pm   9 - 3 - 01

Glendale hills, California; watercolor and white gouache on toned mixed-media paper, 3 x 5 inches

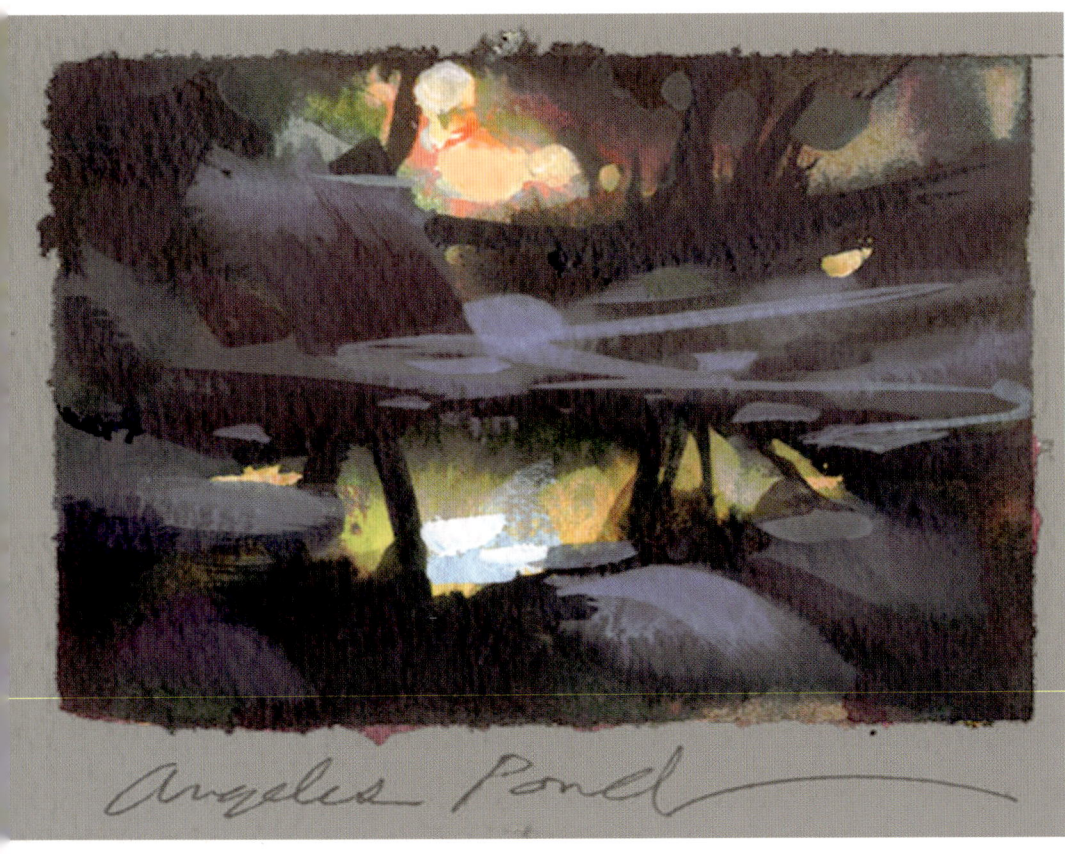

Angeles Pond

Angeles National Forest pond, California; watercolor and white gouache on toned mixed-media paper, 4 x 6 inches

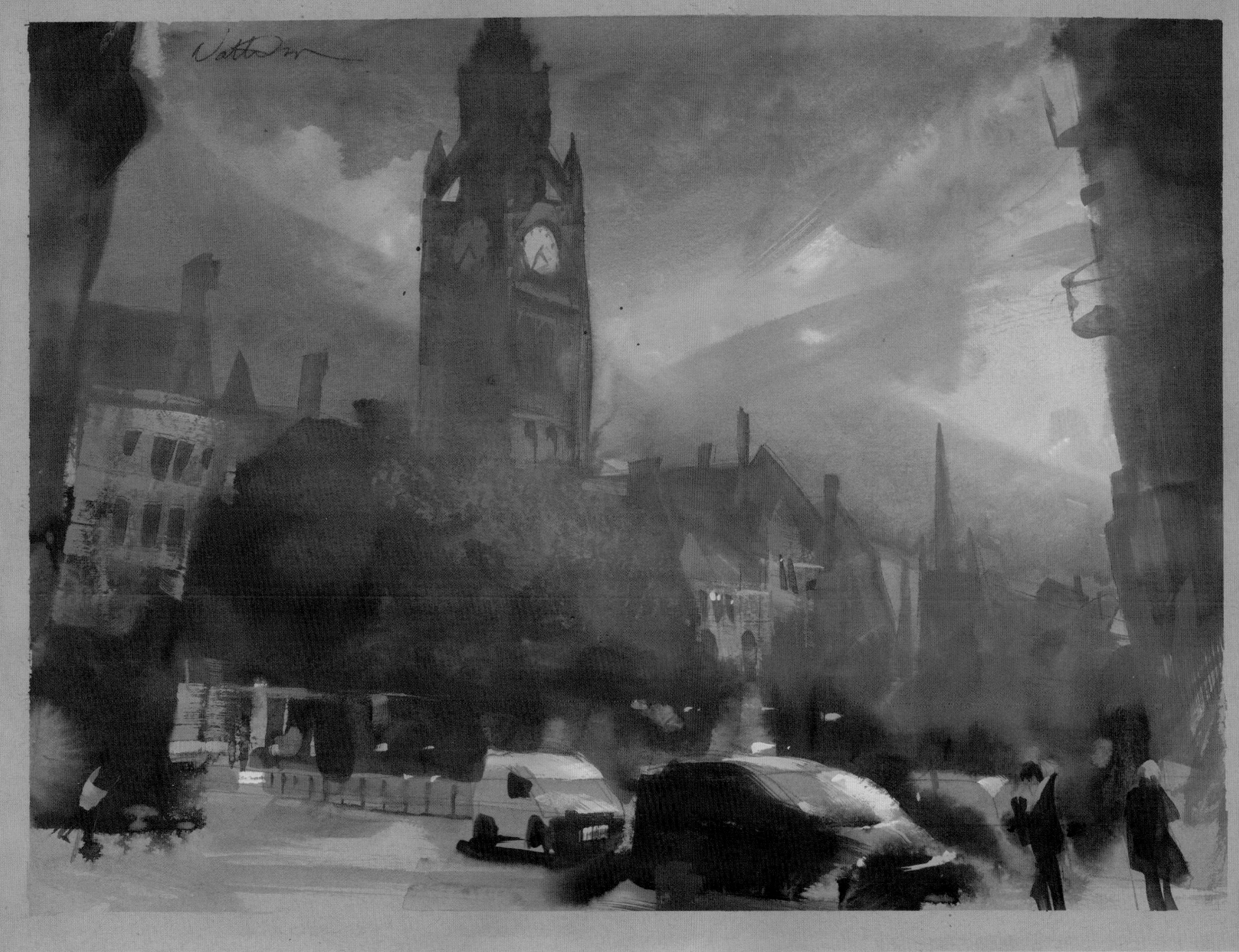

Clock tower, Warsaw, Poland; watercolor and white gouache on
toned mixed-media paper, 11 x 14 inches

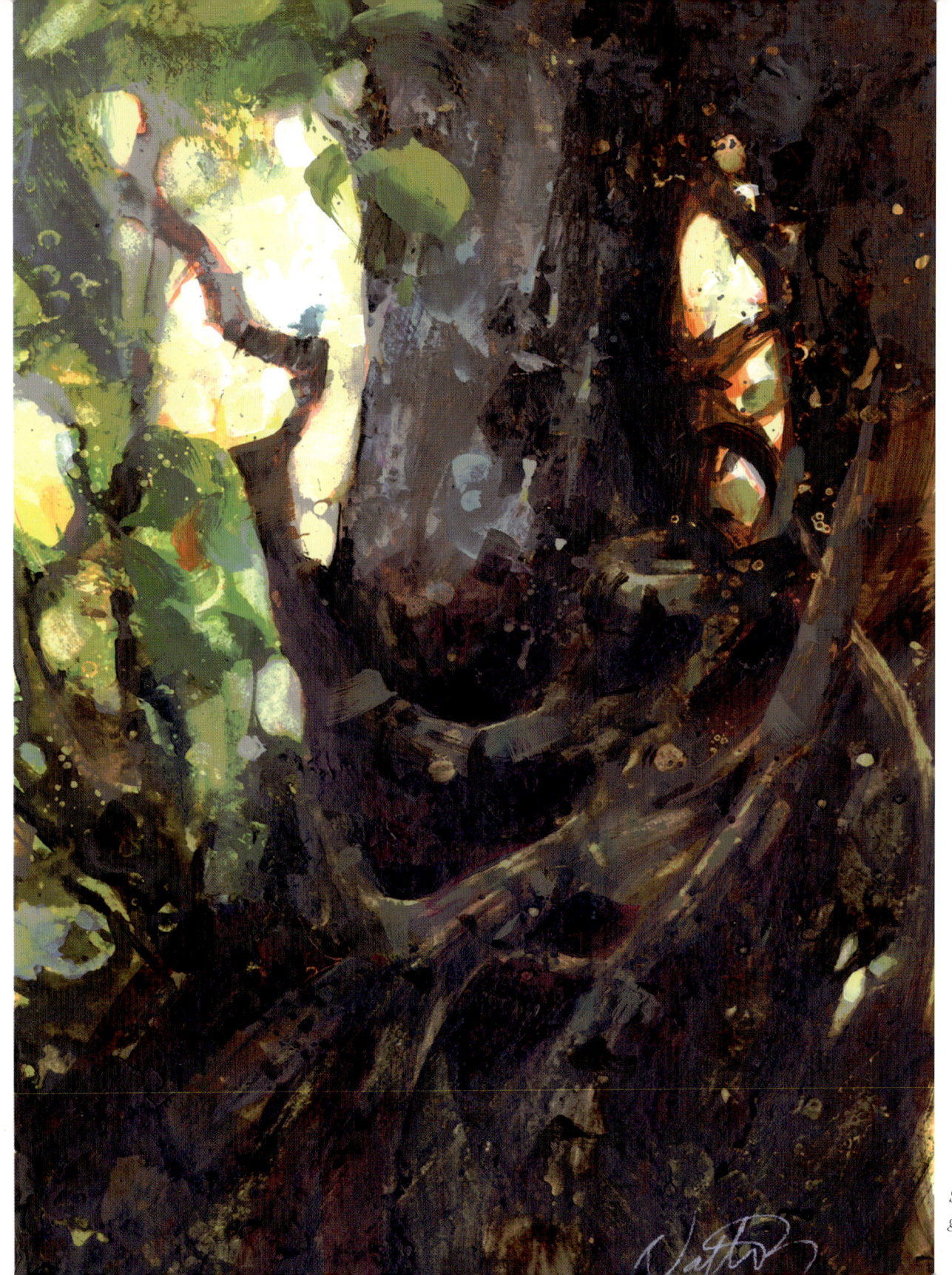

Strangler fig, Costa Rica; watercolor and white gouache on Arches cold-pressed paper, 16 x 10 inches

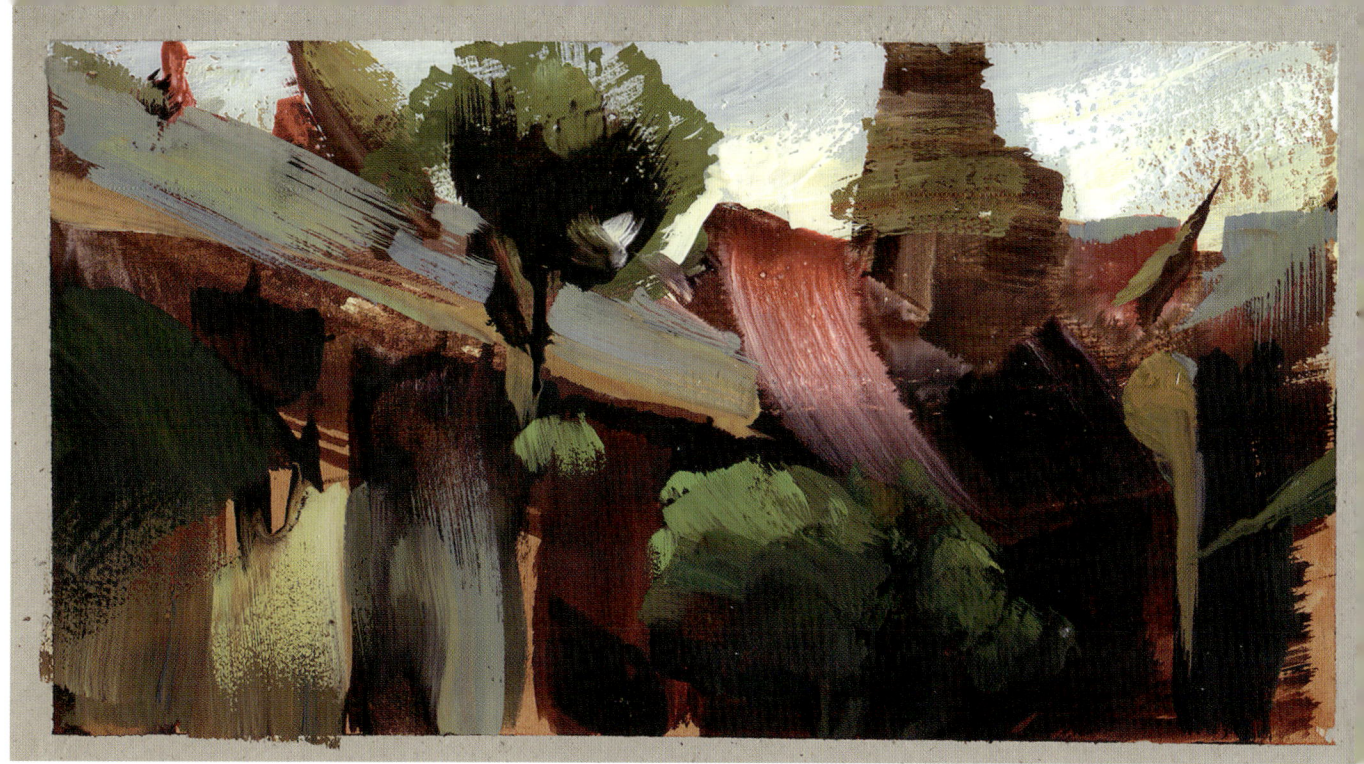

Bangkok, Thailand; watercolor and white gouache on toned mixed-media paper, 4 x 7 inches

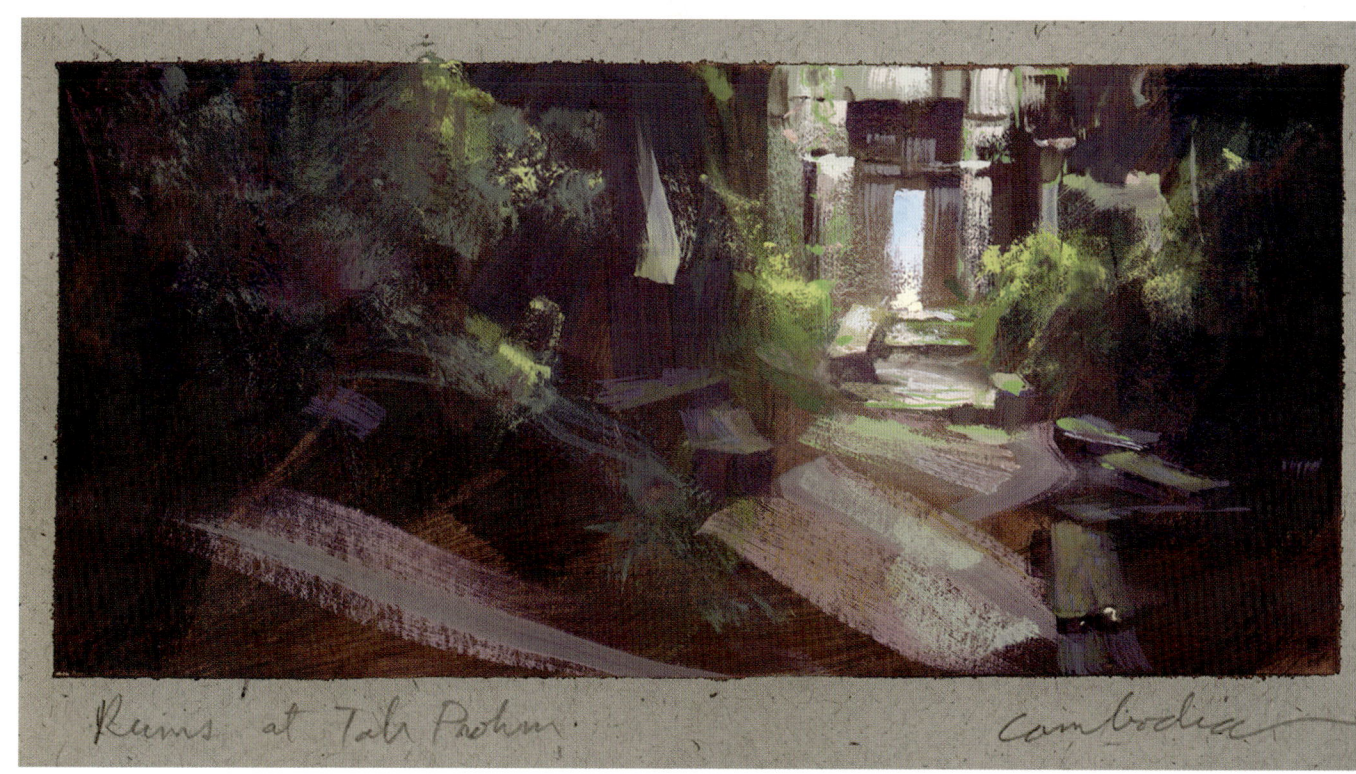

Ta Prohm ruins, Siem Reap, Cambodia; watercolor and white gouache on toned mixed-media paper, 3 x 6 inches

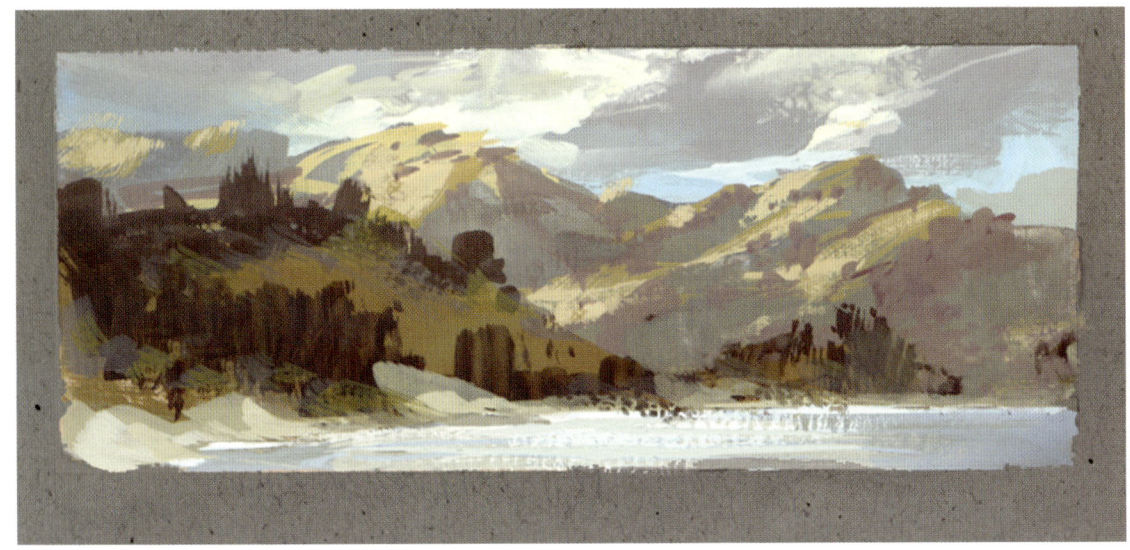

Castaic Lake, Los Angeles County, California; watercolor and white gouache on toned mixed-media paper, 2 x 4 inches

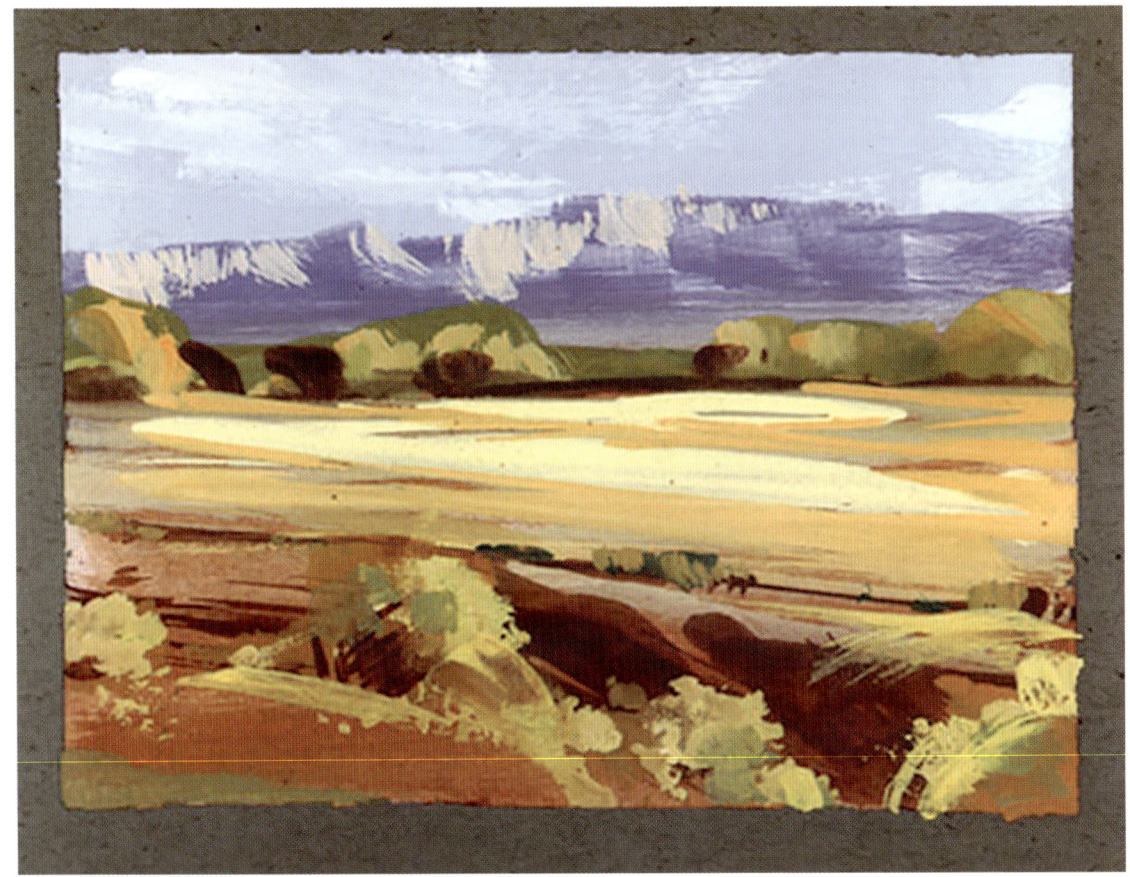

Cedar City, Utah; watercolor and white gouache on toned mixed-media paper, 4 x 5 inches

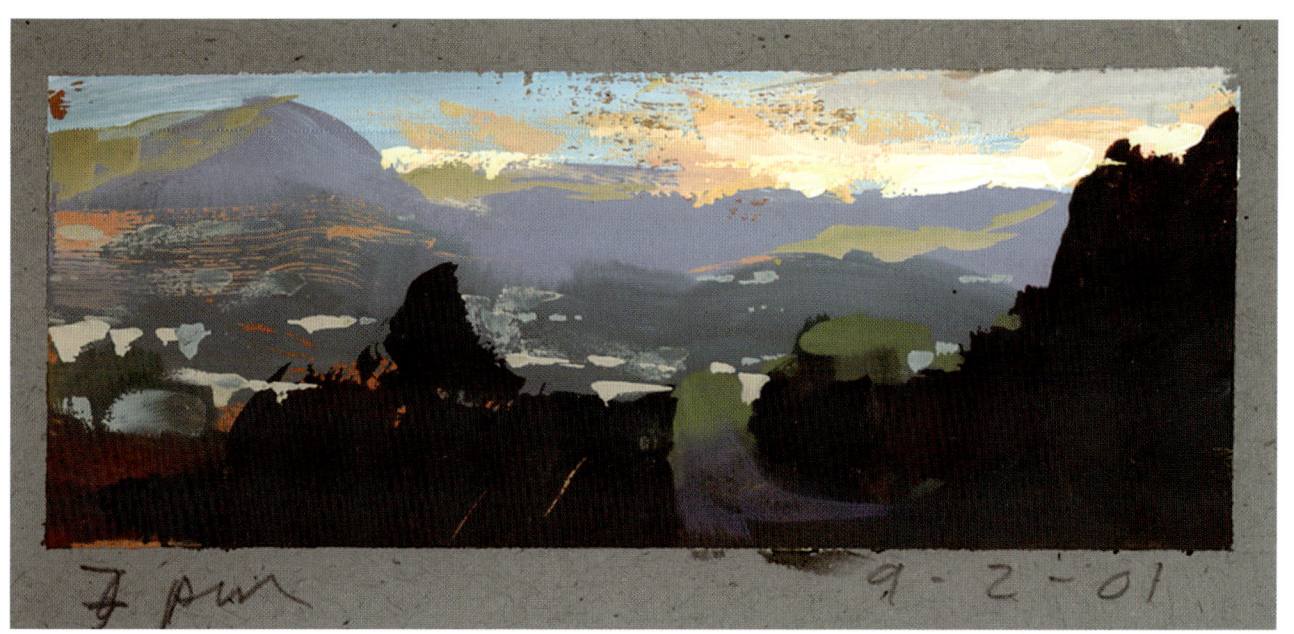

Santa Barbara, California; watercolor and white gouache on toned mixed-media paper, 3 x 6 inches

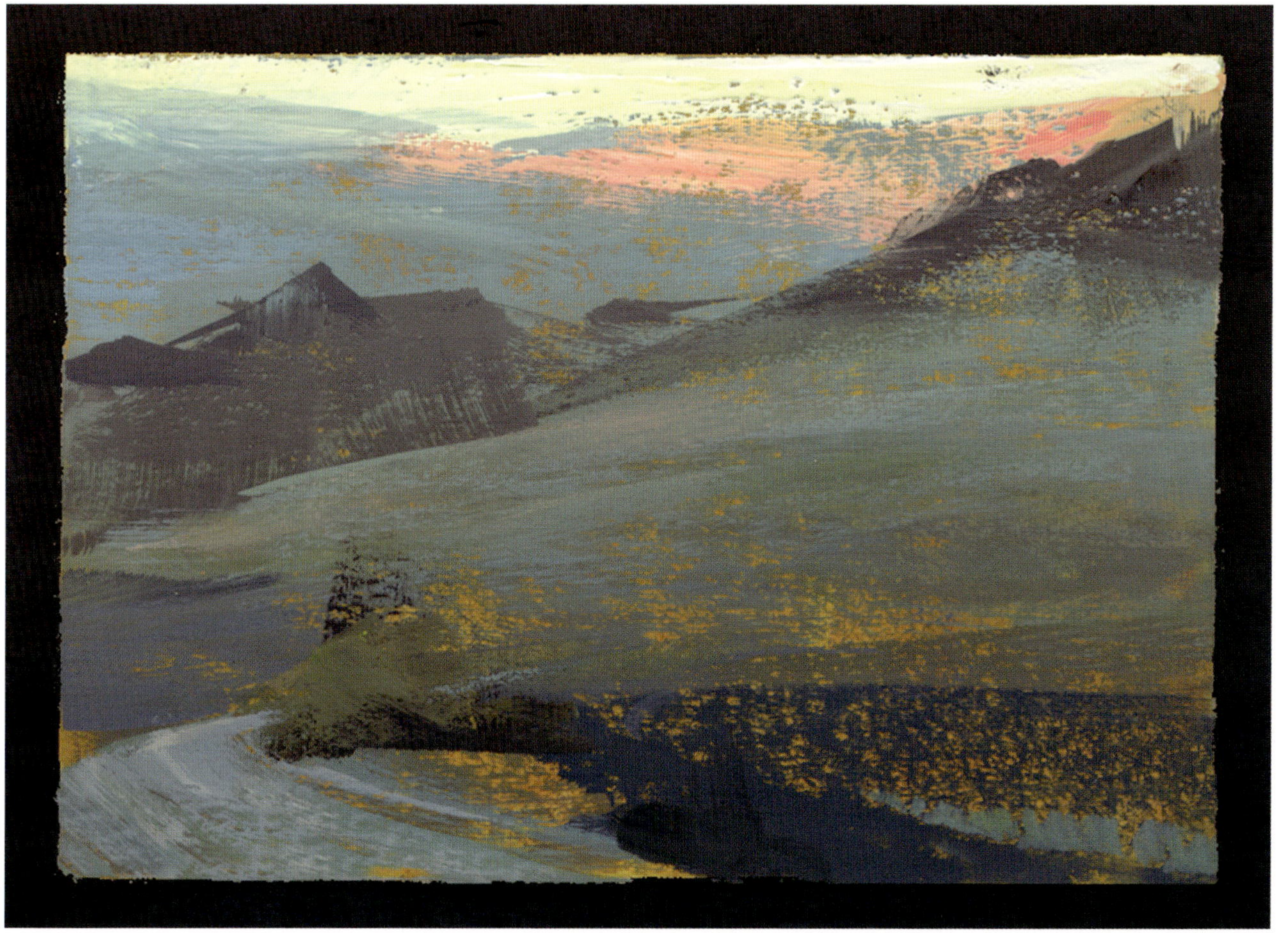

Death Valley, California; watercolor and white gouache on toned mixed-media paper, 4 x 5 inches

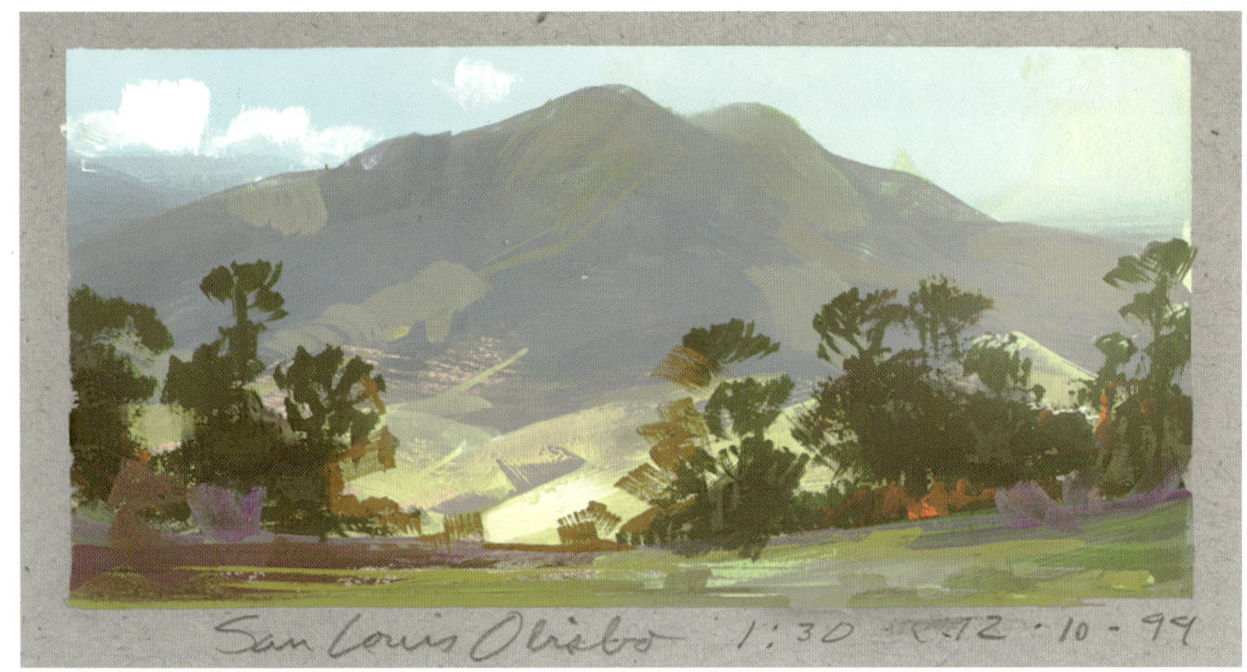

San Luis Obispo, California; watercolor and white gouache on toned mixed–media paper, 4 x 7 inches

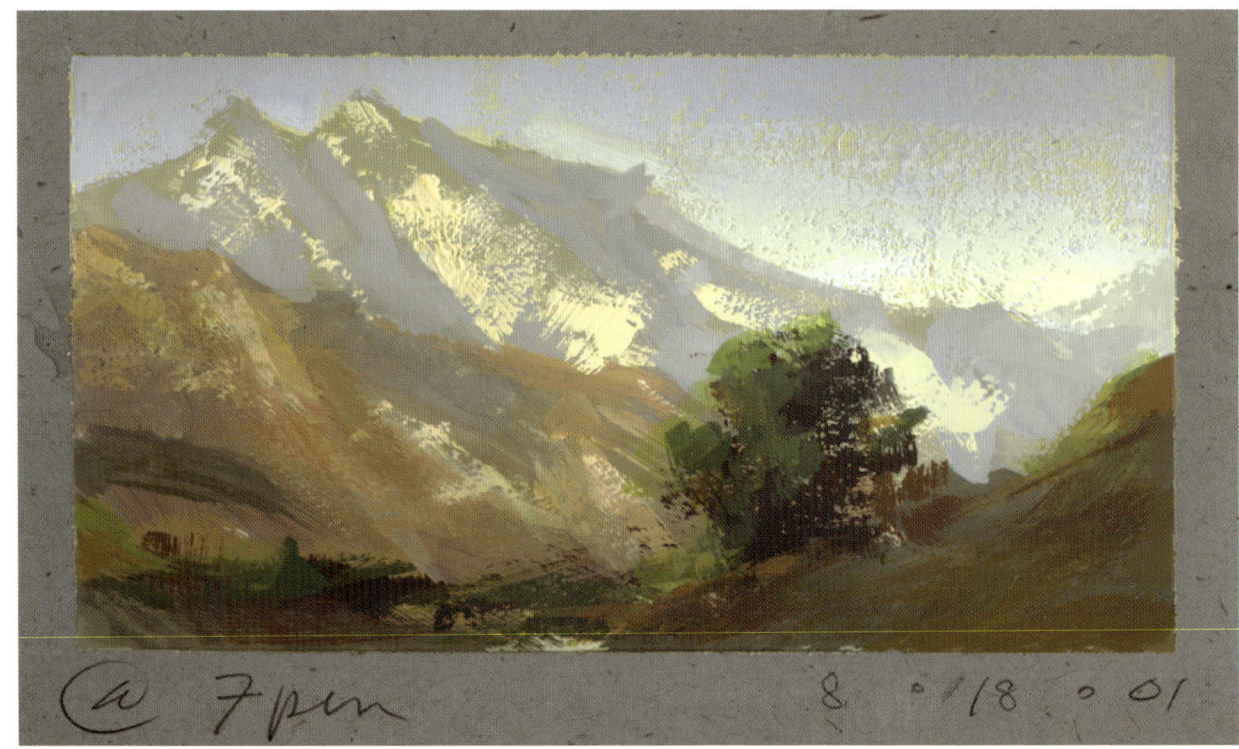

Angeles National Forest, Los Angeles County, California; watercolor and white gouache on toned mixed–media paper, 3 x 5 inches

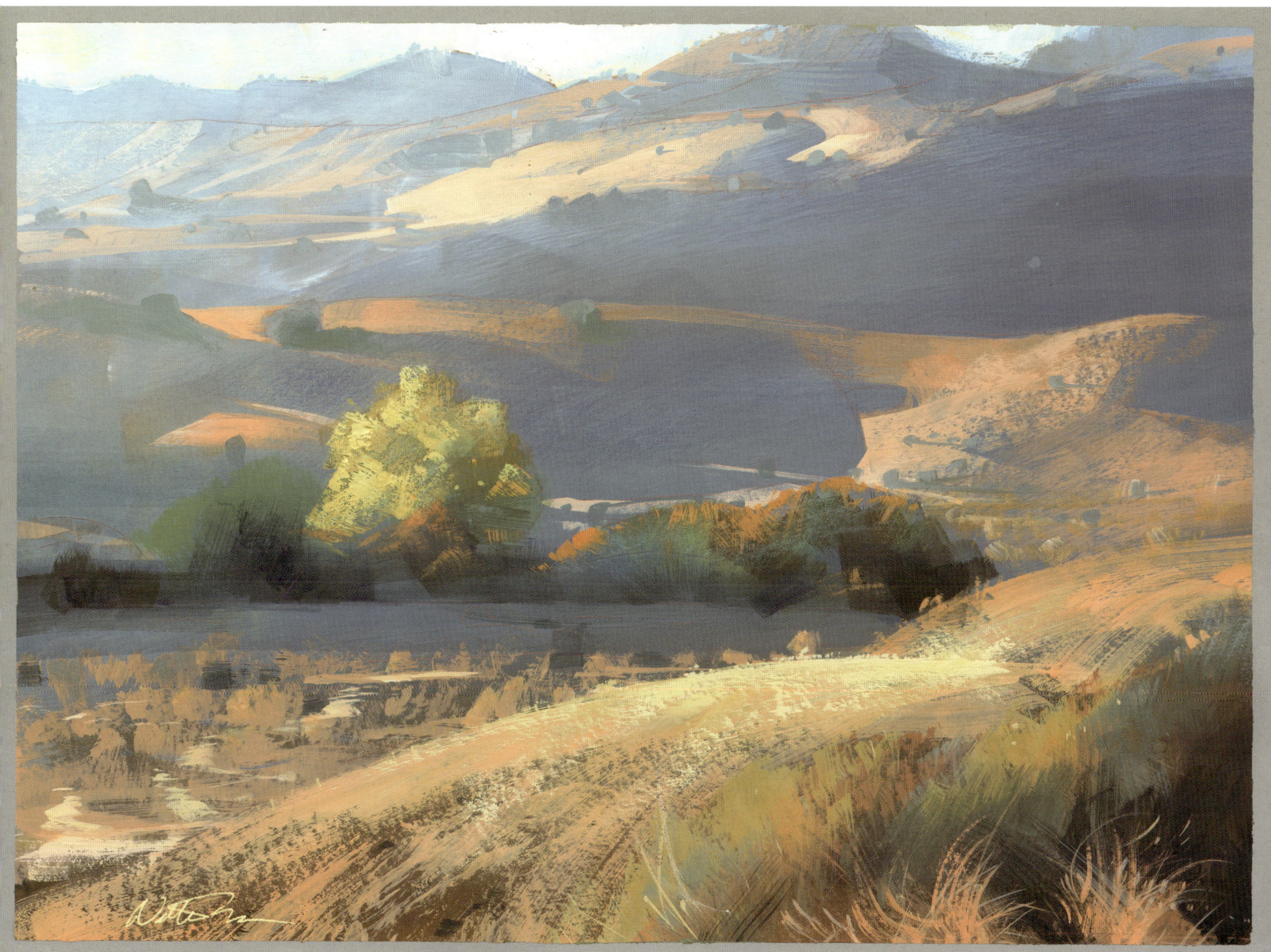

*Coalinga hills, California; watercolor and white gouache
on toned mixed-media paper, 11 x 14 inches*

Here are a handful of reference photos from some of the demonstrations; I thought it would be helpful to see some of the actual locations being painted. Keep in mind that I'm never trying to mindlessly copy a scene the way a camera does, but rather represent the spirit and emotion of the landscape.

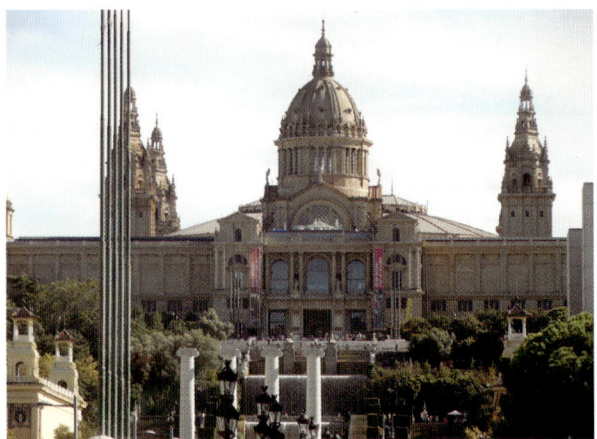

See page 18

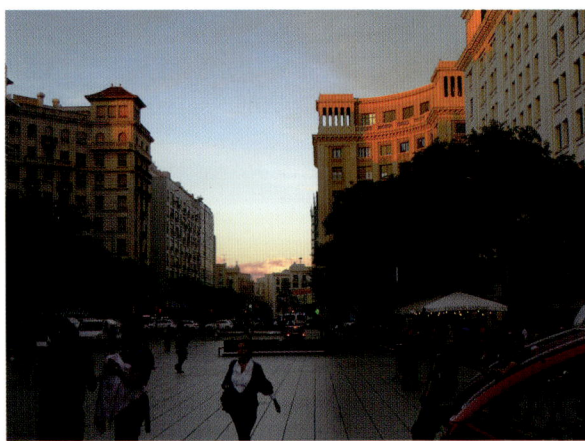

See page 20

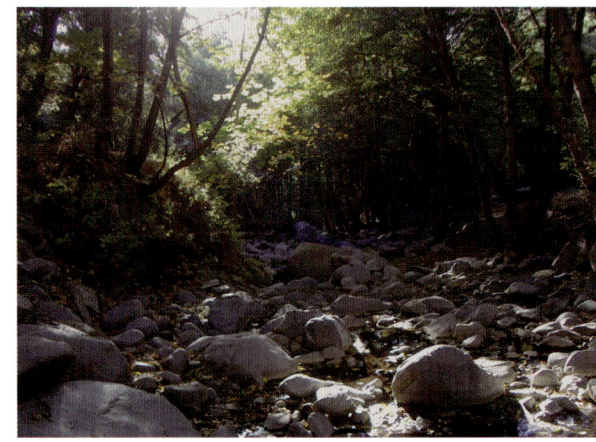

See page 22

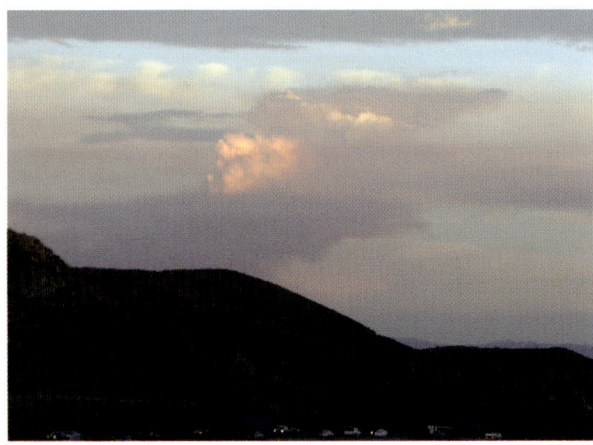

See page 46

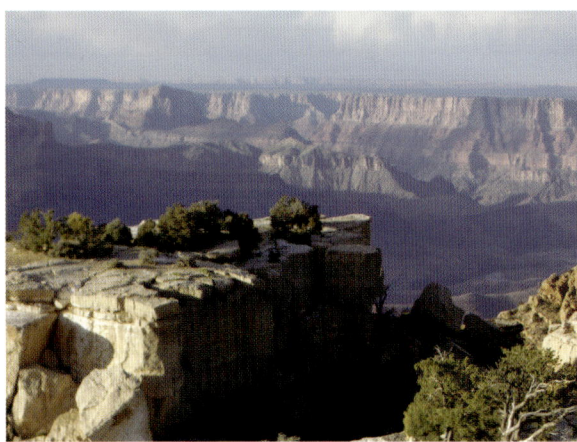

See page 54

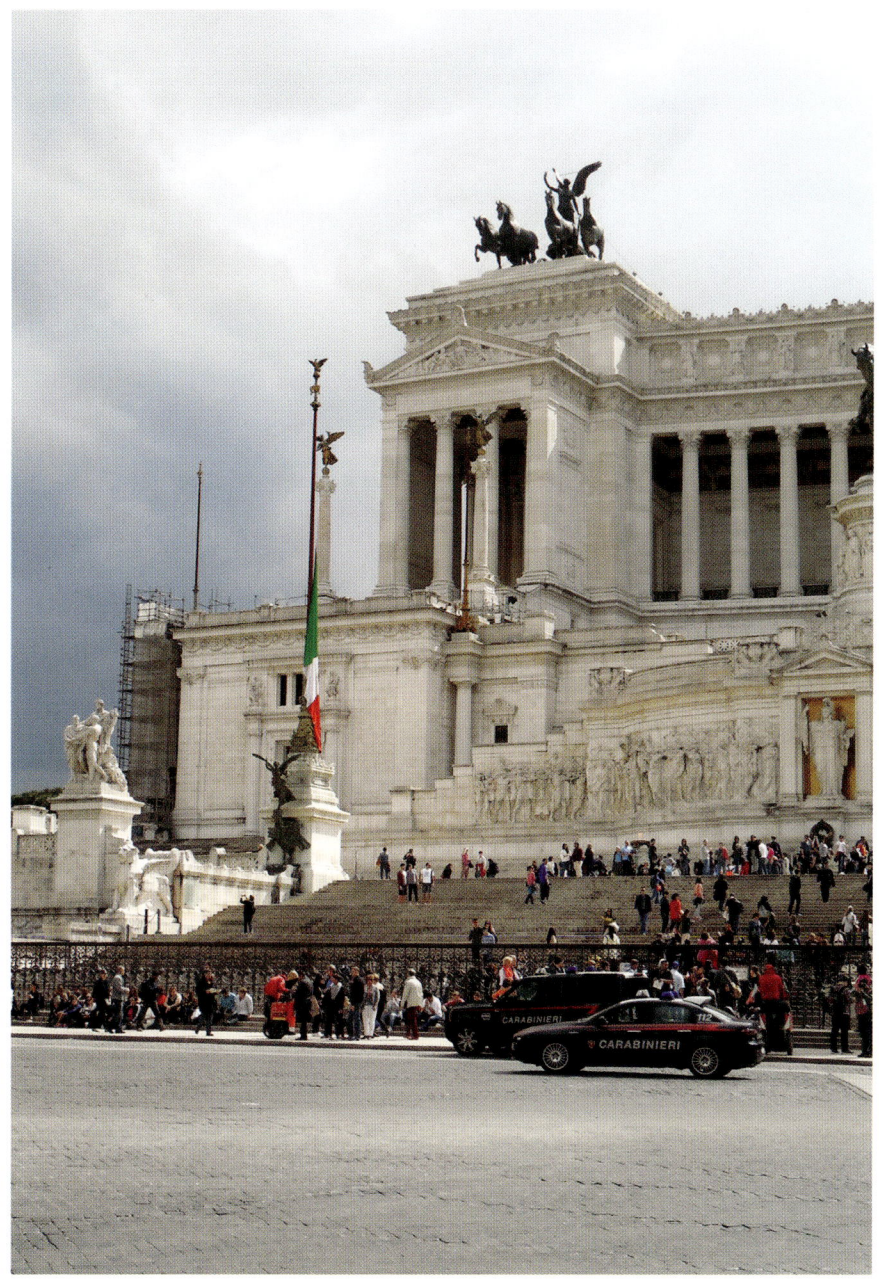

See page 32

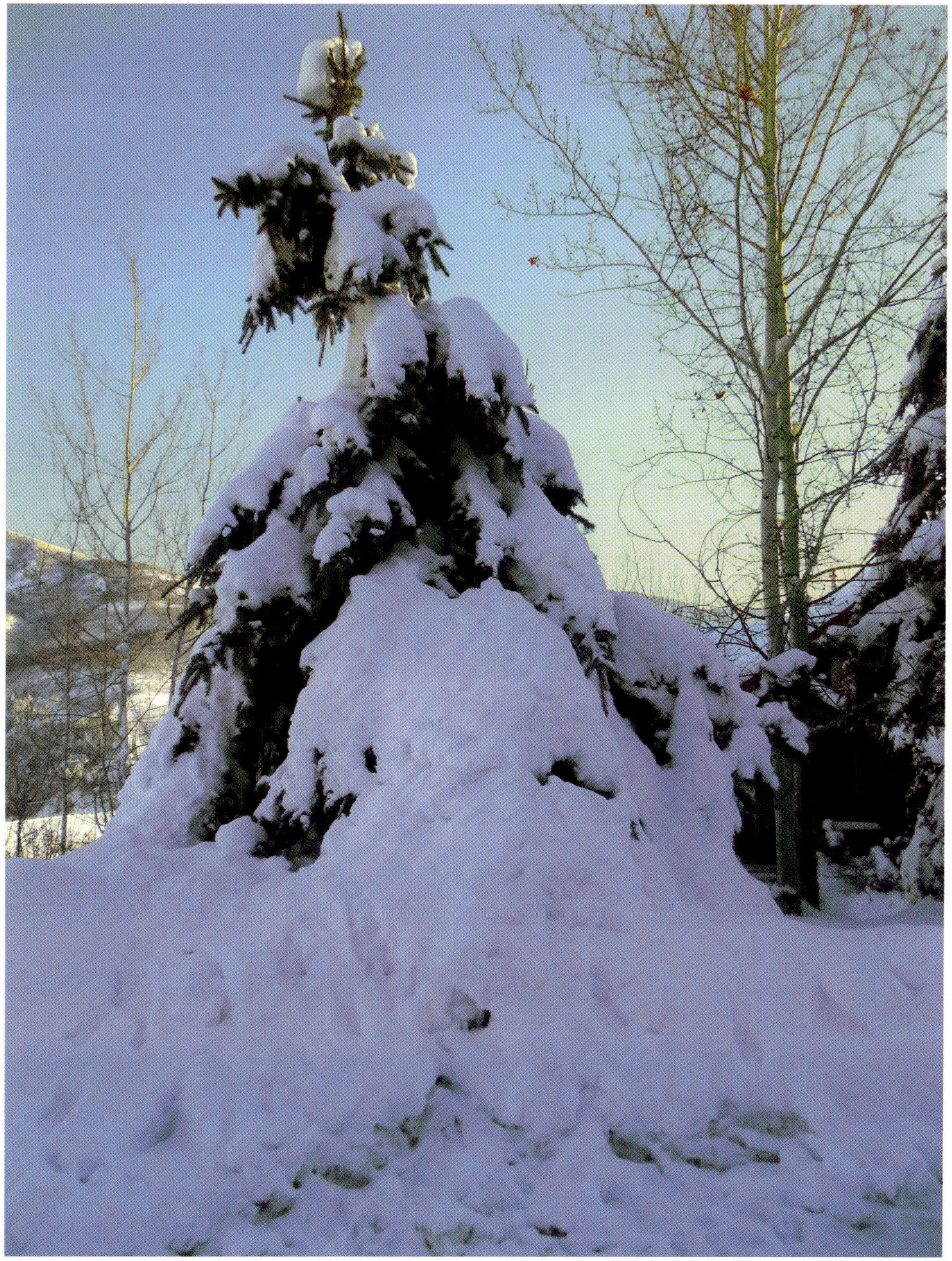

See page 100

Afterword

When I got out of art school in the early '90s, I was proud of what I had done: I had worked as hard as I knew how and focused as much as I was able. I did find professional work as an artist, but I was painfully aware of how much I still had to learn, so I set up a daily program of practice and study. I tried to use any time I could find at lunch, in the evenings, and on weekends to keep practicing—I was desperate to do better.

All of us work very hard and need to take a break. There's nothing wrong with spending an hour watching a show or playing some video games to wind down. But sometimes one hour flows into the next, and before we know it, two or three hours have evaporated! I caught myself doing this, so I forced myself to get away from the TV and into my studio to practice.

Still, the TV would call to me from the next room, and when the inevitable frustrations of learning something new would hit, the TV was just too tempting of an escape. I realized that I could never have the level of focus that I needed as long as there was a constant distraction right there in the next room. So I bit the bullet, I did the hard thing that had to be done: I took my TV set and threw it out the window, metaphorically speaking.

And, yes, I know it's annoying to hear someone smugly go on and on about how they're above watching TV, but that's not it at all! I had the opposite problem—I loved TV too much! But my definition of sacrifice is to give up something good in the hope of gaining something even better.

And so, with as many impediments removed as possible, I built my little art kingdom. I studied and practiced into the dark of the night, and got outside to sketch nature by light of day. And I made the personal commitment that I would not let a day go by without some form of daily practice, a commitment that I have held to in all the years since then. Today, as my responsibilities seem to grow greater as the years pass, I'm grateful that I forged the habits back then that help me to continue to focus today, and I hope the same for all of you.

So, go ahead, play some video games, watch a good show, there's so much great entertainment out there. I know . . . I created some of it at my day job in animation! But do set your standards very high in how much you are willing to sacrifice to develop your artistic chops. Take a moment right now to identify the thing that holds you back the most and eliminate it. Really, do it right now, don't let the moment pass you by.

About the Artist

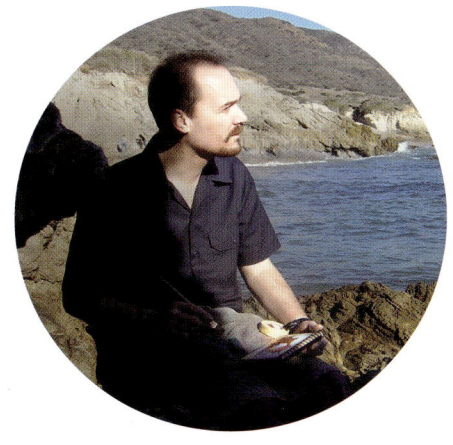

*The artist on a studio research field trip
for the DreamWorks–animated film*
How to Train Your Dragon

Nathan Fowkes is a world-renowned entertainment and fine artist who has been teaching drawing, painting, color, and design since 1999.

He studied traditional painting and entertainment design at the prestigious ArtCenter College of Design, where he graduated with honors, and wrote the best seller *How to Draw Portraits in Charcoal* from Design Studio Press. Currently a conceptual artist for animated films, Nathan's clients include DreamWorks, Disney, Blue Sky Studios, and Paramount Animation. His film credits include such popular movies as *The Prince of Egypt*, *Spirit*, *How to Train Your Dragon*, *Wonder Park*, and several projects within the *Shrek* universe.

The magazines Art of Watercolour, Pratique des Arts, and American Artist Watercolor have featured his watercolor artwork, which has also appeared in solo and group exhibitions at Gallery Nucleus in Los Angeles.

Q & A

Do you find there is a resurgence of interest in traditional landscape painting by younger generations?

Absolutely! When I was in art school in the early '90s, the fine-art faculty and students eschewed traditional landscape painting, and the trendy illustration styles ignored it. But in the past decades, working artists have transitioned toward animation and video game design, where a sense of lighting, mood, and environment is exceptionally important. These people have been "flocking to the hills" with their paints to gain an understanding of those qualities of environment.

Can many of your lessons in the book also be applied to digital painting?

In my opinion, the lessons of landscape painting must be applied to digital painting. Digital painting makes it possible to render every little nuance, and to use photo textures to bring hyperrealism to every surface. But a painting that forcibly shows you everything, quickly loses its sense of purpose and leaves the audience feeling like they've been talked down to. A painting that has well-crafted "lost and found" allows the viewer to participate, they fill in the gaps and the painting becomes that much more engaging.

This is exactly the lesson of the one-hour landscape sketch: train yourself to identify the special quality that led you to paint a particular place, then emphasize those qualities. Much of digital painting is about visual storytelling, so we go through the same process and emphasize the special qualities of story, ignoring anything that might distract from it. In my mind, the conceptual process of landscape painting and digital painting is the same.

On average, how much digital versus traditionally painting do you do?

My "day job" is working as a conceptual artist for animated movies and that work is all painted digitally. And with so many hours of digital painting, I find myself itching to get out the traditional paints in my free time. Ideally, that means getting outside, but I also have a pull-out table underneath my computer desk with my watercolor palette and brush all set to go. I'll take a break and do some sketching while looking at sketches and photo reference on my monitor that I've shot on location. Then deadlines start looming and I switch back to my digital painting projects. This is my way of being extra productive, to take a break from painting by doing more painting.

Is it difficult to shift from medium to medium?

Because I've spent so many years working in both mediums, it's not a problem to switch back and forth. It's kind of like being bilingual and speaking one language at work and another at home—it's automatic.

If you were to compare one of your pure on-site landscape paintings to a studio painting with the same time and material constraints, would they look that different?

They do have a tendency to look a little different. I try to give myself a time limit in the studio to avoid paintings that look overly "studied," but the on-location paintings tend to have a "flying-by the-seat-of-your-pants" look that can be more energetic and spontaneous.

What do you find most valuable about mastering quick landscape painting?

It's a do-or-die situation. Creating a clear, simple statement is an absolute necessity, and this is, in my opinion, one of the most important skills an artist can have.

While a very basic question, can you share what you consider the benefits of gouache vs. watercolor are?

It's a good question, and it actually requires a discussion of oil paint. I began this book by discussing my travails with oil paint and how I finally settled on watercolors with white gouache after much trial and error. The truth is I really love oil paint, I used it throughout art school, and I taught oil portraiture for many years, I just don't love it for on location painting. What I like about it so much is the way you can combine washes and opaque painting, I wanted that quality in my landscapes, but I also needed convenience. As mentioned in this book, I experimented with acrylic and gouache on location but found myself constantly fighting the medium as the paints dried out in my palette despite all kinds of schemes to keep them wet.

Watercolor dries out just as quickly, but it just takes a spritz of water to bring them back to life, but the quality of opacity that I liked in other mediums was mostly absent. For that reason, I've been willing to take on the extra trouble of using white gouache with the watercolors. I just squeeze out fresh white rather than trying to dig into the dried white on the palette. Admittedly I go through a lot of white! So in the end, oils, acrylics, and gouache are strictly "in-studio" mediums for my way of working.

Many of your fans have pointed out that they could tell a painting was yours even before seeing your name. What qualities in your painting do you feel make them truly yours?

It's a nice compliment to have anyone feel that I paint in a distinctive way, at the same time it tempts me to change things up so that my paintings are always about the distinctiveness of the place, rather than the technique. I will say, however, that mark making is part of the fun of landscape painting, I usually use flat brushes to get a bit of calligraphic "thick and thin" in my brushstrokes.

There are some similarities between your charcoal work and watercolor paintings in terms of the varying block-like brushstrokes as well. Can this be considered a very Fowkes-esque approach?

Yes, you're right about this, same artist, same way of thinking. I like to block in the big simple statement then add the flourishes of variety. This reminds me of the period when I was teaching at the Los Angeles Academy of Figurative Art. My demonstrations had the approach of getting the clear idea down first, then adding the variety. There was another excellent instructor there at the time that had the opposite approach. He would lay down expressive strokes and textures of paint, then pull the simplicity of the subject out of that.

This drove some students crazy. They felt like I was telling them to do one thing and the other instructor was telling them to do another. But this is why I always say that principles are far more important than techniques. The other instructor and I were teaching exactly the same principles, we just had different techniques for applying them. This is a very important distinction as it allows everyone to paint in their own way while taking advantage of time-honored principles, rather than mindlessly copying one particular teacher's technique.

It's clear you have a romance with travel. Is this something you developed at an early age?

My parents both grew up on farms in middle America, and when I was a kid, I thought other people were more cosmopolitan than we were, because our family vacations were spent traveling back from Central California to the heartland to visit relatives. I did draw a great deal on those early trips to the family farms. Until age 12 I was quite sure that I was going to be a natural scientist of some kind; I spent all my drawing time on things like the local crayfish and strange bugs!

Then my folks, being the exceptional people they were, began taking us on trips to other countries when I was in high school. That's when I first caught the travel bug. And when I started working in animation, I would take a few weeks off after every project to travel to a new place with my sketchbook. Many of the sketches in this book are from those trips.

Over the past decade, I've been doing short-term consulting work for animation and video game studios in many cities around the world. It's been an unbelievable opportunity and something I never expected, but I've taken full advantage of it by filling my sketchbooks with as much work as possible during free time, and by doing studio paintings back home from my sketches and photos.

For those who cannot travel to faraway places to capture unique scenes and colors, what do you suggest they do to diversify their subjects and challenge themselves?

This is an important question, because in all the years I've been teaching, I've noticed a strong tendency for students to try to develop a single formula or technique to deal with the complexities of landscape painting. But this means that the wide variety of places and the momentary qualities of light will all be funneled through the same formula and made to be uniform; what makes each location special is likely to be lost!

This book spends a great deal of time discussing the importance of identifying the unique quality of each landscape and demonstrates many different approaches to describe those qualities. A convenient painting kit that is geared toward one-hour location studies, means that everywhere you look there is a painting to be made. So even if an artist is landlocked, there's a great variety all around, including the changing of light and seasons.

Your paintings in this book, as quickly as they're done, appear effortless. What does it take to achieve this?

When I teach my painting classes and go on and on about how much practice is required, and brag about how I've squeezed it in to every spare moment throughout my life, I can't help but wonder if the students are thinking, This guy has no life! I won't admit to that, but putting tens of thousands of hours into painting has made all the difference, and of course has required a good amount of sacrifice.

Special thanks to the crack design and publishing team at Design Studio Press.

My online Landscape Painting class and demonstrations can be found at schoolism.com.

For classes, events, workshops, and social media, visit nathanfowkesart.com, and for my portfolio, visit nathanfowkes.com.

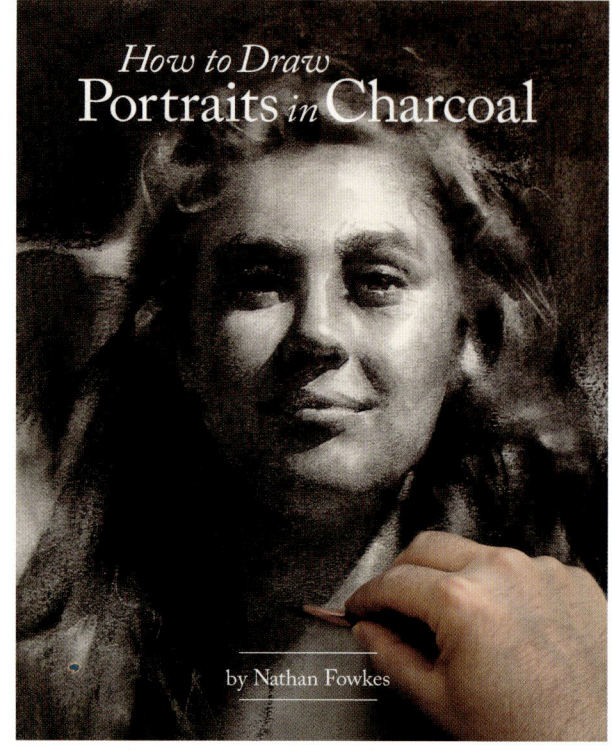
How to Paint
Landscapes *Quickly*
and Beautifully
in Watercolor and Gouache

Published by
Design Studio Press

Website: www.designstudiopress.com
Email: info@designstudiopress.com

Editor: Teena Apeles
Graphic Design: Alyssa Homan

10 9 8 7 6 5 4

Printed in China
First edition, October 2019
Revised edition, March 2021

ISBN: 9781624650499
Library of Congress Control Number: 2019947506